ABHANDLUNGEN

DER AKADEMIE DER WISSENSCHAFTEN IN GÖTTINGEN

ABHANDLUNGEN
DER AKADEMIE DER WISSENSCHAFTEN
IN GÖTTINGEN

PHILOLOGISCH-HISTORISCHE KLASSE
DRITTE FOLGE
Nr. 125

GÖTTINGEN · VANDENHOECK & RUPRECHT · 1982

MITTEILUNGEN
DES SEPTUAGINTA-UNTERNEHMENS (MSU) XVI

Text History
of the Greek Numbers

Von

John William Wevers

GÖTTINGEN · VANDENHOECK & RUPRECHT · 1982

Vorgelegt in der Sitzung vom 3. Juli 1981

CIP-Kurztitelaufnahme der Deutschen Bibliothek

Wevers, John William:
Text History of the Greek Numbers / von John William
Wevers. - Göttingen : Vandenhoeck und Ruprecht, 1982.
(Mitteilungen des Septuaginta-Unternehmens 16) (Abhandlun-
gen der Akademie der Wissenschaften in Göttingen, Philo-
logisch-Historische Klasse ; Folge 3, Nr. 125)
ISBN 3-525-82411-4

NE: Septuaginta-Unternehmen: Mitteilungen des
Septuaginta-Unternehmens; Akademie der Wissenschaften
⟨Göttingen⟩ / Philologisch-Historische Klasse: Abhandlungen
der Akademie . . .

Research for this monograph was generously supported by grants
from The Social Science and Humanities Research Council of Canada
to whom the writer tenders his thanks.

Table of Contents

Table of Contents

Chapter 1   The *x* Group

In THGG 152 it was stated that mss. 71 and 619 commonly go together in the second half of Genesis and contain a large number of unique readings. It was similarly noted in THGD 54 that 71'-527 often have readings at variance with 121-318-392 of the *y* group. For Numbers it is abundantly clear that these form two distinct groups. To the former group, which I have arbitrarily designated the *x*-group one may with some hesitation add ms 509. That these constitute distinct groups should be clear from the following two lists. In *List* 1 are given instances of *y*-readings in which at least two out of the three remaining *y* mss (with only random support from other mss) attest to the reading. *List* 2 consists of *x*-readings, i.e. readings supported by at least all but one of the extant *x*-mss. with no more than random support from other mss. By random support is meant ms support by individual rather than textual group support.

List 1

7_{78} Ἀχιρέ] αχιρεν y^{-318}
14_{44} om τήν A y^{-318}
15_{22} διαμάρτητε] -ρτυρητε A K(vid) y^{-318}
15_{35} λίθοις] pr εν 16-46 y^{-121} = 𝔐
20_{16} ἐν] εκ G 46* 129 y^{-318}
20_{19} om τε 414 y^{-392} 319 Phil II 87^{ap}
22_{11} ἐξελήλυθεν] εξηλθεν y^{-392} 126
24_{25} ἀποστραφείς] post αὐτοῦ tr 54-458 y^{-392}

26_{28} Βαριαΐ] βαραι A y^{-392} 59 Arm
26_{44} Νοεμάν 1°] νοεμα A 15-82 y 55
27_{19} ἔναντι 1°] εναντιον K 29-64 y 59 Tht Nm 224
$33_{31\ 32}$ Βαναιακάν] βανικαν A y^{-392} 407
33_{47} Γελμών] δελμων y^{-392} 128^{mg}-669
35_{19} ἀποκτενεῖ 1°] -κτεινει 413-616* 246 y^{-121}

The shortness of this list reemphasizes the colorless character of the *y*-group as a group as indicated for Genesis in THGG 139ff. It is also clear that its text is related to codex A.

List 2

1_2 om υἱῶν B *x* Bas II 145 ^{Lat}cod 100
1_{12} Ἀμισαδαί] μισαδαι x^{-509} 59
1_{20} om τῇ x^{-509}
1_{21} ἔξ — fin] χιλιαδες πεντακοσιοι τεσσαρακοντα εξ x^{-509}
1_{22} om αὐτῶν 1° 82 x^{-509}
1_{23} ἐννέα — fin] χιλιαδες τριακοσιαι πεντηκοντα εννεα x^{-509}
1_{24} om αὐτῶν 1° 458(‖) x^{-509}
1_{24} κατά 2°] και x^{-509}
1_{26} om πᾶς — (27) Ἰσσαχάρ 44 x^{-509}
1_{38} om πᾶς — (39) Δάν 44-107 x^{-509}
1_{50} αὐτῆς 1°] ⌒2° 44 129^{txt}(c pr m) x^{-509}

2_3 πρῶτοι] κατα νοτον (νωτ. 619) B *x* ^{Lat}cod 100
2_9 om καί ἑξακισχίλιοι x^{-509}
2_{18} παρά — Ἐφράιμ 2°] bis scr x^{-509}
2_{18} Ἐμιούδ] σαμιουδ x^{-509}
2_{24} τρίτοι] πρωτοι 767* x^{-509}
2_{25} Ἀμισαδαί] σαδαι x^{-509} 407; but cf σαδε 68'-120
2_{32} om τῶν 1° x^{-509}
2_{32} ἑξακόσιαι] -σιοι 707 528 x^{-509}
3_9 τοῖς υἱοῖς] τους υιους 15-426* x^{-509} 120 59 Tht Nm 192^{ap}
3_{10} τῆς σκηνῆς] την σκηνην x^{-509} 126

3₁₃ ἦ ἡμέρᾳ] η αν ημερα x⁻⁵⁰⁹; tr 509
   Phil I 250ᵃᵖ
3₁₅ om κατὰ συγγενείας αὐτῶν B x 55
   Aethᶜ Arab Sa = 𝔐
3₁₈ Λοβενί] λουβενι x⁻⁵⁰⁹ Boᴬ
3₁₉ om Ἰσαάρ x⁻⁵⁰⁹
3₂₁ om τῷ x
3₂₇ καί 1°] ∩2° 54 343 x⁻⁵⁰⁹
3₃₀ τοῦ] των x⁻⁵⁰⁹
4₂₃ om καί 2° B x⁻⁶¹⁹ Arm Sa = 𝔐
4₄₆ om αὐτῶν 1° B x⁻⁶¹⁹ Latcod 104(vid)
   = Ra
6₁₄ ἐνιαυσίαν 963] -σιον V 618* 528-529ᶜ
   321 x⁻⁵⁰⁹ 319
6₂₅ om σε 2° B 963 x⁻⁶¹⁹
7₇₅ om ἕνα 3° A V 82 16-46-528 767 x⁻⁶¹⁹
   18-126
9₁₃ om τό 2° 58-72′ 458 28 74-76 x⁻⁷¹ 59
11₂₀ ὅς] ο x⁻⁵⁰⁹ 120′
11₂₆ om τό B x⁻⁶¹⁹
11₂₉ μοι] εμε B x⁻⁵²⁷ 392
11₂₉ προφήτας] + ειναι x⁻⁵⁰⁹ Chr IX 192
   XVI 520 Sev 513 Tht Nm 206ᵃᵖ
11₃₄ om ὅτι B x
12₁₂ om γένηται — θανάτῳ x⁻⁵⁰⁹
13₃ ἀποστελεῖς] -στειλας B x⁻⁵⁰⁹
13₅ Ζακχούρ] ζακχυρ B 509; ζαχηρ x⁻⁵⁰⁹
13₆ Σαφάτ] σαφα x⁻⁵⁰⁹ Latcod 100
13₈ Ἰγαάλ Ra.] ιλααλ B x
13₁₃ Γαμαλί] γαμαι B x 319 Arm
13₁₆ Μακχί] μακοσι Bᵐᵍ 509; μοκοσι 71′;
   μοσκωση 527
13₂₀ τειχήρεσιν] τειχηραις (c var) εισιν x⁻⁵⁰⁹
   318
13₂₃ Ἐνάκ] εναχ B F 129 x Sa = Ra; cf
   αιναχ 767
13₂₇ Καδής] καδδης 707ᶜ 528-529 71′-527ᶜ
   55ᶜ
13₂₇ om καί 5° x⁻⁵⁰⁹
13₂₉ ὀχυραί] ισχυραι x⁻⁵⁰⁹
13₂₉ Ἐνάκ] εναχ B 129 x Sa = Ra
13₃₃ fin] + εκει B x⁻⁵⁰⁹ Latcod 100
14₃ εἰσάγει] -γεις 551 x⁻⁵⁰⁹
14₃ om ἡμῖν Bᶜ x⁻⁵⁰⁹
14₁₀ om ἐν 3° B x Aeth
14₁₂ om καί πολύ μᾶλλον x⁻⁵⁰⁹
14₁₄ πορεύῃ] -ρευση x⁻⁵⁰⁹
14₂₂ om ταύτῃ B 58 x AethᶜᴳG Arab Co =
   𝔐
14₃₄ κατεσκέψασθε] επεσκεψασθε Bᶜ G x
14₄₀ τό] pr εις Bᶜ x
14₄₃ ἀπεστράφητε] -φησθε x⁻⁵⁰⁹
15₃ καθ'] κατ 46ˢ 127 x⁻⁵⁰⁹; but cf κατα b
15₄ τό δῶρον] τα δωρα x⁻⁵⁰⁹
15₁₀ εἰς] επι x⁽⁻⁵⁰⁹⁾
15₁₀ ὀσμήν] οσμη F 64*-707 314 x⁻⁵⁰⁹
15₁₅ ἔσται 1°] εστιν 528 x⁻⁵⁰⁹

15₂₀ ἅλωνος] αλω B x⁻⁵⁰⁹ Cyr VI 568 = Ra
15₂₄ om καί 3° x⁻⁵⁰⁹
15₂₅ πάσης] της 29 x⁻⁵⁰⁹
15₃₈ πτερυγίων] ιματιων 72 414-417 129
   x⁻⁵⁰⁹ 799 Syhᴳ
15₄₁ εἶναι] pr του x⁻⁵⁰⁹
16₅ ὁ θεός] κς 426 767 x⁻⁵⁰⁹ Tim II 2₁₉
   Or IV 303 447 539 La
16₇ om ἐπίθετε ἐπ' αὐτά 2° 106-125 x⁻⁵²⁷
   319 799
16₇ om ἄν B x 59 Cyr I 860
16₇ ἐκλέξηται] εκλελεκται Bᶜ x Cyr I 860
16₁₉ om τῇ x⁻⁵⁰⁹
16₂₆ συναπόλησθε] ουν απολησθε (c var)
   x⁻⁵⁰⁹ 59
16₂₇ ἐξῆλθον] -θοσαν 130ᵐᵍ x⁻⁵⁰⁹ 319
16₂₈ om ἀπ' x⁻⁵⁰⁹
16₃₄ οἵ] ο x⁻⁵⁰⁹
16₃₇ ἡγίασαν] -σε x⁻⁵⁰⁹ 68′ Cyr I 616
16₃₈ περίθεμα] επιθ. x⁻⁵²⁷
17₂ ἐπίγραφον] ad fin tr x⁻⁵²⁷
17₁₀ εἶπεν] ελαλησε(ν) x⁻⁵²⁷
18₁₀ om οἱ M 313-615-616* 30 x⁻⁶¹⁹
18₁₂ om καί 2° B 426 x⁻⁶¹⁹
18₂₇ ἅλωνος] αλω B 426 x⁻⁶¹⁹ Cyr I 844
   = Ra
18₂₇ om ὡς 2° B 129 x⁻⁶¹⁹ 319 Cyr I 844
   Bo Sa¹ = Ra
18₃₁ ἀντί] απο Bᶜ x⁻⁶¹⁹
19₈ om comma 72 84 x⁻⁶¹⁹
26₃ om μετ' αὐτῶν B 58-82 x⁻⁶¹⁹ Aethᶜ
   Arm Sa = Ra
26₆ τῷ 1°] του x⁻⁶¹⁹ 407 Syh
26₆ Ἀσρών] αρσων x⁻⁶¹⁹ 68′-120
26₈ Ἐλιάβ] ∩(9) 29 19 x⁻⁶¹⁹ 121
26₁₇ Ἀσρών] αρσων x⁻⁶¹⁹
26₁₇ Ἀσρωνί] αρσων(ε)ι M x⁻⁶¹⁹
27₂ om ἔναντι 2° 72-381′ 44-125 x⁻⁶¹⁹ 126
   319 Arab Sa
27₄ πατρός 2°] pr του 707 44 x⁻⁶¹⁹
29₁₃ om κάρπωμα Bᶜ M′ V x⁻⁶¹⁹ 318 407
29₂₁ om αὐτῶν 1° 44 x⁻⁵⁰⁹
29₂₂ om αὐτῶν 1° x⁻⁵⁰⁹
29₂₅ om αὐτῶν 1° x⁻⁵⁰⁹
29₂₈ om αὐτῶν 1° x⁻⁵⁰⁹
29₃₀ om αὐτῶν 1° 125 x⁻⁵⁰⁹
29₃₁ om αὐτῶν 1° x⁻⁵⁰⁹
29₃₃ om αὐτῶν 1° x⁻⁵⁰⁹
29₃₄ om αὐτῶν 1° x⁻⁵⁰⁹
29₃₉ om ὑμῶν 5° 125 84ᵗˣᵗ(c pr m) x⁻⁵⁰⁹
   Latcod 104
29₃₉ om ὑμῶν 6° 72 125 x⁻⁵⁰⁹
30₂ om Μωυσῆς 72 x⁻⁵⁰⁹
30₂ om λέγων 72 x⁻⁵⁰⁹
30₂ om ὅ 344*(c pr m) x⁻⁵⁰⁹
30₃ αὐτοῦ 2°] τουτο x⁻⁵⁰⁹
30₇ om καί x⁻⁵⁰⁹

8

30₉ αὐτήν 963] εαυτην x⁻⁵⁰⁹
30₁₁ om αὐτῆς 3° x⁻⁵⁰⁹
30₁₃ ἀκούσῃ 963] εξελθη x⁻⁵⁰⁹
30₁₃ ἐξέλθῃ 963] εξηλθεν x⁻⁵⁰⁹
31₅ ἐξηρίθμησαν] -σεν 72 129 30 x⁻⁵²⁷ 407 59 799 Bo
31₉ ἐπρονόμευσαν 1°] επροεν. x⁻⁵⁰⁹
31₁₉ om ὁ 2° 29-72 73'-422 x⁻⁵²⁷ 392 18-630
31₂₈ ὄνων] αιγων B Fᵃ V 82 129 x⁻⁵²⁷ 407 319 Arm Sa
31₃₆ ἑπτακισχίλια] -λιαι Bᶜ x
31₃₆ πεντακόσια] -κοσιαι B 127 (vid) x⁻⁵²⁷ 407
31₄₃ ἑπτακισχίλια] -λιαι 321 x⁻⁵⁰⁹
31₄₈ καθεσταμένοι] κατεστ. B V 129 767 x⁻⁵⁰⁹ 407 319
31₅₂ κυρίῳ] pr τω x⁻⁵⁰⁹
32₃ Σεβαμά] εσαβαμα 71-527; εσσαβαμα 619
32₃ Ναβαύ] βαναυ x⁻⁵⁰⁹
32₄ παισίν σου] πασιν ου x⁻⁵⁰⁹
32₆ καθήσεσθε 963] καθησθε 71; καθεισθε 527-619
32₁₂ υἱός] pr ο 963*(c pr m) 72 52'-313 x⁻⁵⁰⁹
32₁₄ σύστρεμμα] συντριμμα Bᶜ x
32₁₅ ἀνομήσετε] -σητε (c var) 75 x 319 799
32₁₇ προφυλακῇ] φυλακη x 407
32₂₁ om ἄν 29 x⁻⁵⁰⁹ 407
32₂₅ ἐντέλλεται] εντελειται B* x⁻⁵⁰⁹
32₂₇ om δέ 15-72 x⁻⁵⁰⁹ 18-628 BoᴮB
32₃₀ αὐτῶν 1°] ∩2° F 72-381' 106 56ᵗˣᵗ x⁻⁵⁰⁹
32₃₀ συγκατακληρονομηθήσονται] -μησονται 82 x⁻⁵⁰⁹

32₃₉ om εἰς B x
33₃ Ῥαμεσσή] -σσων B 71; -μεσων 527; -μαισων 619; -σσω 509
33₅₄ αὐτῶν 2°] ∩3° 528 19 125 x⁻⁵⁰⁹ 392 126-669ᵗˣᵗ
33₅₄ ὑμῶν 2°] αυτων 53 x⁻⁵⁰⁹ 319 Aethᴹ
34₁₀ Ἀσερναίν] σεναειρ 71'; σεναηρ 527
34₁₂ om ἡ 2° Bᶜ V 963 52* 129 x 59 319
34₂₂ om ἄρχων 72-82 246 x⁻⁵⁰⁹ 126 Latcod 104
34₂₂ Βακχίρ] βαχειρ V 527'-619ᶜ
34₂₃ τῶν υἱῶν] της φυλης 246*(c pr m) x⁻⁵⁰⁹ Arab
34₂₆ Ὀζά] ζα x⁻⁵⁰⁹ 319
34₂₈ Φαδαήλ] φαλαηλ x⁻⁶¹⁹ 407
34₂₈ Βεναμιούδ] βενιαμιουδ Bᶜ x⁻⁵⁰⁹ 319; βενιαμειουδ B*
35₇ om ἅς B V 82 129 344ᵗˣᵗ x 407 319 Latcod 100 Arm = Ra
35₁₂ φυγαδευτήρια] pr εις x⁻⁵⁰⁹ = 𝔐
35₁₂ ἔναντι] απεναντι 417 x⁻⁵⁰⁹
35₁₅ φυγεῖν] φευγειν A 29 129* x⁻⁵⁰⁹
35₁₆ πατάξῃ] pr ου x⁻⁵⁰⁹
35₃₀ ψυχήν 2°] ψυχη 426 129 x 55
35₃₄ κατασκηνῶν ἐν μέσῳ] κατασκηνωσεως x⁻⁵⁰⁹
36₅ om υἱῶν x⁻⁵⁰⁹
36₆ om ὁ 707 x⁻⁵⁰⁹
36₆ γυναῖκες 1°] ∩2° Bᵗˣᵗ 528-616ᵗˣᵗ 767 x⁻⁵⁰⁹ 318 628 Latcod 104 Aethꟳ
36₇ om ὅτι x⁻⁵⁰⁹ 126
36₇ προσκολληθήσονται] pr και B x
36₁₁ om init — Σαλπααδ 106 x⁻⁵⁰⁹
36₁₂ δήμου 2°] δημον Bᶜ 761ᶜ(vid) 129 x⁻⁵⁰⁹

That these texts constitute a group seems clear from the above. Though the inclusion of 509 in the group might seem dubious, an analysis of the variants, particularly of the spelling of proper names, makes it clear that a definite relationship does obtain.

Ms 527 has a number of omissions in Numbers; these are 1₁₇—₄₄ 2₉ συν — 3₃₉ 3₄₃ τρεις — 8₂₂ 10₈ υμων — 10₃₆ 18₅—19₂₂ 25₁₆—30₁₇ 33₂₉—₄₇ and 34₄ και 5°—34₉. Ms 619 is the product of three scribes. One scribe wrote 1₁—11₁₆ Μωυσην and 18₈ ελαλησε — 29₁₄ ενι 1°; a second copied 11₁₆ κυριος — 18₈ και 1° and 29₁₄ τοις — 32₂₅ λεγοντες, and a third wrote the remainder of the book. Close affinities between 71 and 619 are especially apparent for the texts copied by the second and third scribes.

An analysis of the above list indicates far more instances of omissions than of additions (67 over against 12). Most omissions are of one word only. Longer omissions may be the result of homoioteleuton as at 1₅₀ 3₂₇ 19₈ 26₈ 32₃₀ 33₅₄ 36₆ ₁₁. Omissions of phrases or clauses obtain at 1₂₆ ₃₈ 2₉ 3₁₅ 12₁₂ 14₁₂ 16₇ and 26₃.

Omissions of single words usually involve pronouns (1$_{22}$ $_{24}$ 4$_{46}$ 6$_{25}$ 14$_3$ $_{22}$ 29$_{21}$ $_{22}$ 25 28 30 31 33 34 39 (twice) 30$_{11}$ 35$_7$). The article is omitted at 1$_{20}$ 2$_{32}$ 3$_{21}$ 9$_{13}$ 11$_{26}$ 16$_{19}$ 18$_{10}$ 31$_{19}$ 34$_{12}$; $καί$, at 2$_{31}$ 4$_{23}$ 13$_{27}$ 15$_{24}$ 18$_{12}$ 30$_7$, and $δέ$, at 32$_{27}$. Prepositions are involved at 14$_{10}$ 16$_{28}$ 27$_2$ 32$_{39}$, the particle $ἄν$, at 16$_7$ 32$_{21}$, and $ὅτι$, at 11$_{34}$ 36$_7$. Other omissions which obtain in the list are of $υἱῶν$ (1$_2$ 36$_5$), $Ἰσαάρ$ (3$_{19}$), $ἕνα$ 3° (7$_{75}$), $κάρπωμα$ (29$_{13}$), $Μωυσῆς$ and $λέγων$ at 30$_2$, and of $ἄρχων$ in 34$_{22}$.

Only 12 instances of a longer text obtain in the above list and these involve but one word in all but one instance, viz. a dittograph of $παρά$ — $Ἐφράιμ$ 2° in 2$_{18}$. Of the remaining 11 three involve the articulation of a noun (27$_4$ 31$_{52}$ 32$_{12}$), one, the articulation of an infinitive (15$_{41}$), two, the addition of the preposition $εἰς$ before a noun (14$_{40}$ 35$_{12}$). The particle $αν$ is inserted between $ἦ$ and $ἡμέρᾳ$ in 3$_{13}$; the conjunction $και$ is added in 36$_7$, the infinitive $ειναι$, at 11$_{29}$, and the adverb $εκει$, in 13$_{33}$. The addition of $ου$ before $πατάξῃ$ in 35$_{16}$ substantially changes the meaning; it is, however, the result of dittography since the preceding word is $σιδήρου$.

Change in nominal inflection may involve gender, case or number. Change in gender usually involves the gender of compound numbers: of 600 at 2$_{32}$, of 500 at 31$_{36}$, and of 7000 at 31$_{36}$ $_{43}$; cf also $ενιαυσιον$ for $ἐνιαυσίαν$ at 6$_{14}$. The change of $ὅς$ to o at 11$_{20}$ must be palaeographically based since the masculine is demanded by the context, the antecedent being $κυρίῳ$.

Change in case is also rare. Case after $ἐπί$ is changed from genitive to accusative in 3$_{10}$ and from accusative to dative in 35$_{30}$. The dative pronoun $μοι$ modifying $ζηλοῖς$ at 11$_{29}$ is changed to $εμε$. The dative article $τῷ$ in the formulaic "$τῷ$ PN, $δῆμος$ + genitive gentilic noun" is changed to the genitive at 26$_6$. The accusative becomes a nominative at 15$_{10}$. The occurrence of the accusative for $δήμου$ 2° in 36$_{12}$ obtains under the influence of the immediately preceding $τὴν φυλήν$. Change in number occurs only three times. Two of these involve an article before a proper noun. At 3$_{30}$ for $τοῦ Καάθ$ the article appears in the plural since $τῶν δήμων$ precedes it. At 16$_{34}$ the singular article obtains in $πᾶς Ἰσραὴλ οἱ κύκλῳ αὐτῶν$, because $Ἰσραήλ$ is grammatically singular. The only other change in number obtains at 15$_4$ where $τὸ δῶρον$ is changed to the plural.

Change in word order is equally rare. Two instances of change in order of compound numbers obtain in 1$_{21}$ $_{23}$; the only other change in word order occurs at 17$_2$.

Change in verbal inflection often involves tense. Thus at 13$_3$ a future indicative is changed to aorist participle, a present tense is changed to aorist at 14$_{14}$ and to future at 32$_{25}$. An original future indicative becomes present indicative in 15$_{15}$ but present imperative at 32$_6$. An original aorist is changed to the present at 35$_{15}$ and to the perfect at 16$_7$.

Changes in mood occur three times: at 30$_{13}$ a subjunctive is changed to the indicative, and the reverse obtains at 32$_{15}$; for 16$_7$ cf the preceding paragraph. Change in voice is attested twice, at 14$_{43}$ a passive is given a middle ending,

10

and at 32₃₀ a middle inflection obtains for a passive. Change in number obtains at 14₃ 16₃₇ 31₅. At 16₂₇ the Hellenistic εξηλθοσαν is found for the classical ἐξῆλθον. And finally at 31₉ the augment of an aorist form obtains doubly, i.e. both before the stem and before the compound element in the variant επροενομευσαν.

One of the more interesting variations in text involving change in lexical stem is found at 35₃₄. Num reads ἐγὼ κύριος κατασκηνῶν ἐν μέσῳ τῶν υἱῶν Ἰσραήλ. The x variant changes the participle into κατασκηνωσεως and omits ἐν μέσῳ. Many lexical changes are simply errors palaeographically or phonetically conditioned. Such are the changes of κατά to και 1₂₄, τειχήρεσιν to τειχηραις εισιν in 13₂₀, ὀχυραί to ισχυραι 13₂₉, πάσης to της 15₂₅, συναπόλησθε to ουν απολησθε 16₂₆, παισίν to πασιν 32₄ and of σου to ου in the same verse. Other changes are obviously due to the influence of the immediate context and illustrate scribal carelessness in copying the parent text. Such are the changes of πτερυγίων to ιματιων in 15₃₈, of ἀκούσῃ to εξελθη 30₁₃, ὄνων to αιγων 31₂₈, ὑμῶν 2° to αυτων 33₅₄ and of τῶν υἱῶν to της φυλης 34₂₃.

Change of preposition is attested at 15₁₀ of εἰς as επι and at 18₃₁ of ἀντί as απο. Pronominal change occurs at 30₃ with τουτο for αὐτοῦ 2°, and at 30₉ with εαυτην for αὐτήν. The substitution of synonyms or near synonyms occurs but rarely. The only ones attested are αλω for ἅλωνος at 15₂₀ 18₂₇, of κ̅ς̅ for ὁ θεός at 16₅ and of ελαλησε(ν) for εἶπεν at 17₁₀. Only wandering attention on the part of a scribal parent can explicate the substitution of πρωτοι for τρίτοι at 2₂₄ and of κατα νοτον for πρῶτοι at 2₃.

Change in compound element occurs at 14₃₄ with κατεσκέψασθε to επεσκ. and in 16₃₈ with περίθεμα to επιθ. Change of simplex to compound obtains with απεναντι for ἔναντι at 35₁₂, and the reverse at 32₁₇ of φυλακη for προφυλακή. Lack of assimilation produced κατεσταμενοι at 31₄₈ and κατ (for καθ᾽) at 15₃; cf also συντριμμα at 32₁₄.

That these four mss constitute an independent group is particularly evident from common errors in the tradition of the spelling of proper names. In the following list the Num spelling is given in parenthesis after the variant. 1₁₂ μισαδαι (Ἀμισαδαί), 2₁₈ σαμιουδ (Ἐμιούδ), 2₂₅ σαδαι (Ἀμισαδαί), 3₁₈ λουβενι (Λοβενί), 13₅ ζακχυρ or ζαχηρ (Ζακχούρ), 13₆ σαφα (Σαφάτ), 13₈ ιλααλ (Ἰγαάλ), 13₁₃ γαμαι (Γαμαλί), 13₁₆ μακοσι, μοκοσι or μοσκωση (Μακχί), 13₂₃ ₂₉ εναχ (Ἐνάκ), 13₂₇ καδδης (Καδής), 26₆ ₁₇ αρσων (Ἀσρών), 26₁₇ αρσων(ε)ι (Ἀσρωνί), 32₃ εσ(σ)αβαμα (Σεβαμά), 32₃ βαναυ (Ναβαύ), 33₃ ραμεσ(σ)ω(ν) or ραμαισων (Ραμεσσή), 34₁₀ σεναειρ or σεναηρ (Ἀσερναίν), 34₂₂ βαχειρ (Βαχχίρ), 34₂₆ ζα (Ὀζά), 34₂₈ φαλαηλ (Φαδαήλ) and 34₂₈ βενιαμιουδ (Βεναμιούδ).

A major characteristic of the above list is the frequent occurrence of B or Bᶜ indicating random support of the x variant text. The B text (or that of its corrector) supports the variant text 45 times whereas codex A occurs but twice. On the other hand the short list of 16 variants shown in list 1 as unique

11

or almost unique variants of the *y*-group are supported by A five times and never by B.

This affinity of the *x*-group to the B tradition is further confirmed in the following list of variants in Codex B in which random support by one or more members of the *x*-group occur.

List 3

1₄₄ om αὐτῶν B F*(c pr m) V 19 71-509 319 ᴸᵃᵗcod 100 = Ra

2₈ αὐτοῦ] αυτων B 246ᶜ¹ 509-527

3₁₈ αὐτῶν] ∩(19) Bᵗˣᵗ 16-46 127ᵗˣᵗ 509 628 ᴸᵃᵗcod 100

3₄₀ λάβε] λαβετε B F 71

4₂₆ om init—μαρτυρίου Bᵗˣᵗ707ᵗˣᵗC⁻¹³¹ᵐᵍ- 46-552ᵗˣᵗ-615-761ᵗˣᵗ 458 71

4₄₆ om αὐτῶν 2° B 71 ᴸᵃᵗcod 104

5₄ om τῷ B 509

7₇₉ πλήρῃ] -ρης B 707 610 458-767 84 509 319

8₈ σεμίδαλιν 963] -λεως B 71 68′-120′ 59 = Ra

9₁₈ om καί B* 509-619 Sa

11₃₂ ἔψυξαν] εσφαξαν B 509

13₂₄ κλῆμα] κληματα B 509 319

20₄ ἀνηγάγετε] -γαγες B* 129 74-76-84 71-509

20₈ τὴν συναγωγήν 1°] τη συναγωγη B 509

24₁₁ ἐστέρησέν] -ρεσεν B* 509

25₄ om θυμοῦ B* G*(vid; c pr m) 16-46- 417 458ᵗˣᵗ 527 319 Phil III 223 Sa¹²

25₇ υἱοῦ] υς B 509

26₂₀ om ὁ 1° B 426 53′ 71

26₂₆ Ἀροαδί 2°] αροδει B* 71

26₃₄ Χέλεκ] χελεγ B 376 129 71 407 Arm = Ra

26₃₄ Χελεκί] χελεγ(ε)ι B 129 71 407 Arm = Ra

26₃₆ om τῷ 2° B 82 509 319 Arm

31₃₄ om καί 1° B V G-82-376 44 129 509 407 319 Bo Syh

31₃₇ ἑξακόσια] -σιοι B*(vid) 376 528 527

32₂₄ οἰκοδομήσετε] -σητε B* 528 127 71′ 59

33₁₃ Αἰλούς] αιλειμ B 509-619

33₁₄ Αἰλούς] αιλειμ B 71′

33₃₃ Ἐτεβάθα] σετ. B* 54′ 619 ᴸᵃᵗcod 100

35₁₄ om ἐν τῷ B 71′ 126-628

35₁₅ om καί 2° B* 509 319

The *x* group in its loyalty to the B text tradition is sometimes along with B a witness to Num over against almost all other witnesses. In the following list only B and *x* together with no more than random support witness to LXX.

List 4

1₁₈ ἐπηξονοῦσαν (επεξ. 509; επιξ. 619) B *x*] επεσκεψαντο (-ψατο 54-75′) *d* 129 *n t* 18; επεσκεφθησαν 53′; *disposuerunt* ᴸᵃᵗcod 100; *recensuerunt eos* Aeth Sa; επεσκεπησαν (c var) rell

1₄₅ υἱῶν B V G-426 53* 71-509] των 58; pr των rell

3₃₇ πασσάλους (c var) B V 44-125 71-509 799 ᴸᵃᵗcodd 100 104] + αυτης *z* 646; + αυτων rell

5₆ τῶν 1° A B G *x*⁻⁶¹⁹ Anast 376 Arab Sa] πασων 126 55; pr πασων (παντων 29) rell

5₁₃ μετ᾽ αὐτῆς 2° B *x*⁻⁶¹⁹ 59 Cyr I 909] μετα ταυτης 963; κατ αυτης rell

6₁₄ ὁλοκαύτωσιν (-τησιν 963*c pr m) B V 963 *x*⁻⁶¹⁹ 319 Cyr I 1052] -τωμα rell

6₂₁ ἥν B *x*⁻⁶¹⁹ Cyr I 1053] η[... 963; ος 537; ης rell

7₈₅ τῶν ἁγίων B 963 458 *x*⁻⁶¹⁹] τω αγιω rell = Ra

9₇ αὐτόν (-των 426) B 426 71-509 Cyr I 1081 Sa Syh] αυτους rell

9₇ προσενέγκαι B V 71-509 126 319 Cyr I 1081 Bo] ωστε (> 127 527 Chr) προσενεγκειν *n* 527 Chr II 877; pr του *b*; pr ωστε του 619 68′-120′; ωστε προσεγγισαι 55; pr ωστε rell

13₃₃ πᾶς B V 426 *x* Boᴬᴮᶜ Sa] και G C″ 799; > Boᴮ*; pr και rell

14₃ παιδία B M′ 129 *x* Cyr I 373] τεκνα ημων *b*; + υμων 44-107′ 321; + ημων rell

16₁ Αὔν B *x* Cyr I 857] αμναν *b*; αναν 72; ανθαν *c*I⁻⁷⁶¹*-551; αβ[.]αν 761*; ανναν rell

18₈ ἀπαρχῶν B V 82 129 *x*⁻⁶¹⁹ Cyr I 837 ᴸᵃᵗcod 100 Sa] εντολων μου Procop 844; απαρχιων μου 44; + μου rell

36₁ ἄρχοντες B V 72 129 *x* 407-630 319 Aeth Arm Sa] + (+ των O) πατριων rell

12

It remains to determine the place of the x group within the text tradition of the book. In the final list variants are given support by x and no more than three other text groups. As usual random support is disregarded. Text groups other than x are indicated in parentheses.

List 5

1₂ (d n t) om αὐτῶν 1° B 414′ d n⁻⁷⁶⁷ t x 18 Bas II 145 Cyr VI 453 X 624 ᴸᵃᵗcod 100 PsBas *Is* I 5 Arm

1₂ (d n t) om αὐτῶν 2° B V d n⁻⁷⁶⁷ t x 18 319 Bas II 145 Cyr VI 453 X 624 ᴸᵃᵗcod 100 Hi *Eph* II 3 PsBas *Is* I 5 Arm

1₂ (d t) om αὐτῶν 3° B 19 d 127 t x 18 319 Cyr VI 453 X 624 ᴸᵃᵗcod 100 Arm = 𝔐

1₃ (b d t) ἄρσην] αρσεν 72 131ᶜ¹ b d 458 t x⁻⁵⁰⁹ 126-669* 319

1₂₁ (O n) ἐπίσκεψις] -σκοπη B O n x⁻⁵⁰⁹ 18 319

1₃₄ (d) om πᾶς—(35) Βενιαμίν 44-107′ x⁻⁵⁰⁹

1₃₆ (d) om πᾶς—(37) Γάδ 44-107′ x⁻⁵⁰⁹

1₄₇ (O f) οὐ συνεπεσκέπησαν] ουκ (ου G) επεσκ. (επισκ. 53) B O⁻⁵⁸ f 75 x⁻⁵²⁷ 319

2₁₃ (cI b n) τριακόσιοι] τετρακ. 707 cI b 54-75′ 344*(c pr m) x⁻⁵⁰⁹ 646 BoB

2₂₂ (d t) Γαδεωνί] γεδεων 77 d 458 t x⁻⁵⁰⁹ BoB

2₂₃ (d t) τετρακόσιοι] τριακ. 44-106*-107′ t x⁻⁵⁰⁹ 799

2₂₇ (C) Ἀσήρ 1°] ασσηρ C⁻⁵²⁹ 106 53 x⁻⁵⁰⁹ 126-628 Bo Sa¹²

2₂₇ (C) Ἀσήρ 2°] ασσηρ C⁻¹⁶ ⁵²⁹ x⁻⁵⁰⁹ 126 Bo Sa¹²

3₁ (f) ᾗ ἡμέρᾳ] tr f 30 x⁻⁵⁰⁹ 126 55

3₉ (b) μοί] μου 15 b x⁻⁵⁰⁹ 318

3₂₀ (z) Μουσί] ομουσιν x⁻⁵⁰⁹ 68′-120′

3₂₅ (O) Γεδσών] γηρσων O⁻⁵⁸ 767* x⁻⁵⁰⁹ Syh; γηρσσων 767ᶜ

4₂₂ (f) τούτους] τους 56′-129 x⁻⁶¹⁹ 121 18

4₂₆ (b) om καί 4° B b x⁻⁶¹⁹ 392 319 ᴸᵃᵗcod 100 AethM Arm Bo Sa⁴

4₃₅ (f) om τὰ ἔργα B f x⁻⁶¹⁹ 319 ᴸᵃᵗcod 100 Sa

6₅ (n) om τῆς εὐχῆς B 963 664 54-75′ 28-85 x⁻⁶¹⁹ 628 799 Cyr I 1041 Arm Sa⁴

6₅ (cI n) κυρίῳ 963] pr τω 72-426 73′-413-414-552-761 75′-767 30 x⁻⁷¹ 68′ Tht *Nm* 198

6₆ (z) κυρίῳ 963] κ̄ῡ S* x⁻⁶¹⁹ 18′-126-628-669 ᴸᵃᵗcod 100; του κ̄ῡ 68′-120′

6₁₄ (oI n) κυρίῳ 963] pr τω M′ V oI-72 16-46-413-417-422 44 75′-127 30 84 x⁻⁷¹ 318 799

7₂ (z) om οἱ 2° 82 x⁻⁶¹⁹ 120′-126-128-628-669 319

7₂₄ (b f n) Χαιλών] χελων F V 963 15-72-82-376 77-414 b 125-610 f⁻⁵⁶ 54-75′ 130* 76-84 x 318 669 319

7₃₉ (t) ἕνα ἐνιαύσιον] tr 29 t x⁻⁶¹⁹ 392

7₇₂ (oI b) Φαγαιήλ 963] φαγεηλ B V G-72-707*-oI⁻¹⁵ 77 118′-537 125 54-458 30 76 x 392ᶜ 319 Co

7₇₇ (oI) Φαγαιήλ 963] φαγεηλ B V oI⁻¹⁵ 77 127 30 76 x⁻⁵⁰⁹ 392 Co

7₈₁ (n) om ἕνα 3° A* V 29ᵗˣᵗ(c pr m)-82 529 107′ 56 n⁻⁷⁶⁷ x⁻⁶¹⁹ 392 120 319 ᴸᵃᵗcod 100

8₁₄ (O d t) τῶν 963] > A B O⁻⁵⁸ d 127-767 t x⁻⁶¹⁹ 121 = Ra

8₁₆ (b) ἀποδεδομένοι 963] -νον (-διδ. 376) M′ V 376 413 b 610 134 x⁻⁵⁰⁹ Arm Bo

10₁₂ (O d) om τοῦ 1° B V O⁻⁵⁸ 44′-125 x⁻⁶¹⁹ = Ra

11₁₂ (O f n) τὸν πάντα] tr B V O⁻⁵⁸ 422 f n x⁻⁶¹⁹ Phil III 6 Chr I 476 Tht *Nm* 204ᵃᵖ = Ra

11₃₅ (O n) om τῆς B F V O′⁻²⁹ ⁵⁸ 129 54-75′ x 392 59 319 799 = Ra

12₄ (cI′) om καί 4°—fin 376-381′ 77-cI′⁻⁴⁶ 56 54 x⁻⁵⁰⁹ 18-68-126 319 Cyr II 600 Aeth Bo

12₁₀ (d n t) πρός] επι B V d 129 n⁻⁷⁵ 321′ᵐᵍ t x 319 Arab Arm Co = Ra

12₁₅ (n) ἕως] + ον 54-75′ 84 x⁻⁵⁰⁹ 319 Cyr II 593

12₁₅ (z) Μαριάμ 2°] pr η x⁻⁵⁰⁹ 121 68′-120′

13₂₅ (C′′) Φάραγξ] -γγα C′′ x⁻⁵⁰⁹ 318 ᴸᵃᵗcod 100 Aug *Loc in hept* IV 36

13₂₇ (f) ῥῆμα] ρηματα f x⁻⁵⁰⁹ Sa

13₂₉ (d n t) om αἱ B F*(c pr m) V 29 d n⁻⁷⁶⁷ t x Cyr I 373

14₁₃ (t) ἐν] τη B 44′ 129 127-767 t x⁻⁵⁰⁹ = Ra

14₁₄ (n s) κύριε] κ̄ς̄ 58 528 n⁻⁷⁶⁷ 28-30-85′-346 x⁻⁵⁰⁹

13

14₂₀ (oI) εἰμι] εσομαι οΙ⁻¹⁵-29 x⁻⁵⁰⁹ Arm Co

14₂₇ (b n) τὴν πονηράν / ταύτην] tr b 44 n x⁻⁵⁰⁹ 392 ᴸᵃᵗcod 100 Arm

14₃₃ (b f y) om ἄν A B* F*(c pr m) 707 77 b 44 f⁻¹²⁹ 458-767 x⁻⁵⁰⁹ y 126 55 319 624

15₁ (d t) ἐλάλησεν] ειπε(ν) B V d 129 t x Cyr I 1029 = Ra

15₃ (d t) κάρπωμα] ολοκαυτωματα B d t x Cyr I 1029 = Ra

15₃ (d n t) ὁλοκαύτωμα] ολοκαρπωμα B d 129 n t x 319* Cyr I 1029 = Ra

15₇ (d n) κυρίῳ] pr τω 72-426 422 44-107′ n⁻¹²⁷ 74-76 x 121 18(2°)-628

15₁₁ (O) ποιήσεις] -σει G-72-426 x Syh

15₁₄ (d t) γένηται] προσγεν. 551 d 127 t x

15₃₂ (n) τῇ 2°] pr εν A 376 n⁻¹²⁷ x⁻⁵⁰⁹ 318 319 ᴸᵃᵗcod 100 Syh

15₃₆ (O d) om ἔξω τῆς παρεμβολῆς 2° M′ O′(⁻⁵⁸)-82-381′ d′(⁻¹⁰⁶) x⁻⁵²⁷ Arab Syh

15₃₉ (d n t) om ὀπίσω 2° B V d 129 n⁻⁷⁶⁷ t x 319 Tht Nm 211 ᴸᵃᵗcod 100 Arm Co

16₁ (C″ f) Ῥουβήν] ρουβ(ε)ιμ 72-376-381′ C″ 106 f⁻¹²⁹ 75ᶜ 84 x⁻⁵⁰⁹ 126-669ᶜ 59 799

16₅ (d) ἑαυτόν 1°] ⌒2° 551 d⁻⁴⁴ 75′ 84-370 x⁻⁵⁰⁹ 126-628 Aeth

16₉ (n) ὁ θεὸς Ἰσραήλ] κυριος 54-75′ x⁻⁵⁰⁹

16₁₉ (d t) τὴν θύραν] τας θυρας A V 29-82 d(⁻⁴⁴) 129 30′ t x(⁻⁵²⁷) 121 Sa

16₂₂ (b n) θεὸς θεός] o (> 82) θεος ο θεος 82-707 b 129 54′-458 x

16₂₂ (z) om τήν V x z⁻⁶²⁸

16₂₉ (b) εἰ καί] tr b x⁻⁵⁰⁹ ᴸᵃᵗFac Def XII 3 Syh

16₂₉ (b) κατ’] κατα b x⁻⁵⁰⁹

16₄₅ (O) ἔπεσον] -σαν Bᶜ G-29-426 x⁻⁵²⁷

18₉ (d n t) om τῆς B 82 d n⁻⁷⁶⁷ t x⁻⁶¹⁹ Cyr I 837 = Ra

20₁₀ (d f n) ἐξάξομεν] εξαξωμεν 15-707 313-417-615* 19′ 106-107′ f⁻²⁴⁶ 75′-767 84 x⁻⁶¹⁹ 628 55 59 319 799

26₄ (O n) καί 2°] pr συ (σοι 767) B V O n x⁻⁶¹⁹ 407 ᴸᵃᵗcod 100 Arm Syh

26₃₇ (O) om ταῦτα Bᶜ F O′⁻⁵⁸ ⁷⁰⁷ 129 x⁻⁶¹⁹ 59 Arm Sa Syh = 𝔐

26₃₇ (b) Μααλά] μαλα A B 72*-82 413 b 767 321 x⁻⁶¹⁹ 319 = Ra

26₄₂ (t) Ἀχιράν] ιαχ(ε)ιραν B V t 509; ιαχηραν 106 71

26₅₀ (d n t) om πέντε καί b Fᵃ V 963 d 129 n t x⁻⁶¹⁹ 319 Arm Bo

27₁₈ (d f t) τόν 963] > Bᶜ F K (vid) M′ 72-426 46ᶜ-52′ d f⁻²⁴⁶ 767 t x⁻⁶¹⁹ 18-126 59 646

28₃ (C″ s) κυρίῳ] pr τω 29-376 C″ 44 53 458 s x⁻⁶¹⁹ 392 424 646 Or IV 184

28₁₀ (O s) σαββάτοις] σαββασιν (+ αυτου O Syh) O 30′-85ᵐᵍ-321′ᵐᵍ x⁻⁶¹⁹ 68′-120 Syh

29₁₅ (f) τέσσαρας καὶ δέκα] δεκα τεσσ. (c var) B M′ 82-376 77 f x 126-407 319

29₁₇ (f t) idem B M′ V 963 82-376′ 77-417 106 f t x 18-126-407-669 319

29₂₀ (d f t) idem B M′ V 82-376 77 d(⁻¹⁰⁶ᵗˣᵗ) f t x 18-126-407

29₂₃ (f) idem B V 963 72-82-376 77 44′ f x 126-407 416

29₂₄ (d) om αὐτῶν 1° d⁻¹⁰⁶ x⁻⁵⁰⁹

29₂₆ (d f t) τέσσαρας καὶ δέκα] δεκα τεσσ. (c var) B V 58-72-82-376 77 d f t x 126-407 416

29₂₇ (d) om αὐτῶν 1° d⁻¹⁰⁶ x⁻⁵⁰⁹

29₂₉ (d f t) τέσσαρας καὶ δέκα] δεκα τεσσ. (c var) B V 963 58-72-82-376 77 d⁻⁴⁴ f(⁻⁵³) t x 126-407 416 = Ra

29₃₂ (d f t) idem B V 963 58-72-82-376 77 d f t x 126-407 416

30₃ (d n t) ἢ ὁρίσηται/ὁρισμῷ] tr B Fᵃ 963 82 d 129 n t x 407 319 Or II 306 ᴸᵃᵗcod 100 Arm

30₅ (n) ἀκούσῃ] -σει 58 57′ 53 75′-767 85 84 x 318 59 319

30₈ (n) παρασιωπήσῃ] -σει 58 75′-767 730 x⁻⁵⁰⁹ 318 59 319

30₉ (b n t) ἀνήρ 2°] + αυτης 29 b 106(ᵐᵍ) 129-246 n t x⁻⁵⁰⁹ 392 55 Co Syh

30₁₄ (C″ d f) αὐτῇ] αυτην F 72-376 C″(⁻⁴¹⁷) 19 d⁻¹⁰⁶ 53′-129 30′-130ᶜ-343 134*-370* x⁻⁵⁰⁹ 318 126-407 624

30₁₅ (oI y) αὐτῆς 2°] αυτη A 72-426-oΙ⁻¹⁵ 53′ 134 x⁻⁵⁰⁹ y 407 55 416

30₁₅ (d) ἤκουσεν] ⌒(16) 72 d⁻¹⁰⁶ x⁻⁵⁰⁹

31₁₀ (C″ d t) om ἐν 2° Bᶜ G-82-426 C″⁻⁴¹⁴ ⁴¹⁷ d 53 127-767 t x⁻⁵²⁷ 407 55 319 624

31₂₉ (oI) κυρίου] κ͞ω G-72-oΙ⁻¹⁵ 46*-414 44 53′ 30 x⁻⁵²⁷ 59 ᴸᵃᵗcodd 100 104

31₃₂ (t z) ἐπρονόμευσαν 963] προεν. 618 52 106 127-767 t x⁻⁵⁰⁹ z⁻¹²⁶ ⁴⁰⁷ 55ᶜ 799

31₄₇ (oI z) ἕν] ενα V 246 x⁻⁵⁰⁹ 18′-126-407-628-630′ 55 319 624

31₅₄ (C″ s) εἰσήνεγκαν] -γκεν A B F 376′ C″⁻⁵²⁹ ⁷⁶¹ᶜ 127 s⁻³⁰′ 84 x 59 Cyr I 340 = Ra

32₃ (b f n) Δαιβών] δεβων F 58-707 46*-77-414-529 b f 54-75-767 30′-343 76 x⁻⁵⁰⁹ 18 59 319

14

32_{11} ($b\,n\,t$) Ἰσαάκ] pr τω 381′ b 129 n^{-458} 30′ t x^{-509} 407

32_{11} ($b\,n\,t$) Ἰακώβ] pr τω 381′ b 129 n^{-458} 30′ t^{-84} x^{-509} 407

32_{13} ($s\,y$) ἐξανηλώθη] εξαναλ. A F^b 963 G 422(vid) 129 767 $s^{-30′}$ x^{-509} y^{-392} 68′-120′ 799

32_{25} (d) ἡμῶν] ημιν A d^{-106} x^{-509} 799 Aeth Sa^{12}

32_{30} (b) ἐν τῇ γῇ] εις γην 417 b x^{-509}

32_{31} ($b\,n$) om αὐτοῦ B F 29-72 b n^{-127} 30′-344 x 392 120′ 59 319 ^{Lat}codd 100 104

32_{33} ($d\,n$) Σηών] σιων 58* 528-739 108 d 53′ n^{-127} 28-30 370 x 318 120-122-630* 55 319

33_6 (O) ἀπῆραν] απαραντες A V G-82-426 129-246 x^{-509} 68′-120′ Arm Syh

33_{14} ($d\,t\,z$) πιεῖν ἐκεῖ] tr B^c M′ V 15′ d 129-246 t x^{-527} 126-128-407-628-630′

33_{17} ($O\,f$) τῆς ἐπιθυμίας] om τῆς B M′ V O′$^{-58}$72 f x^{-509} = Ra; > 509

33_{26} ($d\,t$) Κατάαθ] κααθ d t x^{-509} ^{Lat}cod 100

33_{27} ($d\,t$) idem d^{-125} t x^{-509}

33_{29} ($d\,n\,t$) Ἀσελμωνά] σελμ. B d^{-125} 129 $n^{-54\bullet}767$ t x 18 799 Arm Sa = Ra

33_{35} (O) εἰς] εν B^c M′ V O^{-58}-82 129 x

33_{43} (n) Ὠβώθ] σωβωθ (σοβ. 58 619; -βοθ 458) B V 58 n^{-75} x 319 ^{Lat}cod 104

33_{44} (n) ἐξ Ὠβώθ] εκ σωβωθ (σοβ. 58 619; -βοθ 458) B M′ 58 n^{-75} x ^{Lat}cod 104 Sa^1

33_{52} (b) σκοπιάς] κοπιας M b^{-537} 106*-107*(c pr m) 75′ 130 370* x 319

34_9 ($d\,n$) Ζεφρώνα] εφρ. B^c F^a 707$^{(mg)}$ 106-125-610* 129-246 n 76 x 319 Arm(vid) Sa^1

34_{13} ($d\,f\,y$) τῷ ἡμίσει] το ημισυ (c var) 29-58-72-376 313-615 19′ 44′-125 53′-246 730 x^{-527} y^{-121} 55 319 799

34_{26} ($d\,t$) Φαλτιήλ] φατιηλ 376 46-417 d 730 t x^{-509} 392 416 ^{Lat}cod 104

35_6 ($b\,f$) om ἅς 1° B V 963 82 b f x 407 319 Cyr I 865 = Ra

35_7 (d) om καί 1° 72-82 d^{-44} 458 x^{-509} 126 319

35_8 (b) ἐλάττω] -ττονα 29 b 246 x^{-509} 318

35_{11} (oI) φυγεῖν] φευγειν A oI 129 30′ x^{-509}

35_{21} ($d\,n\,t$) θανάτῳ 1°] ⌒2° d 246 n^{-767} t x^{-527} 319 Aeth^c Bo

36_3 ($oI\,b\,z$) om υἱῶν oI b 53-129 75′ 76* x^{-527} 18′-126-628-669 Arm

36_4 ($d\,n\,t$) om ἡ 1° 72-376′ d 54-75′ t x^{-509} 799

36_{10} (n) θυγατέρες] pr αι 72-82-376 16-422 129 n x^{-509}

The following table indicates the approximate relationships of the x-group to the other textual groups. For these tables the subordinate groups of the Catena group have not been distinguished; thus C'' may stand for C, cI, cII or any combination of these. Column A indicates the number of instances of support for an x-group variant by one group; column B, by two groups, and column C, by three groups. The total number is given in the last column.

	A	B	C	Total
O	6	9	1	16
oI	4	4	1	9
oII	—	—	—	0
C''	4	4	3	11
b	9	5	9	23
d	8	15	24	47
f	6	6	11	23
n	10	12	19	41
s	—	5	—	5
t	3	12	24	39
y	—	2	2	4
z	5	2	2	9

From this table it is clear that the x-group is closer to the Byzantine text represented by d, n and t than to any other tradition, the total number of instances of common support being d 47, n 41 and t 39. Then follow b and f each with 23 instances, O with 16, C'' with 11, and oI and z with 9 each. If O and oI are taken together its 25 instances would place it ahead of b and f. For s and y no instance of single group support obtain and only a few instances of double group support; these are quite insignificant. It is noteworthy that x and y are demonstrably at opposite ends of the tradition, and should therefore be considered as quite distinct textual groups.

Chapter 2   The Byzantine text

That the *d* text group constitutes the Byzantine text family was already quite apparent from the study of the Lectionary texts in THGG 176 ff. Furthermore it was also clear that the *t* group is intimately related with *d* and could from Genesis ch. 21 onwards be regarded as a subgroup of *d* (THGG 136f). The *n* text for Genesis presented a somewhat complicated picture; for chh. 34—43 the *n* group was fully submerged in that of *d*, and outside these chh. showed closer relationship to *d* than to other groups (cf THGG 106—111). In Deuteronomy where the *n* group was subjected to further analysis (THGD 17ff) its close relationship to the *d t* tradition also shows that it can justifiably be called a second subordinate group in the Byzantine tradition.

For Numbers only two lections obtain in the texts edited by Høeg and Zuntz[1], viz. 11₁₆—17 24—29 and 24₂—₃ ₅—₉ 17—18. Their collation demonstrates as in Genesis their witness to the Byzantine text. I present only the majority reading of the Lectionary texts in the following collation.

11₁₆ Ἰσραήλ] τον λαου Lect Sa¹²
11₁₆ πρὸς τὴν σκηνήν B *d* 130ᵐᵍ-321′ᵐᵍ *t x* Cyr II 461] εν τη σκηνη 46 *b*; επι την σκηνην Bas II 285; εις την σκηνην Tht *Nm* 204 Lect rell
11₂₅ αὐτόν] μωυσην aut μωσην Lect; μωυσην *d t* Arm; μωσην *n*
11₂₅ παρείλατο] περιειλετο *d* 246 *t z* 55ᶜ 646 Lect
11₂₅ ἐπροφήτευσαν] προεφ. (c var) Fᵃ 58ᵐᵍ-72-376-o*I* C′′⁻⁷⁷ ¹³¹ ³¹³ ⁵⁰⁰′ ⁵²⁸ ⁵²⁹′* ⁶¹⁵ *d* 246 *n* 30′-321-346*ᵉᵗ ᶜ² *t* 71′ *z* 55ᶜ 424 646 Lect; + εν (> cod 104) τη παρεμβολη V 376 *n* ᴸᵃᵗcodd 100 104 Arm Bo Lect
11₂₆ πρὸς τὴν σκηνήν B V 82 *d* 129 *t x*⁻⁵²⁷] επι τ. σκ. 624; εν τη σκηνη 15 121 ᴸᵃᵗcod 100; om τήν 527; εις τ. σκ. Lect rell
11₂₆ ἐπροφήτευσαν] προεφ. Fᵇ 72-376-o*I* C′′⁻⁷⁷ ¹³¹ ³¹³ ⁴²² ⁵⁰⁰′ ⁵²⁸ ⁶¹⁵ ⁶¹⁶* *d* 54′-458 *t* 71′ 121 55ᶜ 319 424 Lect
11₂₇ ἀπήγγειλεν] ανηγγ. (-γγιλ. 458) *n*⁻⁷⁶⁷ Lect
11₂₇ εἶπεν] + αυτω 58-376 118′-537 *d*⁽⁻⁴⁴⁾ *f*⁻¹²⁹ *n t* Arm Lect
24₃ παραβολήν] παρεμβ. 707*(vid) 414-616 129 127*-458 343 84 527 318 18-126 59* 319 Boᴮ Lect
24₇ om Γώγ Fᵇ o*I*-72′ 739ᶜ *f*⁻¹²⁹ 767 527 121 68′-120′-669ᶜ 59 799 Eus VI 18 Lect
24₇ om ἡ βασιλεία αὐτοῦ 72-381′ 767 619 121 68′-120′-126-669ᶜ 55 799 Lect
24₉ εὐλόγηνται] -γημενοι 16-46 19′ *d n* 130ᵐᵍ-321′ᵐᵍ-344ᵐᵍ *t* 126 Syh Lect
24₁₈ om ἐν 376(vid) C′′⁻¹³¹ᶜ ⁴²² ⁷⁶¹ᶜ 30′ 84 71 799 Lect

Except for 11₁₆(1°) which is a unique reading, 24₃, ₇(twice) ₁₈, Lect supports the reading of *d n* or *t* text. When *d n t* do not support a common variant Lect tends to support *n*.

---

[1]) *Monumenta Musicae Byzantinae*: Vol I *Prophetologium* ediderunt Carsten Høeg et Günther Zuntz. Hanniae, 1939—1970.

It is proposed to subject this text type to somewhat closer scrutiny in this chapter, first of all, to determine whether or not it betrays recensional characteristics based on some immediate or mediate acquaintance with the Hebrew text tradition, and secondly to gain some insight into the general character of this divergent text as a whole.

A. Since the work of Origen strongly affected the subsequent text tradition throughout, the extent of hexaplaric influence on the Byzantine is first examined. In the list below are given the instances in which an asterisked variant is supported by the Byzantine group. Since these are understood to be = 𝔐, this fact is not recorded in the list.

List 1

1₄₆ init] pr (※ G 127 Syh) και εγενοντο παντες οι επεσκεμμενοι (aut επισκ.) O⁻⁵⁸ d n t 799 Arm Syh

1₅₁ ἀναστήσουσιν] + (※ G) αυτην (+ ※ Syh) οι λευιται (λευειται G 127; λεβειται 767) O-707 44 n t 55 319 799 Arab Arm Syh; + αυτην A b Co

6₆ εὐχῆς 963] + (※ G Syh) αυτου Fᵇ M′ V O⁻⁵⁸ d n 85′ᵐᵍ-321′ᵐᵍ-344ᵐᵍ t⁻⁸⁴ 319 Tht Nm 198 Arm Bo Sa⁴ Syh

6₆ κυρίῳ 963] sub ※ Sᶜ; pr (※ S G Syh) τω (το 376) M′ Sᶜ O-82 52′-313-414 d n 28-85′ᵐᵍ-321′ᵐᵍ-344ᵐᵍ t Tht Nm 198 Bo Syh

6₂₁ fin] + (※ G) αυτου (+ κυριω 376; + τω κω 767; + τω κω ουτως ποιησει d t 799) V O′ d 767 t 318 799 Arab Sa⁴

11₁₀ θύρας] + (※ Syhᴸ) της (> 58*) σκηνης O d n t 527 Arm Syh

11₃₂ ἡμέραν 1°] + (※ G Syh) εκεινην (εκην. 767*; εκηνειν 376) O d f⁻¹²⁹ n t 18′-126-628-669 646 Syh

13₂₇ ἔδειξαν] + (※ G Syh) αυτοις V O-29 d t 121 319 ᴸᵃᵗcod 100 Aeth Bo Pal Syh

13₃₃ κατασκέψασθαι] sub ※ Syh; + (※ G Syh) αυτην O′⁻¹⁵ ⁵⁸ n⁽⁻⁴⁵⁸⁾ 319 Aeth Arm Pal Sa¹¹ Syh

14₇ κατεσκεψάμεθα] (c var) παρηλθομεν κατασκεψασθαι d t 799; pr (※ G) παρηλθομεν εν αυτη (+ ※ Syh) και O Arab Syh: cf 𝔐 עברנו בה לתור
The change of κατεσκεψάμεθα to an infinitive in d t seems at first blush to be based on the Hebrew, but is probably due to the influence of 13₃₃.

14₂₂ σημεῖα] + (※ G) μου (+ ↙ Syh) V O d t 799 Arab Syh

14₂₇ ἐγόγγυσαν] pr (※ G Syh) αυτοι V O d 129 t 18′-126-628-630′ Syh

15₂₈ fin B F V 72′ f⁻²⁴⁶ n⁻¹²⁷ x 59 ᴸᵃᵗcod 100 Aeth Arab Arm Sa] + και αφεθησεσθαι (-σθε 44) αυτω d t⁻⁸⁴; + (※ Gᶜ Syhᴸ; ÷ G*) και αφεθησεται (c var) αυτω (> 82) rell = 𝔐

16₂₇ Κόρε B F M′ V 72-707ᵗˣᵗ f n x 392 68′-120′ 59 319 799 ᴸᵃᵗcod 100 Aeth Arm Co] + (※ G Syh) και (> O 125 = 𝔐) δαθαν (θαν 426*c pr m) και αβιρων (c var) rell

18₉ ἁμαρτιῶν] + (※ Syhᴸ) αυτων F O-29 d f⁻⁵⁶ n t x⁻⁵⁰⁹ z⁻¹²⁸ ⁶⁶⁹ 646 Cyr I 837 ᴸᵃᵗcod 100 Arm Sa¹¹¹ Syh = edd

20₁₂ ἐπιστεύσατε] + μοι (μου 458 Thtᵃᵖ) M′ V 82 b d n⁻⁷⁶⁷ 130ᵐᵍ-321′ᵐᵍ t 527 319 Chr I 506 X 332 Tht Nm 216 ᴸᵃᵗcod 100 Aethᶜ Arab Arm; + (※ G Syh) εν εμοι O Bas I 440 Syh

22₂₂ ἐνδιαβάλλειν αὐτόν] pr (÷ Syh mend pro ※) εν (> 407) τη οδω (> 120) O n 527 120*-407 Or IV 409 ᴸᵃᵗcod 100 Bo Syh
It should be noted, however, that a variant επι της οδου after αὐτόν is widely supported as well.

22₂₃ ἐπάταξεν] + (※ Syh) βαλααμ M′ᵐᵍ V O d n t 527 Or IV 409 ᴸᵃᵗcod 100 Arab Syh

22₃₇ ἀπέστειλα] pr (※ Syhᴸ) mittens ᴸᵃᵗcod 100 Syh; pr αποστελλων 426-oI⁻⁶⁴ᵗˣᵗ 246 18′-628-630′; pr αποστειλας 376 b d⁻¹²⁵ n t 319

23₂₃ Ἰακώβ 2°] pr (※ Syhᴸ) τω Fᵇ O⁻³⁷⁶ 414 d n⁽⁻⁴⁵⁸⁾ t 527 Or III 223 Cels II 420 Tht Nm 220 Syh; τω ιακακωβ 376

27₁₀ κληρονομίαν] + (※ Syh) αυτου O⁻⁵⁸ 417-616 *b* 44-106⁽ᵐᵍ⁾-107 127-767 *t* 18'-407-628-630' 799 Arm Bo Syh

30₅ αὐτῆς /ὁ πατήρ] tr 82 *b d n t* 126 Cyr I 1060 Or II 306; + (※ Syh) αυτης O⁻ᴳ 730 Armᵗᵉ Syh = 𝔐; ※ αυτης↙ G

30₆ ὁρισμούς] + (※ Syh) αυτης A O-82-381' *b* 106⁽ᵐᵍ⁾ *n* 134 *y*⁻³¹⁸ Cyr I 1060 ᴸᵃᵗcod 100 Aug *Num* 57 Co Syh

30₁₅ αὐτῇ 1°] + (※ G) ο ανηρ αυτης O⁽⁻⁵⁸⁾-15 *d t* Bo Syh

32₃₇ Ἐλεαλή] pr (※ G Syh) την O⁻⁴²⁶ 422 *b f*⁻¹²⁹ *n* 799 Syh

33₃₈ ἱερεύς] + επι (εις 56'-664 84 Arm Compl; + ωρ 799) το ορος (του ορους pro τ. ο. 458) 29-82 *d* 56'-664 *n*⁻⁷⁶⁷ *t* 799 Arm Bo = Ald Compl; + (※ G Syh) εις ωρ το ορος O⁻⁵⁸ 767 ᴸᵃᵗcod 104 Arab Syh = 𝔐; + πλησιον του ορους A

34₂ αὕτη] + ※ η γη ↙ η G; + (※ 85) η γη (+ ※ 344) ητις (> M' 58-426 799 Syh) M' O⁻ᴳ-82 *d n*⁻⁷⁵ 30'-85ᵐᵍ-130-321'-343' *t* 392 799 ᴸᵃᵗcod 100 Arab Syh

34₁₄ Ῥουβήν] + (※ G) κατ οικους πατριων αυτων (> 246) O⁻⁵⁸-82 *b*⁻³¹⁴ 246 54' *t*⁻⁸⁴ 799 ᴸᵃᵗcodd 100 104(vid) Arab Syh

35₁₀ αὐτούς] + (※ G; ÷ Syh mend) οτι O⁻⁵⁸-15 *b d n t* Syh

36₃ (τῶν φυλῶν) υἱῶν] pr (※ Syh) των 29-82-376 551 44-125'-610ᶜ 54' *t*⁻⁷⁶* 55 319 799 Syh = Ald: contra 𝔐, but cf τῶν] pr (※ G) των νιων G-426 = 𝔐

36₉ οἱ υἱοί] (※ 344 Syh; + και 44 La) αι φυλαι (αι φ. sub ※ Gᶜ et sub ÷ G*; + των C'' 44 30'-85-344 392 646) νιων(bis scr 82) O-82 C'' *d n* 30'-85ᵐᵍ-344ᵐᵍ *t* 392 646 799 ᴸᵃᵗcodd 100 104 Syh

That the Byzantine text form was somewhat influenced by the hex recension is apparent from the above list. It is, however, not a primary witness to *O* as the chapter on The Hexaplaric Recension (pp. 43ss) clearly shows.

A few instances in the above list need special comment. At 6₂₁ the final clause reads ἣν ἂν εὔξηται κατὰ τὸν νόμον ἁγνείας. The hex text reads ης αν ευξηται ουτως ποιησει κατα τον νομον αγνειας αυτου with ουτως ποιησει and αυτου sub ast; this corresponds to the Hebrew אשר ידר כן יעשה על תורת נזרו. The Byzantine text witnesses to αυτου τω κυριω ουτως ποιησει after ἁγνείας. Thus the αυτου corresponds to *O*, but the remainder is inexact. The nominal τω κυριω has no basis in the Hebrew and is an epexegetical gloss. ουτως ποιησει may be due to *O* influence but it is in the wrong place.

At 20₁₂ Num rendered האמנתם בי simply by the absolute ἐπιστεύσατε. Origen, as might be expected, added εν εμοι, an exact equivalent for בי. The Byzantine text adds μοι to the verb. This need not actually be dependent on the *O* tradition, however, since this text tends to render explicit that which is implicit.

At 22₃₇ Num does not render the free infinitive שלח in the expression שלח שלחתי. This deficiency is filled by Origen by the addition of the present participle αποστελλων (ἀπέστειλα), whereas the Byzantine text adds the aorist form αποστειλας. Again unfortunately there are no hex notes extant to give one a hint as to possible independent recensional activity.

The inversion of αὐτῆς and ὁ πατήρ by the Byzantine text at 30₅ is only formally similar to the *O* tradition; it is probably only a stylistic change. The Hebrew context is והחריש לה אביה, rendered in Num by καὶ παρασιωπήσῃ αὐτῆς ὁ πατήρ, i.e. Num did not apparently render לה. *O* changed αὐτῆς to αυτη and

19

added αυτης sub ast. The αυτη tradition was present in The Three as the margin of 344 shows.

Finally the variants at 33₃₈ need comment. The Hebrew text reads ויעל אהרן הכהן אל הר ההר which is rendered in Num by καὶ ἀνέβη Ἀαρὼν ὁ ἱερεύς; i. e. the prepositional phrase is omitted. This was "corrected" by Origen through the addition of εις ωρ το ορος. The Byzantine text, on the other hand, has added επι το ορος. This is by no means necessarily due to the influence of the O text, however, since επι το ορος may simply represent an independent amplification of the text. The use of the preposition επι seems to me to indicate the fact that the plus is not based on any acquaintance with the Hebrew text or Hebraizing recensions/translations.

Other instances of possible hex plusses also attested by the Byzantine text tradition but without an asterisk are given in list 2. Only variants supported by at least one member of the primary O witnesses (including Syh) are listed as probably hex in character. Since these additions are understood to be = 𝔐, this fact is not indicated.

List 2

3₃₄ ἑξακισχίλιοι] εξ χιλιαδες (tr 458) και διακοσιοι n; + και (> 58 d) διακοσιοι O b d t Latcod 100 Arab Arm (but cf *List* 4)
3₄₉ τῶν 1°] pr παρα G-426 d⁻¹⁰⁶ f 54′ 343′ t 646 799 Syh
4₃₅ ἕως] pr και 58-426 n⁻⁷⁵
8₁₅ αὐτούς 2° 963] + αποδομα (aut -δωμα) Fᵃ V 44′ 129 130ᵐᵍ-321′ᵐᵍ t y⁻³¹⁸ 319 Arm; + δομα (aut δωμα; -ματα 19′) 58-376 b f⁻¹²⁹ n Latcod 100(datum)
13₂₁ πίων] + εστι(ν) 426 d 246 n t 319 Arm(vid) Bo Pal
14₁₄ ὀπτάζῃ] οπτανη (c var) συ n; + (+ οτι 58) συ O 129 Eus VI 240 Arm Syh
15₃₂ τῇ 2°] pr εν A 376 n⁻¹²⁷ x⁻⁵⁰⁹ 318 319 Latcod 100 Syh
21₃₃ αὐτοῖς] + αυτος V O⁻⁵⁸ d n t 527 Sa¹² Syh
26₅₉ Μωυσῆν] pr τον 106-125′ t 619 z 319; τον μωυση 44-610; τον μωσην 426 77 127-767; lmwš̄' Syh
27₉ κληρονομίαν] + αυτου V 963 82-376′ C'' b d 129 n s⁻³⁰ t 392 z 319 624 646 Arm Co Syh

The addition of the pronoun is also attested in 963 and was therefore already in the tradition before Origen's time. If his LXX parent text did not have it, he reintroduced it as is clear from the support by 376′ Syh.

27₁₉ συναγωγῆς 963] pr της 426 d 53′-56ᶜ-129 n t⁻⁷⁶ 619 y⁻³⁹² 68′ 319 Tht *Nm* 224
27₂₁ (αὐτὸς καὶ) οἱ] pr παντες O⁻⁵⁸ b d⁻¹²⁵ n⁻⁷⁶⁷ t; παντες 125 767
    This is certainly hex since Syh attests to παντες sub ast before αὐτός.
27₂₂ συναγωγῆς] pr της 381′-426 422 125 53′ n 28-85⁽ᵐᵍ⁾ 619 55 319
30₁₅ ὁρισμούς] + αυτης (αυτους 107*) A 426 d 127-458 730 t Armᵃᵖ Sa
30₁₇ πατρός 2° 963] + αυτης 426 b 44-107′ n⁻⁷⁵ t Arm Co Syh
31₁₉ ἀνελών] + ψυχην M′ V O′ b d f⁻¹²⁹ n t 799 Latcodd 100 104 Arab Bo Syh
31₂₇ συναγωγῆς] pr της (τη 75) A O⁻⁴²⁶-381′ 414 106⁽ᵐᵍ⁾ 129 n t⁽⁻³⁷⁰⁾ 527 Cyr I 333bis
32₂₈ Ἰσραήλ] pr των υιων 707 106 127 t 527; pr υιων 376′-618 54-75′ 799 Arab Bo Syh = Compl
32₃₃ Ἀμορραίων] pr των A 58-376 73′ b d f⁻¹²⁹ n⁻⁴⁵⁸ t 55 799
34₅ διέξοδος 963] + αυτου O d 129-246 n t 628 Arm Sa¹ Syh
34₂₂ Δάν 963] pr υιων 426 d⁻¹²⁵ 246 n t Syh

Also considered hex are changes in word order to fit that of 𝔐. The following list is limited to those supported by at least one of the primary witnesses to the O text.

List 3

7₈₈ ἑξήκοντα ἐνιαύσιαι] tr V O n⁻⁵⁴ 126

16₉ ὑμᾶς 1°] post Ἰσραήλ 1° tr B O⁻⁵⁸ d 129 127 t 509 Cyr I 860 Syh = Ra

22₃₃ τρίτον τοῦτο] tr A V 29 118'-537 106 129 767 30 t 319 Or IV 409 Aeth Arm Syh; το τριτον 376' 552 19' 71

22₄₀ πρόβατα] et μόσχους tr 376' n 527 Arm Syh

23₃ μοι δείξῃ] δειξη μοι ο θεος d t; tr 426 59 Arm Syh = 𝔐

24₂ πνεῦμα θεοῦ / ἐπ' αὐτῷ] tr A F O'⁻⁸² C'' 56' n⁻¹²⁷ s 527-619 y z 55 59 799 ᴸᵃᵗcod 100 Ruf Num XVII 2 Aeth Arab Syh

24₁₀ τρίτον τοῦτο] tr A F M' O'⁻³⁷⁶-29-707 C''⁻⁵²' ³¹³ ⁷⁶¹ 19 d 53'-56 s 527 y 18'-126-407-628-630' 59 799 Arm Bo Syh

27₉ θυγάτηρ αὐτῷ] tr V 963 (vid) O⁻⁵⁸-82 414 b d 129 n t x⁻⁶¹⁹ 55 624 ᴸᵃᵗRuf Num XXII 1 Syh

That 963 had the transposed order is practically certain. The line in question reads [η αυτω θυγατ]ηρ δωσε, and 10 letters is precisely what is lacking. Thus the variant order was already in the tradition by the time of Origen.

33₄ τὴν ἐκδίκησιν / κύριος] tr O⁻⁵⁸-82 53' n⁻⁴⁵⁸ 76 ᴸᵃᵗcodd 100 104 Ruf Num XXVII 8 Aeth Syh

35₁₂ αἱ πόλεις / ὑμῖν] υμων αι πολεις G; tr O⁻ᴳ n Arm Bo Syh

Post-hexaplaric activity resulting in the omission of materials which Origen had placed under the obelus is examined in the chapter on the Hexaplaric Recension. This is also represented in list 4. That the omission is = 𝔐 is not noted.

List 4

1₂ αὐτῶν 3°] sub ÷ G; > B 19 d 127 t x 18 319 Cyr VI 453 X 624 ᴸᵃᵗcod 100 Arm

3₃₄ καὶ πεντήκοντα] sub ÷ G Syh; > 15-58 b d n⁻⁷⁶⁷ t ᴸᵃᵗcod 100 Aethᶜ Arab Arm (but cf List 2)

6₃ ἀπὸ οἴνου 2°] sub ÷ G Syh; > 58-72-381' d f n⁽⁻⁴⁵⁸⁾ t 619 59 319 Cyr I 1041 Eus VIII 2.116 ᴸᵃᵗcod 100 Aethᶜᴳ Arm Sa

6₆ πάσῃ] sub ÷ G Syh; > 58 n⁻⁷⁶⁷ Arm

10₄ πάντες] pr ÷ Syh; > 58 n⁻⁷⁶⁷ 527 319 Arm

11₈ αὐτό 1°] sub ÷ Syh; > n 527 121 628 319 Tht Nm 203 ᴸᵃᵗcod 100 Arm

11₂₇ λέγων] sub ÷ Syh; > b d⁽⁻⁴⁴⁾ n t 126 Aeth Arm Sa

20₁₆ κύριος] sub ÷ G; > 58 552 d 53' 126 Arab

31₈ σύν—fin] sub ÷ G; > 58-426 d⁻¹⁰⁶ 527 Arab

33₅₂ αὐτά] sub ÷ G Syh; > 72-381' d 664 55 799 ᴸᵃᵗcod 104 Spec 44 Aeth Arm

It is of course possible that the obelus was lost in the tradition. In the following list are given omissions in the Byzantine text group which are equal to 𝔐 but for which no obelus tradition is extant.

List 5

5₈ om ὁ A oI n 130 68' 55 Tht Nm 195

8₆ τῶν υἱῶν Ἰσραήλ] om τῶν B O⁻⁵⁸ d⁻⁶¹⁰ 127-767 t⁻⁸⁴ 509 55 319

8₁₄ idem A B O⁻⁵⁸ d 127-767 t x⁻⁶¹⁹ 121

10₁₂ τοῦ Φαράν] om τοῦ 44'-125 767

10₁₇ οἱ υἱοὶ Γεδσών] om οἱ O⁻⁵⁸-707 C⁻¹⁶-417 d⁻⁴⁴ 129 75 321* 509* 392* 319

13₃₀ om ποταμόν V O⁻⁵⁸ d n⁻⁷⁶⁷ t 319 Latcod 100 Arab Arm Co Pal Syh

14₁₀ τοῖς υἱοῖς Ἰσραήλ] om τοῖς n⁻⁴⁵⁸

15₃₆ om πᾶσα ἡ συναγωγή 2° O⁽⁻⁵⁸⁾-82-381' d⁻¹⁰⁶ f⁻¹²⁹ 509-619 Arab Syh

15₃₆ om ἔξω τῆς παρεμβολῆς 2° M' O⁽⁻⁵⁸⁾-82-381' d⁽⁻¹⁰⁶⁾ x⁻⁵²⁷ Arab Syh

18₉ τῆς πλημμελείας αὐτῶν] om τῆς B 82 d n⁻⁷⁶⁷ t x⁻⁶¹⁹ Cyr I 837 = Ra

18₂₃ τὰ ἁμαρτήματα αὐτῶν] om τά 15-618*(c pr m) d⁻¹⁰⁶ 509

18₃₀ om ἀπό 1° n 319 Bo

18₃₀ om ἀπό 2° n 319 Latcod 100 Bo

19₁₂ om καί 2° 15*-82-376 550' 118'-537 53'-129 n⁻¹²⁷ 30 619 126 416 799 Eus VI 12 Bo

21₇ om ὅτι 1° V O⁻⁵⁸ 44 n⁻¹²⁷ 30 619 z 646 Latcod 100 Aeth Arm Syh

22₂₂ ὁ ἄγγελος τοῦ θεοῦ] om ὁ 72 b d 527

24₈ ταῖς βολίσιν αὐτοῦ] om ταῖς d⁻⁴⁴ t

26₅₈ om καί 1° 58-72-82 n 76 392 126 Bo

30₁₁ om ἐν 528 d⁻¹⁰⁶ 53' 509 128

31₂₂ om καί 2° 3° 4° d 71'

33₆ om τι O⁻⁵⁸-29-82 739* d⁻¹⁰⁶ f⁻¹²⁹ 54-75' 84 527 18'-126-630' LatPsAmbr Mans 3 Co Syh

35₃₁ om παρά d⁻¹⁰⁶ 84

35₃₄ τῶν υἱῶν Ἰσραήλ] om τῶν V 29-82-376 422 b d 129 n t x 392 407-630 55 59 319

36₃ τὴν κληρονομίαν τῆς φυλῆς] om τήν B V G-82-426 d 129 n t x 319 = Ra

36₁₂ τοῦ πατρὸς αὐτῶν] om τοῦ 82 b n⁻⁷⁶⁷ 126 319

The above list includes the omission of articles which only formally correspond to 𝔐; since the noun modified is a bound form it cannot be articulated in Hebrew, and these instances are to be discounted in any evaluation of possible hex influence on the text tradition (these are 8₆ ₁₄ 10₁₇ 14₁₀ 18₉ ₂₃ 22₂₂ 24₈ 35₃₄ 36₃ ₁₂).

A proper evaluation of the extent of possible hex influence on the Byzantine text must involve a comparison of the above lists with the corresponding lists in ch. 3. Such a comparison shows that hex influence is comparatively minimal.

It remains to discover whether or not the Byzantine text shows direct or indirect Hebrew influence which is nonhexaplaric in origin. In the list below are given all instances of formal correspondences to the text of 𝔐 which seem not to stem from Origen; the reading of 𝔐 is given in each instance.

List 6

1₄ ἀρχόντων] αρχων d n⁻⁷⁶⁷ t 18 319 Arm: ראש

The variant singular need not be due to Hebrew influence since it could be created by syncopation as well.

1₄ πατριῶν] + αυτων 16-46 106-107' t 392 319 Co: cf אבתיו

It is unlikely that the variant is due to the influence of 𝔐, but rather to that of the oft-recurring formula κατ' (οἴκους) πατριῶν αὐτῶν throughout the ch. (cf. e.g. vv. 20 22 24)

1₅ τῶν (Ρουβήν)] τω A 29 d n⁻⁷⁶⁷ 30 t 121 18 55* Arm: לראובן

1₆ τῶν (Συμεών)] τω A 528-551 d n⁻⁷⁶⁷ t 121 18 Arm: לשמעון

22

1₇ τῶν (Ἰούδα)] τω A d n⁻⁷⁶⁷ t 121 18 Arm: ליהודה
1₈ τῶν (Ἰσσαχάρ)] τω Aᶜ 46ˢ d n⁻⁷⁶⁷ t 18 Arm: ליששכר
1₉ τῶν (Ζαβουλών)] τω Aᶜ d n⁻⁷⁶⁷ t 18 Arm: לזבולן
1₉ τῶν (Ἐφράιμ)] τω 73'-550'-761* d n t 18 Arm: לאפרים
1₁₀ τῶν (Μανασσή)] τω 618 d n t 18 Arm: למנשה
1₁₁ τῶν (Βενιαμίν)] τω d n⁽⁻⁷⁵⁾ t 18 Arm: לבנימן
1₁₂ τῶν (Δάν)] τω d n t 18 Arm: לדן
1₁₃ τῶν (Ἀσήρ)] τω d n t 18 Arm: לאשר
1₁₄ τῶν (Γάδ)] τω 551 d n t 18 Arm: לגד
1₁₅ τῶν (Νεφθαλί)] τω d n t 18 Arm: לנפתלי

In each of the above instances (vv. 5—15) the dative article of the variant text correctly renders the Hebrew preposition whereas the genitive plural of Num constitutes a free interpretation.

2₁₇ μέσον] pr εις d n t 799: בתוך
2₃₁ (κατὰ) τάγμα (αὐτῶν)] -ματα (συντ. 528) M' V G-82-707-oI⁻¹⁵ C'' b⁻¹⁹ d 53'-56 s 509 y⁻¹²¹ 55 Cyr I 725 ᴸᵃᵗcod 100: לדגליהם

The origin of the variant is uncertain as its mixed support indicates.

3₂₃ υἱοί] pr οι δημοι 58 799; οι (> V 54-75') δημοι V O⁻⁵⁸ d n t Arm Sa Syh: משפחת

This may well represent a prehexaplaric revision already present in Origin's parent text.

4₂₇ (καὶ) ἐπισκέψῃ] -ψασθε (c var) n⁻⁷⁶⁷ 84-134 Arm; -ψεσθε d 74-76' Arab: ופקדתם

The command is to Moses alone (cf. v. 21), and Num is consistently singular from vv. 21—28, but then becomes plural in v. 29 (singular in 𝔐, and v. 32 (as 𝔐)). The number of the verbs is too mixed in the tradition to posit Hebrew influence in v. 27.

4₄₈ ὀγδοήκοντα] pr και 44 54'-767 t⁻⁸⁴ Syh: ושמנים

The tradition of compound numbers is complicated by the fact that numbers are often represented in the mss by short forms. It would be dangerous to posit Hebrew influence in the presence (or absence) of a conjunction.

7₈₇ αἱ θυσίαι αὐτῶν] pr και B* 707 d f⁻¹²⁹ n t 319 Arm Sa: ומנחתם

The correspondence of the variant text and 𝔐 is by no means evidence of Hebrew influence. The και of the variant text comes between δώδεκα and αἱ and may be palaeographically conditioned. For the secondary nature of και cf p. 100.

9₁₃ κυρίῳ] (+ του 381') κυ A F 72-376ᶜ-426-oI⁻¹⁵ 73' 106 n⁻⁵⁴ 30 x⁻⁵⁰⁹ 392 z⁻¹²⁰' 319 Aeth Bo Syh: יהוה (קרבן)
9₂₁ ἤ (νυκτός)] και 707 d 127 730 t 71 Sa: ולילה
10₈ ταῖς σάλπιγξιν] pr εν V oI⁻¹⁵ b d n t 527-619 Bo: בחצצרוח
10₁₂ ἐν τῇ ἐρήμῳ 1°] εκ της ερημου d n⁻⁴⁵⁸ t Arab Arm: ממדבר
11₁₂ (λάβε) αὐτούς] αυτον B O⁻⁵⁸ d 56* n⁻⁷⁶⁷ t x⁻⁶¹⁹ Phil III 6ᵗᵉ Chr I 476 Tht Nm 204 Arm Boᴮ Syh = Ra: שאהו

23

It should be noted that the Byzantine text is strangely inconsistent, since earlier in the verse it has (ἔτεκον) αὐτούς where 628 799 Phil III 6te Chr I 476 Tht Nm 204 have αυτον corresponding to Hebrew's ילדתיהו.

14$_{42}$ καὶ πεσεῖσθε] και ου πεσ. M′ d n^{-75} t: cf ולא תגפו

The introduction of the negative particle corresponds to 𝔐. It could have been introduced from the context however without Hebrew influence, since the clause is preceded by μὴ ἀναβαίνετε οὐ γάρ ἐστιν κύριος μεθ' ὑμῶν. The intent of the Hebrew is "lest you be smitten" which is hardly met by the variant text and it is more likely that the simple negative was thoughtlessly introduced under the influence of the context.

18$_{15}$ λυτρωθήσεται] λυτρωση d^{-125} n^{-767} t 319 Arm; redimis ^{Lat}cod 100: תפדה

The variant text is not necessarily due to Hebrew influence, since λυτρώσῃ occurs in the next clause.

20$_9$ συνέταξεν] + αυτω V 72 b d n t 527 319 Aeth^F Arm: צוהו

The context reads καθὰ συνέταξεν κύριος for 𝔐's כאשר צוהו. It should be noted that V 319 also omit κύριος. The introduction of the pronoun may well be ex par, since the formula is a common one.

20$_{24}$ εἰσέλθητε] εισελθη b d 129 n t 527 318 319 ^{Lat}cod 100 Arm^{te}: יבא

The context reads "let Aaron be gathered to his people, for not will ye (he) enter the land." The LXX "corrected" the Hebrew text since both Moses and Aaron would die before the conquest διότι παρωξύνατέ με. The Byzantine text simplifies the text and its correspondence with 𝔐 may be a coincidence.

21$_1$ Χανανίς] χαυανι 321′ t 121^c 18′-126-628-630′ 646; χαναναιος (χαναιος 53; χαναναι 54) A 72-426 53′-56*-129 n 527 Procop 856 ^{Lat}cod 100 Arab Arm^{ap} Bo Sa^{1012}; χαναav d Aeth Syh: הכנעני

21$_3$ Χανανίν] χαυανι (-νη 343) A M*(vid) s^{-2885} t 71-509 y^{-392} 18′-126-628-630′ 416 646; χαναναιον 72-426-oI 53′-129 n 527-619 ^{Lat}cod 100 Arm Sa^{1012} Syh; χαναav d$^{(-44)}$ Aeth: הכנעני

21$_5$ ἐξήγαγες (ἡμᾶς)] -γαγετε (c var; εξαγ. 509) A M′ V 82 d 129 n 321*(vid) t x^{-619} 121 55 Sa^{412}: העליתנו

𝔐 is vocalized as a plural verb. The context requires a plural verb: καὶ κατελάλει ὁ λαὸς πρὸς τὸν θεὸν καὶ κατὰ Μωυσῆ. Note how the LXX avoids the plain speech of the Hebrew by using two different prepositions in the context as well as using the singular ἐξήγαγες. The rebellious challenge is thereby mitigated and only Moses is said to have brought the people from Egypt in order to die in the desert. The variant text is probably simply due to the plural context rather than to Hebrew influence.

22$_{22}$ τοῦ θεοῦ] κυ 376 314 d t 527 Aeth Bo: יהוה
24$_{10}$ ἐπί (Βαλαάμ)] προς n^{-127} 509 ^{Lat}cod 100: אל בלעם
24$_{14}$ ἰδού] + εγω 64-381 d f^{-56*} 127 t 319: הני

24₂₀ (καὶ τὸ σπέρμα) αὐτῶν] αυτου 376 b d 246 n⁽⁻⁷⁶⁷⁾ 30′-344ᵐᵍ t(370 inc) 318 319 ᴸᵃᵗRuf
Num XIX 1ᵃᵖ: ואחריתו

The referent is ἀρχὴ ἐθνῶν Ἀμαλήκ (ראשית גוים עמלק). The translator's plural pronoun refers to ἐθνῶν (or possibly Ἀμαλήκ), whereas the simpler referent of the variant must be Ἀμαλήκ.

25₄ τῷ Μωυσῇ] πρὸς μωυσην (-ση M′; μωσει 72) A M′ 58-72-oI d s t 619 y 55 319: אל משה
26₁₉ καὶ (υἱοί)] > n 126 319 ᴸᵃᵗcod 100: בני
26₄₀ οὗτοι] pr και d⁽⁻⁴⁴⁾ t: ואלה
26₄₆ υἱοί] pr ουτοι (+ οι 54) 106-125 n 321′-344ᵐᵍ 319 ᴸᵃᵗcod 100; ουτοι 44-107′ t: אלה בני
28₁₃ δέκατον 1°] pr και b d n t 646 ᴸᵃᵗcod 100 Aethᶜ Arab Arm Sa: ועשרן
29₁₁ ἡ θυσία αὐτῆς 963] pr και d n t Aeth Arab Arm Sa: ומנחתה
29₁₃ ὁλοκαυτώματα 963] -μα F 29-376-381′ n⁻¹²⁷ 28-85 84 ᴸᵃᵗcodd 100 104 Aeth Bo: עלה
29₂₁ (καὶ) ἡ σπονδὴ (αὐτῶν)] αι σπονδαι 52′ b d⁽⁻¹⁰⁶ᵗˣᵗ⁾ n⁽⁻⁷⁵⁾ t ᴸᵃᵗcod 100: ונסכיהם

The variant happens to correspond to 𝔐 but this is meaningless. ἡ θυσία and ἡ σπονδή in v. 18 and ἡ θυσία in v. 21 are also in the plural in the Byzantine text.

29₃₆ ὁλοκαυτώματα] -μα F G-29-376-381′-707 d⁻¹²⁵ 56′ n t 319 Cyr I 1124 Aeth: עלה
30₄ ἢ (ὁρίσηται)] και d n t ᴸᵃᵗcod 100 Bo: ואסרה
31₅₄ τῶν υἱῶν] τοις υιοις 82 b n 799 ᴸᵃᵗcodd 100 104 Ruf Num XXVI 2: לבני
32₉ Φάραγγα] pr εις Fᵇ M′ 58-426 f⁻¹²⁹ n Aeth Arm Bo; εκ φαραγγος d t; pr εως oI: עד נחל
32₁₄ ἰδού] pr και 707 d n t 126 55 799 Cyr I 404 Aeth Syh: והנה
33₇ (στόμα) Εἰρώθ] pr επι 58 d n t; επειρωθ 82 321′ᵐᵍ-344ᵐᵍ; επιρωθ B* 129 319 Arm: פי החירת

At first blush the introduction of επι might seem related to פי but this can hardly be correct since the translator rendered it by στόμα. The reading of B shows that it was palaeographically conditioned; the initial ει was carelessly copied as επι yielding επιρωθ, or as seems more likely επειρωθ. This in turn produced either επιρωθ or επειρωθ (or επι ειρωθ). Since στόμα is preceded by ἐπί as well, the process of corruption was made easier.

33₁₄ (ἐν) Ῥαφιδίν] -διμ (-δειμ 761) 426 761 d t Syh: ברפידם
33₁₅ (ἐκ) Ῥαφιδίν] -διμ (-δειμ 761) 426 761 d t Armᵗᵉ Syh: מרפידם
33₄₀ Χανανίς] χαναναιος (χαναναι 134) 82 d 129 n t ᴸᵃᵗcodd 100 104 Aeth Syh: הכנעני
34₁₄ ἔλαβεν] ελαβον d t 799 Aeth Bo: לקחו

The subject of the verb is compound: φυλή ... καὶ φυλή ... καὶ τὸ ἥμισυ φυλῆς in which case the translator normally uses a singular verb. The Hebrew usually does so as well. The plural verb is equally justifiable from a Greek point of view and the change need not be due to the Hebrew text.

36₂ καὶ τῷ κυρίῳ] + ημων (υμ. 44) 29-72 d n t 59 Co; + μου O⁽⁻³⁷⁶⁾ 246 126-128-669 Syh: ואדני

The addition of ημων is hardly due to the Hebrew text but to the occurrence of τῷ κυρίῳ ἡμῶν earlier in the verse.

36₄ πατριᾶς (ἡμῶν)] πατριων 𝔐ᵗˣᵗ d⁽⁻¹⁰⁶⁾ n⁻⁴⁵⁸ t 646: אבתינו

B. Whether or not the Byzantine text was recensionally conditioned by the Hebrew text either immediately or mediately as the above instances might be interpreted to indicate can only be determined by an investigation of the general character of the text type. Thus if the text has many omissions an occasional omission which corresponds to 𝔐 is probably mere coincidence. Or if a verbal inflection is commonly changed to fit the context an occasional correspondence to 𝔐 has little meaning.

In list 6 above omissions involve καί or the article, as well as one of a pronoun. The addition of κα occurs a number of times as does the change of conjunctions (ἤ to και). Plusses involve pronouns, prepositions or the negative particle. Changes may involve number, case, preposition, lexical stem or the spelling of proper names. Each of these will be investigated as to whether it is a common tendency in the Byzantine tradition. All instances are contra 𝔐.

1. Variants involving the addition or omission of κα are common in this text type. As in list 6 the addition of κα occurs more often than its omission (39 times over against 24). Since these are all contra 𝔐 there is little point to detailing all the evidence. The interested reader is referred to the apparatus in Num. Additions of κα occur at 2₁₆ 3₃ ₁₉ 4₂₃ ₂₇ ₂₉ 5₁₅ 6₅ ₉ 7₈₅ ₈₈ 9₁₃ ₁₅ ₂₂ 10₃₅ 11₃₅ 13₂₉ ₃₄ 14₂ ₁₈ 15₁₄ ₁₅ 18₁₂ ₁₆ ₂₆ 19₁₁ 20₁₃ 21₈ 22₃₈ 26₅ ₆(twice) ₃₃ 28₂₁ 29₁₀ 31₃₇ 32₁₈ ₂₀ 33₃. Omissions of καί obtain at 1₄₆(twice) 2₁₅ ₂₀ 4₃ ₄₄ 5₂₈ ₂₉ 7₈₅ 9₃ 10₃₄ 11₃₂ 16₄₂ 18₂₃ 26₁ ₃₆ ₅₁ 31₈ ₃₂(twice) ₅₂ 34₄ 35₆ ₇.

It is interesting to observe that και is substituted for ἤ in only one instance in opposition to 𝔐, viz. 30₁₁ ἤ] και d Aeth

2. The Byzantine group is characterized by much more nominal articulation than is Num. Nouns are articulated in 78 instances where Num has the noun unarticulated. Over against this the article is omitted only 22 times. Furthermore the article (used as relative pronoun) is added before ἐν τοῖς κτήνεσιν in 3₄₁, before ὑπ' αὐτῶν in 4₂₇, before πρὸς αὐτόν in 5₈, before πρὸς λίβα 2° in 34₃, and before πρὸς βορρᾶν in 34₇. Thus the occasional correspondence of the addition or omission of an article to the Hebrew text is probably mere coincidence.

3. Addition or omission of pronouns.
In the following list all instances are contra 𝔐.

List 7

1₂ om αὐτῶν 1° B 414′ d n⁻⁷⁶⁷ t x 18 Bas II 145 Cyr VI 453 X 624 ᴸᵃᵗcod 100 PsBas *Is* I 5 Arm

1₂ om αὐτῶν 2° B V d n⁻⁷⁶⁷ t x 18 319 Bas II 145 Cyr VI 453 X 624 ᴸᵃᵗcod 100 Hi *Eph* II 3 PsBas *Is* I 5 Arm

14₂ om αὐτῶν 1° 44-107′

4₇ σπένδει] + εν αυτοις 803 d n t

4₁₄ αὐτοῖς] + επ αυτο 44′-125(2°) 127 t Sa; + επ αυτων n⁻¹²⁷

4₃₁ om αὐτῆς 1° B V d 54-75′ t x⁻⁶¹⁹ 319 ᴸᵃᵗcod 104 Arm Sa¹² = Ra

4₃₅ ἔργα] + αυτου d t

5₁₆ om αὐτήν 1° n⁻⁷⁶⁷ Tht *Nm* 196 Arm

5₂₂ γαστέρα] + σου d n t Aeth Arm Bo Syh

7₈₇ om αὐτῶν 1° *d* Bo

7₈₈ αὐτόν 963] + αυτα *d n t* 799

9₁₀ om ὅς *d t* 126 319

9₁₄ om πρὸς ὑμᾶς *d t*

11₈ ἔτριβον] + αυτο 413-422 44-107′ 730 *t* 509 392 799 Aeth Bo Syh[L]; + αυτον 125

11₁₁ ἐπιθεῖναι] + μοι (με 107 Tht[ap]) *d* 767 *t* 527 319 Tht *Nm* 204 Arm

11₁₇ λαοῦ] + τουτου 58 *d* n⁻⁷⁵ *t* Bas II 285 Tht *Nm* 204 Aeth Arab Arm Co

11₂₇ εἶπεν] + αυτω 58-376 118′-537 *d*⁽⁻⁴⁴⁾ *f*⁻¹²⁹ *n t* Arm

14₁₅ λαόν] + σου 376 *d*⁻¹²⁵ 54′ *t* Arm

14₂₇ om ἅ B* V *d*⁻⁴⁴ 75 *t* 318 319 [Lat]cod 100 Sa

14₃₇ ἄνθρωποι] + εκεινοι *b d*⁽⁻¹²⁵⁾ *n t* 799 Aeth⁻[CG] Arm Syh

15₃₉ om ὑμῶν 2° B 15-82 c*I*-551 *d* 129 n⁻⁷⁶⁷ *t*⁻⁸⁴ x⁻⁵⁰⁹ z 319 Tht *Nm* 211 [Lat]cod 100

16₁₁ om σου 15 *d* 120*(c pr m)

16₁₃ ἐρήμῳ] + ταυτη 58-376 *d* 127-767 *t* 799 [Lat]cod 100 Co

16₁₃ ἄρχων] pr συ *b d* 127 *t* Arm Bo

16₁₅ εἴληφα] + τι *d t*

16₃₄ om αὐτῶν 1° *d*

17₂ om αὐτοῦ 1° 58-72-381′ 52-529 n⁻⁷⁶⁷ 527 799 [Lat]cod 100 Arm Bo Sa¹

18₄ προστεθήσονται] + και ουτοι *d*⁽⁻¹²⁵⁾ *t*

18₉ καρπωμάτων] + αυτων *d t* Arm[ap]

18₁₆ συντίμησις] + αυτου 29-72-376 131[c] 54-75′ 59 Arab Arm Sa¹² Syh

18₁₉ δέδωκα] + αυτα *d* 54-75′ *t* [Lat]cod 100 Co

19₂ om ᾗ V *d* 53′-129 54-75′ *t* 71 318 59[c] 319 Arm Bo

19₅ om αὐτῆς 2° *d*⁻¹⁰⁶ 458 319 [Lat]PsAug *Serm Cai* II 38.2

19₁₄ οἰκία 2°] + εκεινη V *d t* 799

19₁₅ om ἐπ' αὐτῷ *b d t* 126 799 Phil I 281 II 261 Eus VI 12

19₂₁ ἔσται 1°] + τουτο *d*⁽⁻¹²⁵⁾ n⁻⁷⁵ *t* 121 799 [Lat]cod 100

19₂₂ om αὐτοῦ 82 *d* 54′ *t* [Lat]cod 100

19₂₂ ψυχή] + εκεινη *d* 54′-767 *t* 799

20₁₇ ἀγρῶν] + σου *d* 53′-129 127-767 *t* 527 319 Arm

22₈ νύκτα] + ταυτην *b d n t* 527 [Lat]cod 100 Aeth Arm Co Syh

22₂₅ om ἑαυτήν n⁻¹²⁷ 527

22₃₂ om αὐτῷ 246 n⁻¹²⁷ 126[txt]

22₃₅ ἀνθρώπων] + τουτων 58-376 *d n t* Aeth Arm Co

22₃₈ βάλῃ] + μοι n⁽⁻⁷⁶⁷⁾ 28-85′[mg]-321′[mg]-344[mg] 527 319 [Lat]cod 100

23₃ om σου *d* 53 *t*

23₁₁ ἰδού] + συ *d* 127 *t* 527

23₂₆ θεός] + προς με 106 *t*

24₁₀ om μου 414 *d t* [Lat]cod 100

26₄ καί 2°] pr συ B V *O n* 71-509 407 [Lat]cod 100 Arm Syh

26₃₇ om αὐτῷ 552 n⁻¹²⁷ [Lat]cod 100 Arm

26₅₅ ὀνόμασιν] + αυτων n⁻¹²⁷ Arm[ap]

27₁ om αὐτῶν *d*⁻¹⁰⁶

27₁₁ ὦσιν] + αυτω 16-46 44-106⁽ᵐᵍ⁾-107 54′-767 *t* 318 799 Bo

29₂₄ om αὐτῶν 3° *d*⁻¹⁰⁶

29₂₇ om αὐτῶν 1° *d*⁻¹⁰⁶ x⁻⁵⁰⁹

30₅ ὁρισμοί] + αυτης V 414 *b d* 129 767 *t* 407 55 319 Cyr I 1060 Sa

30₉ ἀνήρ 2°] + αυτης 29 *b* 106⁽ᵐᵍ⁾ 129-246 *n t* x⁻⁵⁰⁹ 392 55 Co Syh

30₁₁ ὁρισμός 963] + αυτης *d f*⁻¹²⁹ n⁽⁻⁷⁶⁷⁾ *t* x⁻⁵⁰⁹ 628

30₁₃ ὁρισμούς 963] + αυτης 29 529 *d* 129 54-458 *t* 509 318 z⁻⁴⁰⁷ 319 646 Arm Co

31₇ fin] + εν αυτη V *d f*⁻⁵⁶* *t*

31₁₀ om αὐτῶν 1° 72 *d*

32₂₆ om ἡμῶν 1° *d*⁻¹⁰⁶ [Lat]cod 104

32₂₆ om ἡμῶν 2° *d*⁻¹⁰⁶

32₃₁ om αὐτοῦ B F 29-72 *b* n⁻¹²⁷ 30′-344 x 392 120′ 59 319 [Lat]codd 100 104

32₃₃ om αὐτοῖς M′ *d n t* 799 Arm Bo

33₅₂ om αὐτῶν 3° *d*⁻¹⁰⁶

35₁₉ αἷμα] + αυτου *d t*

35₁₉ ἀποκτενεῖ 1°] + αυτον *d* n⁻⁷⁵ *t*

35₂₁ ἀποκτενεῖ] + αυτον *d*⁻¹²⁵ *n t* Aeth Arm

In the above list of 69 instances, 39 constitute additions of pronouns or pronominal phrases, and 30, of omissions. There seems to be a greater tendency towards amplification than towards the reverse in this text group. In list 6 there were four instances of pronouns added and only one omission; whether these were due to Hebrew influence rather than part of the general character of this text type must remain uncertain. In general the Byzantine text seems to betray a fair amount of freedom with respect to the pronominal tradition.

4. Addition, omission or change of preposition.

3₈ κατά] και 376 528-739* 106-107' n⁻⁷⁶⁷ t Tht Nm 192 Arab Arm

4₉ ὅσοις] εν οις d n t 71

4₁₄ ὅσοις] εν οις F V d f n t ᴸᵃᵗcod 100

6₇ ἐπ' (αὐτοῖς) 963] εν 72 C'' n 84*(vid) 392 Bo

7₃ ἐναντίον 963] εναντι 376 b n 392 319

9₁₁ ἐν (τῷ μηνί)] > n⁻⁷⁶⁷ 527

9₁₁ πικρίδων] pr επι 376-707 b d 246 n t 527 319 ᴸᵃᵗcod 100 Aethᶜᴳ

10₅ ἀνατολάς] pr κατα (aut κατ) b d n t 527 392 Aeth

10₆ λίβα] pr κατα 537 n⁻¹²⁷ Aeth; pr προς d t ᴸᵃᵗcod 100 Ambr Sat II 107 Or Matth 52

10₆ παρά] προς 77 d s⁽⁻³⁴³⁾ 646 ᴸᵃᵗcod 100 Ambr Sat II 107; κατα Mᵐᵍ 73'-413-528'-551 b⁻¹⁹ n ᴸᵃᵗOr Matth 52 Aeth

10₃₅ χιλιάδας] pr εις C'' d n 28-30'-85'ᵐᵍ t ᴸᵃᵗcod 100 Aeth Arm

11₁ ἔναντι] -τιον C-46 d⁻⁴⁴ 54' t 527

11₁₀ ἔναντι] -τιον V 29-72 C-46 d n t 527 318 55 624

11₁₈ ἔναντι] -τιον oI⁻¹⁵-72 C'' d s t x⁻⁵⁰⁹ 126 799 Cyr I 389 Or II 388

14₅ ἐναντίον] εναντι V 376 d 129 127-767 t 319ᵐᵍ 624

14₁₀ ἐν (λίθοις)] > F*(c pr m) M' 72 n⁻⁵⁴ 30 624

14₃₁ ἥν] αφ ης Mᵐᵍ d n⁻⁷⁶⁷ t ᴸᵃᵗcod 100 GregII Tr 11

14₃₇ ἔναντι] -τιον 29 d⁻⁴⁴ t

15₅ om ἐπί 1° d⁻¹⁰⁶

15₅ ὀσμήν] pr εις 414 d t 392 59 Aeth Arm

15₁₄ ὀσμήν] pr εις d t 509 ᴸᵃᵗcod 100 Arm Boᴮ

15₁₅ ἔναντι] -τιον F 381' C'' d s⁽⁻¹³⁰⁾ t 55 59

15₃₉ om ὀπίσω 2° B V d 129 n⁻⁷⁶⁷ t x 319 Tht Nm 211 ᴸᵃᵗcod 100 Arm Co

16₂ ἔναντι] -τιον 16-46 d n t

16₃₇ om πρός 29-72-381' d⁻¹⁰⁶ ᴸᵃᵗcod 100 Bo

16₄₆ ἀπὸ προσώπου] παρα 29-72ᵐᵍ n⁻¹²⁷ 319 Arm

17₇ ἐν τῇ σκηνῇ] επι της σκηνης d n t⁻⁸⁴ 527; επι την σκηνην 84

18₁₈ om κατά A 618*(c pr m) d 54-75' t ᴸᵃᵗcod 100 Arm

18₁₉ τῶν ἁγίων] pr απο V b d 127-767 t⁻⁷⁶ 319 Arm Sa⁴; απο τ. αιγων 54-75; εκ τ. αιγων 458

18₁₉ ἔναντι] -τιον 16-46-422 d t

19₁₃ ἐπ' (αὐτόν)] περι 381' d 370

19₂₀ ἐπ' (αὐτόν)] περι d⁽⁻¹²⁵⁾ 370

20₆ πρός (αὐτούς)] επ V O'⁻¹⁵ d 246 n t 527' 128 Arm Bo Syh

21₅ om ἐν 2° C'' n⁻⁷⁶⁷ s 527 646

21₂₃ om εἰς 2° 82 d 370

22₆ ἐκ] απο 376 d n 85'ᵐᵍ-321'ᵐᵍ-344ᵐᵍ t 527' 392 55

23₃ εὐθεῖαν] pr εις 58 d t; pr επ Fᵇ n 527' Tht Nm 219

23₂₁ ἐν αὐτῷ] μεν αυτου 376 n 527

23₂₆ τῷ (Βαλάκ)] προς 376 C''⁻⁵²'³¹³⁴¹⁷ 106 54 t

23₂₇ πρὸς (Βαλαάμ)] τω n 527

24₁ ἔναντι] -τιον A F 64-72-381 d t 619 y⁻³¹⁸ 630 55

24₁₃ παρ' (ἐμαυτοῦ)] απ 376 d n t

25₁₃ διαθήκη] εις διαθηκην (-κης 75) 58-376 d n⁻⁴⁵⁸ t 407 ᴸᵃᵗLuc Parc 1 Bo

26₃ μετ' αὐτῶν] αυτοις Mᵗˣᵗ oI C'' d n 30'-85'ᵗˣᵗ-321'ᵗˣᵗ-343' t 392 z⁻⁶⁸'¹²⁰ 55 319 646 ᴸᵃᵗcod 100 Bo

27₁₉ ἔναντι 2° 963] -τιον A 29-58-oI d n t 619 y⁻³⁹² 68' 55 319 Tht Nm 224

27₂₂ ἐναντίον 1° 963⁽ᶜ⁾] εναντι A 15-72 C''⁻⁵²'³¹³ 125 129 n 28-30'-85'⁽ᵐᵍ⁾-343-344ᵗˣᵗ 84* 121 55 646

28₉ ἐν (ἐλαίῳ) 963] > 73' d⁻¹⁰⁶ 53'

28₁₃ ὀσμήν] pr εις 376-707*(vid) b d n t Aeth Armᵗᵉ

28₂₄ κατά] και 529 d 53'

30₁₂ αὐτῇ 1°] pr εν d 54'-75 t

30₁₂ αὐτῇ 2° 963] pr εν 106-107' 127 t

31₃ ἔναντι] -τιον d t 630

31₁₀ ἐν (πυρί)] > Bᶜ G-82-426 C''⁻⁴¹⁴⁴¹⁷ d 53 127-767 t x⁻⁵²⁷ 407 55 319 624

31₁₂ om πρός 2° V 414 d 129 t 624 ᴸᵃᵗcod 100 Bo
31₄₃ ἀπό 963] > V 16-46 d n⁻⁷⁶⁷ t
31₄₇ ἀπὸ τῶν 3°] om ἀπό 422 799 ᴸᵃᵗcodd 100 104; > d⁻¹⁰⁶
31₄₉ ἀπ' (αὐτῶν)] > d⁻¹⁰⁶ Phil II 240 (sed hab 192)
33₁₃ ἐν] εις O'⁻¹⁵⁴²⁶-72 d n t x⁻⁵⁰⁹ 121 799
33₁₄ ἐν] εις 58-72 d 129 n t 527 121 319
33₁₅ ἐν τῇ ἐρήμῳ] εις την ερημον 29 d n⁻⁴⁵⁸ t Armᵗᵉ
33₁₇ ἐν] εις 72 d f⁻¹²⁹ n t 318
33₁₈ ἐν] εις M' V oI d n t 18'-126-628-630' 799
33₁₉ ἐν] εις d n⁽⁻⁴⁵⁸⁾ 30' t 799
33₂₀ ἐν] εις O-29 422 d n 30' t 392 799
33₃₆ ἐν τῇ ἐρήμῳ] εις την ερημον 422 d n t 121
33₄₄ ἐν 1°] εις d 129 n t
33₄₇ ἐπί] εις d 246 t Aeth Arm
33₄₉ παρά] επι oI-72-82 52'-417-422-761*(c pr m) b d⁻¹⁰⁶ 246 n⁽⁻⁴⁵⁸⁾ 321 509-527 y⁻¹²¹ z
34₄ παρελεύσεται 2°] εις d⁻¹⁰⁶; + εις 376 52 106 n 730* t 318 799 Bo
34₁₀ τά] pr εις d⁽⁻¹²⁵⁾ 246 n⁻¹²⁷ t⁻³⁷⁰ 799; εις το 370
34₁₀ ἀνατολῶν] pr απ(ο) V G-376 b d⁽⁻¹²⁵⁾ 246 n t 126 Arm Bo
35₁ παρά 963] επι n⁻¹²⁷
35₁₂ ἔναντι] -τιον d 129 n⁻¹²⁷ t
35₁₅ om εἰς 82 n⁻⁷⁶⁷ 407 55 Aeth Arm
36₇ ἐπί 963] εις G-707 b d n t 126 59 799 ᴸᵃᵗcodd 100 104 Aeth Arm = 𝔐

This list shows that the Byzantine text betrays a certain amount of freedom in the matter of prepositions over against the Num text. In list 6 there are seven instances involving prepositions in which the variant text equals 𝔐. Four involve the addition of a preposition: of εις in 2₁₇ 32₉, of εν in 10₈ and of επι in 33₇. In list 8, wherever such additions do not equal 𝔐, a similar pattern emerges, that is επι is added at 9₁₁ and εις in 10₃₅ 15₅ ₁₄ 23₃ 25₁₃ 28₁₃ 34₉ ₁₀. It is quite possible that the correspondence to 𝔐 in the instances from list 6 is a coincidence. Change of preposition in list 6 is indicated at 10₁₂ (ἐν to εκ) and 24₁₀ (ἐπί to προς). The above list shows numerous instances of change of preposition, and too much importance must not be attached to the occasional correspondence of such a change to 𝔐. Similarly the change of τῷ Μωυσῇ to a προς construction which is = 𝔐 is paralleled in the above list in 23₂₆ (and exactly the reverse in 23₂₇).

5. At 14₄₂ a positive statement was changed into a negative statement thereby formally corresponding to 𝔐. It was there (*List 6*) argued that this was due to the context rather than to Hebrew influence.

It is interesting to note that such changes occur in the Byzantine text type in places where it is contrary to 𝔐.

4₂₀ ἀποθανοῦνται] pr ουκ V 319; pr ου μη 417 318 55; ου μη αποθανωσιν d n t ᴸᵃᵗcod 100
    Arm Bo
7₉ ἔχουσιν] pr ουκ d t
22₃₈ δυνατὸς ἔσομαι] pr μη n 527 Co; μη δυνησομαι d t
27₃ διὰ ἁμαρτίαν] pr ου V b d n⁻⁷⁶⁷ t Phil II 309
29₇ κακώσετε] pr ου d t
35₃₂ φυγεῖν] pr μη M'ᵐᵍ 417 d 54'-75 t

29

In all these cases as at 14₄₂ a negative particle in the context obtains which may have influenced the tradition.

6. Change in number in list 6 is a common phenomenon and may involve verbs, nouns or pronouns. It is, however, a characteristic of the Byzantine text group also against the Hebrew text as the following list amply demonstrates.

List 9

1₄₄ ἐπεσκέψατο] -ψαντο (επισκ. 107′) B F$^{c\,pr\,m}$ M′ d 127^c 74^c-76′ Aeth Arm Bo^{ABc} Sa^1
Syh = Ra
A compound subject obtains here.

1₄₄ πατριᾶς] -ριων F V 29-376 d 53′ n 130^{mg}-346^{mg} t 318 68′ 59 ^{Lat}cod 100 Arm Co Syh

2₁₀ τάγμα] -ματα C′$^{-761}$-414′-422 d 53′-56 75′ x 68′-120′-126-628 646 Bo^A

2₁₇ ἐχόμενος] -νοι 72 d 54′-458 t; -νοις 767

2₁₈ τάγμα] -ματα 131 d f^{-246} 75 730 74-76′ 68′-126 Bo^A

3₄ ἐτελεύτησεν] -σαν 29-72 C′′$^{-73′}$ d 246 n^{-458} s$^{-343\,344c\,pr\,m}$ t 71′ 318 319 799 ^{Lat}cod 100 Aeth
With compound subject.

3₄ ἱεράτευσεν] -σαν F M′ oI-82-707 C′′ d f n s$^{-343\,344c\,pr\,m}$ t y z^{-628} 319 624 799 ^{Lat}cod 100 Aeth Arm
With compound subject.

3₂₄ πατριᾶς] -ριων 417 d n t 799 ^{Lat}cod 100 Aeth^{CG} Arm Co

4₄ ἅγιον] αγια d n^{-127*} t 646 Arm^{ap}

4₁₃ ἐπιθήσει] -σουσι(ν) M^{mg} C′′ d n 85^{mg}-346^{mg}-730 t 319 416 Cyr I 852 ^{Lat}cod 100 Aeth Arm Bo

4₄₂ δῆμος] δημοι d 127-767 t ^{Lat}cod 104 Arm

7₈₉ ἤκουσεν] -σαν n^{-767} Arm

7₈₉ δ] α V d^{-125} 54′-767 t 799 Arm Bo

8₂₅ ἀποστήσεται] -σονται (c var) O^{-58} 19 246 n 527-619 318 z^{-126} 319 646 Arm Bo Syh; -στησ^τ 126

9₃ ποιήσεις 1°] ποιειτωσαν (ποιητ. d) d t 55; -σουσιν (c var) b n 319 Arm

9₃ ποιήσεις 2°] -σουσιν (c var) d n t Arab Arm

10₅ σαλπιεῖτε] σαλπιει d

11₄ ἐπεθύμησαν] -σεν (c var) B O^{-58} 313* 106-125′ n^{-458} t x^{-619} 624 Phil II 298 Cyr I 389 II 461 Arm^{ap}

13₂₈ αὐτῷ] αυτοις V 72-376 106 n^{-767} 71* ^{Lat}cod 100 Aeth Arab Arm Co

13₃₀ κατοικεῖ 2°] -οικουσιν d n t 628 Aeth Co Pal

14₂₃ ἀγαθὸν οὐδὲ κακόν] αγαθα ουδε (η 54-767) κακα b d n t 319

14₄₃ ὁ Χαναναῖος] οι χαναναιοι M′ d t

15₆ ποιήσεις] -σετε d$^{(-125)}$ t

15₆ ἀναπεποιημένης] -μενα V d$^{(-125)}$ n t 319 ^{Lat}cod 100 Sa

15₉ idem d n t ^{Lat}cod 100

15₃₉ τῶν διανοιῶν] τη διανοια d^{-106}

16₁₉ τὴν θύραν] τας θυρας A V 29-82 d$^{(-44)}$ 129 30′ t x$^{(-527)}$ 121 Sa

16₃₉ προσέθηκαν] περιεθηκεν (c var) 107′-125 n^{-767} t 527 Syh

17₃ πατριῶν] -ριας d 54′-458 t 527$^{c\,pr\,m}$ 319

17₅ ᾆ] ον d 129 n t 527 Arm Bo

17₉ ἔλαβον] -βεν V 58-72 C′′$^{-46\,52′\,313}$ 19 d^{-125} f^{-129} n 30-85* t x y^{-318} z$^{-126\,407}$ 646 799 Aeth Arm; cf εβαλεν B

17₁₁ ἐποίησεν] -σαν n 527 Aeth Arm Bo
With compound subject.

18₁₀ φάγεται] φαγεσθε (c var) 29-82 414 b n^{-127} Cyr I 837

18₁₀ ἔσται] εσονται d t 319

18₃₂ αὐτό] αυτα V d n^{-458*} t 319 Arm

19₁₈ λήμψεται] ληψονται (c var) 72 d n t Eus VI 12 Aeth Arm Bo

20₈ ποτιεῖτε] ποτιει (ποτεει 44) V d 319 Latcod 100
20₂₂ ἀπῆραν] -ρεν (απειρεν 319) 72-376-618 d⁻¹²⁵ 54-75-767 t 527 628 319
23₁₂ τοῦτο] ταυτα oI-707ᶜ 414-761 d 246 n 85′ ᵐᵍ-321′ ᵐᵍ-344ᵐᵍ t 527 y⁻³¹⁸ 18′-126-628-630′ LatRuf Num XVI 1 Bo Syh
24₁₄ ἐσχάτου] -των V 58-82-376*-707 414 d 53′-129-246* n 130ᵐᵍ-321′ ᵐᵍ-344ᵐᵍ t 55
24₁₉ σωζόμενον] -νους (-νου 120*) 58 b d t 120 Aeth Arm
24₂₁ πέτρᾳ] -ραις (c var) oI d n⁻⁷⁶⁷ t 319 Arm
25₆ τὴν θύραν] τας θυρας F V 58-72-376 b d n t 527-619 z 59 319 Bo
28₁₉ κάρπωμα] -ματα B* K 58-82-426 d⁻⁴⁴ f n⁻⁴⁵⁸ 74′-370 624 = Ra
28₂₄ δῶρον] δωρα d⁻¹⁰⁶
29₁₃ κάρπωμα 963] -ματα B* 58-82 n⁻⁴⁵⁸ Arm Sa = Ra
29₁₈ ἡ θυσία] αι θυσιαι V 618*(vid) 52′ b 106 n t 407 Latcodd 100 104(vid) Arm
29₂₁ ἡ θυσία] αι θυσιαι 52′ b d⁽⁻¹⁰⁶ᵗˣᵗ⁾ n⁽⁻⁷⁵⁾ t 509 Latcodd 100 104
30₃ τὸ ῥῆμα] τα ρηματα d t
30₉ πᾶσαι αἱ εὐχαί] πασα η ευχη d
30₁₃ μενεῖ] μενουσι(ν) d n⁽⁻⁷⁶⁷⁾ t Bo Syh
33₅₅ ἔσται] εσονται 963 58-376 d n 344ᵐᵍ t 799 Latcod 104 Aeth Arm Sa Syh
33₅₅ ἐχθρεύσουσιν] -ρευσω (c var) n
36₈ αὐτῆς] αυτων oII⁻⁷⁰⁷ 16*-77-131-422-500-550-551ᶜ-739* d 246 n 85ᵐᵍ-344ᵐᵍ t x⁻⁵⁰⁹ 392* 18′-126-407-628-630′ 799 Aeth⁻ᶜ Co

From this list it appears that change in number occurs commonly in this text group both for verbs and nouns but only once (36₈) for pronouns.

7. Change in case was attested in list 6 outside of the consistent change of τῶν to τω in 15—15 only twice: in 9₁₃ κυριον for κυρίῳ, and in 31₅₄ τοις υιοις for τῶν υἱῶν. In both cases a dative is involved over against a genitive, which corresponds respectively in Hebrew to a ל phrase over against the second element in a bound phrase.

The Byzantine text attests a large number of variants involving case which in view of the fact that case inflection does not exist in Masoretic Hebrew can have nothing to do with Hebrew influence. In the following list only such variants are given that could conceivably reflect the Hebrew distinction mentioned above, i.e. genitive/dative variants. In each case the relevant Hebrew text is given as well.

List 10

15₈ κυρίῳ] κυριον d 343 t Latcod 100: ליהוה
15₁₄ κυρίῳ 2°] κυριον V 376 125 129 n⁻⁴⁵⁸ 346ᶜ 319 Latcod 100: non hab 𝔐
18₂₈ (ἀφαιρεμάτων) κυρίου] κυριω 82-426-oI⁻¹⁵ b d 53 n t x⁻⁶¹⁹ 318 319 Latcod 100 Aeth Syh: תרומת יהוה
27₂₀ (δώσεις) τῆς δόξης (σου)] τη δοξη 72 d⁻¹⁰⁶: מהודך
31₃₇ κυρίῳ] κυριον 72-426-oI⁻¹⁵ 761*(c pr m) d n 321ᵐᵍ(vid)-343-344ᵐᵍ t 619 392 799 Aeth: ליהוה
31₃₈ κυρίῳ] κυριον 72 d n⁻⁷⁶⁷ 30′-343-344ᵐᵍ-346ᵐᵍ t 799 Aeth: ליהוה
31₃₉ κυρίῳ] κυριον 426 d n⁻⁴⁵⁸ 30′-343-344ᵐᵍ t 799 Aeth Bo: ליהוה
31₄₁ κυρίῳ] κυριον 72 413-414 b d n 346ᵐᵍ-730 t Bo: non hab 𝔐
32₂₅ (ὁ κύριος) ἡμῶν] ημιν A d⁻¹⁰⁶ x⁻⁵⁰⁹ Aeth⁻ᶜᴹ Sa¹²: אדני
35₁₆ (ἐν σκεύει) σιδήρου] -ρω d n t 624: בכלי ברזל

Again the text group under discussion exercises a certain freedom within the text tradition which has nothing to do with immediate or mediate Hebrew influence.

31

8. Change in lexeme under possible Hebrew influence was attested in list 6 only at 3₂₃ υἱοί] δημοι and 22₂₂ τοῦ θεοῦ] κυριον. Such change is much more common in contrast to 𝔐 as the following list indicates.

List 11

1₃₃ διακόσιοι] τριακοσιοι B d⁻¹⁰⁶ᶜ 54′ t 392 799 ᴸᵃᵗcod 100 Arm

1₃₅ τετρακόσιοι] τριακοσιοι d⁻¹⁰⁶ᶜ 85*(vid) t 392 799

1₄₄ ἄνδρες] αρχοντες Aᶜ d 54′-458 t Arm

2₂ σήμέας] σημασιας (c var) V 58 b d f 767 30′-85ᵐᵍ-130-321′ t 71ᶜ-619 318 18′-126-628-669 319 799

2₁₆ παρεμβολῆς] φυλης 107′-125 n Arm

2₂₁ διακόσιοι] τριακοσιοι A*(vid) V 413*(c pr m) d n⁻⁷⁶⁷ t 55 799 ᴸᵃᵗcod 100 Arm

2₂₃ τετρακόσιοι] τριακοσιοι 44-106*-107′ t x⁻⁵⁰⁹ 799; γ̅ 458

2₂₄ ἑκατόν 2°] διακοσιοι d⁻¹⁰⁶ᶜ n⁻⁷⁶⁷ t 318 799 Arm

2₃₂ πεντακόσιοι] και (> d⁻⁴⁴) εξακοσιοι d⁻¹²⁵* n⁻⁷⁶⁷ t 799 Arm Bo

2₃₈ ἑξακόσιοι] τριακοσιοι d n⁻⁷⁶⁷ t 799 Arm

3₃₆ αὐτῶν 1°] τουτων d⁻¹²⁵ n⁻⁷⁶⁷ t Arm

3₃₆ αὐτῶν 2°] τουτων d^(⁻⁴⁴) n⁻⁷⁶⁷ t Arm

4₃ εἰσπορευόμενος] εκπορ. V d 370 y⁻¹²¹

4₉ ἀγγεῖα] αγια A 58-72 d 53′-56-129^(mgᶜˡ) 54-767 t 71 318

4₁₂ δερματίνῳ 803] δερματι A b n Aeth

4₂₇ ἀρτά 1°] εργαλ(ε)ια d 54-75′ t 509 318 799

4₄₇ ἔργων] αγιων 29-58 44′ n⁻⁷⁶⁷ 85′ ᵐᵍ-321′ ᵐᵍ t 68′-120′ 799 ᴸᵃᵗcod 100 Arm

5₂₂ πρῆσαι] πρισαι (-σε 799) 29 46ˢ-414-529ᶜ b d⁻⁴⁴ 127-458 343 t⁻⁸⁴ 71 319 799 Chr II 917

7₈₄ οὗτος ὁ ἐγκαινισμός] τουτο το δωρον (+ του εγκαινισμου 376) 376 d⁻¹⁰⁶; ταυτα τα δωρα 106

11₂₀ αὐτοῦ] κυριου 107′-125 Arab

11₂₅ αὐτόν] μω(υ)σην d n t Arm

11₂₅ παρείλατο] περιειλετο (-λατο 55*) d 246 t z 55 646

13₃ κατὰ δήμους] κατ οικους Mᵐᵍ d 127 t 392 55 416 799 Arm; + (+ αυτων 458) κατ οικους V n⁻¹²⁷

13₁₈ ἀπέστειλεν] εξαπ. 29 d^(⁻⁴⁴) n t 799

14₁₇ ἰσχύς] χειρ A M′ 29-72-376 16-46 d 129 n t 392 59 799 Eus VI 240 ᴸᵃᵗQuodv *Prom* II 17 Arab Arm

14₃₇ πληγῇ] γη 107′ t

14₄₃ οὗ εἵνεκεν] διοτι d⁻¹⁰⁶

15₁ ἐλάλησεν] ειπε(ν) B V d 129 t x Cyr I 1029 = Ra

15₃ ὁλοκαύτωμα] -καρπωμα B d 129 n t x 319* Cyr I 1029 = Ra

15₉ προσοίσει] ποιησεις V 29 d t

15₁₄ γένηται] προσγεν. 551 d 127 t x

15₂₄ αὐτοῦ] τουτου 29-72 d n⁻⁴⁵⁸ t

16₂ ἀνέστησαν] αντεστ. V d 75′-127 t

16₃ συνέστησαν] επισυν. V d⁻¹²⁵ n t 319

16₅ ἐλάλησεν] ειπε(ν) 376 d t Aeth

16₄₁ ἀπεκτάγκατε] -κτεινατε (c var) Fᵇ O⁻⁵⁸-72 52-414 d⁻¹⁰⁶ 129 75 126 799

16₄₃ εἰσῆλθεν] εστη d n t; steterunt Arm

18₁ ἁμαρτίας 1°] απαρχας B Mᵗˣᵗ oI d t x⁻⁵²⁷ 68′-120′-126 416 799 Cyr I 837

18₂ φυλήν] νιους d t 319

18₂₀ ὅτι] ετι d t

18₂₄ κλήρῳ] -ρονομια d n t Arm(vid)

18₃₂ υἱῶν] αγιων 72-618 414 d⁻¹⁰⁶ 28 669

19₂₀ τῆς συναγωγῆς] των νιων ιηλ̅ d t 799

20₆ ἦλθεν] εισηλθεν (c var) V C″ d n 30′-85′ ᵐᵍ-321′ ᵐᵍ t 527 646 ᴸᵃᵗcod 100

20₁₃ ἀντιλογίας] λοιδοριας (c var) M′ ᵐᵍ 82 n 130ᵐᵍ-321′ ᵐᵍ-344ᵐᵍ 527 319 ᴸᵃᵗcod 100 Arm

20₁₄ σύ] εν d t

21₈ Μωυσῆν] αυτον d Sa¹⁰

21₉ ἔστησεν] επεστ. d n t 527

21₁₁ ἐξάραντες] απαρ. V 29 414 d 343 t 669⁽ᶜ¹⁾

21₂₃ τῶν ὁρίων] της γης n 527

21₃₂ ὄντα] κατοικουντα B V O-82 d 53'-129 n t x⁻⁶¹⁹ Arm Syh

21₃₄ καθώς] καθα d t

22₈ κατέμειναν] εμειναν (-νον 127*) b d n⁻⁷⁶⁷ t 527 126

22₁₁ κεκάλυφεν] κατεκαλυψε(ν) d n t 527

23₆ ἐφειστήκει] παριστ. (c var) n 527

23₂₄ ἀναστήσεται] αναβησ. d t 630

24₁₀ Βαλαάμ 2°] αυτον 72 d⁻¹⁰⁶ 126

24₂₃ εἶπεν] εφη d⁻¹⁰⁶

25₆ ἀδελφόν] λαον d⁻¹⁰⁶

25₈ πληγή] οργη 58ᵐᵍ d n t 319 Sa¹

25₁₃ ἀνθ' ὧν] οτι d n t Aeth

26₄₅ ἑξακόσιοι] τριακοσιοι d⁻¹⁰⁶ n t 319 Bo; ⅃ 106

26₅₄ καθώς] καθα n

27₈ περιθήσετε] (+ θυγατηρ d⁻¹⁰⁶) δωσετε d⁻¹⁰⁶ ᴸᵃᵗRuf *Num* XXII 1 Aeth Bo

27₈ τῇ θυγατρί] τω αδελφω d⁻¹⁰⁶

27₁₄ ἀντιπίπτειν] αντειπειν (c var) K 29-707 d n 30'-85' ᵐᵍ-321' ᵐᵍ-344ᵐᵍ t 319 799 ᴸᵃᵗcod 100 Aeth Bo

27₂₃ συνέταξεν] ενετειλατο b n

28₉ προσάξετε] προσεταξε 73' d

29₂₃ τέσσαρας καὶ δέκα] δωδεκα 107'-125 t

31₂ ἔσχατον] υστερον V d t

31₁₁ σκῦλα 963] σκευη d⁻¹⁰⁶ t 407 Bo

31₁₈ οἶδεν] εγνω (-νωσεν 85) A F 15-29-72 107'-125 129 n 85' ᵐᵍ-321' ᵐᵍ y⁻¹²¹

31₃₆ ἐκπεπορευμένων] -πορνευμ. d 127* 74-76'-84'*(vid)-134*

32₁₅ ἀποστραφήσεσθε] αποστησεσθε 707 n 85ᵐᵍ-321' ᵐᵍ 799

32₄₁ ἐπαύλεις 1°] πολεις d⁽⁻⁴⁴⁾ 129 n⁻¹²⁷ t 319 Arab Arm Sa

33₂ ἀπάρσεις] απαρτιας d t

33₈ ἀπέναντι Εἰρώθ] εκ μαγδωλου (c var) 58 d⁽⁻⁶¹⁰⁾ n 344 t

33₄₂ παρενέβαλον] απηλθον d⁻¹⁰⁶

34₁₇ κληρονομήσουσιν] κατακλ. d n t 71'

Many of these variants are due to the influence of the context; others are palaeographically conditioned; still others are stylistic changes. A substantial number of instances involve change in numbers. These are probably due to the common use of letters used to indicate numbers, and confusion in the text tradition easily results from this practice.

9. Particularly characteristic of the Byzantine text type is the variant tradition in the transcription of proper names. Little purpose would be served in presenting a list of all such variants. Since many of these show great divergence from the original transcription the following list is presented to illustrate this divergence by placing the Num transcription and the text of 𝔐 in parentheses after the variant. For the ms support the reader is referred to the apparatus of Num. The list is merely illustrative.

List 12

3₂₄ 7₄₂ ₄₇ ελισαφαν (Ἐλισάφ: אֱלִיסָף); 3₃₃ ομοσι (Μουσί: מוּשִׁי); 7₇₈ ₈₃ 10₂₇ αχιραν (Ἀχιρέ: אֲחִירַע); 10₂₂ ελισα (Ἐλισαμά: אֱלִישָׁמָע); 13₈ γαδ (Ἰγαάλ: יְגְאָל); 13₂₂ εφρααθ (Ἐμάθ: חֲמָת);

33

21₁₁ αχελσειν εν γειν (Ἀχελγαί: עיי‎); 21₁₄ βοοζ (Ζωόβ: והב‎); 21₁₅ σηιρ (Ἠρ: ער‎); 21₂₆ σινα (Σηών: סיחן‎); 26₁₃ σααρ (Ζάρα: זרח‎); 26₁₇ εσρωμ (Ἀσρών: חצרן‎); 26₂₂ σαδρι (Σάρεδ: סרד‎); 26₄₂₄₄ βαλακ (Βάλε: בלע‎); 26₄₉ ιεσσααρ (Ἰέσερ: יצר‎); 32₃₇ ελεαηλ (Ἐλεαλή: אלעלא‎); 33₂₃ σασαφαρ (Σάφαρ: שפר‎); 33₂₆₂₇ κααθ (Κατάαθ: תחת‎); 33₃₂₃₃ γαδ (Γαδγάδ: גדגד‎); 34₈ αιθαμ (Ἐμάθ: חמת‎); 34₁₁ σεμφαμαρ (Σεπφάμ: שפם‎); 34₂₃ αιηλ (Ἀνιήλ: חניאל‎); 34₂₅ φεναχ (Φαρνάχ: פרנך‎); 34₂₈ σελεμιουδ (Βεναμιούδ בן עמיהוד‎).

The above list represents various types of errors which are to be found in the Byzantine text type. This tradition concerning proper names is on the whole quite untrustworthy; it represents a late and often corrupt textual tradition. Should the *d n t* text on occasions actually be closer to 𝔐 than Num, this is probably accidental, since there is no compelling evidence in this tradition of a revision based on acquaintance with the Hebrew text.

C. Since both in Genesis and Deuteronomy the Biblical text used by Chrysostom and Theodoret seems to represent a late and mixed text (cf THGG ch. 10 and THGD 25—30) it remains to investigate whether the Byzantine text group might have been their text.

Since the book of Numbers was not quoted by these fathers extensively the results can hardly be conclusive, and in order that one may receive a complete picture of the problems posed by their text a full list of their variant readings is given in the following list.

List 13

3₅ ἐλάλησεν] ειπε 125 Tht *Nm* 192

3₅ om λέγων 125 Tht *Nm* 192

3₆ Λευί] pr του 29-426 52′ 767 126 Tht *Nm* 192ᵗᵉ

3₇ ἔναντι] -τιον 646 Tht *Nm* 192

3₈ κατά] και 376 528-739* 106-107′ *n*⁻⁷⁶⁷ *t* Tht *Nm* 192 Arab Arm

3₉ Ἀαρών B V O⁻⁵⁸ 46⁸ *x* 121 ᴸᵃᵗcod 100 Arab Sa Syh] τω αδελφω σου 246; + τω αδελφω σου Tht *Nm* 192 rell

3₉ δεδομένοι] -νον V 64-381ᶜ-618 C″ 53′ 30′-85 509 319 Tht *Nm* 192ᵗᵉ

3₉ οὗτοί μοί εἰσιν] εισιν ουτοι Tht *Nm* 192ᵗᵉ Arm; αυτοι (aut αυτη) Tht *Nm* 192ᵃᵖ: cf App I

5₆ ὅστις ἂν ποιήσῃ] ει τις ποιησει Tht *Nm* 194ᵗᵉ; οστις ποιησει *b n*

5₆ τῶν ἁμαρτιῶν A B G *x*⁻⁶¹⁹ Anast 376 Arab Sa] pr παντων 29; πασων αμαρτιων 126; πασων 55; pr πασων Tht *Nm* 194 rell = 𝔐

5₈ om ὁ A *oI n* 130 68′ 55 Tht *Nm* 195 = 𝔐

5₈ πρὸς αὐτόν] pr το (τω 107′-125 767) 707ᶜ *d* 127-767 85′ ᵐᵍ-346ᵐᵍ *t* Tht *Nm* 195

5₈ κυρίῳ B *b* 509] του κ̄ῡ 72; > 16-46 53′; pr τω Tht *Nm* 195 rell

5₈ ἐν αὐτῷ] ad fin tr 414 *b d f n t* Tht *Nm* 195 Bo

5₁₂ αὐτοῦ] κατα του ανδρος αυτης Chr II 917

5₁₃ om αὐτῆς 2° 82 Chr II 917 ᴸᵃᵗcod 100

5₁₃ καί 3°] ⌒4° Chr II 917

5₁₃ om αὐτή 2° Chr II 917 Arm

5₁₄ αὐτῷ 1° 963] pr επ 72-82-376 761 *b* 509 68*-122 55 799 Chr II 917 = 𝔐; τω ανδρι αυτης *d n t* Arm Bo

5₁₄ om καί 2°—αὐτοῦ 2° Chr II 917

5₁₄ μεμιαμμένη] μεμιασμενη 381′ 77-528 53-664*(vid) *n*⁽⁻⁴⁵⁸⁾ 84* 619 126 55ᶜ Chr II 917 Cyr I 909

5₁₅ δῶρον] + (※ G Syh) αυτης O Chr II 917 Syh = 𝔐

5₁₅ ἐπιχεεῖ 963] -χεεις F*(c pr m) 551 *b* 509 Chr II 917

5₁₅ ἐπιθήσει] -σεις F *b* 509 Chr II 917

5₁₅ μνημοσύνου] + (+ και 125) θυσια *d*⁻¹⁰⁶ *n t* Tht *Nm* 196 Arm

34

5₁₆ om αὐτήν 1° n⁻⁷⁶⁷ Tht Nm 196 Arm

5₁₆ αὐτήν 2° 963] τὴν γυναικα 44′ n t Tht Nm 196 Arm

5₁₇ om ὁ ἱερεύς 1° Chr II 917

5₁₇ ζῶν] sub ÷ Gᶜ Syh; > Chr II 917 ᴸᵃᵗApocEvang Inf H 51 Aethᶜ Fa: cf 𝔐; + εναντι κυριου Tht Nm 196ᵗᵉ

5₁₇ τῆς γῆς] pr απο K V O C'' 767 30′-130ᵐᵍ-321′ᵐᵍ z Chr II 917 Syh = 𝔐

5₁₇ om τῆς 3°—καί ult Chr II 917

5₁₈ (ἐπὶ) τὰς χεῖρας] των χειρων Tht Nm 196ᵗᵉ

5₁₉ παραβέβηκας] παρεβης Chr II 917

5₁₉ ὑπό] προς A Chr II 917

5₁₉ ἀθῷα] αθωος Fᵇ 551 n Tht Nm 197ᵗᵉ; σωα Chr II 917

5₂₀ σύ—οὖσα] παρεβης Chr II 917

5₂₀ ἤ] και V 767 30′-321′ᵐᵍ 319 Chr II 917 Aeth

5₂₀ μεμίανσαι] pr συ (σοι G) O b d n⁻⁷⁶⁷ t Tht Nm 197 ᴸᵃᵗcod 100 Syh

5₂₀ καί] η Tht Nm 197

5₂₀ om αὐτοῦ 610* 84ᵗˣᵗ(c pr m) Tht Nm 197

5₂₁ om init—γυναικί d t 619 Chr II 917 Tht Nm 197

5₂₁ κύριός σε] σε (σοι 616ᶜ 54 Thtᵃᵖ; + o 552) κ̅ς̅ A M′ V oI C'' b n s 619 126 55 319 624 Tht Nm 197

5₂₁ om τόν—καί ult Chr II 917

5₂₁ πεπρησμένην 963] εμπεπρισμενην Chr II 917

5₂₂ ἐπικαταρώμενον] -τηραμενον Chr II 917

5₂₂ om τοῦτο—σου 1° Chr II 917

5₂₂ πρῆσαι] πρισαι 29 46ˢ-414-529ᶜ b d⁻⁴⁴ 127-458 343 t⁻⁸⁴ 71 319 799 Chr II 917

5₂₂ γαστέρα] την γ. σου Chr II 917; + σου d n t Aeth Arm Bo Syh

6₂ κυρίῳ] pr τω 414 d 53′ n 321*(vid) t 126-128 799 Tht Nm 197ᵗᵉ

6₅ κυρίῳ] pr τω 72-426 73′-413-414-552-761 75′-767 30 x⁻⁷¹ 68′ Tht Nm 198

6₆ εὐχῆς 963] + (❊ G Syh) αυτου Fᵇ M′ V O⁻⁵⁸ d n 85′ᵐᵍ-321′ᵐᵍ-344ᵐᵍ t⁻⁸⁴ 319 Tht Nm 198 Arm Bo Sa⁴ Syh = 𝔐

6₆ κυρίῳ 963] sub ❊ Sᶜ; pr (❊ S G Syh) τω (το 376) M′ Sᶜ O-82 52′-313-414 d n 28-85′ᵐᵍ-321′ᵐᵍ-344ᵐᵍ t Tht Nm 198 Bo Syh

6₁₂ αἱ 1°—ἔσονται] αλογιστοι εσονται αυτων (αυτωᵃᵖ) αι προτεραι ημεραι Tht Nm 198 Cf αλογιστοι pro ἄλογοι in d n⁻⁷⁶⁷ t

6₁₂ κεφαλή 963] pr η O′⁻⁵⁸-72 C'' 44′-610 f n x⁻⁷¹ y⁻³⁹² 18-68-122ᶜ 55ᶜ 624 799 Phil II 131ᵃᵖ Cyr I 1041 Tht Nm 198

6₁₂ εὐχῆς 2°] pr της Tht Nm 198

6₂₇ ἐπὶ σέ] επι σοι Tht Nm 199s

9₂ εἶπον] ειπε (ειπαι 458) n⁻⁷⁶⁷ Chr X 331

9₂ om oἱ 376* 458 319 Chr X 331

9₇ ἀκάθαρτοι] + εσμεν 56ᵐᵍ-246 Chr II 877 ᴸᵃᵗcod 100; cf pr (❊ Syh) εσμεν O Syh

9₇ om oὖν 319 Chr II 877 ᴸᵃᵗcod 100

9₇ προσενέγκαι] (+ ωστε n⁻¹²⁷) προσενεγκειν n 527 Chr II 877

9₇ κυρίῳ] κυριον 426 44 n 527-619 68′-120′ Chr II 877 Aeth Syh = 𝔐

9₉ λέγων] ⌢(10) 72 75′ 669ᵗˣᵗ 59 Chr II 877 Sa¹²

9₁₀ om ἄνθρωπος 2° Fᵇ 72 d 75′ 126 319 Chr II 877 Cyr I 1081 ᴸᵃᵗcod 100 Bo Sa¹²

9₁₀ μακράν] -ρα O⁻³⁷⁶-72 414 56 75 Chr II 877 ᴸᵃᵗcod 100 Syh(vid) = 𝔐

9₁₀ om ἤ 2° 376 106 54′-458 527 Chr II 877 Arm Syh

9₁₀ om καί Chr II 877 Aeth Arm Sa¹²

9₁₀ om κυρίῳ 72 52 84 55 Chr II 877

9₁₄ om ὑμῖν καί Tht Ios 277

10₂ ἀργυρᾶς ἐλατάς] tr B V b d 129 n t⁻⁸⁴ᵗˣᵗ x⁻⁶¹⁹ 319 Chr II 881 Cyr I 397 V 773 X 837 ᴸᵃᵗcod 100 Ambr Sat II 107

10₆ σαλπιοῦσιν] -πιειτε Tht Nm 201

10₆ αὐτῶν] υμων Tht Nm 201

10₉ om δέ Tht Nm 202

10₁₀ σαλπιεῖτε] pr και Chr II 881 Aeth⁻ᶜ = 𝔐

10₁₀ ὁλοκαυτώμασιν Tht *Nm* 202] + υμων O Chr II 881 ᴸᵃᵗOr *Matth* 52 Aeth Bo Saˡˡ Syh = 𝔐

10₁₀ om ἐπί 2° Chr II 881 ᴸᵃᵗAmbr *Sat* II 107 Bo

10₁₀ ἔναντι] -τιον M′ C′⁻⁴¹⁴′-57 s 619 z 646 Cyr X 580 Tht *Nm* 202

11₄ κρέα] κρεας B* 618* C″ 458* 71′ Chr I 476

11₅ ἐμνήσθημεν] + γαρ Fᵃ d n⁻¹²⁷ t 527 Chr I 476 ᴸᵃᵗQuodv *Prom* II 14 Arm

11₅ ἰχθύας] ιχθυς 246*(c pr m) 319 Chr X 331

11₅ om δωρεάν 610 458 318 Chr I 476 X 331

11₅ om καί 1° Phil III 19ᵃᵖ Chr X 331 ᴸᵃᵗQuodv *Prom* II 14 = 𝔐

11₅ om καί 3° 799 Chr X 331 ᴸᵃᵗQuodv *Prom* II 14

11₅ om καί 4° 730 799 Chr X 331 ᴸᵃᵗcod 100 Quodv *Prom* II 14

11₅ om καί 5° Chr X 331

11₅ σκόρδα] -ροδα Fᵇ 376-707ᶜ-οI⁻¹⁵* 16-46-77-414′-529′ᶜ-761ᶜ b d⁻⁶¹⁰ 767ᶜ 28-85-343 84 71 126-128-407-628-630′ 55ᶜ ᵖʳ ᵐ 59 416 646 Phil III 19ᵃᵖ Chr I 476 X 331 Cyr I 389 II 461 Or II 388

11₆ νυνί] νυν F 72 422-529 54-75′ 343′ 59 Chr I 476 X 331

11₆ κατάξηρος—μάννα] κατακενος επι τω μαννα Chr IX 291 (sed hab passim)

11₈ ἤληθον] ηλεθον 58ᵐᵍ 77 d t⁻⁷⁶* 392 68′-120′ Tht *Nm* 203ᵗᵉ

11₈ om αὐτό 1° n 527 121 628 319 Tht *Nm* 203 ᴸᵃᵗcod 100 Arm = 𝔐

11₈ ἤ V b 319 ᴸᵃᵗcod 100 Bo] και Tht *Nm* 203 rell = Ra

11₈ om αὐτό 2° b Tht *Nm* 203 ᴸᵃᵗcodd 94—96 100 Arm = 𝔐

11₈ om αὐτό 3° Tht *Nm* 203 Arm

11₁₁ κύριον] τον θεον Chr I 476

11₁₁ ἐπιθεῖναι] + μοι (με 107 Thtᵃᵖ) d 767 t 527 319 Tht *Nm* 204 Arm

11₁₂ τὸν πάντα] om πάντα Tht *Nm* 204ᵗᵉ ᴸᵃᵗcod 100; tr B V O⁻⁵⁸ 422 f n x⁻⁶¹⁹ Phil III 6 Chr I 476 Tht *Nm* 204ᵃᵖ = Ra

11₁₂ αὐτούς 1°] αυτον 628 799 Phil III 6ᵗᵉ Chr I 476 Tht *Nm* 204 = 𝔐

11₁₂ λάβε] pr οτι 799 Tht *Nm* 204ᵗᵉ; αρον Chr XI 411 XVII 34

11₁₂ αὐτούς 2°] αυτον B O⁻⁵⁸ d 56* n⁻⁷⁶⁷ t x⁻⁶¹⁹ Phil III 6ᵗᵉ Chr I 476 (sed hab passim) Tht *Nm* 204 Arm Boᴮ Syh = Ra 𝔐

11₁₂ εἰς τὸν κόλπον σου] > 126 Chr XVII 34

11₁₂ ὡσεὶ ἄρα] ως αν αρη Chr XI 411; ωσει (+ ανᵃᵖ) λαβοι Tht *Nm* 204

11₁₂ ὤμοσας] -σα (c var) 29 C″⁻¹³¹ᶜ f⁻¹²⁹ 458 28-85 527 121 55 646 Chr I 476 Tht *Nm* 204ᵃᵖ Bo

11₁₅ ἔλεος] χαριν F O⁻⁴²⁶ 551 76 Chr I 476 Co: cf App I

11₁₅ παρὰ σοί] εναντιον σου Chr I 476

11₁₆ αὐτὸς σύ] om σύ 417⁽ᵐᵍ⁾ Cyr II 461 Did 548 Tht *Nm* 204 205ᵃᵖ; > 58 Tht *Nm* 205ᵗᵉ = 𝔐

11₁₆ οὗτοί] αυτοι C″⁻⁵²⁸ s 424 799 Tht *Nm* 204ᵗᵉ Arm

11₁₆ πρός 2°] εις A F M′ V O″ C″⁻⁴⁶ f n s⁻¹³⁰ᵐᵍ ³²¹′ᵐᵍ y z 55 59 319 624 Tht *Nm* 204

11₁₇ λαοῦ] + τουτον 58 d n⁻⁷⁵ t Bas II 285 Tht *Nm* 204 Aeth Arab Arm Co

11₁₈ καλὸν ἡμῖν ἐστιν] καλως ην ημιν Chr III 338 XVII 835

11₂₀ om ἡμερῶν 64ᵗˣᵗ(c pr m) Tht *Nm* 205

11₂₀ φάγεσθε] + κρεα Tht *Nm* 205 Bo

11₂₁ χιλιάδες] + εισι Chr I 506 Isid 1488

11₂₂ om αὐτοῖς 1° 129 730* 84 128-669 Phil III 6 Chr I 506 Isid 1488 Arm Bo

11₂₂ om καὶ ἀρκέσει αὐτοῖς 1° 414 f⁻¹²⁹ Phil III 6 Chr I 506 Isid 1488 Aeth

11₂₂ ὄψος] οψον Fᵇ M′ οI-707 414′-528-761ᶜ 108-118′ 458 730 646 799 Phil III 6ᵃᵖ Chr I 506 Isid 1488

11₂₂ om αὐτοῖς 3° A οI 16-46 75 55 Phil III 6 Chr I 506 Isid 1488 ᴸᵃᵗcod 100 Arm Bo

11₂₃ μοι] εμοι Chr XVI 520 Cyr VII 720

11₂₃ τίς] + αν Tht *Nm* 206ᵗᵉ

11₂₃ δψη] δω V G 75 319 Chr X 331 Tht *Nm* 206ᵃᵖ

11₂₃ πάντα] απαντα Chr X 331

11₂₃ προφήτας] + ειναι x⁻⁵⁰⁹ Chr IX 192 XVI 520 Sev 513 Tht *Nm* 206ᵃᵖ

12₂ λελάληκε(ν) B 72 44 74-76 630] ελαλησε(ν) Chr X 331 Cyr II 592 593 rell

12₂ κύριος 1°] ο θεος 129 319 Chr X 331

36

12₃ πραΰς σφόδρα] πραοτατος Chr V 134 VII 313 IX 191 379 XII 716 Tht III 1393

12₃ παρά—ὄντας] παντων ανθρωπων (ανδρων IX 379) των Chr VII 313 IX 191 379; om ὄντας 246 55 Chr XII 716

12₃ om τούς 1° 417 n⁻⁵⁴ 84 126 Cyr II 592 597 Tht III 1393

12₆ ὑμῶν] υμιν Cyr II 600 Tht Nm 208ᵗᵉ

12₆ om κυρίῳ Cyr VI 172 Tht Nm 208

12₆ λαλήσω αὐτῷ] tr n Tht Nm 208ᵗᵉ

12₇ ὁ Β G-426 f⁻²⁴⁶ 54-75′ x Cyr VI 172 Bo Syhᴸ] ως 707* 767*; pr ως Cyr passim Tht III 700 Nm 208 rell

12₁₄ ὁ πατὴρ αὐτῆς] om αὐτῆς Chr XI 59; post ἐνέπτυσεν tr Chr III 203 XI 59 (sed hab XIV 248)

12₁₄ πτύων] εμπτ. 376 f⁻¹²⁹ Chr III 203 XI 59 Tht Nm 209; > Chr XIV 248 ᴸᵃᵗRuf Num VII 4 Bo

12₁₄ om αὐτῆς 2° Chr III 203 (sed hab XI 59)

12₁₄ ἐντραπήσεται] (+ αν Chr) ενετραπη Chr III 203 Tht Nm 209ᵃᵖ

12₁₄ ἀφορισθήτω] -θησεται A 54-75′ 799 Cyr II 592 Tht Nm 209ᵗᵉ; μεινατω Chr III 203

12₁₄ ἑπτὰ ἡμέρας 2°] > A F V 29-58-72-376 b 44 f⁻¹²⁹ 458-767 130 619 121 z 55 59 799 Cyr II 592 Tht Nm 209; post παρεμβολῆς tr G C′⁻⁷³ᶜ¹³¹⁵²⁹′⁷⁶¹-46-414-422 Anast 384 Chr III 203 Aeth Bo

14₁₆ δύνασθαι] δυνηθηναι Tht II 993

14₁₆ τὸν λαὸν τοῦτον] αυτους A Mᵐᵍ V οI C′′ 28-30′-85′ᵗˣᵗ-321′′ᵗˣᵗ-343′ 121 55 319 624 Tht II 993 ᴸᵃᵗQuodv Prom II 17 Aeth

14₁₆ ὤμοσεν] επηγγειλατο Tht II 993

14₁₆ αὐτοῖς] τοις πατρασιν αυτων 75′ 121 Tht II 993

14₁₆ κατέστρωσεν] κατηναλωσεν Tht II 993

14₂₁ ἀλλά] αλλ η n⁻¹²⁷ 509 319 Tht II 41

14₂₁ ζῶν] ζη V 72 414 d⁻¹²⁵ 129*(c pr m) t 319*(c pr m) Cyr III 545 Procop 1936 Tht II 41 Nm 210ᵗᵉ ᴸᵃᵗcod 100 Bo

15₃₀ ὑπερηφανίας] -νιαν F*(c pr m) G* 414-417ᶜ Bas III 668ᵃᵖ Tht Nm 210 ᴸᵃᵗcod 100 Aeth Armᵗᵉ Bo

15₃₁ ἡ ἁμαρτία] αμ. γαρ d n t Tht Nm 211 Arm

15₃₉ μνησθήσεσθε] αναμν. (-σθαι 246ᶜ ᵖʳ ᵐ) 246 121 z⁻¹²⁶ Tht Nm 211ᵗᵉ(αναμνησεσθεᵃᵖ)

15₃₉ πασῶν τῶν ἐντολῶν] πασας (> 610*) τας εντολας d n t Tht Nm 211

15₃₉ καὶ ποιήσετε] ποιησαι d n t Tht Nm 211 Arm

15₃₉ om ὀπίσω 2° B V d 129 n⁻⁷⁶⁷ t x 319 Tht Nm 211 ᴸᵃᵗcod 100 Arm Co

15₃₉ om ὑμῶν 2° B 15-82 cI-551 d 129 n⁻⁷⁶⁷ t⁻⁸⁴ x⁻⁵⁰⁹ z 319 Tht Nm 211 ᴸᵃᵗcod 100

16₁₅ προσσχῇς 64-381 46′-57-77-422-615-761 343 630] προσεχης 246; προσχες 799; προσθης 458; προσχης (-χεις 19 75) Procop 840 Tht Nm 212 rell = Ra

16₂₂ ὀργή B F 15-29-58-72-426 528* 129 767 x 628 55 59] pr η Tht Nm 213 rell

16₄₀ μηθείς] μηδεις A F M′ V 58-οI′ C′′ b 56′ n⁻¹²⁷ s 76 y z⁻¹²⁶ 55 59 Tht Nm 213

17₁₂ ἀπολώλαμεν] + εξολωλαμεν Chr XVII 858

18₃₁ οὗτος ὑμῖν] υμων οντος V Tht Nm 214 Arm; tr 73′ b 54-75; υμιν οντως 458-767

19₂₀ ἄν] εαν B 376′ 413 d n t 71 799 Eus VI 12 Tht Nm 215ᵗᵉ = Ra

19₂₀ om μιανθῇ καί Tht Nm 215

20₁₀ ἐξάξομεν] εξαξω 125 246 126 Tht I 1732 Nm 216ᵗᵉ

20₁₀ ὑμῖν ὕδωρ] tr Chr X 332

20₁₂ ἐπιστεύσατε] + μοι M′ V 82 b d 54′-75 130ᵐᵍ-321′ ᵐᵍ t 527 319 Chr I 506 X 332 Tht Nm 216ᵗᵉ ᴸᵃᵗcod 100 Aethᶜ Arab Arm

20₁₂ υἱῶν] pr των A M′ V οI 413-422 b d n 30′ t 527-619 392 319 Chr I 506 X 332 Cyr II 489 492 VI 452 Tht Nm 216

20₁₂ om ὑμεῖς 58 Chr I 506 Bo = 𝔐

20₁₂ δέδωκα] εδωκα A M′ V G-οI⁻¹⁵ C′′⁻⁴¹³ 53′-129 n⁻⁴⁵⁸ s 527 y⁻³⁹² 18-126 55 319 Chr I 506 X 332 Cyr II passim Tht Nm 216

23₃ εὐθεῖαν] pr επ Fᵇ n 527′ Tht Nm 219

23₈ ἤ] και b d n⁻¹²⁷ t 527 319 799 Bas II 653 Tht Nm 219 Aeth⁻ᶜᴳ Bo = 𝔐

23₈ om ὁ C′′⁻⁴¹⁴ Tht Nm 219ᵗᵉ

23₁₀ ἐξηκριβάσατο Tht *Nm* 219ᵃᵖ] -βωσατο Fᵇ oI^{-15} b 53′ 75ᶜ 84 619 $z^{-120'}$ 55ᶜ 59* Tht
  Nm 219ᵗᵉ; εξακρ. Tht *Nm* 219ᵃᵖ
23₁₀ om τό 1° 29 b d^{-106} 53′ Tht *Nm* 219ᵗᵉ
23₁₉ εἶπας] ειπων (-πον 610*) 761ᶜ d 127-767 t 527 628 Tht *Nm* 219
23₁₉ οὐχί 2°] ουκ F V 82-376′ d 56′ n t 527 624 799 Tht *Nm* 219
23₂₀ ἀποστρέψω] -στραφω b n^{-767} 527 Tht *Nm* 219 Aeth
23₂₃ οὐ γάρ ἐστιν] ουκ εσται Or III 223 Tht *Nm* 220
23₂₃ Ἰακώβ 2°] pr (※ Syhᴸ) τω Fᵇ O 414 d $n^{(-458)}$ t 527 Or III 223 *Cels* II 420 Tht *Nm* 220
  Syh
24₂ ἐπ'] εν B b^{-19} Tht *Nm* 221 = Ra
24₂₄ Κιτιαίων] χετιημ Tht *Nm* 221ᵗᵉ; χετ(τ)ιειμ (c var) 761ᵗˣᵗ d 127ᶜ-458ᵗˣᵗ t 319 Tht *Nm*
  221ᵃᵖ
25₅ οἰκεῖον] πλησιον Chr I 477
25₁₁ om υἱοῦ—ἱερέως d^{-106} Tht I 812
25₁₁ κατέπαυσεν] εστησε Tht I 812
25₁₁ ζηλῶσαί] + (÷ G) αυτον V O^{-58} Tht I 812 Bo = 𝔐
25₁₁ μου 2°] post ζῆλον tr V O^{-58} 509 Tht I 812 ᴸᵃᵗcod 100 Ambr *Ps 118* XVIII 10 Hi *Mal* 2
  Hil *Ps* CXVIII 3 Arm Syh = 𝔐
25₁₈ om ὅσα δολιοῦσιν ὑμᾶς Tht *Nm* 222 Bo
27₁₉ om αὐτόν Tht *Nm* 224
27₁₉ ἔναντι 1° 963] -τιον K 29-64 y 59 Tht *Nm* 224
27₁₉ ἔναντι 2° 963] -τιον A 29-58-oI d n t 619 y^{-392} 68′ 55 319 Tht *Nm* 224
27₁₉ συναγωγῆς 963] pr της 426 d 53′-56ᶜ-129 n t^{-76} 619 y^{-392} 68′ 319 Tht *Nm* 224
27₁₉ om καί 3°—fin 44-125 71 319 Tht *Nm* 224
27₂₀ ἄν 963] > F 767 Procop 877 Tht *Nm* 224 Syh
27₂₁ ἔναντι 1° 963] -τιον 29 C'' s 318 646 Tht *Nm* 224
31₈ ἐν ῥομφαίᾳ] εν τω πολεμω μαδιαμ Anast 573 Chr XV 193
31₈ σύν—fin] μετα των τραυματιων Anast 573 Chr XV 193
31₁₆ Ἰσραήλ] + εις (> Anast) σκανδαλον Anast 573 Chr XV 193 Bo
31₁₆ ἀποστῆσαι 963] -στηναι (c var) 29 52′-313 d n^{-767} t Tht *Nm* 222ᵗᵉ
31₁₆ Φογώρ] φεγωρ 529 59 Chr XV 193 Tht *Nm* 222ᵃᵖ
31₁₆ ἡ 963] > 376-oI n^{-767} 71′ 799 Tht *Nm* 222

Though Chr and Tht do not quote Numbers extensively certain interesting
conclusions may be drawn. It is obvious, first of all, that a large number of
unique or almost unique readings obtain in the above list. These need not be
taken seriously since in most instances they do not reflect a true textual tradition but rather the individualistic freedom of the church father over against
the Biblical text.

Secondly the text of Chr/Tht has been influenced by the work of Origen.
In at least ten instances from the list additions to the text almost certainly
are due to the hexapla. These are 5₆ τῶν ἁμαρτιῶν] pr πασων; 5₁₄ αὐτῷ 1°] pr
επ; 5₁₅ δῶρον] + αυτης; 5₁₇ τῆς γῆς] pr απο; 6₆ εὐχῆς] + αυτου; 6₆ κυρίῳ] pr τω;
9₇ ἀκάθαρτοι] + εσμεν; 10₁₀ ὁλοκαυτώμασιν] + υμων; 23₂₃ Ἰακώβ] pr τω, and
25₁₁ ζηλῶσαί] + αυτον.

Furthermore the Chr/Tht citations betray the strong influence of the Byzantine text type. If one analyzes the above list quantitatively it appears that
of variants supported by no more than three text families in the list the *d n t*
families are best represented. The following table makes this clear. Column *A*
gives the number of instances in which one group supports the variant; *B*,
two groups, and *C*, three groups.

	A	B	C	Total
O	7	—	—	7
oI	1	4	1	6
C''	3	4	2	9
b	5	3	2	10
d	2	7	13	22
f	2	1	1	4
n	14	5	11	30
s	—	2	3	5
t	—	7	13	20
x	1	1	—	2
y	1	—	—	1
z	1	—	2	3

It thus appears that Chr/Tht variants are supported by the families to the following extent: n 30, d 22, t 20, b 10, C'' 9, O 7, oI 6, s 5, f 4, z 3, x 2 and y 1. That the Chr/Tht were strongly influenced by the Byzantine type text is clear.

It must be borne in mind, however, that this does not thereby fully identify their text. Equally important are the instances in which the Byzantine text is known, but is unsupported by Chr/Tht. Thus at 5₁₄ αὐτῷ 1° appears as επ αυτω in Chr but as τω ανδρι αυτης in d n t Arm Bo. In fact, of the 70 instances involved in this analysis 28 are not supported by representatives of the Byzantine group, i.e. have a text opposed to the group.

One question remains: is this Byzantine text type to be equated with the Lucianic recension? It has already been noted that this text shows little if any influence from the Hebrew text apart from the influence of hex.

On the other hand, the question remains whether the text contains doublet traditions, i.e. is it characterized by the commonly accepted mark of Lucianic work, the presence of doublets. To examine this possibility the plusses in the d n t tradition are given in the following list. It should be mentioned that none of these plusses comes from the Hebrew tradition.

List 14

1₂₀ δυνάμει] + ιηλ̄ 58-376-707 d n t 18 Arm Syh
1₅₃ ἐναντίοι] εναντιον (εναντι 127 55) κ̄ν̄ B* M′ᵐᵍ V d n^{-767} t 55; + κυριον Bᶜ
2₂ οἴκους πατριῶν αὐτῶν] + παρεμβολαι αυτων d n^{-767} t
3₁₀ καὶ πάντα τὰ κατὰ τὸν βωμόν] + και παντα (> 125) τα (> 125) του θυσιαστηριου 707ᵐᵍ d t 799
3₂₉ σκηνῆς] + του μαρτυριου 44′ t
3₄₁ πάντων τῶν πρωτοτόκων 2°] των κτηνων τ. πρωτ. d $n^{(-767)}$ t
3₄₃ πρωτότοκα] + εν (> 125) τοις υιοις ισραηλ d n t
4₂₀ ἅγια] + των αγιων d^{-610} n t; pr των αγιων 610
4₃₆ αὐτῶν 2°] + κατ οικους πατριων αυτων V d^{-125} t
4₄₈ ἐπισκεπέντες] επισκεφθεντες (επεσκ. 84) παντες d t; + παντες 71 y 799

5₁₅ θυσία μνημοσύνου] + (+ και 125) θυσια d⁻¹⁰⁶ n t Tht Nm 196 Arm

5₂₀ μεμίανσαι] pr συ (σοι G) O b d n⁻⁷⁶⁷ t Tht Nm 197 ᴸᵃᵗcod 100 Syh

6₁₉ ἐπιθήσει 963] + ο ιερευς d n t 55 Arm

7₃ ἅμαξαν 963] αμαξα μια d 370; + μιαν 58-376 n t⁻³⁷⁰ Aeth Arm

7₁₀ ἅρχοντες 1° 963] + ιηλ V b 44′ t ᴸᵃᵗcod 100

7₈₄ ἔχρισεν αὐτό] + μωυσης V d t ᴸᵃᵗcod 100

7₈₉ τοῦ ἱλαστηρίου] pr ανα μεσων των δυο χερουβιμ 767; + (+ και 74-76) ανα μεσον των δυο χερουβιμ (c var) d⁻¹²⁵ 54′ t 799 Arm

8₂ μέρους] pr του ενος d t Arm

8₁₁ ἔργα] + της (τη 54-458) σκηνης d n⁻⁷⁶⁷ t Arm

11₇ σπέρμα κορίου ἐστίν] + λευκον (-κα 527) d n⁻⁷⁵ t 527: ex Exod 16₃₁

11₉ παρεμβολήν] γην επι (> 16-46) της παρεμβολης 16-46 d t

11₃₂ καὶ ἔψυξαν] pr και εσφαξαν (-ξεν 767) 58-376 d f⁻¹²⁹ n t 55 Arm

13₁₇ γῆν] + χανααν (-ναν 54*) V d⁻⁴⁴ n 130ᵐᵍ-321′ᵐᵍ t 392 55 319 799 Arab

13₁₈ Μωυσῆς] + εκ της ερημου φαραν M′ 29-58-376-oI d⁽⁻⁴⁴⁾ n t 799 Arm

14₁₂ πατάξω] pr αφες με (> 458) και (> 799) M′ 58-376 d n t 55 799 Arm

15₁₄ ἡ συναγωγή] pr και (> 75) ο προσηλυτος και M′ d n⁻⁷⁶⁷ t Arm

15₂₀ ἅρτον ἀφαίρεμα ἀφοριεῖτε αὐτό] pr (+ αρτον 767) και δωσετε (c var) κω n Armᵃᵖ Syhᵀ

15₃₁ ἁμαρτία] + γαρ d n t Tht Nm 211 Arm

15₃₈ τῶν πτερυγίων] pr των ιματιων και d⁻¹⁰⁶

16₉ ἐκ (συναγωγῆς)] + μεσου d 127 t Arab Sa

16₉ Ἰσραήλ 2°] pr υιων d 246 75′ t ᴸᵃᵗcod 100

16₁₃ ἀνήγαγες ἡμᾶς] + εξ αιγυπτου V 58 b n⁻¹²⁷

17₃ κατὰ φυλήν] bis scr 127 t 527

17₁₃ σκηνῆς] + του μαρτυριου V d n t 527 ᴸᵃᵗcodd 91 92 94—96 100 Arm

18₃ (σκηνῆς) σου] του μαρτυριου Fᵇ d f⁻¹²⁹ n t 527 126-628 799 Arm

18₁₉ δέδωκα] + αυτα d 54-75′ t ᴸᵃᵗcod 100 Co

18₂₁ Ἰσραήλ] pr υιοις d 53′-129 54-75′ t

19₁₀ init—δαμάλεως] pr και λουσεται το σωμα αυτου n Arm; + και λουσεται το σωμα (τω σωματι pro τ. σ. 610) αυτου d t Aethᶜ: ex 8

19₁₀ τοῖς υἱοῖς Ἰσραήλ] pr εις την (> d⁻¹⁰⁶ 75) συναγωγην 58-376 d n t 799 ᴸᵃᵗcod 100 Arm

19₁₄ οἰκίαν] + ακαθαρτος εσται d t 799: ex sq; + εκεινην ακαθαρτος εσται V

19₁₉ καὶ λούσεται] + το σωμα αυτου (> 64 Eus) 58-oI⁻¹⁵ b d n t 619 18 799 Eus VI 12 Aeth Arm

20₂ ὕδωρ] + εκει d⁻⁶¹⁰ n⁻⁷⁶⁷ t 527 Armᵃᵖ Sa¹²

20₂ συναγωγῇ] + πιειν (ποιειν 458) 58 d n t 527 ᴸᵃᵗcod 100 Arab Arm Sa¹²

20₅ συκαῖ] pr εισι(ν) n 527; + εισιν d t

20₁₅ ἐν Αἰγύπτῳ] pr εκει 52′-313 d⁻⁴⁴ n t 527 646

20₂₅ συναγωγῆς] + (+ των 527) υιων ιηλ 82-376 b d⁽⁻¹²⁵⁾ n t 527 ᴸᵃᵗcod 100

22₈ εἶπεν πρὸς αὐτούς] + βαλααμ (c var) d 246 n t 527 ᴸᵃᵗcod 100 Arab Sa¹² Syhᵀ

22₁₅ ἀποστεῖλαι ἅρχοντας ... τούτων] + προς βαλααμ (-λαακ 107ᶜ) d⁻¹⁰⁶

22₂₅ ἅγγελον τοῦ θεοῦ] + εν τοις (ταις 376) αυλαξι(ν) (αυξασι 44) 376 d⁻¹²⁵ n t 527

22₂₅ μαστίξαι αὐτήν] + βαλααμ O⁻⁴²⁶ n t 527 Sa¹²

22₃₈ τὸ ῥῆμα] pr ρημα πλην d t Bo

23₁₄ παρέλαβεν αὐτόν] + εκειθεν n t⁽⁻³⁷⁰⁾ 527 318

23₁₈ ἀναλαβών] + βαλααμ (c var) M′ᵐᵍ d⁻¹²⁵ n⁻⁴⁵⁸ t 527 55

23₂₂ ἐξ] εκ γης 376-381′ b d n 85′ᵐᵍ-321′ᵐᵍ-344ᵐᵍ t 527 ᴸᵃᵗcod 100 Aeth Armᵃᵖ

23₂₈ ἐπὶ κορυφήν] pr (+ και 58-376 La) ανεβιβασεν (c var) αυτον O⁻⁴²⁶ d⁻¹²⁵ n t 527 ᴸᵃᵗcod 100: ex 22₄₁

24₁₃ πονηρὸν ἤ καλόν] pr μικρον η μεγα 58 d n t

24₁₅ ἀναλαβών] + βαλααμ d 127 t 55

24₂₂ init] pr (c var) ασσυριοι σε αιχμαλωτευσουσιν 106-107′ n t 55

24₂₃ fin] + (∼ Syh) επι της γης Mᵐᵍ d n t 416 Syhᵀᵐᵍ

26₄ καὶ 2°] + ησαν d t

26₄₃ fin] + (c var) τω αραδι δημος ο αραδι V 44-107′ t: cf 44; + τω αραδιν 125; + τω αραδι δημος 106; cf + (※ Syhᵀ; c var) τ ι ουφαμ δημος ο ουφαμι O 767 Arab Syh = 𝔐

27₁₈ πνεῦμα] + θεου Fᵃ M′ V 707 b d n t 55 319 ᴸᵃᵗcod 100 Ruf Num XXII 4 Syh

40

28₇ τοῦ ἴν] + (∼ Syh) οινου Mᵐᵍ 376 44′-107 85ᵐᵍ-344ᵐᵍ t Syh; + μετρου (> 127) του
    οινου n
29₁₉ fin] + τοις μοσχοις τοις κριοις d⁻¹⁰⁶
30₂ ὃ συνέταξεν κύριος] + λεγων d⁻¹²⁵ 129 n t
30₃ ἄνθρωπος ἄνθρωπος] + των υιων ισραηλ n⁻⁴⁵⁸ t; ανθρωπος των υιων ι̅η̅λ̅ d 458
30₆ ἀνένευσεν] pr ανανευων d n t
30₉ οἱ ὁρισμοί] pr παντες d n t Arm
30₁₃ (τοὺς ὁρισμοὺς) τούς] ους ωρισατο (aut ορ.) 82 d t 121 Bo
30₁₆ περιέλῃ] + ο ανηρ Fᵃ 29-58-376-οI 106 t 59 416 ᴸᵃᵗAug Num 59.2ᵃᵖ Arm
31₄ Ἰσραήλ] + χιλιους εκ φυλης t: ex praec
31₃₇ ἑξακόσια ἑβδομήκοντα πέντε] pr χιλιαδες d⁻¹⁰⁶ᶜ 71′; + χιλιαδες V 19 t⁻⁸⁴ 669ᶜ 319 799
    Armᵃᵖ Bo
32₇ κύριος] + ο θεος d 767 t Cyr I 404
32₁₀ ὤμοσεν] + κ̅ς̅ n t
32₁₃ κατερρέμβευσεν αὐτούς] + κ̅ς̅ 72 106 n t
32₂₂ κυρίου 1°] + εις πολεμον και παρελευσεται υμων πας οπλιτης d⁻¹⁰⁶: ex 20s
32₃₂ διαβησόμεθα] + τον ιορδανην d n t Syh
32₄₂ ἔλαβεν] + τας πολεις αυτων ηγουν d: cf ₄₁ ἐπαύλεις 1°] πολεις
33₇ καὶ παρενέβαλον 2°] pr (c var) και απηραν απο στοματος επι ειρωθ 58 d⁽⁻¹²⁵⁾ n 344ᵐᵍ
    t⁽⁻⁸⁴ᵗˣᵗ⁾ 121: cf ₈
33₃₈ ἀνέβη ... ἱερεύς] + επι το (του 458) ορος (ορους 458) 29-82 d n⁻⁷⁶⁷ t⁻⁸⁴ Bo
34₁₃ συνέταξεν κύριος] + τω μωυση (μωση n) B* d⁽⁻⁴⁴⁾ 246 n t Syh = Ra
35₄ ἔξω] + τειχους (τοιχ. 610ˢᵘᵖ ʳᵃˢ) 82 d⁻⁴⁴ n t ᴸᵃᵗcod 104 Armᵃᵖ: ex praec
36₉ προσκολληθήσονται] + τη εαυτου φυλη d n t 799

From the above list it would appear that the Byzantine text type is an expansionist type text. Over against this, however, it must be said that this text, particularly in the d family, has a large number of omissions so that it would be quite incorrect simply to designate this text as expansionist.

An examination of the above list shows that most of the expansions are easily explained. They often constitute importations from the context, clarifying glosses such as the addition of subject or object or the rendering explicit what is implicit, or are due to familiar phrases such as "(tent) of testimony," "(spirit) of God," "(before) the Lord," "upon the land," "among the sons of Israel," "(holy) of holies," or "(land) of Canaan."

There are, however, surprisingly few genuine doublets in the list. At 3₁₀ it is said that Aaron and his sons are to guard their priesthood καὶ πάντα τὰ κατὰ τὸν βωμόν to which our text adds και παντα τα του θυσιαστηριου. In F V 72-82-707ᵗˣᵗ b 767 392 z 59 646 Aeth Arm Bo Sa⁴ this text also appears but as substitute for καὶ πάντα τὰ κατὰ τὸν βωμόν. The doublet has no basis in 𝔐.

At 4₃₆ the census of the sons of Kaath is recorded κατὰ δήμους αὐτῶν to which our text adds κατ οικους πατριων αυτων. This is undoubtedly due to the fact that the longer text occurs in the parallel verses 34, 38, 40, 42, 44 and 46.

An apparent doublet appears in 11₃₂ in the account of the gathering of the quails. The people spent, it is said, an entire day and night as well as the following day in gathering quails to which 𝔐 adds וישטחו להם שטוח סביבות המחנה, "and they spread them out throughout around the camp." This was interpreted by the translator as καὶ ἔψυξαν ἑαυτοῖς ψυγμοὺς κύκλῳ τῆς παρεμβολῆς. The Byzantine text adds και εσφαξαν before this clause, whereas B 509 have εσφαξαν for ἔψυξαν. I suggest that the gloss originated in an attempt to clarify a difficult text. The text was understood as referring to the cooling of the bodies of the gathered quails (cf the text of the old Latin *fecerunt {s}ibi refrigeratoria*); thus the fowl were caught, slain, and allowed to cool. For the equivalence of ψύχω/שטח cf also Sam II 17₁₉ Jer 8₂. Actually the interpretation was probably intended in the sense of "to dry out," then "to spread out for drying"; cf ψυγω and references in LS. Incidentally the note in BHS equating the reading of B with וישחטו is misleading since the B 509 reading is the result of parablepsis (within the longer text) due to homoioteleuton. Nor is it at all likely that the gloss was due to Hebrew influence. The notion that ישטחו was misread as ישחטו by a revisor (then what about שטוח?) is historically unlikely.

At 24₁₃ Balaam protests his inability to transgress the word of the Lord ποιῆσαι αὐτὸ πονηρὸν ἢ καλὸν παρ᾽ ἐμαυτοῦ for the Hebrew לעשות טובה או רעה מלבי. This is expanded in our text to include the phrase μικρον η μεγα immediately before πονηρόν. The expansion may well have been exegetically inspired to emphasize the absolute inability of a seer to go beyond (παραβῆναι) the word of the Lord, i.e. neither in small matters or large ones. It should be noted that the marginal reading of M′ substitutes μικρον η μεγα for πονηρὸν ἢ καλόν.

It can hardly be said that the Byzantine text group is characterized by doublets. It represents a text development which can be explained on the whole as an inner Greek one; that it is the result of a thoroughgoing recension does not appear to be correct. That this text type constitutes the Lucianic recension is possible but remains unproven.

Chapter 3   The Hexaplaric Recension

The principal witnesses to hex are mss G-58-376-426 and Syh; of these ms 58 is the most aberrant. G, a IV. to V. Century uncial ms, has many hex signs as does Syh; it is unfortunately incomplete. Folios which contained 7₈₅—11₁₈ 18₂—₃₀ 20₂₂—25₂ and 26₃—29₁₂ are no longer extant. Syh is almost entirely extant in two Bible mss, Syh^L and Syh^T; only the following texts are lacking: 1₁—₃ and 6₇—7₇.

Primary evidence for hex activity is to be found in the additions to Num which are sub ast. Though the asterisk tradition is not consistently correct in the mss., all of it is presented in the following list. If the possible source of the hex reading is known it is given in parentheses at the end of the citation.

List 1

1₂₂ κατά 3°] pr (※ G Syh) αι (και G-376; η 767) επισκεψεις (-ψις G-376 767) αυτων O 767 Syh = Sam: cf 𝔐

1₄₆ init] pr (※ G 127 Syh) και εγενοντο παντες (-ταις 376 75) οι επεσκεμμενοι (c var) O⁻⁵⁸ d n t 799 Arm Syh = 𝔐

1₅₁ ἀναστήσουσιν] + (※ G) αυτην (+ ※ Syh) οι λευιται (c var) O-707 44 n t 55 319 799 Arab Arm Syh = 𝔐

1₅₃ ἁμάρτημα] + (※ G) επι την (τοις 376) συναγωγην (-γης 376) O⁻⁴²⁶-15 318 Arab Syh = 𝔐

2₉ ἑκατόν] + (※ G Syh) χιλιαδες (χειλ. G) O⁻³⁷⁶ Syh = 𝔐

2₉ ὀγδοήκοντα] pr (※ G) και A F M′ O′’⁻⁽⁶⁴ᵗˣᵗ⁾⁷² C′⁻⁵⁵²-46-417*-422 b 129 s⁻³⁴³ᵐᵍ y⁻³¹⁸ z⁻¹²⁶ ⁶²⁸ 55 59 624 646 Bo^B Syh = 𝔐; et quadraginta Bo^A

2₃₄ init—Μωυσῇ] sub ※ 344 (vid)

3₂₅ σκηνή] + (※ G Syh) και η σκεπη O 767 Syh = 𝔐

3₂₆ σκηνῆς] + (※ G Syh^T) και επι του θυσιαστηριου κυκλω O 767 Arab Syh = 𝔐

3₃₈ κατά—σκηνῆς] pr ※ contra tabernaculum contra orientem ↙ Syh^{mg}; + (※ G) απο ανατολων κατεναντι της σκηνης G-426 = 𝔐

3₄₇ πέντε] + (※ G) πεντε O⁻⁵⁸ = 𝔐

4₃ πεντήκοντα ἐτῶν] pr (※ G^{c}vid; ÷ G*) υιον G-376 18′-126-628-669 Syh = 𝔐

4₇ ἱμάτιον ὁλοπόρφυρον] sub ※ (÷*) G (mend)

4₇ καί 2°] pr ※ Syh; > G*(c pr m); + (※ G) δωσουσιν επ αυτης ([αυ]την 803) 803 O 767 Arab Syh = 𝔐

4₈ κόκκινον] + (※ G Syh) διαφορον (διφ. V) V O⁻⁵⁸ 767 Syh = 𝔐

4₁₆ ἔργοις] + (※ G Syh) αυτου O⁻⁴²⁶ 646 Syh = 𝔐

4₁₉ ἕκαστον] + (※ G Syh) επι την δουλ(ε)ιαν αυτου O 767 Arab Syh = 𝔐

4₂₃ ἐπάνω] + (※ G) εκει O⁻⁴²⁶: contra 𝔐

4₂₃ λειτουργεῖν] + (※ G Syh) λειτουργιαν (λιτ. G) O⁻⁵⁸ 767 Syh = 𝔐

4₂₆ αὐλῆς] + και το επισπαστρον (c var) της θυρας (om τ. θ. 767) της πυλης (om τ. π. 29-58-72 131 619 59 646 Aeth) της αυλης (της 1°—αυλης sub ※ G Syh) V O-29-72 131⁽ᵐᵍ⁾ 767 619 59 646 Aeth^C Arab Syh (o′ + και τὸ ἐπίσπαστρον τῆς θύρας (+ τῆς πύλης 344) τῆς αὐλῆς (om τῆς θύρας τῆς αὐλῆς 85) 85′-344; θ′ + και τὸ ἐπίσπαστρον τῆς θύρας τῆς πύλης τῆς αὐλῆς 344)

4₂₆ ὅσα 1°—σκηνῆς] sub ※ G (mend)

4₂₆ μαρτυρίου] + (※ G Syh; c var) και επι τον θυσιαστηριον κυκλω V O-29 767 619
Syh = 𝔐

4₂₇ ἡ λειτουργία] pr (※ G Syh) πασα O-29 619 Sa⁴ Syh = 𝔐

4₃₀ πεντηκονταετοῦς] pr (※ G Syh) υιον O⁻⁴²⁶ Syh = 𝔐

4₃₀ εἰσπορευόμενος] + (※ G Syh) εις την δυναμιν V O Syh = 𝔐

4₃₃ δήμου] pr (※ G) του O⁻⁴²⁶ 413 19 246 126: contra 𝔐; plebum ↙ Syh = 𝔐

4₃₅ πεντηκονταετοῦς] pr (※ G) υιον O⁻⁴²⁶ Syh = 𝔐

4₃₉ ἕως] pr (※ Syh) και A 376′ b ᴸᵃᵗcod 100 Syh = 𝔐; ※ και εως ↙ G

4₃₉ πεντηκονταετοῦς] pr (※ Syh) υιον 58-376 Syh = 𝔐

4₄₃ ἕως] pr (※ Syh) και 18′-628-669 Syh = 𝔐

4₄₇ ἕως] pr (※ G Syh) και O⁻⁴²⁶ Syh = 𝔐

5₃ παρεμβολῆς] + (※ G Syh) εξαποστειλατε αυτους O Syh = 𝔐

5₆ καὶ παριδὼν παρίδῃ] κ. παριδών sub ※ G; + (※ Syh) εν κυριω O 619 68′-120′ Arab
Syh = 𝔐

5₇ ἁμαρτίαν] + (※ G Syh) αυτων (-των Gᶜ) O⁻⁵⁸ 318 Syh = 𝔐

5₇ πλημμέλειαν] + (※ G Syh) αυτου O 767 Syh = 𝔐

5₇ τὸ κεφάλαιον] (※ G Syh) το κεφ. αυτου O 318 Syh = 𝔐

5₁₀ αὐτοῦ] + (※ G Syh) αυτω V O 767 319 Syh = 𝔐

5₁₀ καί 2° — fin] sub ※ G Syh mend

5₁₅ δῶρον] + (※ G Syh) αυτης O Chr II 917 Syh = 𝔐

5₁₉ εἰ μή 2°] pr (※ G; + ÷ Syh) και V O 18′-628-669 ᴸᵃᵗOr Matth 110 Syh = 𝔐

5₂₂ σου 2°] sub ※ (mend pro ÷) G; sub ÷ Syh (recte): cf 𝔐

5₂₇ init] pr (※ G Syh) και ποτιει αυτην το υδωρ O⁻⁵⁸ Syh = 𝔐

5₂₇ κοιλίαν] + (※ G Syh) αυτης O 767 Chr II 917 ᴸᵃᵗcod 100 Aug Loc in hept IV 12 Arm
Co Syh = 𝔐

6₅ (τοῦ) ἁγνισμοῦ B 963 58 127 84 x⁻⁶¹⁹ Cyr I 1041 ᴸᵃᵗcod 100 Arm Bo] αφαγν. 44; > 72
319; + (※ G; ÷ Syh) αυτου rell = 𝔐

6₅ κεφαλῆς] + (※ G Syh vid) αυτου (αυτον 56ᶜ) V O-29 f⁻¹²⁹ 767 628 319 Arm Co
Syh = 𝔐

6₆ εὐχῆς 963] + (※ G Syh) αυτου Fᵇ M′ V O⁻⁵⁸ d n 85′ᵐᵍ-321′ᵐᵍ-344ᵐᵍ t⁻⁸⁴ 319 Tht
Nm 198 Arm Bo Sa⁴ Syh = 𝔐

6₆ κυρίῳ 963] sub ※ Sᶜ; pr (※ S G Syh) τω M′ Sᶜ O-82 52′-313-414 d n 28-85′ᵐᵍ-321′ᵐᵍ-
344ᵐᵍ t Tht Nm 198 Bo Syh: cf 𝔐

6₇ πατρί 963] + (※ G Syh) αυτου O⁻⁵⁸ 767 Syh = 𝔐

6₇ μητρί 963] + (※ G Syh) αυτου O⁻⁵⁸ 767 Syh = 𝔐

6₇ ἀδελφῷ] + (※ G) αυτου O⁻⁵⁸ 767 = 𝔐

6₇ ἀδελφῇ] + (※ G) αυτου O 767 = 𝔐

6₉ ξυρηθήσεται 963] + (※ G) αυτην O⁻⁵⁸ = 𝔐

6₁₂ init] pr (※ G) και O⁽⁻⁵⁸⁾ Aeth = 𝔐

6₁₂ ἤ ἡγιάσθη] (※ G 321′-344) διαφυλαξει O⁽⁻⁵⁸⁾ 130ᵐᵍ-321′ᵐᵍ-344ᵐᵍ: והזיר 𝔐
The metobolus is lacking after και in G; cf the immediately preceding citation.
Possibly the first part of v. 12 in Origen's hexapla read ÷ η ηγιασθη ※ και διαφυλαξει
τω ↙ κυριω; cf the texts of ms 58 and 767 in App. I.

6₁₂ κυρίῳ 963] pr (※ G) τω F S O′⁻⁽⁵⁸⁾⁷⁰⁷ 619 z 59: cf 𝔐

6₁₂ εὐχῆς 1° 963] + (※ G) αυτου O⁽⁻⁵⁸⁾-707ᶜ C″ s 319 Arm Bo Sa⁴ = 𝔐

6₁₈ τρίχας] + (※ G) της (> 318) κεφαλης ευχης αυτου (ευχ. αυτ. tr 376) και θησει (om κ.
θ. 318) O 318 = 𝔐

6₂₁ εὐχῆς 1° 963] + (※ Gᶜ; ÷ G*) αυτου O C″ b 610 s 318 Bo Sa⁴ = 𝔐

6₂₁ εὔξηται 2°] + (※ G) ουτως ποιησει (-σειν 318) V O 318 Arab Sa = 𝔐

6₂₁ ἁγνείας 963] + (※ G) αυτου V O′ d 767 t 318 799 Arab Sa⁴ = 𝔐

7₃ προσήγαγον] + (※ G) αυτα O⁻⁵⁸ Bo = 𝔐

7₇₂ ἑνδεκάτῃ] + ※ ημερα ↙ G = 𝔐

7₈₅ ἕν (καὶ ἑβδομήκοντα)] + (※ G Syh) αργυριον O⁻⁵⁸-15 Boᴮ Syh = 𝔐; + αργυρουν
85′ᵐᵍ-321′ᵐᵍ 319; και εβδ. sub ※ G

7₈₆ θυμιάματος] + (※ 85-344-730 Syh) δεκα δεκα (χρυσων M′ V oI 619 55; > 319) η (οι
343) θυισκη (-κοι 343; turabula pro η θυισκη Syh; + η μια V 55) εν τω σικλω τω αγιω
(αγιω σικλω pro σ. τ. α. 30) M′ V O′⁻⁵⁸ s⁻³²¹ 619 y⁻³⁹² 18-126-628 55 319 Syh = 𝔐

44

8₁₂ χεῖρας 963] + (✳ Syh) αντων A O⁻⁵⁸ b 18'-126-628-669 ᴸᵃᵗcod 100 Arm Co Syh
= 𝔐

8₁₉ Ἰσραήλ 4°] + (✳ Syh) εν (> 767 Syh = 𝔐) θραυσει (-σ(ε)ις 767 Syh) O 767 Arab
Syh = 𝔐

8₂₅ τῆς] pr (✳ Syh) της δυναμεως (c var) O 767 Syh = 𝔐

9₃ τόν] pr (✳ Syh) παντα O⁻⁵⁸ Syh = 𝔐

9₃ τήν] pr (✳ Syh) πασαν O⁻⁵⁸ Syh = 𝔐

9₅ init] pr (✳ Syh) και εποιησαν το πασχα V O 106ᵐᵍ Syh = 𝔐

9₅ μηνός] + (✳ Syh) ανα μεσον (μεσων του μηνος 376) των εσπερινων O Arab Syh = 𝔐

9₆ Ἀαρών] pr (✳ Syh) εναντιον O⁻⁵⁸ Syh = 𝔐

9₇ ἡμεῖς] + (✳ Syh) εσμεν O Syh: contra 𝔐

9₁₂ τόν] pr (✳ Syh) παντα O 767 Syh = 𝔐

9₂₁ ἡμέρας] pr (✳ Syh) η O⁻³⁷⁶ Syh (σ' aut die Syh)

9₂₂ ἡμέρας 1° — ἡμέρας 2°] a diebus ✳ ad dies ⦚ Syh

9₂₂ νεφέλης] + (✳ Syh) επι της σκηνης O⁽⁻³⁷⁶⁾ 767 Arab Syh (σ' + super tabernaculum
Syh)

9₂₂ ἀπάρωσιν] + (✳ Syh) και (> oI 619) εν τω αναχθηναι αυτην εξηραν (c var) O' 767 619
Arab Syh = 𝔐

9₂₃ ὅτι] (+ ✳ Syh) οτι δια προσταγματος κυριου (+ εν χειρι μωυση 618*) παρεμβαλουσι(ν)
(-λλουσιν 767; + ⦚ Syh) και O'⁻³⁷⁶ 767 619 Syh = 𝔐

10₃ πᾶσα] pr επι σαι 376; pr (✳ Syh) προς σε V O⁻³⁷⁶ 246 619 z 646 ᴸᵃᵗOr Matth 52 Syh
= 𝔐

10₄ ἀρχηγοί] + (✳ Syh) χιλιαδων O 767 Syh (+ ,ā ἀκύλας 344)

10₉ κυρίου] + (✳ Syh) θεου υμων O Arab Syh = 𝔐

10₃₀ fin] + (✳ Syh) πορευσομαι (-σωμαι 376 75*-767) O f n ᴸᵃᵗcod 100 Aug Loc in hept
IV 25 Aeth Arm Syh = 𝔐

10₃₁ μεθ' ἡμῶν] pr (✳ Syh) εν τη παρεμβολη 426 Syh: cf 𝔐; + και εν τη παρεμβολη O⁻⁴²⁶

10₃₄ σε] + (✳ Syh) απο προσωπου σου 426 767 Arab Syh = 𝔐

11₁ γογγύζων] pr (✳ Syh) ως O⁻⁵⁸ Syh = 𝔐

11₁ ὀργῇ] + (✳ Syh) αυτου O⁻³⁷⁶ Syh = 𝔐

11₄ ὁ 2°] sub ✳ Syhᵀ

11₇ εἶδος 2° B 707 f 509 318 z 624 646 799 Boᴮ] ωσει 𝔐'; ως 106 Sa⁵; pr (✳ Syh) ως
rell = 𝔐

11₁₀ θύρας] + (✳ Syhᴸ) της (> 58*) σκηνης O 107'-125 n t⁻³⁷⁰ Arm Syh = 𝔐

11₁₁ τοῦ λαοῦ] pr (✳ Syh) παντος O⁻⁵⁸ 246 18'-126-628-630' Syh = 𝔐

11₁₄ τὸν λαόν] pr (✳ Syh) παντα O⁻⁵⁸ Syh = 𝔐

11₁₉ δύο] + (✳ G Syh) ημερας O 246 Syh = 𝔐

11₃₂ ἡμέραν 1°] + (✳ G Syh) εκεινην O d⁻⁴⁴ f⁻¹²⁹ n t 18'-126-628-669 646 Syh = 𝔐

11₃₃ κύριος ἐθυμώθη] + (✳ G Syh) οργη O⁻⁴²⁶ f⁻¹²⁹ Arab Syh: cf 𝔐; εθυμ. οργη κυριος
426

12₆ ἀκούσατε] + (✳ G Syh) δη O f⁻¹²⁹ Syh = 𝔐

12₁₂ μητρός] + (✳ G Syh) αυτου O f⁻¹²⁹ 130ᵐᵍ-321'ᵐᵍ 128ᵐᵍ 319 Co Syh = 𝔐

13₃ ἄνδρα ἕνα] + (✳ G) ανδρα ενα G-376 = 𝔐

13₂₄ ἀναφορεῦσιν] + (✳ G Syh) δυσι(ν) V O 767 Syh = 𝔐

13₂₇ ἔδειξαν] + (✳ G Syh) αυτοις V O-29 d t 121 319 ᴸᵃᵗcod 100 Aeth Bo Pal Syh = 𝔐

13₃₃ κατασκέψασθαι] sub ✳ Syh; + (✳ G Syh) αυτην O'⁻¹⁵ ⁵⁸ n⁽⁻⁴⁵⁸⁾ 319 Aeth Arm
Pal Sa¹¹ Syh (+ αὐτήν 85-321'-344)

13₃₄ γίγαντας] + (✳ G) υιους ενακ (αιν. 767ᶜ 18) εκ των γιγαντων O⁻⁵⁸ 246 767 18-126-628-
630 Syh = 𝔐

14₁ φωνήν] pr (✳ Gᶜ Syh) την O⁻⁵⁸ Syh = 𝔐; + (✳ G Syh) αυτων O b Arab Syh = 𝔐

14₅ πρόσωπον] + (✳ G Syh) αυτων O Arab Arm Co Syh = 𝔐

14₅ ἐναντίον πάσης] sub ✳ Syh; + (✳ G Syh) εκκλησιας O⁻⁵⁸ Syh = 𝔐

14₇ κατεσκεψάμεθα] pr (✳ G) παρηλθομεν εν αυτη (+ ✳ Syh) και (bis scr G) O Arab
Syh: cf 𝔐

14₉ ὁ καιρός] + (✳ G) αυτων O⁻⁵⁸ 18'-126-628-630' Co Syh (θ' α' (> Syh) ἡ σκιὰ αὐτῶν
σ' ἡ σκέπη αὐτῶν 108 Syh)

14₂₂ σημεῖα] + (✳ G) μου (+ ⦚ Syh) V O d t 799 Arab Syh = 𝔐

14₂₅ ἀπάρατε] + υμεις αυτοι (sub ※ G Syh) O 18′-628-630′ Syh: cf 𝔐

14₂₇ ἐγόγγυσαν] pr (※ G Syh) αυτοι V O⁻³⁷⁶ d t 18′-126-628-630′ Syh (οἱ λ′ ο′ pr αὐτοί 344); αυτοι γογγυζουσιν 376 129 = 𝔐

14₂₉ οἱ κατηριθμημένοι] pr (※ G) παντες O⁻³⁷⁶ 128-630′ Syh = 𝔐; πανταις οι καριθμουμενοι 376

14₃₁ παιδία] + (※ G) υμων O 767 18′-126-628-630′ Sa Syh = 𝔐

14₃₄ ἐνιαυτοῦ] + (※ G Syh) ημεραν του ενιαυτου O⁻⁵⁸ Syh = 𝔐

14₃₅ τῇ 1°] pr (※ G Syh) παση O 246 18′-126-628-630′ Syh = 𝔐

14₃₆ τήν 2°] pr (※ G Syh) πασαν O⁻³⁷⁶ Aeth Syh = 𝔐; πασαν 376

14₃₉ τά] pr (※ G Syh) παντα O b Arab Syh = 𝔐ᵐˢˢ

14₄₁ ἵνα τί] τί sub ※ Syhᴸ; + (※ G Syhᴸ) τουτο O Syh = 𝔐

14₄₁ ὑμῖν] sub ※ Syhᴸ (mend pro ÷)

15₆ ποιήσεις θυσίαν] pr (※ G Syh) η τω κριω (κρειω G) O⁻⁵⁸ Syh: cf 𝔐

15₁₀ οἶνον] + (※ Syhᵀ) προσοισει (-σεις 376) O⁻ᴳ-15 Syh = 𝔐; + ※ προ ⟋ οισει G | εἰς σπονδήν] sub ※ Syhᴸ (mend)

15₁₁ προβάτων] + (※ G Syhᵀ) η (> G-376′) εκ των αμνων O Syh: contra 𝔐
This hex addition is puzzling. Possibly Origen's Hebrew text had a gloss in it; in any event 𝔐 does not support the plus.

15₁₈ ἐγώ] sub ※ G Syhᵀ (mend)

15₂₃ καθά] κατα παντα (sub ※ G Syhᵀ) α (ως 58) O Syh = 𝔐

15₂₈ fin B F V 72′ f⁻²⁴⁶ n⁻¹²⁷ x 59 Latcod 100 Aeth Arab Arm Sa] + (※ Gᶜ Syhᴸ; ÷ G*) και αφεθησεται (c var) αυτω (> 82) rell = 𝔐

15₃₀ τοῦ] pr (※ G) μεσον O Bas III 668 Syh = 𝔐

15₃₆ λίθοις] pr (※ Syh) εν Α O′ ⁽⁻⁵⁸⁾ C′′ ⁻⁵⁵⁰′ 767 s⁽⁻³⁰⁾ 619 y⁽⁻³⁹²⁾ 18-68′-628 55 319 624 Bo Syh = 𝔐

15₃₆ ἔξω τῆς παρεμβολῆς 2°] (※ G) και απεθανε(ν) O⁽⁻⁵⁸⁾ Syh = 𝔐

16₉ λειτουργεῖν] pr (※ G) εις το O⁻⁴²⁶: cf 𝔐; pr ※ Syh; sub ※ Gᶜ (vid)

16₁₀ ἱερατεύειν] pr (※ G Syh) και γε G-376 18′-628-630′ Arab Syh = 𝔐

16₂₄ Κόρε B F V 72-707ᵗˣᵗ f⁻²⁴⁶ x 59 Aeth Sa¹²] δαθαν και αβειρων (c var) 552ᵗˣᵗ-761 125; + κυκλω και δαθαν και αβιρων 458; + (※ G 344 Syh) και (> G-426 68′-120′ = 𝔐) δαθαν και αβιρων (c var) rell = 𝔐; sub ※ 344 Syhᴸ

16₂₆ ἀποσχίσθητε] sub ※ Syhᴸ; + (※ G Syhᵀ) δη G-376 18′-126-630′ Syh = 𝔐

16₂₆ μή (συναπόλησθε)] + (※ G Syh) ποτε O 246 18′-126-628-630′ Syh = 𝔐; συναπόλησθε sub ※ Syhᴸ (mend)

16₂₇ Κόρε (κύκλω) B F M′ V 72-707ᵗˣᵗ f n x 392 68′-120′ 59 319 799 Latcod 100 Aeth Arm Co] + (※ G Syh) και (> O 125 = 𝔐) δαθαν (c var) και αβιρων (c var) rell = 𝔐; κύκλω sub ※ Syhᴸ (mend)

16₄₁ ἐγόγγυσαν (οἱ υἱοί)] + (※ G Syh; + πασαν 630) πασα η συναγωγη O f⁻¹²⁹ 18′-126-628-630′ 646 Arab Syh (s metob ᴛ) = 𝔐; οἱ υἱοί sub ※ Syhᴸ (mend)

16₄₇ εἰς] + (※ G Syhᵀ) μεσην O f⁻¹²⁹ Syh = 𝔐

16₄₈ τεθνηκότων] sub ※ Syhᴸ (mend)

16₄₈ τῶν 2°] pr (※ G) ανα μεσον O-15 f⁻¹²⁹ Aeth Arab Bo Syh = 𝔐

17₆ ἄρχοντα] + (※ G Syhᴸ) ενα O⁻⁵⁸ Syh = 𝔐

17₁₂ ἀπολώλαμεν] + nos ⟋ omnes Syh; + (※ G) παντες ημεις V O f⁻¹²⁹ = 𝔐

18₁ σου 2° B V 58 529 129 x⁻⁵²⁷ 126 Cyr I 837 Arab Co] + (※ Syh) μετα (sup ras 75) σου (> 628) rell = 𝔐; sub ※ G (mend)

18₁ σου ult] + (※ G Syh) μετα σου (> 56*) O⁻⁵⁸ f⁻¹²⁹ 121 Syh = 𝔐

18₆ Ἰσραήλ] + (※ Syhᴸ) υμιν O⁻⁵⁸-15 56 Syh = 𝔐

18₇ δόμα] pr ※ Syhᴸ; + (※ Syhᵀ) δωσω O⁻⁵⁸ Syh (τὸ σαμ′ δόματι δώσω C′′ ᶜᵒᵐᵐ)

18₈ τῶν υἱῶν] sub ※ Syhᴸ (mend)

18₉ ἁμαρτιῶν] + (※ Syhᴸ) αυτων F O-29 d f⁻⁵⁶ n t x⁻⁵⁰⁹ z⁻¹²⁸ ⁶⁶⁹ 646 Cyr I 837 Latcod 100 Arm Sa¹ ¹¹ Syh = 𝔐

18₁₆ μηνιαίου] + (※ Syh) λυτρωση O Syh = 𝔐

18₁₆ συντίμησις] + αυτου αργυριου (sub ※ Syhᵀ) 376 Arab Syh; + αργυριον V O⁻³⁷⁶: cf 𝔐

18₁₇ στέαρ] + (※ Syhᴸ) αυτων O⁻⁵⁸-15 Bo Syh = 𝔐

18₁₈ κρέα] + (※ Syhᴸ) αυτων O⁻⁵⁸ Sa¹² Syh = 𝔐

46

18₂₆ ἐν κλήρῳ] + (+ ※ Syh^L) υμων O⁻⁵⁸ 767 Syh = 𝔐

18₂₉ ἀφαίρεμα] pr (※ Syh) παν O⁻⁵⁸ 130^mg-321'^mg 18'-126-630' 319 ^Lat cod 100 Syh = 𝔐

18₂₉ ἀπαρχῶν] + (※ Syh^L) αυτου O Syh = 𝔐

18₂₉ ἡγιασμένον (ἀπ' αὐτοῦ)] + (※ Syh^L) αυτου O⁻⁵⁸ Syh = 𝔐; ἀπ' αὐτοῦ sub ※ Syh^L (mend)

18₃₀ ἀπαρχὴν (ἀπ' αὐτοῦ)] + (※ G Syh^L) αυτου O⁻ᴳ˙ Syh = 𝔐; ἀπ' αὐτοῦ sub ※ G* (mend)

18₃₂ ἀπαρχήν] + (※ G Syh) αυτου O 767 Sa Syh = 𝔐

19₄ Ἐλεαζάρ] + (※ G Syh) ο ιερευς O Arab Syh = 𝔐

19₄ αὐτῆς 1°] + (※ G Syh) τω δακτυλω αυτου V O⁻³⁷⁶ 108^mg 767 18'-126-628-630' 646 Aeth^C Arab Syh = 𝔐

19₅ τὸ δέρμα B 82 125 53'-129 x⁻⁶¹⁹ ^LatPsAug *Serm Cai* II 38.2] τα κρεα 319; + (※ G Syh^L) αυτης rell = 𝔐

19₈ αὐτοῦ 1°] + (※ G; + ※ Syh^L) εν υδατι O⁽⁻³⁷⁶⁾ Aeth^C Syh = 𝔐

19₈ τὸ σῶμα αὐτοῦ B F 29-82 129 392 Aeth⁻ᴳ] pr υδατι 628; αὐτοῦ sub ※ Syh^L; + (※ G Syh) εν υδατι O⁽⁻³⁷⁶⁾ Syh = 𝔐; + υδατι (c var) rell

19₈ ἑσπέρας] pr ※ της ↙ G = 𝔐

19₁₂ ἁγνισθήσεται] + (※ G) εν αυτω O-15 Syh = 𝔐

19₁₄ ὅσα] pr (※ G) παντα O Eus VI 12 = 𝔐

19₁₆ τραυματίου] + (※ G Syh^L) ρομφαιας (-φαια G-376') O Eus VI 12 Syh = 𝔐

19₁₈ τά] pr (※ G; + ※ Syh^L) παντα O Syh = 𝔐

20₃ λέγοντες] pr (※ G Syh) και ειπαν (-πον 376) O Syh = 𝔐

20₄ ἡμᾶς] pr (※ G; + ※ Syh^L) εκει O⁻³⁷⁶ Syh = 𝔐

20₅ παραγενέσθαι (εἰς τὸν τόπον)] + (※ G) ημας O 121 Aeth Arab Syh = 𝔐; εἰς τὸν τόπον sub ※ Syh^L(mend)

20₆ πρόσωπον] + (※ G Syh^L) αυτων O Arab Arm Co Syh = 𝔐

20₁₁ τῇ ῥάβδῳ] sub ※ Syh^L; + (※ G) αυτου V O Syh = 𝔐

20₁₂ ἐπιστεύσατε] + μοι M' V 82 b d 54'-75 130^mg-321'^mg t 527 319 Chr I 506 X 332 Tht Nm 216te ^Latcod 100 Aeth^C Arab Arm; + (※ G Syh) εν εμοι O Bas I 440 Syh = 𝔐

20₂₃ Ἀαρών] pr ※ ad ↙ Syh = 𝔐

20₂₆ ἔνδυσον] + (※ Syh) αυτην O 121 Co Syh = 𝔐

20₂₈ ἐξέδυσεν] + (※ Syh) μωυσης (μωσ. 58-426) V O-82 Syh⁻ᴳ = 𝔐

20₂₈ Ἀαρών 2° B F oII 414-529 125 f 71-509 392 z 59 799 ^Latcod 100 Aeth⁻ᶜ Arab Arm Co] pr εκει 551 b⁻¹⁹; + (※ Syh) εκει rell = 𝔐

21₁₃ ἐν τῇ ἐρήμῳ] pr (※ Syh^L) ο (+ ※ Syh^T) εστιν O-15 246 18'-628-630' Syh = 𝔐; + ↙ Syh

22₅ Φαθούρα] pr (※ Syh^L) εις 392 128-669 Syh; εις φατουρα 376 ^Latcod 100

The correctness of the ast is highly questionable. Though εις is present in one hex Greek ms, there is no preposition in 𝔐.

22₁₇ σε] + (※ Syh) σφοδρα O⁻⁵⁸ 246 767 18'-126-628-630' Bo Syh = 𝔐

22₁₉ ὑπομείνατε] pr ※ Syh^L; + (※ Syh) δη O⁻⁴²⁶ Syh = 𝔐

22₂₂ τοῦ θεοῦ] κυριου εν τη οδω 376 527 Bo = 𝔐; + (÷ Syh mend pro ※) εν (> 407) τη οδω (> 120) 426 n 120*-407 Or IV 409 ^Latcod 100 Syh

22₂₃ ῥομφαίαν] + (※ Syh^L) αυτου O⁻⁵⁸ Or IV 409 Co Syh = 𝔐

22₂₃ ἐπάταξεν] + (※ Syh) βαλααμ (balam La) M'^mg V O d n t 527 Or IV 409 ^Latcod 100 Arab Syh = 𝔐

22₂₅ Βαλαάμ] sub ※ Syh^L; + (※ Syh^L; c var) προς τον τοιχον A O'⁽⁻¹⁵⁾-82 C''⁽⁻⁴⁶⁷³'⁵²⁹⁾ 246 s⁽⁻³⁴³⁾ 619 y⁻³⁹² z⁽⁻⁶²⁸⁾ LatAug *Num* 50 Arab Syh = 𝔐

22₂₇ ἐθυμώθη] + (※ Syh) οργη O 246 18'-628-630' Syh = 𝔐

22₃₇ ἀπέστειλα] pr (※ Syh^Lvid) *mittens* ^Latcod 100 Syh = 𝔐; pr αποστελλων 426-oI⁻⁶⁴ᵗˣᵗ 246 18'-628-630'; pr αποστειλας 376 b d⁻¹²⁵ n t 319

23₂ ἀνήνεγκεν] + (※ Syh^T) βαλακ και βαλααμ (-λαμ 376*) O⁻⁵⁸ Arab Syh = 𝔐

23₆ αὐτοῦ 1°] sub ※ Syh(mend); + αυτος O⁻⁵⁸ = 𝔐

Obviously it is αυτος, not αὐτοῦ which belongs sub ast.

23₁₅ παράστηθι] + (※ Syh^L) αυτου V 426 Syh = 𝔐

23₂₀ ἀποστρέψω] + (※ Syh) αυτην O 767 ^LatRuf *Num* XVI 2 Syh = 𝔐

23₂₃ Ἰακώβ 2°] pr (✳ Syh^L) τω F^b O 414 d n^(−458) t 527 Or III 223 Cels II 420 Tht Nm 220 Syh: cf 𝔐

24₂ φυλάς] + (✳ Syh^L) αυτου O Syh = 𝔐

24₃ ὁρῶν] sub ✳ Syh^L

24₃ init — θεοῦ 1°] sub ✳ M 344 Syh

24₈ ἐχθρῶν] pr ✳ Syh^L
　　The tradition of the asterisk must be faulty for the last three citations.

24₁₀ ἐθυμώθη] + (✳ Syh) οργη O^−58 767 Syh = 𝔐

24₁₁ τιμήσω] pr (✳ Syh^L) τιμων O^−58 Syh = 𝔐

24₁₆ ἀκούων] pr (✳ Syh) φησιν O^−58-15 106^c Arab Syh = 𝔐

25₄ κυρίῳ B V 82 d 53′ n^−75* t 71-509 319 Cyr I 908 IV 300] > 75*; pr (✳ G) τω rell: cf 𝔐

25₇ χειρί] + (✳ G) αυτου O-72-82 C'' b 85′-321′ 59 646 Arm Co Syh = 𝔐

25₁₁ ζηλῶσαί] + (÷ mend pro ✳ G) αυτον V O^−58 Tht I 812 Bo = 𝔐

25₁₂ διαθήκην] pr (✳ G Syh^L) την G-426 Syh; + μου 58-426-707^txt 527-619 392 68′-120 59 Syh (ο' θ' διαθήκην μου α' την συνθήκην μου 344)
　　The hex must have had μου rather than την sub ast.

25₁₈ δολιότητι] + (✳ G Syh^L) αυτων O-15 Syh = 𝔐

26₉ οὗτοι] + (✳ Syh^T) δαθαν και αβιρων (c var) O^−58 Lat cod 100 Syh = 𝔐

26₉ ἐπισυστάσει] + (+ ✳ Syh^T) αυτων κατα (+ του 646) O-15 18′-126-628-630′ 646 Syh = 𝔐

26₁₀ καὶ διακοσίους] sub ✳ Syh^L; + ανδρας F V O-15 Lat cod 100 Bo Syh = 𝔐

26₂₉ τῷ 1°] pr (✳ Syh) των νιων βαρια (-ρεια 376) O^−58 Syh = 𝔐

26₃₉ Ἐφράιμ] + (✳ Syh^L) κατα δημους αυτων O-15 Arab Syh = 𝔐

26₃₉ τῷ 2°] pr (✳ Syh; c var) τω βαχαρ δημος ο βαχαρι M' 426 C'' 246 s 392 18-126-628 646 Arab Syh = 𝔐

26₄₃ fin] + (✳ Syh^T; c var) τω ουφαμ δημος ο ουφαμι O 767 Arab Syh = 𝔐

26₄₄ Νοεμάν 1°] + (✳ Syh; c var) τω αδερ δημος ο αδερι M' O'^−376 618txt 56′ 619 18′-126-628-630′ Bo^B Sa Syh = 𝔐

26₅₇ υἱοί] pr (c var) ουτοι επεσκεμμενοι O(426 om υιοι = 𝔐) 246 18′-126-628-630′ = 𝔐; pr ✳ επεσκεμμενων ✓ 85^mg; + επεσκεμμενων 130^mg-321′ mg; + ✳ visitati ✓ Syh

26₅₈ Χεβρωνί] + (✳ Syh; c var) και δημος ο μοολι O-15 246 767 18′-126-628-630′ Aeth^C Arab Syh = 𝔐

26₅₉ Μαριάμ] pr (✳ Syh) την 426 76 Syh = 𝔐

26₆₄ Ἀαρών] + (✳ Syh) του ιερεως O^−58 Syh = 𝔐

27₁ Μαχίρ] + (✳ Syh) υιον μανασση (> 58) O-15 767 Arab Syh = 𝔐

27₁₀ κληρονομίαν] + (✳ Syh) αυτου O^−58 417-616 b 44-106^(mg)-107 127-767 t z^−68′ 120(126) 799 Arm Bo Syh = 𝔐

27₁₁ οἰκείῳ] + (✳ Syh) αυτου O^−58-15 53′ Bo Syh = 𝔐

27₁₅ fin] + (✳ Syh) λεγων O^−58 Syh = 𝔐

27₂₁ αὐτὸς καί] pr ✳ omnes ✓ Syh; + παντες O^−58 b d n t = 𝔐

28₅ ἐλαίῳ] + (✳ Syh) κεκομμενω O^−58 Arab Arm Syh = 𝔐

28₆ εὐωδίας] + (✳ Syh) καρπωμα O Syh = 𝔐

28₈ εἰς] pr (✳ Syh) καρπωμα O Syh = 𝔐

28₉ σπονδήν] + (✳ 85-344) αυτου O 85′ mg-321′ mg-344mg Syh = 𝔐

28₁₂ σεμιδάλεως 1°] + (✳ Syh) εις θυσιαν O Syh = 𝔐

28₁₂ σεμιδάλεως 2°] + (✳ Syh) εις θυσιαν M' O Syh = 𝔐

28₁₃ θυσίαν] pr εις ολοκαυτωμα 58 Arab; (✳ Syh) εις (> 426 Syh) ολοκαυτωμα 376′ Syh = 𝔐

28₁₄ μηνός] + (✳ Syh) αυτου O^−58 Syh = 𝔐

28₁₇ ἡμέρᾳ — ἑορτή] sub ✳ 127(mend)

28₂₃ fin] + (✳ Syh) ποιησετε (c var) O 619 121^mg z^−120 646 Syh = 𝔐

28₂₆ κυρίῳ] pr (✳ Syh) τω O^−58 422 ƒ 407 55 Syh: cf 𝔐

28₂₆ ἑβδομάδων] + (✳ Syh) υμων O^−58-15 Arab Syh = 𝔐

29₆ κυρίῳ] pr (✳ Syh) καρπωμα O-15 Arab Syh = 𝔐

29₇ μηνός] + (✳ Syh) τον εβδομου V O^−58 Arab Bo Syh = 𝔐

29₁₃ κυρίῳ] pr (✳ G) τω O^−426 ƒ^−129 Cyr I 1120: cf 𝔐; pr ✳ Syh; sub ÷ G*

48

29₁₇ μόσχους] + (✶ G Syh) εκ βοων O-15 b Arab Syh = 𝔐
29₃₉ πλήν — ὑμῶν 2°] sub ✶ (mend) G Syh
30₅ αὐτῆς / ὁ πατήρ] tr 82 b d n t 126 Cyr I 1060 Or II 306; αὐτῆς sub ✶ G; + (✶ Syh) αυτης O⁻ᴳ 730 Armᵗᵉ Syh = 𝔐
30₆ αὐτῆς 1°] + (✶ G Syh) αυτη V O⁻⁵⁸ Syh = 𝔐
30₆ ὁρισμούς] + (✶ Syh) αυτης A O-82-381′ b 106⁽ᵐᵍ⁾ n 134 y⁻³¹⁸ Cyr I 1060 Latcod 100 Aug Num 57 Co Syh = 𝔐
30₆ fin] + (✶ G Syh) αυτη O⁻⁵⁸ Syh = 𝔐
30₉ ὁρισμοὶ αὐτῆς] + (✶ G) και διασκεδαση την ευχην αυτης την επ αυτης η την διαστολην των χειλεων αυτης G-376: cf 𝔐
30₁₀ ὅσα] pr (✶ G Syh) παντα O Syh = 𝔐
30₁₁ ἢ ὁ ὁρισμός] (✶ G) η ον ωρισατο ορισμον O = 𝔐
30₁₃ περιέλη] + (✶ G) αυτα G-426-oI Syh (ϑ′ διασκεδάση αὐτά 344)
30₁₃ περιεῖλεν] + (✶ G) αυτα (+ ⬋ Syh) O⁽⁻⁵⁸⁾ Latcod 100 Syh = 𝔐
30₁₄ ὅρκος δεσμοῦ] sub ✶ Syh(mend)
30₁₅ αὐτῇ 1°] + (✶ G) ο ανηρ αυτης O⁽⁻⁵⁸⁾-15 d t Bo Syh = 𝔐
30₁₅ τούς 1°] pr (✶ G) παντας O⁽⁻⁵⁸⁾-15 Bo Syh = 𝔐
30₁₇ θυγατρός] + (✶ G) αυτου O⁻⁵⁸-15-72 54-75 Arm Boᴬ Syh = 𝔐
30₁₇ νεότητι] + (✶ G) αυτης O-82 Co Syh = 𝔐
31₆ ἱερέως] + (✶ G) εις παραταξιν V O⁻⁵⁸-15 Syh = 𝔐
31₉ ἐπρονόμευσαν 1°] + (✶ G Syh) οι (> 58-376′) υιοι ισραηλ O 767 Arab Syh = 𝔐
31₉ τήν 2°] pr (✶ G Syh) πασαν O 767 Syh = 𝔐
31₁₀ τάς 3°] pr (✶ G) πασας O Syh = 𝔐
31₁₇ ἔγνωκεν] + (✶ Syh) ανδρα εις O⁻⁵⁸ f⁻¹²⁹ Syh = 𝔐
31₂₃ πυρί] + (✶ Syh; c var) διαξετε εν πυρι 15-376′ f⁻¹²⁹ LatRuf Num XXV 6 Arab Syh = 𝔐; + και (sup ras) πυρι διεξεται ⬋ G
31₂₄ ἱμάτια] + (✶ G) υμων O⁻⁵⁸ f⁻¹²⁹ Cyr I 329 Latcod 100 Ruf Num XXV 6 Arab Sa Syh = 𝔐
31₃₀ ἕνα] + (✶ G) το κρατουμενον O⁻⁵⁸ Syh = 𝔐
31₃₂ ἐγενήθη] + (✶ G) τα σκυλα O⁻⁵⁸ 56′ Syh (+ τὰ σκῦλα (c var) 130-321′)
31₃₂ ἑβδομήκοντα] + (✶ G) χιλιαδες (c var) A Fᶜ ᵖʳ ᵐ M′ G-29-426-707-oI C″ b⁻¹⁹ 246 s y⁻³⁹² z⁻¹²⁶ ⁴⁰⁷ ⁶⁶⁹* 55 624 Syh = 𝔐
31₃₆ τριακόσιαι] ‚γ̄ 77; + (✶ G) χιλιαδες (c var) A F M′ O″⁻⁷²⁸² C″⁻⁷⁷ 56′ s⁻³⁴³ ³⁴⁴ᶜ 509 y z⁻¹²⁶ ⁴⁰⁷ 55 59 624 799 Syh = 𝔐
31₃₈ τέλος] + (✶ G) αυτων O⁻⁵⁸-15 53′-56-246ᵐᵍ 767 Syh = 𝔐
31₃₈ κυρίῳ] pr (✶ G Syh) τω O-15 53′-56-246ᵐᵍ Syh: cf 𝔐
31₄₇ τό] + (✶ G) κρατουμενον O 56* Syh = 𝔐
31₅₀ ἡμῶν] pr (✶ G; + των 669ᶜ) ψυχων O⁻⁵⁸-15 128-630′ Arab Syh = 𝔐
32₂₆ καί 2°] pr (✶ G; c var) και (non hab 𝔐) αι κτησεις ημων V O-15 f⁻¹²⁹ 767 Arab Syh = 𝔐
32₃₂ κατάσχεσιν] + (✶ G Syh) της κληρονομιας O⁻⁵⁸ Syh = 𝔐
32₃₅ Σωφάρ] pr (✶ G) αταρωθ O⁻⁵⁸ Arab Syh = 𝔐
32₃₇ καί 2°] + (✶ G Syh) την O⁻⁴²⁶ 422 b f⁻¹²⁹ n 799 Syh = 𝔐
32₃₇ καί 3°] + (✶ G Syh) την O⁻⁴²⁶ 53ᶜ-56′-664 343 18 799 Syh = 𝔐
32₃₈ περικεκυκλωμένας] + (✶ G Syh) ονοματι O Syh = 𝔐
32₃₉ εἰς] sub ✶ G(mend)
33₂ σταθμοί] + (✶ G) αυτων και (> 82-707 = 𝔐) O⁻⁵⁸-15-82-707 Arab Syh = 𝔐
33₂₃ Σάφαρ] pr (✶ G) ορος O 767 Arab Syh (οἱ λ′ ὄρος Σάφαρ (c var) M′ 85′-321′)
33₂₄ Σάφαρ] pr (✶ G) ορους (ορος 426) O 68′-120 Syh (οἱ λ′ ὄρος Σάφαρ 344)
33₃₈ ἱερεύς] + (✶ G Syh) εις (επι 799) ωρ το ορος O⁻⁵⁸ 767 799 Latcod 104 Arab Syh = 𝔐
33₄₀ κατῴκει] + (✶ G Syh) εν (> 376) τω νοτω O⁻⁵⁸-15 LatHi Ep LXXVIII 36 Arab Syh = 𝔐
33₅₁ ὑμεῖς] pr (✶ G Syh) οτι O Syh = 𝔐
33₅₂ τὰς σκοπιάς] pr (✶ G Syh) πασας (παντας 376) O-15 Syh = 𝔐
33₅₆ ποιῆσαι] pr (✶ G) του G-376: לעשות 𝔐
34₂ ὑμεῖς] pr (✶ G Syh) οτι O⁻⁵⁸ Syh = 𝔐

34₂ αὕτη] + ※ η γη ⟋ η G; + (※ 85) η γη (+ ※ 344) ητις (> M′ 58-426 799 Syh) M′ O⁻ᴳ-82 d n⁻⁷⁵ 30′-85ᵐᵍ-130-321′-343′ t 392 799 ᴸᵃᵗcod 100 Arab Syh = 𝔐

34₁₁ ἐπὶ νώτου] pr (※ G Syh) και συγκρουσει (c var) G-15-58ᵐᵍ-376-707 b f⁻¹²⁹ 68′-120 Arab Syh = 𝔐

34₁₄ Ῥουβήν] + (※ G) κατ οικους (κληρους 85′-321′) πατριων αυτων (> 246) O⁻⁵⁸-82 b⁻³¹⁴ 246 54′ 85′ᵐᵍ-321′ᵐᵍ t⁻⁸⁴ 799 ᴸᵃᵗcodd 100 104(vid) Arab Syh = 𝔐

34₁₈ ἕνα] + (※ G) αρχοντα (αρχον G) ενα G-426 130ᵐᵍ-321′ᵐᵍ Syh = 𝔐

35₃ αὐτῶν 2°] + (※ G) και τη υπαρξει αυτων O Syh = 𝔐 | καί 3° — fin] sub ※ G(mend)

35₅ δισχιλίους 1°] pr (※ G) επι G-376 Syh: cf 𝔐

35₆ καὶ τὰς πόλεις (ἅς)] sub ※ Syh; καὶ τάς sub ※ G*; ἅς sub ※ G

35₆ ταύταις] + (※ G) δωσετε (-ται 376) O Aeth Arab Syh = 𝔐

35₈ πόλεων] pr ※ αν G*; + (※ G) αυτου O⁻⁵⁸ = 𝔐

35₁₀ ὑμεῖς] pr (※ G; ÷ Syh mend) οτι O⁻⁵⁸-15 b d n t Syh = 𝔐

35₁₁ πόλεις] + (※ G Syh) πολεις O⁻⁵⁸ Syh = 𝔐

35₁₅ init] pr (※ G) πολεις (-λις G) O⁻⁵⁸ Arab Syh = 𝔐

35₂₅ τοῦ ἀγχιστεύοντος] pr (※ G Syh) χειρος O⁻⁵⁸ 767 Syh = 𝔐

35₂₅ κατέφυγεν] + (※ G Syh) εκει O⁻⁵⁸ Syh = 𝔐

35₂₆ πόλεως] + (※ G Syh) του φυγαδευτηριου αυτου O⁻⁵⁸-15 Aethᴹ Arab Syh = 𝔐

35₃₀ ψυχὴν διά] sub ※ Gᶜ; > G*; + (※ G Syh) στοματος O⁻⁵⁸-15 130ᵐᵍ-321′ᵐᵍ Arab Syh = 𝔐

35₃₂ οὐ] pr (※ G Syh) και O⁻⁴²⁶ 739 b 75′ Aeth Arm Bo Syh = 𝔐; sub ※ G*

36₃ τῶν φυλῶν] pr (※ G) των νιων G-426 = 𝔐

36₃ υἱῶν] pr (※ Syh) των 29-82-376 551 44-125′-610ᶜ 54′ t⁻⁷⁶* 55 319 799 Syh: contra 𝔐

36₆ δήμου] + (※ G Syh) της φυλης O 246 126-128-669 Syh = 𝔐

36₈ δήμου (τοῦ πατρὸς αὐτῆς)] + (※ G Syh) της φυλης O⁻⁵⁸ Syh = 𝔐; τοῦ πατρὸς αὐτῆς sub ※ mend G Syh

36₉ οἱ υἱοὶ (Ἰσραήλ)] (※ 344 Syh; + και 44 La) αι φυλαι (αι φ. sub ※ Gᶜ et sub ÷ G*; + των C′′ 44 30′-85-344 392 646) νιων (bis scr 82) O-82 C′′ d n 30′-85ᵐᵍ-344ᵐᵍ t 392 646 799 ᴸᵃᵗcod 104 Syh: cf 𝔐; Ἰσραήλ sub ※ 344ᵐᵍ Syh

36₁₁ αὐτῶν] + (※ Syh) εις γυναικας V O Arm Syh (ο′ α′ αὐτῶν εἰς γυναῖκας 85(s nom)-344)

36₁₃ Μωυσῆ] + (※ G Syh) προς τους υιους ισραηλ O 767 Syh = 𝔐

All of the above citations except one are attested in G or Syh or in both with a hex sign. Occasionally the sign is at the wrong place, or the sign is the wrong one, that is an obelus instead of the asterisk, but the original intent of Origen's work can be reconstructed from the tradition. Of the 305 citations listed above 22 are clearly wrong; these are 2₃₄ 4₇(1°) 2₃(1°) 2₆(2°) 33 5₁₀ 22 14₄₁ 15₁₁ ₁₈ 16₄₈ 18₈ 22₅ 24₃ ₄ ₈ 28₁₇ 29₃₉ 30₁₄ 32₃₉ 35₆ 36₃.

In the remaining 283 Syh attests the hex sign 216 times, whereas G has the sign 183 times. Other witnesses are insignificant; 344 has it six times; 85, four times, and S, 127 321′ and 730 each has one.

In the course of transmission many of the signs were omitted by copyists. The following list details additions in the text tradition which correspond to 𝔐 but without the sign tradition. Citations which seem to be hex in origin are marked with a star. As in *List 1* the possible source as given in the second apparatus is given in parentheses at the end. Since all instances compared equal 𝔐, that fact is not noted.

In order not to weigh down the list with insignificant material, instances in which Aeth Arm or Arab add the conjunction uniquely, i.e. without support in the Greek tradition are not given. These are given in the apparatus, but it is most unlikely that such instances are based on a Greek parent text.

50

1₂* ἀρχήν] pr την 58-426 319 Bo

1₄* ἕκαστος Fᵃ] + εκαστος A F G-29-426 56 y⁻³¹⁸ z⁻¹⁸ 59 624 Syh (o′ + ἕκαστος 344)

1₁₉* ἐπεσκέπησαν] + αυτοι O-72 b 129 68′-120′ 59 Aeth Syh (o′ + αὐτοί 344)

1₄₅* δυνάμει] pr τη O z 646 (o′ pr τῇ 344)

2₄* ἐπεσκεμμένοι] + αυτων O⁻⁵⁸ Syh

2₅* ἐχόμενοι] + αυτον O⁻³⁷⁶-15 767 318 Sa (o′ + αὐτοῦ 344)

2₆* ἐπεσκεμμένοι] + αυτου O Syh

2₈* ἐπεσκεμμένοι] + αυτου O Syh

2₁₁ δύναμις] pr και η 799 ᴸᵃᵗcod 100 Arm

2₁₁* ἐπεσκεμμένοι] + αυτου O Syh

2₁₃* ἐπεσκεμμένοι] + αυτων G-426 = 𝔐; + αυτου 58-376 Syh = Sam

2₁₅ init] pr και η b 319 ᴸᵃᵗcod 100 Arm

2₁₅* ἐπεσκεμμένοι] + αυτων O Syh

2₁₆* ἑκατόν] + και μια V O⁻⁵⁸ 344ᵐᵍ Arab Syh

2₁₆* δεύτεροι] pr και O⁻⁵⁸ f⁻²⁴⁶ Aeth Syh

2₁₇ μέσον] pr εις d n t 799

2₁₇* ἐχόμενος] + αυτον O Syh (o′ (> 130) + αὐτοῦ 85′-344)

2₁₇* fin B V 707 d f⁻²⁴⁶ n t x 392 59 799 Arm Sa⁴¹²] + αυτον 376 C⁻¹⁶-46-417 Bo; + αυτ 16;+ αυτων rell (α′ σ′ + αὐτῶν (αυτου 130) 85′-344; θ′ + αὐτῶν 85′-344; o′ + αὐτοῦ (-των 344) 85′-344)

2₁₉* ἐπεσκεμμένοι] + αυτων O = 𝔐; + eius Syh = Sam

2₂₀* ἐχόμενοι] + αυτων G-58 Arm Bo; + αυτου 376′ f Syh = 𝔐

2₂₁ init] pr και η 799 ᴸᵃᵗcod 100 Arm

2₂₁* ἐπεσκεμμένοι] + αυτων O⁻⁵⁸ Syh

2₂₃* ἐπεσκεμμένοι] + αυτων O⁻⁵⁸ Syh

2₂₄* τρίτοι] pr και O⁻³⁷⁶ 68′-120′ Aeth Syh

2₂₆* ἐπεσκεμμένοι] + αυτων O⁻⁵⁸ Syh

2₂₈* ἐπεσκεμμένοι] + αυτων O⁻⁵⁸ Syh

2₃₀* ἐπεσκεμμένοι] + αυτων O Syh

2₃₁* ἑκατόν] + χιλιαδες (χειλ. G) O⁻⁵⁸ Syh

2₃₄* πάντα] pr κατα F 𝔐ᵐᵍ O′⁻²⁹⁽⁴²⁶ᵗˣᵗ⁾ f⁽⁻⁵⁶ᵗˣᵗ⁾ 85′ᵐᵍ-321′ᵐᵍ 318 z⁻¹²⁶ 59 416 799 Bo Syh (o′ οἱ λ′ pr κατά 344)

3₂ πρωτότοκος] pr ο 53′

3₇* τῶν υἱῶν] pr παντων G-426 18′-126-628-669 646 Syh (o′ pr πάντων 344)

3₂₁* δῆμοι] pr εισι(ν) O⁻⁵⁸ Arm Syh

3₂₅* κάλυμμα] + αυτης O 68′-120′ ᴸᵃᵗcod 100 Syh

3₃₄* ἑξακισχίλιοι] + και διακοσιοι O⁻⁵⁸ 767 (o′ οἱ λ′ + καὶ σ̄ 344) Note also that for καὶ πεντήκοντα which follows immediately and has no counterpart in 𝔐 (sub ÷ in G Syh), 58 b d n⁻⁷⁶⁷ t ᴸᵃᵗcod 100 Arab Arm read διακοσιοι.

3₃₆* τά 2°] pr παντα F⁽ᵃ⁾ O 619 z 646 Syh

3₃₇* πασσάλους B V 44-125 x⁻⁶¹⁹ 799 ᴸᵃᵗcodd 100 104] παλους αυτης 120*; + αυτης z⁻¹²⁰* 646; + αυτων rell = 𝔐

3₄₂* κύριος B V 381′ d⁽⁻¹²⁵⁾ 54′-75 71-509 t 392 ᴸᵃᵗcod 100 Aeth Arm] + τω μωυση 30 ᴸᵃᵗcod 104; + τω μωση 458; + αυτοις b; + αυτω rell = 𝔐

3₄₇* λήμψη 2°] pr και V O⁻⁵⁸ 610 Sa Syh: contra 𝔐 (o′ καὶ λήψη 85′-321-344-346(nom absc)

3₄₉* τῶν πλεοναζόντων] pr παρα G-426 d⁻¹⁰⁶ f 54′ 343′ t 646 799 Syh

3₅₁* Μωυσῆς] + το αργυριον F O′ C″ b f 127-458-767 30′-85′ᵐᵍ-321′ᵐᵍ-343-344ᶜ ᵖʳ ᵐ 619 y⁻¹²¹ z 59 319 646 799 ᴸᵃᵗcodd 100 104(vid) Aeth Arab Bo Syh

4₁* Ἀαρών] pr προς 426 Arm

4₆* ἀναφορεῖς] + αυτης O f Arab Syh

4₈* ἀναφορεῖς] + αυτης A F M′ O″⁻⁵⁸⁷² C″⁻⁵²′ b s 619 y⁻³¹⁸ z⁽⁻⁶⁶⁹ᵗˣᵗ⁾ 55 319 646 799 Syh

4₉* ἐλαίου B V 44′ n t x⁻⁶¹⁹ Cyr I 852 ᴸᵃᵗcod 100 Aeth Arm Co] + αυτης rell

4₉* ἐν αὐτοῖς] pr αυτη O Syh (o′ οἱ λ′ pr αὐτῇ 344)

4₁₁ καλύμματι] pr εν 321′ᵐᵍ

4₁₄* σκεύη 1° B 72 d n t x⁻⁶¹⁹ Cyr I 852 ᴸᵃᵗcod 100 Arm Bo] + αυτου rell

4₁₄* λειτουργοῦσιν] + επ αυτο B V O⁻⁵⁸ x⁻⁶¹⁹ Cyr I 852 Arm Syh = Ra

4₁₆ ἐπίσκοπος] pr και 29* Aeth Armᵗᵉ

4₁₉ τοῦτο] pr και 739 ʃ Aeth

4₁₉* ἕκαστον] pr ενα O Arab Syh

4₂₃* ἕως] pr και 58-426 b⁻⁵³⁷ 319 ᴸᵃᵗcod 100 = 𝔐ᵐˢˢ

4₂₆* τὰ περισσά B 82 d n⁻⁷⁶⁷ t x⁻⁶¹⁹ 319 ᴸᵃᵗcod 100 Aeth Arm Bo Sa¹²] abundantiam eius omnem Sa⁴; + τουτων b; + αυτων rell = 𝔐

4₂₆* τὰ λειτουργικά B M′ V 82 16-46 b d n t x⁻⁶¹⁹ 319 Arm Co] της λειτουργιας (+ αυτων 392) 392 ᴸᵃᵗcod 100; + αυτων rell = 𝔐

4₂₆* ὅσα 2°] pr παντα (παντ V) V O⁻⁵⁸-29 619 Aeth Syh

4₂₈* τῶν υἱῶν] pr του (> 376) δημου (-μους 767) O-29 767 619 Syh

4₃₄ κατ'] pr και 125 Aeth

4₃₅* ἕως] pr και 58-426 n⁻⁷⁵

4₃₆* πεντήκοντα] pr και F 426 16-46-529 509 318 18-68′(2°)-120(2°)-628

4₄₀ τριάκοντα] pr και V 28-85-130ᵐᵍ-321′ᵐᵍ Syh

4₄₃* πεντηκονταετοῦς] pr filii Syh

4₄₇* πεντηκονταετοῦς] pr filii Syh

4₄₈* ἐπισκεπέντες] + αυτων O Syh

4₄₈ ὀγδοήκοντα] pr και 44 54′-767 t⁻⁸⁴ Syh

5₈* τῶν ἁμαρτιῶν A B G x⁻⁶¹⁹ Anast 376 Arab Sa] pr παντων 29; πασων αμ. 126; πασων 55; pr πασων rell = 𝔐

5₇ ἐξαγορεύσει] pr και 64ᶜ-381′ 628 319

5₁₄ αὐτῷ 1° 963] pr επ 72-82-376 761 b 509 68*-122 55 799 Chr II 917 (cf επ αυτον V 319)

5₁₄ αὐτῷ 2° 963] pr επ 761 b⁻¹⁹ 56′-129 509 59 ᴸᵃᵗcodd 91 92 94—96 Syh (cf επ αυτον V 106ᶜ t 319; επ αυτη 19; επ αυτην 106*)

5₁₇* τῆς γῆς] pr απο K V O C′' 767 30′-130ᵐᵍ-321′ᵐᵍ z Chr II 917 Syh

5₂₀* μεμίανσαι] pr συ (σοι G) O b d n⁻⁷⁶⁷ t Tht Nm 197 ᴸᵃᵗcod 100 Syh (o′ pr σύ 344)

6₄* ἕως] pr και O⁻⁴²⁶ 246 18′-628-669 ᴸᵃᵗcod 100 Syh

6₉ ἀποθάνῃ] + θανατω 319

7₁₁* ἄρχων 2°] + εις 426 313⁽*⁾-417 30 Eus VI 353 Syh

7₈₇ αἱ θυσίαι 963] pr και B* 707 d ʃ⁻¹²⁹ n t 319 Arm Sa

8₁₄* ἐμοί] + οι λευιται O 246 18′-126-628-669 Syh

8₁₅ αὐτούς 2°] + αποδομα Fᵃ V 44′ 129 130ᵐᵍ-321′ᵐᵍ t y⁻³¹⁸ 319 Arm

8₁₇ ᾖ] pr εν 376

8₂₀* καθά] κατα παντα α O⁻⁵⁸ Syh (o′ θ′ α′ κατὰ πάντα ⟨ἅ⟩ 344)

8₂₁* ἱμάτια B d 127 t x⁻⁶¹⁹ Arm] + αυτων rell

8₂₄* ἐνεργεῖν B 54 x⁻⁶¹⁹ Phil I 273 ᴸᵃᵗcod 100 Aeth Arm] λειτουργειν V d 75′-127 t 392 319 Arab Sa; in liturgiam Bo; (c var) λειτουργειν λειτουργιαν εν εργοις rell = 𝔐

9₃* καιρούς] καιρον αυτου A M′ O′-707 b ʃ⁻¹²⁹ 619 y 55 Syh

9₅* καθά] κατα παντα α (ως 58) O Syh

9₁₃ ἐξολεθρευθήσεται] pr και n⁻⁷⁶⁷ 527 ᴸᵃᵗcod 100

9₂₁* ἀπαροῦσιν 2°] pr και cI⁻⁵⁷⁽⁵²⁸⁾-551 = 𝔐; και απερ. 246; και εξηραν O⁻⁵⁸

9₂₂* ἡμέρας 1°] pr η O⁻³⁷⁶ (σ′ aut diebus Syh)

9₂₂* ἡμέρας 2°] pr η V 58-72 (σ′ aut tempore Syh)

10₈ ταῖς] pr εν V oI⁻¹⁵ b d n t 527-619 Bo

10₉ ταῖς σάλπιγξιν] pr εν M′ d t 71 799 Cyr X passim

10₁₀ ταῖς σάλπιγξιν] pr εν b 319

10₁₀* ὁλοκαυτώμασιν] + υμων O Chr II 881 ᴸᵃᵗOr Matth 52 Aeth Bo Sa¹¹ Syh

10₂₁* παραγένωνται] + αυτοι O Syh: cf 𝔐

10₂₂* Ἐφράιμ] pr υιων O 52′ 246 18′-126-628-669 646 ᴸᵃᵗcod 100 Syh

10₃₁* μή] + δη 426

10₃₄ διασκορπισθήτωσαν] pr και oI⁻¹⁵-72 C′' 19′ s⁻³²¹ x⁻⁵⁰⁹ ᴸᵃᵗSpec 33 Aeth Arm Bo Sa¹¹

10₃₄ φυγέτωσαν] pr και 72 52′ 767 30 126 ᴸᵃᵗSpec 33 Aeth

11₂₈ εἶπεν] pr και 18 Tht Nm 207ᵃᵖ Syhᵀ

11₂₈* κύριε B V 417ᵗˣᵗ d n t⁻⁸⁴ x 126 319 Tht Nm 206ᵗᵉ 207 ᴸᵃᵗcodd 100 104 Arm Co]
   + μου rell
12₂ ἡμῖν] pr εν A
12₁₁* κύριε] + μου O⁻ᴳ f⁻¹²⁹ Arab Syh
12₁₁* μή] + δη 426
12₁₂* μή] + και O f⁻¹²⁹ Syh (ο' + καί 344)
12₁₃ ἴασαι] + δη 767
13₂₁* πίων] + εστι(ν) 426 d 246 n t 319 Arm(vid) Bo Pal
13₂₇* Ἀαρών] pr προς 426 Arm
13₃₃* πᾶς B V 426 x BoᴬᴮᶜᵒSa] και G C'' 799; > Boᴮ*; pr και rell = 𝔐
14₃* παιδία B M' 129 x Cyr I 373] τεκνα ημων b; + ημων (υμων 44-107' 321) rell = 𝔐
14₄* ἑτέρῳ] + αυτου O Syh (ο' + αὐτοῦ 344)
14₈ εἰσάξει] pr και 126 Arm
14₁₂ θανάτῳ] pr εν V
14₁₆* κατέστρωσεν] pr και G-426 Armᵃᵖ Syh
14₃₁ εἰσάξω] pr και 630
15₃₀* ἐξολεθρευθήσεται (c var) B V 58 x 55 59 Aeth Armᵗᵉ Bo] pr και rell
15₃₃* Ἀαρών] pr προς 426 Armᵃᵖ
15₃₅ λίθοις] pr εν 16-46 y⁻¹²¹
15₃₅* συναγωγή] + εξω της παρεμβολης G-376 74'-84 128-630' ᴸᵃᵗPsAmbr Mans 27
   Arab Syh
16₃* Ἀαρών] pr επι 426 Aeth
16₃* εἶπαν (c var) B V 72 d n t x ᴸᵃᵗcod 100 Arm Boᴬ] λεγουσιν 319; + προς(> 376*)
   αυτους (αυτον 15-64*vid) rell
16₄* πρόσωπον] + αυτου O 246 18'-126-628-630' Arab Arm Co Syh (ο' οἱ λ' + αὐτοῦ 344)
16₃₁ ἡ γῆ] + η V t
16₃₂ τά] pr παντα b
16₃₃ ὅσα B G-426 b 129 n⁻⁷⁶⁷ 509 319 ᴸᵃᵗcod 100 Arm Co] pr παντα rell
16₃₆* Μωυσῆν] + λεγων 376 106ᶜ Arab Syh
16₄₀* Μωυσῆ] + αυτω B O⁻⁵⁸ 129 71' Syh (ο'θ'α' + αὐτῷ 344)
17₁₀* σημεῖον B V 82 129 54-75' x Cyr I 673] pr και εις 246; pr et Bo; signi ᴸᵃᵗcod 100;
   > 319; pr εις rell = 𝔐
18₅* οὐκ ἔσται B 82 129 730 x Bo] ουκετι εσται 381' b d n t 392 799 ᴸᵃᵗcod 100 MissMoz 85
   Arm; + ετι (c var) rell = 𝔐
18₆* ἐγώ] + ιδου V O 56 18'-628-630' 646 Sa Syh (α' ο' θ' + ἰδού 344)
18₈* ἀπαρχῶν B V 82 129 x⁻⁶¹⁹ Cyr I 837 ᴸᵃᵗcod 100 Sa] -χιων μου 44; εντολων μου
   Procop 844; + μου rell = 𝔐
18₉ τῶν καρπωμάτων] pr απο 128-669
18₁₀* ἔσται σοι] + και τοις υιοις σου O⁻⁵⁸ Syh (ο' οἱ λ' + καὶ τοῖς υἱοῖς σου 344)
18₂₈* ἀφαίρεμα] pr το O⁻⁵⁸
19₁₀* τὰ ἱμάτια] + αυτου O⁻⁵⁸-82 b d t 509 Syh
19₁₂ τῇ ἡμέρᾳ 1°] pr εν 376
19₁₃ ἐκτριβήσεται] pr και V 72 b 767 319 ᴸᵃᵗcod 100
19₁₉ τῇ 5°] pr εν A 82 414-550' 54'-75 318 55
20₁₂* Ἀαρών] pr προς 426 Arm
20₁₉* τὰ κτήνη B V 82 d n⁻⁷⁶⁷ t x⁻⁶¹⁹ Phil II 87ᵗᵉ Sa¹²] pecora nostra ᴸᵃᵗcod 100 Aeth; + μου
   rell = 𝔐
21₂* ὑποχείριον] υπο χειρα μοι O⁻³⁷⁶ Syh: cf 𝔐
21₇ ἔλεγον] pr και 392
21₈ ἰδών] pr και V 15-376 b n 527 319
21₉ ὄφις] pr ὁ Fᶜᵖʳᵐ M' 72-376-618 b 53' 127-767 71 y⁻¹²¹ 18'-120'-628-630' 59 319 Cyr
   II 637
21₁₂ ἐκεῖθεν] pr και Fᵇ 619 68'-120' (ο' οἱ λ' pr καί 344)
21₂₆* Ἀμορραίων] + εστιν B O⁻⁵⁸ 129 509 Syh
21₃₃* καί 3°] pr αυτος V O⁻⁵⁸ d n t 527 Sa¹² Syh
22₁ παρενέβαλον] pr και 314
22₁₃ οὐκ] pr quia Aeth Arm

22₁₇* ὅσα (aut α) B* V b⁻³¹⁴ d 53'-129 n t 527 319 ᴸᵃᵗcod 100 Arm Sa] ος 314; o Bᶜ 130ᵐᵍ-
321'ᵐᵍ-344ᵐᵍ 71-509; παντα F 29 C⁻¹⁶-417* 392*; pr παντα Fᵃ rell = 𝔐

22₁₇* εἴπῃς A B oI⁻¹⁵-82 b d 129 n⁻⁷⁶⁷ t x⁻⁶¹⁹ y⁻³⁹² 55 319 ᴸᵃᵗcod 100 Arm] pr μοι M';
+ μοι rell = 𝔐

22₁₈* τοῦ θεοῦ] + μου O 414 343 Arab Syh (o' oἱ λ' + μου 344)

22₂₆* ἦν] + οδος O⁻⁵⁸ Syhᵀ

22₃₁ μάχαιραν] + eius Sa

22₃₃* ἐξέκλινεν 2° B d 129 n t x⁻⁶¹⁹ 319 AethᶠCo] + απ εμου rell

22₃₇* ὄντως] pr η O⁻⁵⁸-15ᶜ 68'-120' Syh

23₃* εἶ] + πως O 619 z Syh (σ' εἰ πῶς 344)

23₅ οὕτως] pr και 669 55 ᴸᵃᵗcod 100 Aeth Arm Pal

23₁₉* ἐμμενεῖ] + αυτω O

23₂₀ εὐλογήσω] pr και 669

23₂₁ τά] pr et Aeth = 𝔐; και 58-72 59; + δε A 121

24₁ οὐκ] pr και F ᴸᵃᵗcod 100

25₇ ἐξανέστη] pr και 130ᵐᵍ-321'ᵐᵍ-344ᵐᵍ 319

26₁* Ἐλεαζάρ] + υιον ααρων O Arab Syh (o' oἱ λ' + υν Ἀαρών 344)

26₄ ἐξ] εκ γης V Arab

26₁₀ κατέπιεν] pr και 246

26₃₁* Ἀσήρ] pr υιων O Syh (o' σ' pr υἱῶν 344)

26₄₀ init] pr και d⁽⁻⁴⁴⁾ t

26₄₁* Ἐφράιμ] pr υιων O Arab Syh (o' pr υἱῶν 344)

26₄₆ υἱοί] pr ουτοι (+ οι 54) 106-125 n 321'-344ᵐᵍ 319 ᴸᵃᵗcod 100

26₅₀* Νεφθαλί] + κατα δημους αυτων O Syh

26₅₄* κληρονομίαν 1°] + αυτου 426 = 𝔐; + αυτων 376 126 Cyr I 349 Co Syh = Tar°

26₅₉* Μωυσῆν] pr τον 426 77 d 127-767 t 619 z 319 Syh

27₉ κληρονομίαν] + αυτου V 963 O⁻⁵⁸-82 C'' b d 129 n s⁻³⁰ t 392 z 319 624 646 Arm Co
Syh

27₁₁* κληρονομίαν] + αυτου O b d⁻⁶¹⁰ 129 54'-767 t 318 126 Bo Syh

27₁₁ δικαίωμα] pr εις d t

27₁₇* ἔστιν] + αυτοις 426 Phil II 104ᵁᶠ

27₁₉* ἐντελῇ 2°] + αυτω O

28₂* εὐωδίας] + μου O⁻⁵⁸ Syh

28₁₀* σαββάτοις] σαββασιν αυτου O Syh

28₁₁* νουμηνίαις] + υμων O Arab Syh

28₁₁* ἐνιαυσίους] pr υιους 376

28₁₂* init] pr και O Arm Syh

28₁₃ init] pr και b d n t 646 ᴸᵃᵗcod 100 Aethᶜ Arab Arm Sa (σ' pr καί 344)

28₁₃* σεμιδάλεως] + εις (> La Aeth Bo = 𝔐) θυσιαν O b ᴸᵃᵗcod 100 Aethᶜ Arab Bo
Syh (o' θ' α' + εἰς θυσίαν 344)

28₁₉* κριόν] pr και O 46ˢ 44 319 624 Aeth Arab Arm Co Syh (o' oἱ λ' pr καί 344)

28₁₉ ἑπτά] pr και b Aeth Boᴬ Sa

29₄ init] pr και d 246 n t Aeth Arm

29₈* ὁλοκαυτώματα] + τω (> 426) κω̄ O Syh (o' oἱ λ' ὁλοκαύτωμα τῷ κω̄ 344)

29₁₁ ἡ θυσία] pr και d n t Aeth Arab Sa

29₁₅ init B M' V 963 O'⁻⁵⁸-82 f⁻²⁴⁶ x 407 319 Cyr I 1120 Aeth Syh] pr και rell

29₁₇* init 963 b 509] pr και rell = Ra

29₁₉ αἱ 1°] pr και 458 Aeth Arm Sa

29₂₀ init] pr και A 129 54 509 392 18 646 Aeth Arab Arm Boᴮ

29₂₉ init] pr και V b 458 Aeth Arm Co

29₃₂ init] pr και b Aeth Arab Arm Co

29₃₃ init] pr και 963 426 Aeth Arab Arm Sa

30₂* Ἰσραήλ B V 963 (vid) 15-oII⁻²⁹ 610 53' x y⁻³⁹² 126-407 ᴸᵃᵗcodd 100 104] > 392;
pr των υιων G C'' 44'-107 n s t 424 646 Cyr I 1060; pr υιων rell = 𝔐

30₉* ὁ ἀνὴρ αὐτῆς] + ανανευση αυτη O⁻⁵⁸ Arab

30₁₅ ὁρισμούς] + αυτης (-τους 107*) A 426 d 127-458 730 t Armᵃᵖ Sa

30₁₇* πατρός 2°] + αυτης 426 b 44-107' n⁻⁷⁵ t Arm Co Syh

31₉   τά 1°] pr παντα 30′

31₁₈* πᾶσαν B 82 129 x⁻⁵²⁷ 407 319] και πασαν δε f⁻¹²⁹; + δε O⁻³⁷⁶ Syh; pr και rell = 𝔐

31₁₉* ἀνελῶν] + ψυχην M′ V O′ d f⁻¹²⁹ n t 799 ᴸᵃᵗcodd 100 104 Arab Bo Syh; αποκτεινας ψυχην (-χης 19*) b

31₁₉* ὁ 2°] pr πας O f⁻¹²⁹ Syh

31₁₉* τῇ ἡμέρᾳ] pr εν O⁻³⁷⁶ 53′-56

31₁₉   τῇ 3°] pr εν 58 53-56′-664ᶜ

31₂₂   κασσιτέρου] pr του 58-72 f⁻¹²⁹ 59

31₂₇* συναγωγῆς] pr της (τη 75) A O⁻⁴²⁶-381′ 414 106⁽ᵐᵍ⁾ 129 n t⁽⁻³⁷⁰⁾ 527 Cyr I 333

31₃₉* τέλος] + αυτων 15-376 b 767

32₂   εἶπαν] και ειπον 458

32₉   φάραγγα] pr εως οI

32₁₄   init] pr και 707 d n t 126 55 799 Cyr I 404 Aeth Syh

32₂₆* ἔσονται] + εκει O f⁻¹²⁹ Syh (o′ οἱ λ′ + ἐκεῖ 344)

32₂₇* κύριος] + μου O⁻⁵⁸ 128-630′

32₂₈* Ἰσραήλ] pr (+ των 707 106 127 t 527) υιων 376′-618-707 106 n⁻⁷⁶⁷ t 527 799 Arab Bo Syh (o′ οἱ λ′ pr υἱῶν 344)

32₃₈* καί 1° B 82-707* b 129 n x 319 799 ᴸᵃᵗcodd 100 104 Aeth Arm Co] pr ναβαυ 106; + την ναβω 707ᶜ; pr (c var) και την ναβω rell = 𝔐

33₃*   init] pr και A O′ y⁻³¹⁸ 18′-126-628-630′ 55 799 Aeth Sa Syh (o′ οἱ λ′ pr καί 344)

33₅   παρενέβαλον] pr και 19

33₁₄* ἦν B M′ V oI d 129-246 n 30 t x 318 126-128-407-628-630′ 319 799 Arm Bo] pr ibi Aug Loc in hept IV 120; + εκει rell = 𝔐

33₃₃   Γαδγάδ] pr του 707 C′⁻⁵⁷′⁵²⁹-46′ s⁻³²¹

33₃₈   μιᾷ] pr εν 82

33₅₅* ἐπί 2° B 963 129 x 407 319 Sa] pr adversos vos ᴸᵃᵗcod 100; pr υμιν (υμων 707* 458 18) rell = 𝔐

34₅*   διέξοδος] + αυτου O d 129-246 n t 628 Arm Sa¹ Syh

34₁₂* διέξοδος] + αυτου O Arm Syh (o′ οἱ λ′ + αὐτοῦ 344)

34₂₀* Συμεών] pr υιων O⁻⁵⁸ Syh (o′ οἱ λ′ pr υἱῶν 344)

34₂₂* Δάν] pr υιων 426 d⁻¹²⁵ 246 n t Syh (o′ οἱ λ′ pr υἱῶν 344)

34₂₅* Ζαβουλών] pr υιων O Aeth Syh

34₂₈* Νεφθαλί] pr υιων O C″ 106 s 392 319 Aeth Sa Syh

35₁₂   φυγαδευτήρια] pr εις x⁻⁵⁰⁹

35₁₅* πόλεις] pr εξ V O 767 126-128-630′ Syh

35₂₁* χειρί] + αυτου O⁻⁵⁸ 767 Arm Co Syh

35₂₁* συναντῆσαι] + αυτον O⁻⁵⁸

35₂₃* παντί] pr εν O⁻⁵⁸ b 407-630 Cyr VII 625 (o′ οἱ λ′ pr ἐν 344)

35₂₅   τῷ 1°] pr εν 29

35₂₈* καταφυγῆς B V 82 106 129 n⁻⁷⁵ t x 407-630 319 Sa] -φυλης αυτου 618; φυγης αυτου M′; + αυτου rell = 𝔐

35₃₂* φυγαδευτηρίων] + αυτου O Syh

35₃₃* fin] + αυτο O ᴸᵃᵗcod 100 Syh (+ αὐτό 130)

35₃₄* κατοικεῖτε] pr υμεις O 121 ᴸᵃᵗcod 100 Syh

36₁*   ἄρχοντες B V 72 129 x 407-630 319 Aeth Arm Sa] + των πατριων O = 𝔐; + πατριων rell

36₂*   κυρίῳ 2°] + μου O⁽⁻³⁷⁶⁾ 246 126-128-669 Syh

List 2 contains a further group of 237 correspondences in the tradition to the text of 𝔐. Of these 161 have been starred, that is to say have been judged to have their origin in Origen's work. Each of these is supported by at least one or more of the main hex witnesses in the tradition; in fact, most of them are supported in the commonly recurring pattern found in List 1, i.e. by O Syh or by O⁻⁵⁸ Syh. These must be taken along with those of List 1 as being primary evidence for the hex recension.

An analysis of the remaining 76 instances which are probably not hex in origin reveals that 34 find only random support and may be dismissed as coincidence. Of the remainder, 14 variants belong to the Byzantine text tradition; cf the discussion of its character on pp. 18–34. Nine are supported by the *b* group; four are found on the margins of *s* mss, for which cf THGG 67f, and four are *f* readings. Five are supported by four or more groups but not by *O* (7₈₇ 10₈ ₃₄ 28₁₃ 29₁₅). One variant (27₉) is supported by at least four groups including *O*; it can hardly be hex in origin since the reading is also found in 963. The support for the remaining variants in *List 2* are scattered singly among the other text groups (*oI C″ s x y* and *z*). It would appear that the only identifiable recensional activity occasioned by "correction" towards the Hebrew in the Numbers text tradition is the hexaplaric.

Further evidence for hexaplaric activity is to be found in changes in word order to correspond to that of Origen's Hebrew text, as was argued in THGG 59f. This evidence is given in *List 3*. Since these correspond in each case to 𝔐, this fact is not noted.

List 3

1₂ κατὰ κεφαλὴν αὐτῶν] post (₃) ἄρσην tr G-376 129 Arab
1₂₄ init — (₃₅) fin] post (₃₇) fin tr *O*⁻⁵⁸ Arab Syh
15₂ ἑαυτοῦ ἡγεμονίαν] ηγ. αυτου (εαυτου G°-426) *O*⁻⁵⁸
2₂ αὐτοῦ / κατὰ τάγμα B V *d n t x* 319] κ. τα ταγματα αυτων 53′; > 416; tr rell = 𝔐
2₁₈ παρὰ θάλασσαν] post αὐτῶν tr *O*⁻⁵⁸ Syh
3₄₀ αὐτῶν] ad fin tr *O*⁻⁵⁸ Bo Syh
5₁₅ ἔστιν — ζηλοτυπίας] θυσια (θυμιαμα 376) γαρ (> 72) ζηλ. εστι(ν) *O*⁻⁵⁸-72 Aeth Arm Bo Syh
5₂₀ τὴν κοίτην αὐτοῦ] post σοί tr *O*⁻⁵⁸ Syh
5₂₃ ὁ ἱερεύς] post ταύτας tr 376′ Syh
5₂₇ τοῦ ἐλεγμοῦ / τὸ ἐπικαταρώμενον] tr *O*⁻⁵⁸ Syh
6₉ ἐξάπινα / ἐπ' αὐτῷ B M′ 963 G-376-707 *d f n t x*⁻⁶¹⁹ 392 799 Bo] εαυτω (επ αυτω^te) αιφνιδιως Phil II 131; επ αυτω αιφνιδιον Clem I 92; om ἐπ' αὐτῷ Cyr I 1048; tr rell = 𝔐
6₁₁ ἐκείνη 963] ad fin tr *O*⁻⁵⁸ Arm
6₁₄ ἐνιαυσίαν ἄμωμον / μίαν] tr *O*⁻⁵⁸ 126 Arm
6₁₉ ἕνα ἄζυμον 963] tr A V 376′-707-*oI C″*⁻⁴⁶⁸ *b s y*⁻³¹⁸ 55 319 624 799 ᴸᵃᵗcod 100 Aeth
6₂₄ comma] post (₂₇) fin tr S°(vid) *O* 669 Thess Aeth° Co
7₅ αὐτοῦ λειτουργίαν] tr *O*⁻⁵⁸ ᴸᵃᵗcod 100
7₈₇ μόσχοι] post δώδεκα 1° tr *O*⁻⁵⁸ 319 ᴸᵃᵗcod 100 Syh
7₈₈ δαμάλεις] post τέσσαρες tr *O*⁻⁵⁸ Syh
7₈₈ ἑξήκοντα 3°] post ἐνιαύσιαι tr V *O n*⁻⁵⁴ 126
8₈ τούτον] post θυσίαν tr *O*⁻⁵⁸ Syh: cf 𝔐
9₆ ἐκείνη 2°] ad fin tr *O*⁻⁵⁸-15-72 417* 392 319 Arm^te
9₁₃ καθαρὸς ᾖ] tr V *O*⁻⁵⁸ 59 ᴸᵃᵗcod 100 Syh; η ακαθαρτος 319
10₂₈ καὶ ἐξῆραν / σὺν δυνάμει αὐτῶν] tr *O*⁻⁵⁸ Syh (et om καί 376)
10₂₉ σε ποιήσομεν] ποιησομεν (-σωμεν 376-426*) σοι (σε 426) *O*⁻⁵⁸ Arm Syh
10₃₂ σε ποιήσομεν] ποιησωμεν σοι 376 Syh = 𝔐; tr 426
10₃₄ init — (₃₅) fin] post (₃₆) fin tr 426 Arab Syh
10₃₅ χιλιάδας μυριάδας] tr *O*⁻⁵⁸ = 𝔐; myriades et millia Syh
11₄ ἡμᾶς ψωμιεῖ] ψωμιει (-μησει 376) ημας *O*⁻⁵⁸ Syh
11₁₅ μου B V *f n x*⁻⁶¹⁹ 319 Cyr II 461 ᴸᵃᵗcod 100] > Bo; ad fin tr rell
11₁₈ ἡμᾶς] post ψωμιεῖ tr G-426 Arm Syh
11₂₅ τὸ πνεῦμα / ἐπ' αὐτούς B *d*^(⁻¹²⁵) 129 *n*⁻⁴⁵⁸ *t x* Arm] om τὸ πνεῦμα 458; tr rell

12₂ Μωυσῆ μόνῳ] μονω μωυση (μωσει 426) 426 422 ᴸᵃᵗRuf *Num* VI 6
12₄ ὑμεῖς / οἱ τρεῖς] tr O⁻⁵⁸
14₂₂ μου / τῆς φωνῆς Β Μ' V d 129 t x Cyr II 609] tr rell
15₈ ἀπὸ τῶν βοῶν / ποιῆτε] tr A F M' O'' C'' b f⁻¹²⁹ s y z 55 59 319 624 Cyr I 1029 ᴸᵃᵗcod
    100 Arab Bo Syh
15₂₀ ἀφαίρεμα 1°] post ἀφοριεῖτε tr O⁻⁵⁸ z Syh
16₅ αὐτοῦ 1°] post συναγωγήν tr O⁻⁵⁸ 417* b 54-75 799 ᴸᵃᵗcod 100 Arm Syh
16₉ ὑμᾶς / ὁ θεὸς Ἰσραήλ] tr B O⁻⁵⁸ d 129 127 t 509 Cyr I 860 Syh = Ra
16₄₀ ἔστιν] post Ἀαρών tr O⁻⁵⁸ Syh (vid)
16₅₀ ἐκόπασεν] ad fin tr G-376 ᴸᵃᵗcod 100 Syh
18₁₅ σοί ἔσται] tr Syh
18₁₉ σοὶ δέδωκα Β Μ' V 82 b 53'-129 127-767 x⁻⁶¹⁹ Arm] συ εστι (-ται*) 319; + αυτα d
    54-75' t ᴸᵃᵗcod 100 Co; tr rell = 𝔐
19₁₀ τὰ ἱμάτια] + αυτου et post δαμάλεως tr O⁻⁵⁸ b Syh
19₁₆ ἑπτὰ ἡμέρας / ἀκάθαρτος ἔσται] tr O⁻⁵⁸ 54-75-767 509 392 Eus VI 12 Aeth Arm
    Bo Syh
22₃₃ τρίτον τοῦτο] tr A V 29 118'-537 106 129 767 30 t 319 Or IV 409 Aeth Arm Syh
22₃₄ ἐν τῇ ὁδῷ / εἰς συνάντησιν] tr (c var) A F M' O''⁻⁷² C'' 56' s 619 y z 55 59 799 Aeth
    Arab Sa Syh
22₄₀ πρόβατα] et μόσχους tr O⁻⁵⁸ n 527 Arm Syh
23₃ μοι 1°] post θεός tr Syh; post συναντήσει tr O = 𝔐
23₃ μοι δείξῃ] tr 426 d t 59 Arm Syh
23₂₇ μοι] post αὐτόν tr 426 Syh
24₁ τὸ πρόσωπον αὐτοῦ] ad fin tr O⁻⁵⁸ ᴸᵃᵗcod 100 Syh
24₂ πνεῦμα θεοῦ] ad fin tr A F O''⁻⁸² C'' 56' n⁻¹²⁷ s 527-619 y z 55 59 799 ᴸᵃᵗcod 100 Ruf
    Num XVII 2 Aeth Arab Syh
24₁₀ εὐλογῶν] post εὐλόγησας tr O⁻⁵⁸
24₁₀ τρίτον] ad fin tr A F M' O'⁻³⁷⁶-29-707 C''⁻⁵²'³¹³⁷⁶¹ 19 d 53'-56 s 527 y z⁻⁶⁸'¹²⁰ 59 799
    Arm Bo Syh
24₁₃ μοι] post δῷ tr F V O'⁻⁵⁸-707 ᴸᵃᵗcod 100 Arm Syh
24₁₃ πονηρόν Β V 82-381' d 53'-129 n⁻⁴⁵⁸ t 71-509 319 ᴸᵃᵗcod 100 Arm Co] + η κακον 458;
    μικρον η μεγα M'ᵐᵍ; et καλόν tr rell
24₂₂ σε αἰχμαλωτεύσουσιν Β Μ' V 82ᵐᵍ-426 d 53'-129 n t 71-509 ᴸᵃᵗcod 100] om σε 82ᵗˣᵗ
    319 Arm; tr rell = 𝔐
25₁₁ μου 2°] post ζῆλον tr V O⁻⁵⁸ 509 Tht I 812 ᴸᵃᵗcod 100 Ambr *Ps 118* XVIII 10 Hi *Mal* 2
    Hil *Ps* CXVIII 3 Arm Syh
25₁₅ τῇ Μαδιανίτιδι / τῇ πεπληγυίᾳ] tr O⁻⁵⁸
25₁₅ ἐστιν] ad fin tr O⁻⁵⁸ Syh
26₁₅ init — (23) fin] post (27) fin tr O⁻⁵⁸ Arab Syh
26₂₈ init — (31) fin] post (47) fin tr O⁻⁵⁸ Arab Syh
26₅₈ δῆμος ὁ Κόρε Β V 963 82 129 n 730 t⁽⁻³⁷⁰⁾ x⁻⁶¹⁹ 319 ᴸᵃᵗcod 100 Arm Bo Sa⁵] > Sa¹²;
    post Μουσί tr rell = 𝔐
27₉ θυγάτηρ αὐτῷ] tr V 963 (vid) O⁻⁵⁸-82 414 b d 129 n t x⁻⁶¹⁹ 55 624 ᴸᵃᵗRuf *Num* XXII
    1 Syh
27₂₂ αὐτῷ κύριος] tr 426 16 44 126 Syh
28₉ ἀναπεποιημένης ἐν ἐλαίῳ Β V 963 15-82 d f n t x⁻⁶¹⁹ 121 319 Cyr I 1113 ᴸᵃᵗcod 100 Arm
    Bo Sa¹] post θυσίαν tr rell
28₂₂ ἕνα] post ἁμαρτίας tr 426 Syh
29₂ ἕνα 1°] post βοῶν tr O⁻⁵⁸ ᴸᵃᵗcod 100 Syh
29₈ ἕνα / ἐκ βοῶν Β Μ V 82 d 53'-129 n t x⁻⁶¹⁹ 407 319 624] om ἐκ βοῶν 126; tr rell = 𝔐
29₂₂ ἕνα] post ἁμαρτίας tr 426 44 126-128 Syh
29₂₈ ἕνα] post ἁμαρτίας tr G-426 Syh
29₃₁ ἕνα] post ἁμαρτίας tr G-426 Syh
29₃₄ ἕνα] post ἁμαρτίας tr G-426 Syh
29₃₆ εἰς ὀσμὴν εὐωδίας] post κάρπωμα tr A O-707 C'' 56' s y z⁻⁴⁰⁷ 646 Cyr I 1124 Aeth
    Arab Syh
29₃₈ ἕνα] post ἁμαρτίας tr G-426 Syh

30₈ καὶ παρασιωπήσῃ αὐτῇ] post ἀκούσῃ 2° tr O⁻⁵⁸ Syh

31₈ Σούρ B M' V 82 b d 129 n t x⁻⁵²⁷ 407 319 ᴸᵃᵗcod 100 Arm Co] et Ῥόκομ tr rell

31₃₀ προβάτων] et ὄνων tr O⁻⁵⁸ ᴸᵃᵗcodd 100 104(vid) Arab Bo Syh

32₂ Ῥουβήν] et Γάδ tr 376' Syh

32₇ κύριος] ad fin tr O⁻⁵⁸ 799 Aeth Syh

32₉ κύριος αὐτοῖς B V 82-381' 414 19' d 129 n t x 318 407] αυτους κϛ 120; om αὐτοῖς 18; tr rell = 𝔐

32₁₆ ὧδε] post ἡμῶν 1° tr O⁻⁵⁸ Syh

32₁₇ ἑαυτῶν τόπον] τοπον αυτων (+ αυτους 799) O⁻⁵⁸ 799 ᴸᵃᵗcod 100 Syh

32₂₃ ὑμᾶς] post καταλάβῃ tr O⁻⁵⁸ Syh

32₂₅ Ῥουβήν] et Γάδ tr O⁻⁵⁸ Syh

32₂₉ πρὸς αὐτούς] post Μωυσῆς tr G-426 30 Sa¹ Syh

32₂₉ Ῥουβήν] et Γάδ tr O⁻⁵⁸ Syh

32₃₁ Ῥουβήν] et Γάδ tr O⁻⁵⁸ 16-46 Syh

32₃₁ ὁ κύριος] post λέγει tr O⁻⁵⁸ ᴸᵃᵗcod 100 Arm Syh

32₃₃ σὺν τοῖς ὁρίοις / αὐτῆς] tr 376' 52' Syh

34₄ ἐξ — κύριος 1°] συν ους επαταξεν κυριος εξ αυτων 426

34₄ τὴν ἐκδίκησιν / κύριος] tr O⁻⁵⁸ 53' n⁻⁴⁵⁸ 76 ᴸᵃᵗcodd 100 104 Ruf Num XXVII 8 Aeth Syh

33₃₈ τεσσαρακοστῷ ἔτει] ετει τω τεσσ. 426

33₅₃ αὐτῶν] ad fin tr G-426: cf 𝔐

34₇ τὰ ὅρια / ὑμῖν B 963 44'-107-610ᶜ t⁽⁻⁸⁴⁾ 509 407 319 Sa¹] τα ορια υμων 125-610*; υμιν ορια 82 799; om ὑμῖν 53' 126; tr rell = 𝔐

35₃ αὐτοῖς / αἱ πόλεις] tr (c var) A F M' O'' C''⁻⁵²⁹ f⁻¹²⁹ s y z⁻¹²⁰' 55 59 Aeth Arab Co Syh

35₁₂ αἱ πόλεις / ὑμῖν] υμων αι πολεις G; tr O⁻ᴳ n Arm Bo Syh

35₂₇ ἔνοχός ἐστιν] tr O⁻⁵⁸: cf 𝔐

35₃₁ ἐνόχου ὄντος] tr O⁻⁵⁸ Syh

35₃₃ οὐκ ἐξιλασθήσεται] post γῇ tr O⁻⁵⁸ Syh

36₁₁ in initio ordinis nominum Μααλά hab A F O'⁻⁸² C'' f⁻¹²⁹ s x⁻⁵⁰⁹ y 68'-120 55 59 Aeth Arab Syh

The changes in word order are also examples of hex activity. In each case one or more of the major hex witnesses attests to the change.

The above lists have also been analyzed in order to discover the spread of hex recensional materials within the text tradition. Instances where more than three text groups (i. e. beyond the O witnesses) support the reading have been disregarded in the table below, as well as random support. Included in s are readings found on the margins of s mss, 85'-321'-344. Support by a text group means support by the majority of mss within the group except for z where support is identified as meaning at least four mss.

In the table below Column A gives the number of instances where the text group is the only group (outside of O) supporting the reading; Column B, where the text group is one of two groups supporting, and Column C, one of three groups. The last column gives the total number of readings involved.

Column	A	B	C	Total
C''	—	3	4	7
cI	1	—	—	1
b	11	4	7	22
d	—	7	11	18

f	23	3	4	30
n	8	4	9	21
s	4	6	5	15
t	1	11	12	24
x	1	—	—	1
y	—	3	3	6
z	37	7	5	49

From this table it is clear that the z group is somewhat more hexaplaric than all others with a total of 49 instances of support (out of a total of 566 readings) followed by f with 30, t with 24, b with 22, n with 21, d with 18, s with 15, C'' together with cI, 8; y with 6, and x with only 1.

Within the n group ms 767 is often aberrant. When its text differs from the n group it shows hexaplaric influence. In the above lists n^{-767} has the hex reading only twice, whereas 767 supports the hex reading over against n 59 times. It is, however, an n text in its major allegiance.

In the following list the possibility of Origenian revision of proper names is explored. The evidence of Syh is not given since Paul of Tella commonly used the Peshitta form rather than his own transcription from the Greek. The list is limited to those names which appear to have been influenced by the Hebrew within the text tradition.

List 4

3₂   Ἀβιούδ] αβιον G-426: אביהוא 𝔐
3₄   Ἀβιούδ] αβιον 426: אביהוא 𝔐
3₄   Σινά] σιναι 58-426 n^{-767}: סיני 𝔐
3₁₄   Σινά] σιναι 426 n^{-767}: סיני 𝔐
3₁₇   Γεδσών] γηρσων O⁻⁵⁸ LatRuf Num IV 1: גרשון 𝔐
3₁₈   Γεδσών] γηρσων O⁻⁵⁸: גרשון 𝔐
3₂₁   Γεδσών 1°] γηρσων G-426 767: גרשון 𝔐
3₂₁   (τοῦ) Γεδσών] γηρσων G-376ᵗˣᵗ-426 767: הגרשני 𝔐
3₂₃   (τοῦ) Γεδσών] γηρσων O 767: הגרשני 𝔐
3₂₄   (τοῦ) Γεδσών] γηρσων G-426; σηρσων 376; γηρσσων 767: לגרשני 𝔐
3₂₅   Γεδσών] γηρσων O⁻⁵⁸ 767* x^{-509}; γηρσσων 767ᶜ: גרשון 𝔐
4₂₂   Γεδσών] γηρσων O⁻⁵⁸ 767: גרשון 𝔐
4₂₄   (τοῦ) Γεδσών] γηρσων O⁻⁵⁸: הגרשני 𝔐
4₂₇   Γεδσών] γηρσων O⁻⁵⁸ 767: הגרשני 𝔐
4₂₈   Γεδσών] γηρσων O⁻⁵⁸: הגרשני 𝔐
4₃₈   Γεδσών] γηρσων G-426: גרשון 𝔐
4₄₁   Γεδσών] γηρσων G-426 767: גרשון 𝔐
7₇   Γεδσών] γηρσων O⁻⁵⁸; γηρσσων 767: גרשון 𝔐
9₁   Σινά] σιναι 426 54'-127; συναι 458: סיני 𝔐
9₅   Σινά] σιναι 426 54-75; συναι 458: סיני 𝔐
10₁₂   Σινά] σιναι O⁻³⁷⁶ n^{-767}: סיני 𝔐
10₁₇   Γεδσών] γηρσων 426; γηρσσων 767: גרשון 𝔐
13₁₅   Ἰαβί] οναφει 426; οναβη 58; οναφση 767: ופסי 𝔐
13₁₆   Γουδιήλ] γουιηλ 426 54'; γονοιηλ 75': גאואל 𝔐
16₁   Ἀβιρών] αβειρωμ G: אבירם 𝔐
16₁₂   Ἀβιρών] αβειρωμ G: אבירם 𝔐
16₂₄   Ἀβιρών] αβειρωμ G: אבירם 𝔐
21₁₁   Ἀχελγαί] αιη 426: עיי 𝔐

21₁₈ *Μανθαναίν*] μαθθανα 426: מתנה 𝔐

21₁₉ *Μανθαναίν*] μαθθανα 426⁽ᵐᵍ⁾: מתנה 𝔐

21₂₄ *Ἰαζήρ*] αζ 767: עז 𝔐

21₃₃ *Ἑδράίν*] εδραει 426; εδραι F 29-58-72 54ᶜ 59: אדרעי 𝔐

26₁₇ *Ἰαμουήλ*] αμουλ 426: חמול 𝔐

26₁₇ (ὁ) *Ἰαμουηλί*] αμουλει 426: החמולי 𝔐

26₂₀ *Σαμράμ*] σαμραν 82-426 767: שמרן 𝔐

26₂₀ (ὁ) *Σαμραμί*] σαμρανει 82-426ᶜ: השמרני 𝔐

26₂₂ *Ἀλλήλ*] ιαλληλ 767; ιαλλη 376; ιαλιηλ 426: יחלאל 𝔐

26₂₂ (ὁ) *Ἀλληλί*] ιαλληλι 426; ιαλλειλι 376; ιαληλ 767: היחלאלי 𝔐

26₂₆ *Ἀροαδί* 1°] αρωδ 426: ארוד 𝔐

26₂₆ (ὁ) *Ἀροαδί*] αροδι 59⁽ᶜ⁾ Bo; αρωδει B* 71; αρωδει 426: הארודי 𝔐

26₄₂ *Ἀσυβήρ*] ασβηλ 426: אשבל 𝔐

26₄₂ (ὁ) *Ἀσυβηρί*] ασβηλει 426: האשבלי 𝔐

26₄₂ *Ἀχιράν*] -ραμ 58-707 246 54-75′; αχειραμ 426 53′ 318; αχηραμ 56: אחירם 𝔐

26₄₂ (ὁ) *Ἀχιρανί*] -ραμει 707; αχειραμι 53′; αχειραμει 426; αχιραμι 58 56′: האחירמי 𝔐

26₄₃ *Σωφάν*] σωφαμ 58-426: שפופם 𝔐

26₄₃ (ὁ) *Σωφανί*] σωφαμι 58; σωφαμει 426: השופמי 𝔐

26₄₄ *Ἀδάρ*] αραδ 426: ארד 𝔐

26₄₆ *Σαμί* 1°] σουαμ 426: שוחם 𝔐

26₄₆ (ὁ) *Σαμί*] σουαμει 426: השוחמי 𝔐

26₄₇ *Σαμί*] σουαμει 426ᶜ: השוחמי 𝔐

26₄₈ *Ἀσιήλ*] ιασιηλ 58-426: יחצאל 𝔐

26₄₈ (ὁ) *Ἀσιηλί*] ιασιηλι 58-426: היחצאלי 𝔐

26₅₇ *Γεδσών*] γηρσων 426 767: גרשון 𝔐

26₅₇ (ὁ) *Γεδσωνί*] γηρσωνει 426; γερσωνι 120′: הגרשני 𝔐

26₆₀ *Ἀβιούδ*] αβιου 426: אביהוא 𝔐

26₆₁ *Ἀβιούδ*] αβιου 426: אביהוא 𝔐

26₆₄ *Σινά*] σιναι (σηναι 458) n⁻⁷⁶⁷: סיני 𝔐

28₆ *Σινά*] σιναι 426 54′-458: סיני 𝔐

31₈ *Εὐίν*] ευει G-426: אוי 𝔐

31₈ *Ρόβοκ*] ροβο 426: רבע 𝔐

32₃ *Σεβάμα*] σεβαμ 426: שבם 𝔐

32₃₅ *Σωφάρ*] σωφαν F 15-29-426 s⁻²⁸ ⁸⁵ y⁻³⁹² Aeth; σοφαν C″ 19 28-85 68′-120 59; ωφαν 82; ζωφαν 624; σεφαν 72: שופן 𝔐

32₃₆ *Ναμβρά*] βηθναμρα 426 Arab; βηθηαμραμ 58; βιθιαμραμ (-αμαρμ 53′) 53′-56: בית נמרה 𝔐

33₃ *Ραμεσσή*] ραμεσσης 426; ραμεσης 82: רעמסס 𝔐

33₅ *Ραμεσσή*] -σσης Bᶜ G-426 509: רעמסס 𝔐

33₆ *Βουθάν*] ονθαμ 426 54-75; οθαμ 799; οθομ 82: אתם 𝔐

33₇ *Βουθάν*] ονθαμ 426 54; οθαμ 799; οθομ 82: אתם 𝔐

33₁₂ *Ραφακά*] δαφακα 767; daphaga Sa¹: דפקה 𝔐

33₁₃ *Ραφακά*] δαφακαν 767; daphaga Sa¹: דפקה 𝔐

33₁₄ *Ραφιδίν*] -διμ 426 d t; -δειμ 761: רפידם 𝔐

33₁₅ *Ραφιδίν*] -διμ 426 d t Armᵗᵉ; -δειμ 761: רפידם 𝔐

33₁₅ *Σινά*] σιναι Mᵐᵍ 426 54′-458 416: סיני 𝔐

33₁₆ *Σινά*] σιναι Mᵐᵍ 426 n⁻⁷⁶⁷ 416: סיני 𝔐

33₂₁ *Δεσσά* Fᵃ] ρεσσα (c var) A F O′-29-707 C″ f⁻¹²⁹ s⁻³⁴⁴ᶜ y⁻¹²¹ 68′-120 LatRuf *Num* XXVII 12: רסה 𝔐

33₂₂ *Δεσσά* Fᵃ] ρεσσα (c var) A F O′-29 C″ f⁻¹²⁹ s⁻³⁴⁴ᶜ y⁻¹²¹ 68′-120: רסה 𝔐

33₂₄ *Χαραδάθ*] -δα 82-426-707 53′-56 68′-120: חרדה 𝔐

33₂₅ *Χαραδάθ*] -δα 82-426-707 53′-56 68′-120 Latcod 104: חרדה 𝔐

33₂₆ *Κατάαθ*] θααθ 58-426 767: תחת 𝔐

33₂₇ *Κατάαθ*] θααθ 58-426 767; τααθ 318: תחת 𝔐

33₂₇ *Τάραθ*] θαρα 426 344ᶜ; ταρα 82: תרח 𝔐

33₂₈ *Τάραθ*] θαρα 426 344ᶜ; ταρα 82: תרח 𝔐

33₂₉ *Ἀσελμωνά*] ασεμ. O⁻³⁷⁶ 68′-120; ασσεμ. 707 56; ασεμονα 53′: חשמנה 𝔐

33₃₀ Ἀσελμωνά] ασεμ. O 56 68'; ασεμονα 53; ασεμμ. 707: חשמנה 𝔐
33₃₃ Ἐτεβάθα] ιετ. M' 58-426; ιεταβ. G-376: יטבתה 𝔐
33₃₄ Ἐτεβάθα] ιετ. M 58-426; ιεταβ. G-376 318 416: יטבתה 𝔐
33₄₉ Βελσαττίμ] αβελ. (c var) 58-82-426-707 b d f⁻¹²⁹ 54-458 t 68'-120: אבל השטים 𝔐
34₄ Ἀκραβίν] -βειμ 29*-381 16-46-528 54; -ββιμ 426: עקרבים 𝔐
34₂₀ Σαλαμιήλ] σαμουηλ 346ᵐᵍ(vid): שמואל 𝔐
34₂₆ Ὀζά] οζαν C-46 d⁻¹⁰⁶: עזן 𝔐

Out of the 90 instances in *List 4* all but six are attested by O witnesses, particularly by 426 and by 58 to a lesser extent. From this fact it would appear that Origen did "correct" a number of proper names, probably on the basis of the text of The Three, even though he does not state this as a principle underlying his hexaplaric activity.

The six instances not attested by O witnesses are to be found at 21₂₄ 26₆₄ 33₁₂ ₁₃ 34₂₀ ₂₆. The last of these, οζαν for Ὀζά, is probably mere coincidence, the result of reading a parent text οζα as though it were οζᾱ. σιναι for Σινά at 26₆₄ is not a hex reading at all, since its support by n⁻⁷⁶⁷ is meaningless. Most of the n mss read σιναι consistently throughout Numbers for Σινά, but do not show particular hex activity otherwise.

It remains to test whether post hexaplaric activity can be demonstrated in the text tradition with respect to the obelus tradition. In the following list are detailed instances in which the tradition omits text under the obelus. Since all of the instances are equivalent to 𝔐, that fact is not noted.

List 5

1₂ αὐτῶν 3°] sub ÷ G; > B 19 d 127 t x 18 319 Cyr VI 453 X 624 ᴸᵃᵗcod 100 Arm
1₃ ἐπισκέψασθε αὐτούς 2°] sub ÷ G; > Aeth^CG
1₁₈ αὐτῶν 3°] sub ÷ G Syh; > 417ᵗˣᵗ 458 ᴸᵃᵗcod 100
1₁₈ πᾶν ἀρσενικόν] ἀρσενικόν sub ÷ G Syh; > Arab
1₂₀ αὐτῶν 4°] sub ÷ G Syh; > b
1₃₀ αὐτῶν 4° — ἀρσενικά] sub ÷ G Syh; > 107'
1₃₂ αὐτῶν 4° — ἀρσενικά] sub ÷ G Syh^T; > 44
1₅₀ ἐν αὐτῇ 1°] sub ÷ G Syh; ἐν sub ÷; om ἐν V 707 537 106* 55 Sa
1₅₃ ἐναντίοι] sub ÷ G Syh^T; > 58-376 Arm Bo
1₅₃ αὐτοί] sub ÷ G Syh^T; > 58 319 Aeth Arm Bo
1₅₄ καὶ Ἀαρών] sub ÷ G Syh; > 15 75
2₂ οἱ υἱοὶ Ἰσραήλ 2°] sub ÷ G Syh; > 75
2₁₄ οἱ — αὐτοῦ] sub ÷ G Syh; > Arab
2₂₂ οἱ — αὐτοῦ] sub ÷ G Syh^T; > Arab
2₂₉ οἱ — αὐτοῦ] sub ÷ G Syh^T; > Arab
2₃₁ σὺν δυνάμει αὐτῶν] sub ÷ Syh^T; > B V O⁻⁵⁸-707 b f⁻²⁴⁶ x 392 Cyr I 724 ᴸᵃᵗcod 100 Aeth Arab Co Syh^L = Ra
2₃₄ ἐχόμενοι] sub ÷ G Syh; > ᴸᵃᵗcod 100 Aeth Arm(vid)
3₉ τοῖς ἱερεῦσιν] sub ÷ G Syh; > 426
3₁₀ ἐπί — μαρτυρίου] sub ÷ G Syh; > Arab
3₁₀ καί 4° — καταπετάσματος] sub ÷ G Syh; > Arab
3₁₂ λύτρα αὐτῶν ἔσονται] sub ÷ G Syh; > Ambr *Cain* II 7
3₁₅ κατὰ συγγενείας αὐτῶν] sub ÷ G Syh; > B x 55 Aeth^C Arab Sa
3₁₆ καὶ Ἀαρών] sub ÷ G Syh; > 417 Arab
3₂₃ καὶ οὗτοι] sub ÷ G Syh; > ᴸᵃᵗcod 100
3₂₄ τοῦ δήμου] sub ÷ G Syh; > 707(vid) 56ᵗˣᵗ 628 646 Sa¹²

3₅₀ σίκλους] sub ÷ G Syh; > A
4₃ πάντα] sub ÷ G Syh; > ᴸᵃᵗcod 104
4₆ ἐπ' αὐτήν] sub ÷ G Syh; > 58
4₇ ἐπ' αὐτήν] sub ÷ G; > 58 Aeth Arm Bo
4₁₄ καί 9° — fin] sub ÷ G Syh; > 58 Arab
4₂₆ τοῦ μαρτυρίου] sub ÷ G Syh; > b 53' 319 Arab
4₄₄ κατ' — αὐτῶν 3°] sub ÷ G Syh; > 426 52' 107'-125 ᴸᵃᵗcod 100
5₆ λέγων] sub ÷ G Syh; > F*(c pr m) 72 73ᵗˣᵗ-320 125 53' 799 Arab
5₈ αὐτῷ 1°] sub ÷ G Syh; > 58 246 Bo
5₉ κυρίῳ] sub ÷ G; > 58 Arab
5₁₈ τούτου] τουτο (sub ÷ G; pr ÷ Syh) G Syh; > 58 b Aeth
5₂₁ ταύτης] sub ÷ G; pr ÷ Syh; > 58
5₃₀ αὐτοῦ 2°] sub ÷ G Syh; > 58 Arm
6₃ ἀπὸ οἴνου 2° 963] sub ÷ G Syh; > 58-72-381' d f n⁽⁻⁴⁵⁸⁾ t 619 59 319 Cyr I 1041
    Eus VIII 2.116 ᴸᵃᵗcod 100 Aethᶜᴳ Arm Sa
6₆ πάσῃ] sub ÷ G Syh; > 58 n⁻⁷⁶⁷ Arm
6₇ ἐπ' αὐτῷ] sub ÷ G; > 58 C'' Arm
6₁₁ ὁ ἱερεύς 2°] sub ÷ G; > 58 z
7₂ δώδεκα] sub ÷ G; > 58 Arab
7₁₂ ἄρχων] sub ÷ G; pr ÷ Syh; > 319
7₈₅ σίκλοι] sub ÷ Syh; > 319 ᴸᵃᵗcod 100
7₈₆ χρυσοῖ] sub ÷ Syh; > 58
7₈₈ ἄμωμοι] sub ÷ Syh; > 58 413(spatium) 126 Arab
7₈₈ μετά 1° — καί] sub ÷ Procop 812 Syh; > 58 Aethᶜ Arab
8₁₃ κυρίου καὶ ἔναντι] sub ÷ Syh; > Aethᶜ Arab Sa
8₁₉ ἀπόδομα] sub ÷ Syh; > 58 Arab
9₈ αὐτοῦ] sub ÷ Syh; > 15-58 552 Aeth
9₁₀ ἀνθρώπου] sub ÷ Syh; > Arab Sa¹²
9₁₄ ἐν — ὑμῶν] sub ÷ Syh; > Arab Bo
9₁₄ αὐτό] sub ÷ Syh; > 58 319 ᴸᵃᵗcod 100
9₁₈ οἱ υἱοὶ Ἰσραήλ 2°] sub ÷ Syh; > Arab
10₄ πάντες] pr ÷ Syh; > 58 n⁻⁷⁶⁷ 527 319 Arm
11₁ παρὰ κυρίου] sub ÷ Syhᵀ; παρά sub ÷ Syhᴸ; om παρά Arab
11₈ αὐτό 1°] sub ÷ Syh; > n 527 121 628 319 Tht Nm 203 ᴸᵃᵗcod 100 Arm
11₈ αὐτό 2°] sub ÷ Syh; > b Tht Nm 203 ᴸᵃᵗcodd 94—96 100 Arm
11₁₆ αὐτὸς σύ] sub ÷ Syhᵀ; > 58 Tht Nm 205ᵗᵉ
11₂₇ λέγων] sub ÷ Syh; > b d⁽⁻⁴⁴⁾ n t 126 Aeth Arm Sa
12₁ Μωυσῆς] sub ÷ G Syh; > Aethᶜ Arab
12₄ εἰς 2° — fin] sub ÷ G; > 58 Sa
12₅ τοῦ μαρτυρίου] sub ÷ G Syh; > Arab
12₆ πρὸς αὐτούς] sub ÷ G; > 58
13₃ αὐτούς] sub ÷ G Syh; > 29 Aeth Bo
13₂₄ καὶ κατεσκέψαντο αὐτήν] sub ÷ G Syh; > Arab
13₃₀ καὶ ὁ Εὐαῖος] sub ÷ G Syh; > Arab Bo
13₃₂ οὐκ ἀναβαίνομεν ὅτι] sub ÷ G Syh; > Arab
13₃₂ μᾶλλον] sub ÷ G Syh; > 126 799
14₁₀ ἐν νεφέλῃ] sub ÷ G; > 58 319
14₁₂ καί 3° — σου] sub ÷ G; καὶ τὸν οἶκον sub ÷ Syh; > Arab
14₁₈ καὶ ἀληθινός] sub ÷ G Syh; > Cyr VI 948 Arab
14₁₈ καὶ ἁμαρτίας] sub ÷ G Syh; > ᴸᵃᵗcod 100 Arab
14₁₈ τὸν ἔνοχον] sub ÷ G Syh; > Arab
14₂₂ ταύτῃ] sub ÷ G Syh; > B 58 x Aethᶜᴳ Arab Co
14₂₃ ἀλλ' — γῆν 2°] sub ÷ G Syh; > Arab
14₃₁ εἰς τὴν γῆν] sub ÷ G; > 58 319 ᴸᵃᵗcod 100 GregIl Tr 11
14₃₁ ὑμεῖς] sub ÷ G; > 58
14₄₁ ὑμῖν] sub ÷ G(υμεις*); sub ✳ Syhᴸ(mend); > 58
15₄ τοῦ οἰφί] sub ÷ G; > ᴸᵃᵗcod 100

15₁₄ ἐν 2° — ὑμῶν 1°] sub ÷ G Syh^T; > Arab

15₁₄ ὑμεῖς] sub ÷ G Syh^L; > Sa

15₁₄ κυρίῳ 2°] sub ÷ G Syh^L; > 58

15₁₉ ἀφόρισμα] sub ÷ G Syh^L; > ^{Lat}codd 91 92 94—96

15₂₀ αὐτό] sub ÷ Syh; > 58

15₂₃ πρὸς ὑμᾶς 2°] sub ÷ G Syh; > ^{Lat}cod 100 Arab

15₂₄ ἄμωμον] sub ÷ G(αμνον) Syh; > 75 Arab

15₂₇ μίαν] sub ÷ G; pr ÷ Syh; > 58 ^{Lat}Hi C Pel I 35

15₃₃ υἱῶν Ἰσραήλ] pr ÷ Syh; sub ÷ G; > 106 319

15₃₅ λέγων] sub ÷ G; > Arab

16₁₃ τοῦτο] sub ÷ G Syh; > 58 319 Bo

16₁₉ αὐτοῦ] sub ÷ G Syh; > 15 84*

16₂₅ πάντες] sub ÷ G Syh^T; > 58 319

16₃₀ καί 2° — αὐτῶν 2°] sub ÷ G Syh; om καί 2° — αὐτῶν 1° 58; > Arab = 𝔐

16₃₇ τὰ χαλκᾶ] pr ÷ Syh; sub ÷ G; > 58 Arab

16₃₉ υἱὸς Ἀαρών] sub ÷ G; > Arab

16₄₄ καὶ Ἀαρών] sub ÷ G Syh^T; > A* 551 Sa¹²

16₄₆ ἐπ' αὐτό 2°] sub ÷ G Syh; > 125

17₈ καὶ Ἀαρών] sub ÷ G Syh^T; > 58 628 Arab

17₁₁ καὶ Ἀαρών] sub ÷ G Syh^T; > 58 Arab

18₁ λέγων] sub ÷ G Syh; > 72 528 125 126 ^{Lat}Ruf Num X inscr Arab Sa¹²

18₃ σου 2°] sub ÷ Syh^T; > B V 58-82 x⁻⁵²⁷ z^{-126 628} 319 646 Aeth^{CG} Sa = Ra

18₈ μοι] pr ÷ Syh^T; > 58 120

18₈ σου μετὰ σέ] sub ÷ Syh^L | μετὰ σέ] pr ÷ Syh^T; > 58-72

18₂₆ ὑμεῖς] pr ÷ Syh^L; > 44

19₃ εἰς τόπον καθαρόν] sub ÷ G^c Syh; > 319 Arab

19₁₃ ἐστιν 2°] sub ÷ G; > 529*

19₁₄ καὶ οὗτος] sub ÷ Syh; καί sub ÷ G^c; om καί Bo

20₅ τοῦτο] sub ÷ G; > 72 71 ^{Lat}cod 100 Arm Bo Sa¹²

20₁₂ ὑμεῖς] sub ÷ G Syh^T; > 58 Chr I 506 Bo

20₁₆ κύριος] sub ÷ G; > 58 552 d 53' 126 Arab

20₁₇ σου 2°] sub ÷ Syh^L; > 16-46 Phil II 87^{UF} Aeth

20₂₀ δι' ἐμοῦ] sub ÷ G Syh; > ^{Lat}cod 100

20₂₅ ἔναντι — fin] sub ÷ Syh; > Arab

21₅ τούτῳ] sub ~ Syh^L; > B 29-426-707* 16-46 71-509 68'-120' Arab Arm Sa = Ra

21₇ πρὸς κύριον 2°] sub ÷ Syh; > Cyr II 637 Arab

21₁₆ πιεῖν] sub ÷ Syh; > 58 551

21₂₁ λόγοις εἰρηνικοῖς] pr ÷ Syh^T; > 58 246 Arab Bo

21₂₂ τῇ ὁδῷ πορευσόμεθα] sub ÷ Syh^L; > 58 319 ^{Lat}PsAmbr Mans 41 Arab

21₂₂ σου 2°] sub ÷ Syh^L; > 128 319 ^{Lat}PsAmbr Mans 41

21₂₄ ἐστιν] pr ÷ Syh^L; > 58

22₆ σύ 1°] sub ÷ Syh; > C'' 53' 75 28-85'-321' 527-619 318 z 55 59 319 ^{Lat}cod 100 Caes Serm CXIII 2 Ruf Num XIII 5 Bo

22₆ σύ 2°] sub ÷ Syh; > 72 44 527 392 ^{Lat}cod 100 Caes Serm CXIII 2 Ruf Num XIII 5 Arm Bo

22₁₀ αὐτούς] sub ÷ Syh^L; > 58 767 319 Bo

22₁₈ ἐν — fin] sub ÷ Syh^T; > 58 319 Arab

22₁₉ ταύτην] sub ÷ Syh; > 58

22₂₀ οὗτοι] pr ÷ Syh; > 58 ^{Lat}Aug Num 48

22₄₁ τι] sub ÷ Syh; > 82 z

23₃ καί 4° — θεόν] sub ÷ Syh; > 426 Arab

23₇ μοι 2°] pr ÷ Syh; > Co

23₁₇ πάντες] sub ÷ Syh^T; > 58

24₁₃ αὐτό] sub ÷ Syh^T; > 500 Aeth

25₂ τῶν θυσιῶν αὐτῶν] sub ÷ Syh; > 58 Arab

25₁₅ Ὀμμώθ] sub ÷ G Syh; > Arab

25₁₆ λάλησον — fin] sub ÷ G; > 58-426 417 84^{txt}(c pr m) 319 Arab

26₉ οὗτοί εἰσιν] pr ÷ Syh^T; εἰσιν sub ÷ Syh^L; > O^(-376) Co
26₁₀ αὐτοῦ] sub ÷ Syh^L; > Sa
26₆₁ ἐν 2° — fin] pr ÷ Syh; > Arab
27₂ ἔναντι 4°] sub ÷ Syh; > 58-618^c 44-125 71 126 319 Arab Sa⁵
27₁₂ Χανάαν] sub ÷ Syh; > 129 392
27₁₂ ἐν κατασχέσει] sub ÷ Syh; > 58 Arab
27₁₃ ἐν — fin] sub ÷ Syh; > Arab
27₁₆ ταύτης] sub ÷ Syh; > 58
27₁₈ λέγων] sub ÷ Syh; > 58 Arab
28₂ λέγων] sub ÷ Syh; > 58-72-82 125 509 Aeth Arab Arm Bo Sa¹²
28₅ καὶ ποιήσεις] sub ÷ Syh; om ποιήσεις 125
28₁₈ ὑμῖν] sub ÷ Syh; > 58 Sa
28₂₃ τῆς διὰ παντός] sub ÷ Syh; > 426 761 75 392
28₂₅ ἐν αὐτῇ] sub ÷ Syh; > 125 ^Latcod 100
28₂₇ ἀμώμους] sub ÷ Syh; > 58 ^Latcod 100 Arab
28₃₀ περὶ ἁμαρτίας] sub ÷ Syh; > 58 Arab
28₃₁ μοι] sub ÷ Syh; > 58 ^Latcod 100 Arm
29₁₁ ἐξιλάσασθαι περὶ ὑμῶν] sub ÷ Syh; > 28-85^txt Arab
29₁₁ κατά — fin] sub ÷ Syh; > 426 Arab
29₁₂ τούτου] pr ÷ Syh; > Arab Co
29₁₂ αὐτήν] sub ÷ G; > V 58-618 106 ^Latcodd 100 104
29₁₃ τῇ 1° — πρώτῃ] sub ÷ G Syh; > Arab
29₂₄ αὐτῶν 4°] sub÷ G; > 72
29₂₈ ἐξ αἰγῶν] sub ÷ G Syh; > 126
29₃₁ ἐξ αἰγῶν] sub ÷ G Syh; > 126
29₃₄ ἐξ αἰγῶν] sub ÷ G; > 126
29₃₇ αὐτῶν 4°] sub ÷ G Syh; > ^Latcodd 100 104
29₃₈ ἐξ αἰγῶν] sub ÷ G Syh; > 126
30₃ ἄνθρωπος 2°] sub ÷ G Syh; > 72 126 Cyr I 1060 Or II 306 ^Latcodd 100 104 Bo
30₆ ἀνανεύων] sub ÷ G Syh; > 125 767 Arm
30₉ οὐ — αὐτῆς 5°] sub ÷ G Syh; > 58-426
30₁₂ αὐτῆς 3°] sub ÷ G; > A F 15'-58-618*(c pr m)-707 C'' 125 53'-56 s^(-85txt) y^(-392) z^(-407) 55 59 416 624 646 ^LatAug Num LIX 2te
30₁₅ αὐτῇ 2°] sub ÷ (※*) G; > 72 246 ^Latcod 100
31₈ σύν — fin] sub ÷ G; > 58-426 d^(-106) 527 Arab
31₁₁ αὐτῶν] sub ÷ G; > 29-58 527 18
31₁₇ πάσῃ] sub ÷ G; > 58 Aeth
31₂₁ τῆς παρατάξεως] sub ÷ G; > 58 126 ^Latcodd 100 104
32₁₁ οὗτοι] εκεινοι sub ÷ G; > 53' Arm
32₁₁ οἱ 3° — ἀγαθόν] sub ÷ G; > 58 Aeth^C Arab
32₃₀ εἰς 1° — Χανάαν 1°] sub ÷ G; > 426 Arab
33₄ ἐν γῇ Αἰγύπτῳ] sub ÷ G Syh; > Arab
33₉ παρά — fin] sub ÷ G Syh; > Arab
33₃₆ καί 3° — Φαράν] sub ÷ G; > 426 Arab
33₅₂ αὐτά] sub ÷ G Syh; > 72-381' d 664 55 799 ^Latcod 104 Spec 44 Aeth Arm
33₅₄ αὐτῶν 1° B^(mg) M' V 963(vid) 58-376'-oI 56^mg-129-664 n t^(-84) 509-527 z 319 ^Latcod 100 Bo Sa¹] ταυτην 799; sub ÷ G Syh; > rell
34₁₃ αὐτήν 2°] sub ÷ G; > 57 129 Aeth
34₁₃ Μανασσή] sub ÷ G Syh; > 82
34₁₈ ὑμῖν] sub ÷ G(※*) Syh; > V 552
35₁₂ τὸ αἷμα] sub ÷ G Syh; > 72
35₂₁ θανάτῳ 2° — φονεύων] sub ÷ G; > V 58-72-381'-426 b 53' 120
35₃₂ ὁ μέγας] sub ÷ G; > 58
36₁ καί 3° — ἱερέως] sub ÷ G Syh; > 426
36₁₃ καὶ τὰ δικαιώματα] sub ÷ G Syh; > 58 458

Most of the above instances of omissions agreeing with 𝔐 are undoubtedly coincidences and should not be taken seriously. It is, however, not without significance that of witnesses to such omissions ms 58 heads the list with 73 followed by Arab with 66 instances. Next in order is Latin codex 100 with 25; 319, with 22, and 426, with 15. For Arab and the influence of Hebrew on it cf J W Wevers, The Textual Affinities of the Arabic Genesis of Bib. Nat.Arab 9, Studies of the Ancient Palestinian World, ed. by J. W. Wevers and D. B. Redford, Toronto 1971. That ms 58 gave evidence of post-hexaplaric activity was shown in THGD 43—47 for Deuteronomy.

From lists 1 and 2 it was evident that hex additions in the text tradition were to be found in O^{-58} more often than in the common witness of O. From List 5 it would seem that the copyist of 58 often omitted materials under the asterisk. It is interesting to speculate whether this copyist tended to omit textual materials under hex signs without distinguishing asterisks and obeluses. On the whole, ms 58 seems to be the result of further hex activity beyond that of Origen. On the other hand, it also presents over against the text tradition as a whole an at times curiously expanded text; thus at 5_{27} ms 58 has introduced an interpretative gloss taken from Josephus Antiq III 273.

Chapter 4   The Texts of B and A

It is the purpose of this study to examine the character of our two oldest complete texts of Numbers, to determine their place within the text history of the book, and to explore whether one can validly speak of a B vs an A text type. This last point is particularly important in the light of the tendency of scholars of former generations to limit Septuagint citations largely to these two codices. Thus Hatch-Redpath's well-known Concordance to the Septuagint is based principally on these two mss. Or if one reads the apparatus to the text of Numbers in Ra it is clear that except for an occasional hex reading Rahlfs limited himself to variants in A & B including the text of their correctors.

It should be said that this last-named practice is a most unfortunate one, particularly with reference to readings from B. The corrections in B are much later than B*, and only first hand corrections deserve to be cited. Bᶜ should be regarded as an independent witness within the text history and not as an adjunct to B. Accordingly readings of Aᶜ and Bᶜ are disregarded in this essay. I have discussed the text of the B correctors in Numbers elsewhere (in a Festschrift for R. J. Williams).

A. The text of Numbers has been copied far more carefully by the B scribe than was the case in Deuteronomy (cf THGD 48f). The following list presents a list of errors in B caused by homoioteleuton or homoiarchon.

List 1

3₁₈ αὐτῶν] ⌒(19) Bᵗˣᵗ 16-46 127ᵗˣᵗ 509 628 ᴸᵃᵗcod 100
4₁₅ ἅγια 1°] ⌒2° Bᵗˣᵗ 528 18 Bo
4₂₅ μαρτυρίου] ⌒(26) Bᵗˣᵗ 707ᵗˣᵗ C⁻¹³¹ᵐᵍ-46-552ᵗˣᵗ-615-761ᵗˣᵗ 458 71
5₁₈ τὴν θυσίαν 1°] ⌒2° B* 130-321′
8₃ om καθά — fin Bᵗˣᵗ
11₃₁ ἐντεῦθεν 1°] ⌒2° B* 618ᵗˣᵗ C⁻¹³¹ᵐᵍ-46 458-767 407 55 319 799
13₃₀ καί ult] ⌒(31) 1° B*
14₃₇ ἄνθρωποι οἱ] om οἱ B*
15₉ τοῦ ἵν] ⌒(10) Bᵗˣᵗ C-46-57* 19 75′ 343 509 121 68′-120 319
16₇ ἐπίθετε 1°] ⌒2° Bᵗˣᵗ 29 46-320 30′ 84 392
16₉ κυρίου — συναγωγῆς 2°] bis scr B
19₁₂ τῇ 6°] bis scr B*
19₁₉ ἑβδόμῃ 1°] ⌒2° Bᵗˣᵗ 500-761 314 d 53′ 85ᵗˣᵗ-343 t 59 Eus VI 12
21₁₈ ἐν 1°] ⌒2° B* 319 Aeth
27₁₃ καί 1°] ⌒2° B*(vid)
28₁₄ ἵν 1°] ⌒2° Bᵗˣᵗ
30₁₅ om ἤ — (16) ἡμέραν B*
33₅₃ ἐν 2°] ⌒(54) Bᵗˣᵗ 106 53-246 84 Arm
35₂₄ αἷμα] ⌒(25) B* 16-528 53′ 126-128-669 319 Arabᵗˣᵗ
36₆ γυναῖκες 1°] ⌒2° Bᵗˣᵗ 528-616ᵗˣᵗ 767 x⁻⁵⁰⁹ 318 628 ᴸᵃᵗcod 104 Aethᶠ

Compared to Deuteronomy the B text of Numbers is carefully copied; copyist errors due to homoioteleuton or homoiarchon are infrequent.

This conclusion is also confirmed by the fact that there obtain relatively few unique readings in B. The following list presents these readings for Numbers. By unique reading is meant a reading found only in B as far as the Greek evidence is concerned.

List 2

1:6 Σουρισαδαί] σουρεισαδαι B
1:14 Ἐλισάφ] ελεισαφ B
1:47 πατριᾶς] pr της B*
2:2 σημέας] σημιας B*
2:16 τῆς] pr εκ B*
2:18 om υἱός B* Aeth[M]
2:21 διακόσιοι] τετρακοσιοι B*
2:26 ἑπτακόσιοι] πεντακοσιοι B*
3:27 Ἰσααρίς] σαριεις B*
3:33 Μοολί] μολει B*
3:35 Ἀβιχάιλ] αβειχαιλ B
4:18 Λευιτῶν] πολειτων B*
4:31 αὐτῶν 2°] των B*
5:6 πλημμελήσῃ] pr πλημμελων B*
5:18 ὁ ἱερεὺς / τὴν γυναῖκα] tr B
5:21 ὅρκοις] λογοις B
6:6 τετελευτηκυίᾳ] -κυιη B
7:15 κριόν] pr και B* Aeth Bo
7:17 κριούς] pr και B* Aeth Bo
7:30 Σεδιούρ] εδισουρ B*
7:60 Γαδεωνί] γαδαιωνει B
7:88 τράγοι ἑξήκοντα] post ἑξήκοντα 3° tr B*
8:13 om καί 2° B*
8:19 om ἐν 2° B
8:26 ἐργάται] εργαζεται B*
9:1 Σινά] σεινα B*
9:5 Σινά] σεινα B*
10:12 Σινά] σεινα B*
10:20 Ἐλισάφ] ελεισαφ B
10:36 ἐν] pr και B*
11:6 om οὐδέν B*
11:16 οἶδας] οιδες B*
11:20 ὑμῶν] + κρεα B*
11:21 Μωυσῆς] + προς κν B* Lat cod 100 Arab
11:21 αὐτοῖς 2°] + φαγειν B = Ra
11:33 ἐπάταξεν κύριος] tr B*
13:5 Σαμού] σαμουηλ B Syh
13:13 Ἀμιήλ] αμειηλ B
13:20 ἀτειχίστοις] ατιχισταις B*
13:24 συκῶν] σικνων B*
14:1 φωνήν] φωνη B Lat cod 100 Aeth
14:13 ἀνήγαγες] ηγαγες B*
15:16 om ὑμῖν 1° B*
15:31 τὸ ῥῆμα] τα ρηματα B*
15:33 συλλέγοντα] -ντες B*

15:39 om ὑμεῖς B*
16:3 ἐπί 1°] οπισω B*
16:7 ἂν ἐκλέξηται] εκλεγεται B*(vid)
16:14 κλῆρον] καιρον B
16:33 αὐτοῖς] αυτων B Lat cod 100 = Ra
16:38 λεπίδας] -δες B*
16:40 προσέλθη] -θητε B*
16:48 θραῦσις] + εν τω λαω B*
17:9 ἔλαβον] εβαλεν B
18:8 τῶν 1°] αυτων B*
19:14 οἰκίᾳ 1°] pr τη B*
19:18 ὕσσωπον] -πιον B*
20:22 om ἡ B*
21:1 Χανανίς] χανανεις B
21:1 Ἀθαρίμ] -ρειν B Sa[4]
21:5 ἵνα τί] + τουτο B
21:7 ἀφ' — fin] sup ras B
21:11 Ἀχελγαί] χαλγλει B
21:13 ἐξέχον] εξον B*
21:20 νάπην] ιανην B
21:23 Ἰάσσα] εισσα B*
22:9 πρός] παρα B*
22:23 ὁδοῦ] + αυτης B*
22:36 ἥ ἐστιν] ητις B*(vid)
22:36 ὁρίων 1° 2°] ορειων B*
22:37 ὄντως / οὐ δυνήσομαι] tr B
24:1 om αὐτοῦ B*
24:4 ὕπνῳ] + ras 1—2 litt B
24:22 Ἀσσύριοί] συριοι B*
25:7 Φινεές] φεινεες B Sa[1]
25:11 υἱοῦ] υιος B* Lat cod 100
25:14 Μαδιανίτιδος] μαδειανειτιδος B*
25:14 Σαλώ] σαλμων B Bo
26:5 Φαλλού] φαυλου B
26:17 ἐγένοντο] -νετο B*
26:18 δῆμοι] δημω B*
26:19 Φουά] φουει B*
26:20 Σαμράμ] σαμαραμ B*
26:20 Σαμραμί] σαμαρανει B*
26:29 Μελχιήλ] μελλιηλ B*
26:29 Μελχιηλί] μελλιηλει B*
26:34 Ἀχιεζερί] αχιεζειρει B
26:48 Ἀσιήλ] σαηλ B*
26:48 Ἀσιηλί] σαηλει B*
26:49 Σελλήμ] σελλη B
26:50 τεσσαράκοντα] τριακοντα B*
26:61 Σινά] σεινα B*

27₁₄ Καδής] pr εν B Aeth Bo
28₆ Σινά] σεινα B; σει[... 963
28₈ κυρίῳ] κ̅υ̅ B*
28₁₅ κυρίῳ 963] κ̅υ̅ B*
28₁₉ om ἑπτά Bᵗˣᵗ
28₂₄ κυρίῳ] κ̅υ̅ B*
29₆ τὸ ὁλοκαύτωμα τό] τα ολοκαυτωματα B*
29₁₂ κυρίῳ 963] κ̅υ̅ B*
29₁₃ κυρίῳ] κ̅υ̅ B*
29₃₆ κυρίῳ] κ̅υ̅ B*
30₉ ἄν] εαν B*
30₁₂ καὶ παρασιωπήσῃ 963] > B*
31₄ χιλίους 1°] χειλιοι B*
31₄₂ τοῦ 963] > B*
32₁ πλῆθος 1°] pr ras 2 litt B
32₄ παρέδωκεν] παραδεδωκεν B
32₂₄ τῇ ἀποσκευῇ] την αποσκευην B*

32₂₄ ποιήσετε] pr τουτο B*
32₃₆ Ναμβρά] ναμραμ B
32₃₇ Ἐλεαλή] λεαλημ B*
32₃₈ om τήν 2° B*
33₂₀ Ῥεμμών] ραμμων B
33₃₀ Μασουρούθ] μασσουρωθ B
34₅ τὰ ὅρια] α ορεια B*
34₉ Ζεφρώνα] δεφρωνα B* = Ra
34₉ Ἀσερναίν] αρσεναειμ B*
34₁₂ ἔσται ὑμῖν] tr B
34₂₅ Ἐλισαφάν] ελεισαφαν B
34₂₆ Φαλτιήλ] φαλτειηλ B
34₂₈ Βεναμιούδ] βενιαμειουδ B*
34₂₉ οὗτοι οἷς] τουτοις B
35₁₄ γῆ] pr τη B
35₂₈ om καί B*
35₃₀ ψυχήν 2°] ψυχης B

It is clear from the brevity of this list that the text of Numbers has been much more carefully copied than that of Deuteronomy. Many of the variants obtain in the spelling of proper names in which B is notoriously inexact elsewhere as well. It should be noted that the B copyist commonly spelled ι as ει in proper names, e.g. σεινα, ελεισαφ, αμειηλ, φαλτειηλ. This particular itacism will not be recorded in the next list, which is an expansion of list 2 through variants which are almost unique to B. By almost unique is meant support by no more than three Greek witnesses beyond that of B. The purpose of this list is to discover whether there are any close relatives to B in the text tradition. It will of course also give some further insight into the character of B's textual aberrancy.

List 3

1₄ κατ' οἴκους] pr και B* 128
1₅ Ῥουβήν] pr νιων B* V Lᵃᵗcod 100 Arab
1₄₅ σύν] εν B* 58-72 59
2₈ αὐτοῦ] αυτων B 246ᶜ¹ 509-527
3₃₂ καθεσταμένος] κατεστ. (-μμενος 71) B G 71
3₄₀ λάβε 803] λαβετε B F 71
3₄₁ om ἐν τοῖς κτήνεσιν Bᵗˣᵗ 669(1°)
3₄₃ διακόσιοι] -σιαι B 414
3₄₅ λάβε] λαβετε B* 127
3₄₆ τριῶν] τρεις B* 376
3₄₆ διακοσίων] -σιοι B* 376
4₁₅ οὐχ] ουκ B* 58 30 318
4₄₆ om καί 2° B*(||) 73*(c pr m)
4₄₆ om αὐτῶν 1° B x⁻⁶¹⁹ Lᵃᵗcod 104(vid) = Ra
4₄₆ om αὐτῶν 2° B 71 Lᵃᵗcod 104
5₃ οὐ] + μη B Cyr I 977 = Ra
5₄ om τῷ B 509
5₁₃ ἤ 2° 963] ην B Cyr I 909 = Ra

6₂₆ ἐπιφάναι 963] pr και B* 121 Lᵃᵗcod 100 FirmMat *Consult* II 5 Aeth Arab Arm
7₂₀ πλήρη 963] -ρης B S 84 59
7₂₉ τράγους πέντε 963] > Bᵗˣᵗ F*(c pr m) 30-343
7₆₂ πλήρη] -ρης B 707 84
7₆₇ πλήρη 963] -ρης B 707 767 84
7₈₄ om τῶν ἀρχόντων B* 319
7₈₇ βόες] + αι B 318; cf βοαι αι 799
7₈₈ ἐγκαίνισις] -νωσις (ενκ. 509) B 426 509 = Ra
8₂₂ καθά] καθως B* 58-72 59 = Ra
8₂₅ ἐργάται] εργαζεται B 130
9₁₈ om καί B* 509-619 Sa
9₂₁ om καί 4° — (22) ἤ B 129 71-509 Sa = Ra
10₂₉ Ὡβάβ] οβαβ B 343 71 799 Procop 817
11₃₂ ἔψυξαν] εσφαξαν B 509
11₃₃ λαόν] + αυτου B* 44

12₄ om παραχρῆμα B* 618ᵗˣᵗ 126
12₄ om εἰς 1° B 72 59
12₁₂ om καί B* 799 Bo
13₅ Ζακχούρ] ζακχυρ B 509
13₂₂ Ἐμάθ] εφααθ B 376 509 Latcod 100 Sa¹ = Ra
13₂₄ κλῆμα] κληματα B 509 319
13₃₃ τῆς γῆς] pr επι B* 610
14₁ ἔδωκεν] ενεδωκεν B 130ᶜ-346ᵐᵍ 319
14₁₀ om ἐν λίθοις B* 126
14₁₄ σὺ πορεύῃ] συνπορευη B* 129; cf συμπορευη Bᶜ 376
15₁₅ om τάς B 129 509 = Ra
15₂₅ ἐξιλάσεται] + περι αυτου B* 19; cf + περι αυτω 458
15₃₃ om αὐτόν 2° B 129 Arm
15₃₆ ἐλιθοβόλησαν] -σεν B 767 527'
16₁₇ θυμίαμα] θυμιαματα B* 72*
16₄₆ ἐξίλασαι] εξ(ε)ιλασεται B* 126
16₄₇ ἐνῆρκτο] -κται B* 29 106ᶜ
17₂ om αὐτοῦ 2° B Cyr I 672
17₅ ἄν] εαν B 129 = Ra
18₁ om καί 4° B* V 246 458
18₈ Ἀαρών] ααρων B(|) 610*
18₉ om αὐτῶν 2° B* 72
18₁₈ om καθά B* 318
18₂₈ om κυρίῳ B 319 Latcod 100 Arab
18₃₀ ἅλωνος] αλω B G 71 Cyr I 844 = Ra
20₁ πρώτῳ] τριτω B* 106
20₅ ἀνηγάγετε] -γαγες B* 129 Latcod 100
20₅ τὸν πονηρόν Fᵃ] > B* F 59
20₈ τὴν συναγωγήν 1°] τη συναγωγη B 509
20₂₈ om αὐτά B* 381' 71 Latcod 100 Aeth
21₄ om τήν B 82 54-75 = Ra
21₂₄ μαχαίρας] -ρης B*(vid) 129 = Ra
22₆ ἄν 1°] εαν B 376 458 = Ra
22₆ ἄν 2°] εαν B 376 458 = Ra
22₈ ἄν] εαν B 376 Cyr I 440 = Ra
22₁₅ ἔτι] post Βαλάκ tr B 29 = Ra
22₂₉ om μου B 426
23₈ ἀράσομαι] -σωμαι B 75-767 = Ra
23₈ καταράσομαι] -σωμαι B 767* 30 = Ra
23₂₂ om ὁ 1° B(|) 509 = Ra

24₆ παράδεισοι] -σος B* Eus VI 18 409
24₁₁ ἐστέρησέν] -ρεσεν B* 509
25₇ υἱοῦ] υς B 509
25₁₅ Ὀμμώθ] ομμοθ B 82-426 Sa¹¹
26₂₆ Ἀροαδί 1° 2°] αροδει B* 71
26₃₄ Χελεκί] χελεγει B 129 407 Arm; cf χελεγι 71 = Ra
26₃₅ Συχεμί] συχεμεει B* 82
26₃₆ om τῷ 2° B 82 509
26₄₂ Ἀχιράν] ιαχειραν B V 509
26₄₂ Ἀχιρανί] ιαχειρανει B V
26₄₄ Νοεμάν 1°] νοεμανει B 129 30*
26₆₀ ἐγεννήθησαν] εγενηθησαν B 58 71
27₈ ᾗ] ην B 71
27₁₂ πέραν] περα B* 799
27₁₄ οὐχ] ουκ B* 767 30 392
31₂₃ om ὅ B* 730
31₂₃ ἄν] εαν B* G = Ra
31₃₀ ἡμίσους] -συς B* G 392
31₃₀ τοῦ 2°] τουτων B* 53'
31₃₆ ἑπτακισχίλια] πεντακισχ(ε)ιλιαι B* 407
31₃₇ ἑξακόσια] -σιοι B*(vid) 376 528 527
32₁₃ κατερρέμβευσεν] κατερομβ. (-σαν G*) B G
32₁₇ προφυλακῇ] -κην B V 82 Cyr I 404
32₄₂ Κανάθ] κααθ B 16-46 56
33₇ Εἰρώθ] επιρωθ B* 129 319 Arm
33₈ om αὐτοί B* 72 77 799 Bo
33₁₃ Αἰλούς] αιλειμ B 509-619
33₁₄ Αἰλούς] αιλειμ B 71'
33₃₃ Ἑτεβάθα] σετεβαθα B* 54' 619 Latcod 100
33₃₄ ἐξ Ἑτεβάθα] εκ σετεβαθα B* 246 54' Latcod 100
33₄₄ πέραν] περα B* 799
33₅₀ om λέγων B* 44 Arab
34₄ Σέννα] εννακ B 68'-120
34₁₁ Χενέρεθ] χεναρα B 376 509 Latcodd 100 104(vid) Arm Bo = Ra
35₁₄ om τάς 1° B* 528
35₁₅ καί 2° 963] > B* 509 319
36₁₀ τῷ Μωυσῇ] om τῷ B 527 = Ra

As might well be expected an examination of list 3 yields no clear results. If one disregards all correspondence occurring five times or less, the following results obtain: B and 509 agree 20 times; B and 71, 13 times; further agreements in descending order of frequency are: 129, ten times; 376, eight times; 72 and 319, six times, and Cyril, six times. That two members of the x group should head the group is not surprising in view of what was said about that group in chapter 1. Ms 129 belongs to the f group but it frequently diverges from it; when it does it often goes with B. That Cyril's text should be a B type text is particularly interesting since Cyril was an Alexandrian.

In Deuteronomy it was noted that there were traces of recensional activity present in the B text. In the list below I give the instances where the text of B corresponds to 𝔐 over against Num. Should the reading of B be attested in Apparatus II that equation is given together with the source(s). Otherwise the text of 𝔐 is given for comparison.

List 4

1₂₁ ἐπίσκεψις] επισκοπη B *O n x*⁻⁵⁰⁹ 18 319: = *o′* 85′-344

1₄₇ οὐ συνεπεσκέπησαν] ουκ (ου G) επεσκ. (επισκ. 53) B *O*⁻⁵⁸ *f* 75 *x*⁻⁵²⁷ 319 = Ra: = *α′ σ′ ϑ′* 85′-344 et *o′* 344

2₁₀ σὺν δυνάμει] δυναμις B G-426 54′-75ᶜ Arm (pr *et*) Syh: = *o′* 344

2₃₁ σὺν δυνάμει αὐτῶν] sub ÷ Syhᵀ; > B V *O*⁻⁵⁸-707 *b f*⁻²⁴⁶ *x* 392 Cyr I 724 ᴸᵃᵗcod 100 Aeth Arab Co Syhᴸ = Ra 𝔐

3₁₅ κατὰ συγγενείας αὐτῶν (πᾶν)] sub ÷ G Syh; > B *x* 55 Aethᶜ Arab Sa: כל 𝔐

3₁₆ ἐπεσκέψατο] -ψαντο B M′ *O* 106-125′ 767 *t* Aeth Arab Arm Bo Syh = Ra: = *o′* 344

4₃ ἕως] pr και B F M′ V 833 *O*-29-707 19 *d*⁻¹²⁵ *t x*⁻⁶¹⁹ 392 *z* 59 799 Syh = Ra: ועד 𝔐

4₁₄ λειτουργοῦσιν] + επ αυτο (αυτω Cyr) B V *O*⁻⁵⁸ *x*⁻⁶¹⁹ Cyr I 852 Arm Syh = Ra: ישרתו עלין 𝔐

4₂₃ καὶ (ποιεῖν)] > B *x*⁻⁶¹⁹ Arm Sa: לעבד 𝔐

4₄₆ κατ′ οἴκους] pr και B Aeth: ולבית 𝔐

5₁₀ καὶ (ἀνήρ)] > B* = Ra: איש 𝔐ᴸ

6₂₁ τὸν (νόμον) 963] > B M′ V 16-46 19 130-321′ *x*⁻⁶¹⁹ 319 Cyr I 1053 = Ra: תורת 𝔐

7₁₂ τῇ ἡμέρᾳ] pr εν B Cyr I 705: ביום 𝔐

8₆ τῶν (υἱῶν) 963] > B *O*⁻⁵⁸ *d*⁻⁶¹⁰ 127-767 *t*⁻⁸⁴ 509 55 319 = Ra: בני 𝔐

10₁₂ τοῦ (Σινά)] > B V *O*⁻⁵⁸ 44′-125 *x*⁻⁶¹⁹ = Ra: סיני 𝔐

13₂₈ εἰς (ἥν)] > B 46-413-550′ 610 *x*⁻⁵⁰⁹ 799: אשר 𝔐

14₂₂ (καὶ ἐν τῇ ἐρήμῳ) ταύτῃ] sub ÷ G Syh; > B 58 *x* Aethᶜᴳ Arab Co: ובמדבר 𝔐

14₃₅ ἦ μήν] ει μη B* Arm: אם לא 𝔐

16₉ ὑμᾶς / ὁ θεὸς Ἰσραήλ] tr B *O*⁻⁵⁸ *d* 129 127 *t* 509 Cyr I 860 Syh = Ra: אלהי ישראל אתכם 𝔐

18₃ (τῆς σκηνῆς) σου] sub ÷ Syhᵀ; > B V 58-82 *x*⁻⁵²⁷ *z*⁻¹²⁶⁶²⁸ 319 646 Aethᶜᴳ Sa = Ra: האהל 𝔐

21₅ (ἀποκτεῖναι) ἡμᾶς] > B V 381′-426 767 71-509 55 Cyr I 384: למות 𝔐

21₅ (τῷ διακένῳ) τούτῳ] sub ~ Syhᴸ; > B 29-426-707* 16-46 71-509 68′-120′ Arab Arm Sa = Ra: הקלקל 𝔐

21₁₃ καὶ (ἐκεῖθεν)] > B *O*⁻⁵⁸-82 *C*′′⁻⁵²′³¹³⁴¹⁷ *d*⁻⁴⁴ 53′-129 *n*⁻⁴⁵⁸ *t x*⁻⁶¹⁹ 68′-120′ Arab Armᵗᵉ Syhᵀ: משם 𝔐

21₁₆ (τοῦτό) ἐστιν Fᵇ] > B F 82-426-707* *f n*⁻⁴⁵⁸ 71-509 392 Aeth⁻ᶜᴳ Syh: הוא 𝔐

21₂₄ Ἀμμάν 2°] αμμων B V 426 *b* 246 767 30′ 18 319 ᴸᵃᵗcod 100 Arab Syh = Ra: עמון 𝔐

21₂₆ τῶν Ἀμορραίων] + εστιν B *O*⁻⁵⁸ 129 509 Syh: האמרי הוא 𝔐

22₂₈ πεποίηκάς] εποιησα B *O*⁻⁵⁸ 106 *n t* 527 = Ra: = *o′ οἱ λ′* 344

24₈ ὁ (θεός)] > B V 82-426 *d*⁻⁴⁴ *t* 71-509 319 Eus VI 409 Or IV 250 = Ra: אל 𝔐

25₄ τοὺς ἀρχηγούς] pr παντας B Fᵃ *O*⁻⁵⁸-82 *d* 53′ *n* 130ᵐᵍ *t* 71-509 799 Phil III 223 Cyr I 908 IV 300 ᴸᵃᵗcodd 91 92 94—96 100 Co Syh = Ra: = *o′ϑ′* 344

28₂₀ (καὶ) ἡ (θυσία αὐτῶν)] > B *oI*⁻¹⁵ Cyr I 1088: ומבההם 𝔐

35₃₂ τῶν (φυγαδευτηρίων) 963] > B* V 53′-129: מקלטו 𝔐

36₃ τὴν (κληρονομίαν)] > B V G-82-426 *d* 129 *n t x* 319 = Ra: נחלת 𝔐

Not all of the instances in the above list are due to Hebrew influence. Particularly omissions which happen to correspond to 𝔐 may well be due to coincidence. Thus the omission of an article at 6₂₁ 8₆ 36₃ only formally corresponds to 𝔐 and the correspondence has no significance. On the other hand, a number of instances in the list are clearly hex in origin. This certainly applies to the additions in 4₃ ₁₄ 21₂₆ 25₄ as well as to the change in word order at 16₉. The text of B is not entirely free from hex influence, but it is not an important factor; the text of B remains indeed the best witness to Num that we have.

B. Before comparing the text of B to that of A an investigation into the peculiarities of the A text would seem appropriate.

It should be noted that the ms contains a large number of readings sup ras. These readings are not included in the subsequent discussion.

List 5 presents unique readings of A; as in the case of list 2 uniqueness applies here only to the primary Greek tradition.

List 5

1₂₁ om ἐκ — Ῥουβήν A*
1₃₂ Μανασσή] μανν. A Latcod 100
1₄₉ υἱῶν Ἰσραήλ] των αδελφων αυτων A*
2₃ οἵ] ουτοι A*
2₃ om καὶ ὁ ἄρχων A*
2₆ τέσσαρες] τεσσερες A
2₁₄ φυλή] φυ A
2₁₇ μέσον] pr ανα A
2₂₉ Αἰνάν] αιμαν A
3₄ om Ἀαρών A*
3₉ μοί] μονοι A
3₁₅ Λευί] ααρων A*(vid)
3₂₀ υἱοί] pr ουτοι A Latcod 100
3₃₀ om ὁ A*
3₃₉ μηνιαίον] μηνιου A*
3₅₀ om σίκλους A = 𝔐
4₃ εἴκοσι καὶ πέντε ἐτῶν] εικοσαετους A; sed cf x̄ ετους 458
4₁₃ init — ἐπιθήσει] και επιθησεις τον καλυπτηρα A
4₁₈ ὀλεθρεύσητε] εξολεθρ. A
4₃₁ fin] + της σκηνης A
4₄₀ om init — αὐτῶν 1° A
4₄₀ δισχίλιοι] bis scr A*
4₄₈ ὀγδοήκοντα] και πεντηκοντα A
4₄₉ ἐπεσκέψατο] pr ους A
5₂ παρεμβολῆς] συναγωγης A
5₄ om αὐτούς A
6₄ πάντων] πασων A
6₅ ὅσας 963] ας A
6₁₂ ὅτι] οτε A
7₂ παρεστηκότες] παραστηκοντες A
7₆ Λευίταις] λευιτας A*
7₂₀ om δέκα χρυσῶν Atxt
7₆₂ χρυσῶν] χρυσω A*
7₆₉ ἐνιαύσιον] + αμωμον A
7₇₇ om τό A*
7₈₆ θυμιάματος] + φιαλαι αργυραι δωδεκα (δεκα δεκα pro φ.α.δ.*) η θυισκη εν τω σικλω των αγιων A
8₄ om αὐτῆς 1° A
8₇ ἁγνισμόν 963] αγνιασμον A

8₇ πᾶν 963] > A
9₁₅ σκηνῆς] γης A
9₂₂ παρεμβαλοῦσιν] -λωσιν A
10₃₂ ὅσα] α A
10₃₃ τοῦ ὄρους] τους ορους A*
11₂ om ὁ λαός A*
11₁₀ ἐπὶ τῆς θύρας] κατα την θυραν A
11₁₀ Μωυσῆ] κ̄ῡ A*(c pr m)
11₁₂ ἔτεκον] τετοκα A
12₁₀ Ἀαρών] αρων A*
13₁₅ Ναβί] ναβα A
13₁₇ υἱόν] υιος A
13₂₂ κατεσκέψαντο] -ψατο A*
13₂₃ Ἀχιμάν] αχικαμ A
13₂₃ Σεσί] σεμει A
14₃ ἔσονται] post διαρπαγήν tr A
14₁₁ σημείοις] θαυμασιοις A
15₁₂ om ἄν A
15₁₆ τῷ 1°] πρω A
16₆ αὐτοῦ] εαυτου A
16₄₆ om ὀργή A*(vid)
17₃ Ἀαρών] αυτου A
18₂ om σοι 1° A
18₁₅ πᾶν] πας A
18₃₂ οὐ λήμψεσθε] ουτοι λημφονται A
19₁₁ ἡμέρας] + εως εσπερας Amg
19₁₈ τόν 2°] του A
19₁₉ τρίτη] + επι τα A
20₁₅ ἡμέρας πλείους] post Αἰγύπτιοι tr A
20₁₉ παρελευσόμεθα 2°] πορευομεθα A
21₁₆ om συνάγαγε τὸν λαόν A
21₂₂ om τῇ A
21₃₂ κατελάβοντο] -βετο A Armap Co
22₁₀ αὐτούς] αγγελους A
22₂₁ ἀρχόντων] ανδρων A
22₃₈ τὸ στόμα] την καρδιαν A
23₉ βουνῶν] pr των A
23₉ om οὐ A AethM
24₁ εὐλογεῖν] ευλογει A*
24₄ θεοῦ 1°] + ισχυρου A
25₁₈ ἀδελφήν] pr την A
26₁ Μωυσῆν] + λεγων A

71

26₁₇ Ἀσρών] αστρων A
26₃₈ ἑπτακόσιοι] πεντακοσιοι A
26₃₉ Σουτάλα] θωσουσαλα A
26₃₉ Σουταλαΐ] θουσαλαι A
26₄₆ Σαμί 1°] σαμειδη A
26₄₆ Σαμί 2°] σαμειδηι A
26₄₆ οὗτοι] ουτω A*
27₇ ὀρθῶς 963] pr ως A
27₁₈ ἐπιθήσεις 963] -σει A*
28₁₄ αὐτῶν] αυτω A
28₁₇ τούτου 963] + ποιηθησεται A
28₁₉ om ἄμωμοι A
28₂₂ om περὶ ἁμαρτίας A
29₂₁ αὐτῶν 1°] ⌒2° A
30₈ ἀνήρ] πηρ A*
30₁₄ ψυχήν 963] αυτην A
31₈ ῥομφαίᾳ] -φαιαις A Latcod 100
31₁₇ ἀποκτείνατε 2°] -κτενειτε A
31₂₂ χαλκοῦ] καλκου A
31₂₃ διελεύσεται 2°] pr ον A
32₄ γῆ κτηνοτρόφος] tr A
32₇ διαβῆναι 963] αναβηναι A
32₁₄ ἐπὶ Ἰσραήλ 963] επ ισραηλ A
32₁₆ ἀποσκευαῖς] κατασκ. A
32₁₇ ἑαυτῶν] -τω A

32₂₁ ἕως] ως A
32₂₆ καί 1° — ἡμῶν 2°] post ἡμῶν 3° tr A
32₂₉ Γάδ 963] γαλααδ A
32₃₅ Σωφάρ] pr γην A
32₃₆ Βαιθαράν] -ρρα A
32₃₆ om καί ult A
32₃₈ καί 1°] pr και την βαμω A
33₆ Σοκχώθ] σοκχω A
33₉ ὑδάτων] bis scr A
33₁₁ om Σίν A(|)
33₁₂ om Σίν A(|)
33₅₆ ποιῆσαι] ποιησεται A
34₃ λίβα 1° 963] βορρα A
34₆ τὰ ὅρια 2° 963] το οριον A = 𝔐
34₁₇ ὁ τοῦ] υιος A
34₂₄ Σαβαθά] -θαν A
35₂₁ ἀποκτενεῖ] παταξει A
35₂₅ ἀποκαταστήσουσιν — συναγωγή 2°] post φυγαδευτηρίου tr A
35₃₃ οὐκ ἐξιλασθήσεται] ου μη εξιλ. A
36₂ κύριος δοῦναι] tr A
36₇ καί 963] > A
36₉ om οὐ A
36₁₂ ἐγενήθησαν] + αυτοις A Bo

The list of unique readings is not particularly large. Many of the readings are easily identified as copyist errors and are of no significance. Of more interest is an expanded list in which random support up to three Greek witnesses join A. This list might give indication of possible close textual relatives within the tradition. List 6 gives these instances.

List 6

1₁₀ Μανασσῆ] μανν. A 458 121
1₁₈ om τήν A 72
1₃₃ Μανασσῆ] μανν. A 121 Latcod 100
1₅₀ om καί ult A 59 319 Bo
2₄ ἐπεσκεμμένοι] ηριθμημενοι (ηρθ. M) A Mmg 121
2₆ ἐπεσκεμμένοι] ηριθμημενοι (ηρθ. M) A Mmg 121
2₁₅ ἐπεσκεμμένοι] ηριθμημενοι A 121 319
2₁₇ τῶν 2° Fa] > A* F
2₁₇ ἐξαροῦσιν] αναζευξουσι(ν) A 118mg 121 319
2₂₀ Μανασσῆ 1°] μανν. A 121 Latcod 100
2₂₀ Μανασσῆ 2°] μανν. A 458 121 Latcod 100
2₂₅ Ἀμισαδαί] σαμισαδαι A 59
3₃ οἱ 2°] pr και A 121
3₁₃ ἡγίασα] -σας A 376 121
3₁₅ ἐπίσκεψαι] -ψετε A* 121
3₂₇ Ἀμραμίς] αμβρααμεις A 126
3₃₄ om πᾶν ἀρσενικόν A* 414
4₂ Καάθ] καθ A 343 509

4₁₄ διεμβαλοῦσιν] εμβαλουσι(ν) A 121 126 59
4₃₂ κάλους] κλαδους A 121txt
5₁₃ ἤ 1° Fb] pr μη A F 55 799
5₁₉ ὑπό] προς A Chr II 917
7₁₂ τῇ 1° — πρώτῃ] post αὐτοῦ tr A 126 Arm Bo
7₅₄ Μανασσή] μανν. A 127 121
9₁₂ συντρίψουσιν] -ψεται A 767
9₁₃ ποιῆσαι] pr του A 318
9₁₃ προσήνεγκεν] -γκαν A* 28 121
10₆ om παρά A 72
10₂₃ Μανασσῆ] μανν. A 121
10₂₉ Μαδιανίτῃ] -νιτι A 318
12₈ κυρίου] μου A Cyr II 592
12₁₀ ἀπέστη] απηλθεν A 376
12₁₂ γένηται] γενοιτο A Phil I 81ap
12₁₅ ἐκαθαρίσθη] καθερισθη A 72
13₄ ἐξαπέστειλεν] απεστ. A 126
13₅ Σαμού] σαμαλιηλ A 72-618 19
13₅ Ζακχούρ] ζαχρου A 121
13₂₀ αὐτῆς] αυτην A 121

14₃₁ ἔσεσθαι] εσονται A V 75 319 Aeth
Arm Syh
14₃₃ ὑμῶν 2°] αυτων A 121
14₃₆ περί] επι A 125 527
15₂ κατοικήσεως] κατασχεσεως A 458 121
15₆ θυσίαν 1°] ⌒2° A 707ᵗˣᵗ 416
15₂₀ ἀπαρχήν] -χων A 121
15₂₆ τῷ 2°] pr και A 121 55
17₈ ἐξήνεγκεν] εξηνθησεν A 55
19₁₂ ἔσται 1°] εστιν A 121 59
19₁₈ τραυματίου] -ματος A 121
20₅ σπείρεται] σπερειται (-τε 56) A 56* 121
20₁₉ τε] δε A 55
21₁₄ λέγεται] λεγετε A 120
21₁₈ Μανθαναίν] -νιν A 52-414 55* Arm
21₂₂ ἀμπελῶνα] + σου A 121
21₃₀ ἀπολεῖται] -λειτε A 376 509
22₆ ἄρασαί] καταρασαι A 121
22₆ εὐλογήσῃς] ευλογης A 121
22₈ ῥήματα] πραγμα A 426*(c pr m) Cyr
I 440
22₁₈ Βαλαάμ] βαλαμ A 118′ Latcod 100
22₁₈ om καί 2° — Βαλάκ 1° A* 125
22₁₈ καί 3°] η A 55
22₂₂ om καί αὐτὸς ἐπιβεβήκει A 121ᵗˣᵗ
22₂₉ εἰ Fᵇ] η A F 376
22₃₀ om σου 1° A 29 319
23₃ εἴ μοι] εμοι A* 59*
24₁ οἰωνοῖς] ονοις (ων. A) A* 318
24₂₁ Καιναῖον] καινεον A Mᵗˣᵗ 30
26₂₀ Σαμράμ] αμβραν A 75 619
26₂₆ om τῷ 2° — fin A 707 509 121
26₃₂ Μανασσή] μανν. A 75′ 121 Latcod 100
26₃₃ idem A V 458 121 Latcod 100
26₃₈ idem A 75 121 Latcod 100
26₄₀ Σουτάλα 963(vid)] θουσαλα A 53′ 68
26₄₂ Ἀχιρανί] αχιραι A 318

26₆₃ οἵ] οτι A 121
27₁ Μανασσή 963] μανν. A 458 121
27₁₁ om Ἰσραήλ A 73′
28₇ σπονδήν 1°] σπονδη A 55
28₂₃ om τῆς 2° A 44 121
29₈ ἄμωμοι] αμωμους A 129 121
30₃ κυρίῳ] pr τω A 739 767
30₆ πάσας 963] > A V 129-246
30₁₀ ὅσα ἄν] οσαν A 59
30₁₅ om τούς 2° A 730
31₂₂ χρυσίου] et ἀργυρίου tr A 127 121 Bo
32₂ ἄρχοντας] ανδρας A 392
32₁₁ om τῷ A 121
32₂₀ ἐξοπλίσησθε 963] -πλισθησεσθε (c var)
A 59 319
32₂₂ om καί 4° A 321′ 628 Aeth
32₃₂ γῆν] pr την A 392 18-628
32₃₃ Μανασσή] μανν. A 458 121 Latcod 100
32₃₉ ₄₀ ₄₁ idem A 458 121
32₄₂ Κανάθ] κααναθ A 121
33₃₂ om τό A 121
34₈ Σαραδά] σαδαδακ A 29-58 55
34₁₃ Μανασσή] μανν. A 246 458 121 Latcod
100
34₁₄ idem A 246 458 121
34₁₇ om ὑμῖν A 126 Sa
34₂₂ Ἐγλί] εκλι A 30′ Latcod 104
34₂₃ Μανασσή] μανν. A 246 121
34₂₇ Ἀχιώρ] αχιωβ A 121 68′
35₃ om καί 3° — fin A 72 126 59 Arab:
homoiot
35₂₅ αὐτοῦ 963] > A 707 84 Cyr I 581
VII 625 Aeth Arm
36₁ Μανασσή] μανν. A 75 121
36₃ προστεθήσεται] -σονται A 129
36₈ om ἐκ τῶν φυλῶν A 761
36₁₂ Μανασσή 963] μανν. A 121

An analysis of the above list shows that one manuscript stands out as closely related to codex A; ms 121 joins A in the list 51 times, whereas the next in line is ms. 458 with only 12, followed by 55 and 59 with eight each, and by 126 and 319 with six each. No other witness appears more than five times. The high number of agreements between A and 121 is in part due to the fact that the name Manasseh is commonly spelled with a double "n" in both witnesses. If these instances were to be disregarded there would still remain 32 agreements between A and 121, though only one would still obtain between A and 458. It is obvious that ms 121 is closely related to A.

In the next list possible recensional influence on the text of codex A is examined. All instances of correspondence between the text of A and that of 𝔐 over against Num are given in list 7. Since all instances equal 𝔐, that fact is not noted, but the 𝔐 text is given except where the variant text is attested in Apparatus II in which case that equation is recorded.

1₄ ἕκαστος Fᵃ] + εκαστος A F G-29-426 56 y⁻³¹⁸ z⁻¹⁸ 59 624 Syh = o′ 344

1₅ τῶν (Ρουβήν)] τω A 29 d n⁻⁷⁶⁷ 30 t 121 18 55* Arm: לראובן 𝔐

1₆ τῶν (Συμεών)] τω A 528-551 d n⁻⁷⁶⁷ t 121 18 Arm: לשמעון 𝔐

1₇ τῶν (Ἰούδα)] τω A d n⁻⁷⁶⁷ t 121 18 Arm: ליהודה 𝔐

1₁₈ συνήγαγον] εξεκκλησιασαν (c var) A M′ᵗˣᵗ oI-29-707ᵐᵍ (vid) C″ b s 318 55 624 = oi λ′ 344ᵗˣᵗ

1₄₉ τὴν (Λευί)] > A 72 b 106-125 127-458 x⁻⁵²⁷ 392 319 Cyr I 845: לוי 𝔐

1₅₁ ἀναστήσουσιν] + αυτην A b Co; + (※ G) αυτην (+ ※ Syh) οι λευιται (c var) O-707 44 n t 55 319 799 Arab Arm Syh: יקימו אתו הלוים 𝔐

2₁₇ καθ᾽ ἡγεμονίαν] κατα ταγμα (-ματα 131-528 s 126) A M′ᵗˣᵗ 29-58ᵗˣᵗ-72-oI C″ b 246 30′-85′ᵗˣᵗ-321′ᵗˣᵗ-343′ y⁻³⁹² z 55 319 646 Latcod 100: cf σ′ κατὰ τάγματα (ταγμα 85; -τος 130) 85′-344

2₁₇ fin B V 707 d f⁻²⁴⁶ n t x 392 59 799 Arm Sa⁴ ¹²] + αυτου 376 C⁻¹⁶-46-417 Bo; + αυᵗ 16; + αυτων rell: = α′ σ′ ϑ′ αὐτῶν (aut αυτου) 85′-344

3₁₇ οἱ (υἱοί)] > A M′ G-64-426 C⁻¹⁶-528 44-125 246 130-321′ x⁻⁵⁰⁹ z⁻¹⁸ ¹²⁶ 55 624 799: בני 𝔐

3₃₈ ἁπτόμενος] προσπορευομενος (προπορ. 618; -ρεβομ. 54) A M′ᵗˣᵗ oI-29 16-46 b 54 28-30′-85′ᵗˣᵗ-321′ᵗˣᵗ-343′ 619 121 55: = ϑ′ 344ᵗˣᵗ

3₅₀ σίκλους] sub ÷ G Syh; > A: non hab 𝔐

4₈ (καὶ διεμβαλοῦσιν) δι᾽ αὐτῆς] > A F M′ O″⁻⁵⁸ ⁷² C″ b s 619 y⁻³¹⁸ z⁽⁻⁶⁶⁹ᵗˣᵗ⁾ 55 319 646 799 Aeth Arab Syh: ושמו 𝔐

4₈ ἀναφορεῖς] + αυτης (αυτοις 319*) A F M′ O″⁻⁵⁸ ⁷² C″⁻⁵² b s 619 y⁻³¹⁸ z⁽⁻⁶⁶⁹ᵗˣᵗ⁾ 55 319 646 799 Syh: בדיו 𝔐

4₉ ἐλαίου] + αυτης A F M′ O″ C″ b 107′-125 f⁽⁻¹²⁹ᵗˣᵗ⁾ s 619 y z 55 59 319 646 799 Arab Syh: שמנה 𝔐

4₁₄ σκεύη 1°] B 72 d n t x⁻⁶¹⁹ Cyr I 852 Latcod 100 Arm Bo] + αυτου rell: כליו 𝔐

4₂₆ περισσά] + αυτων A F M′ V O″⁻ ⁸² C″ f 767 s 619 y z 55 59 646 799 Arab Syh: מיתריהם 𝔐

4₂₆ λειτουργικά] + αυτων A F O″⁻⁽⁷²⁾ ⁸² C″⁻¹⁶ ⁴⁶ f s 619 y z 55 59 646 799 Aeth Arab Syh: עבדתם 𝔐

4₃₉ ἕως] pr (※ G Syh) και A O⁻⁵⁸ b Latcod 100 Syh: ועד 𝔐

5₈ ὁ ἀγχιστεύων] om ὁ A oI n 130 68′ 55 Tht Nm 195: גאל 𝔐

6₅ τοῦ ἁγνισμοῦ B 963 58 127 84 x⁻⁶¹⁹ Cyr I 1041 Latcod 100 Arm Bo] αφαγν. 44; > 72 319; + (※ G; ÷ Syh mend) αυτου rell: נזרו 𝔐

6₁₉ ἕνα ἄζυμον 963] tr A V 376′-707-oI C″⁻⁴⁶⁸ b s y⁻³¹⁸ 55 319 624 799 Latcod 100 Aeth: מצה אחת 𝔐

6₂₁ τῆς (εὐχῆς αὐτοῦ)] > A M′ oI C″⁽⁻⁵²⁸ᵗˣᵗ⁶¹⁶⁾ s⁽⁻¹³⁰⁾ 71 121 55 624: נדרו 𝔐

8₁₂ χείρας 963] + (※ Syh) αυτων A O⁻⁵⁸ b 18′-126-628-669 Latcod 100 Arm Co Syh: ידיהם 𝔐

8₂₁ (τὰ) ἱμάτια B d 127 t x⁻⁶¹⁹ Arm] + αυτων rell: בגדיהם 𝔐

9₃ ποιήσεις 1°] -σετε A F Mᵐᵍ 58-426ᶜ-oII⁻⁸² C″⁻⁵²′³¹³*⁶¹⁶ s⁻³⁰ 121 68′-120′ 59 416 Aeth Arab Syh: תעשו 𝔐

9₃ κατὰ καιρούς] κατα καιρον αυτου A M′ O′-707 b 56′ 619 y 55 Syh: במועדו 𝔐

11₇ εἶδος 2° B 707 f 509 318 z 624 646 799 Boᴮ] ωσει M′; ως 106 Sa⁵; pr (※ Syh) ως rell: כעין 𝔐

11₁₅ μου / τὴν κάκωσιν B V f n x⁻⁶¹⁹ 319 Cyr II 461 Latcod 100] om μου Bo; tr rell: ברעתי 𝔐

11₂₈ ἐκλεκτός B V 376ᵗˣᵗ 129 n⁽⁻⁷⁶⁷⁾ x 319 Tht Nm 207 Latcodd 100 104 (vid) Arm Bo] + αυτου rell: מבחריו 𝔐

11₂₈ κύριε B V 417ᵗˣᵗ d n t⁻⁸⁴ x 126 319 Tht Nm 206ᵗᵉ 207 Latcodd 100 104 Arm Co] + μου rell: אדני 𝔐

12₂ ἡμῖν] pr εν A: בנו 𝔐

13₂₆ ἀπέστρεψαν] επεστρ. A M′ 29-58-707-oI C″⁻⁵²′⁵⁵¹ b 129 n s⁻³⁰′ y⁻³⁹²: = α′ ϑ′ 344

13₂₉ ἐπ᾽ αὐτῆς] την γην A F M′ O″⁻³⁷⁶ C″ b 56′ s y z 59 624: בארץ 𝔐

13₂₉ καὶ (μεγάλαι)] > A F M′ 58-oI′ C″ 56′ 30′-85′ᵗˣᵗ-321′ᵗˣᵗ-343′ 84 y z 55 59 624 799 Latcod 100 Aeth Arab Syh: גדלת 𝔐

13₃₃ πᾶς B V 426 x Bo^ABᶜ Sa] και G C'' 799; > Bo^B*; pr και rell: וכל 𝔐

14₃ (καὶ τὰ) παιδία B M' 129 x Cyr I 373] τεκνα ημων b; + ημων (νμ. 44-107' 321) rell: וטפנו 𝔐

14₂₂ μου / τῆς φωνῆς B M' V d 129 t x Cyr II 609] tr rell: = σ' 344

14₂₈ ἢ μήν] ει μη A G 417 56* 54 321 318 59ᶜ 799 ᴸᵃᵗcod 100 Arm: אם לא 𝔐

14₄₄ τὴν (κορυφήν)] > A y⁻³¹⁸: ראש 𝔐

15₃ (καὶ) ποιήσεις] -σητε (aut -σετε aut -σατε) A F M' O''⁻ᴳ⁸² C'' b d 56 -129 s t y 18-68'-128-407-630-669ᶜ 55 59 Cyr I 1029 verss: ועשיתם 𝔐

15₄ ἐν 1° — fin] (c var) εν τεταρτω του ιν ελαιω A F M' V O''⁻²⁹⁴²⁶ C''⁻⁴¹⁴ b⁻¹⁹ s 392 55 59 319 624 Arab Sa Syh^L: ברבעית ההין שמן 𝔐

15₈ ἀπὸ τῶν βοῶν / ποιῆτε] tr A F M' O'' C'' b f⁻¹²⁹ s y z 55 59 319 624 Cyr I 1029 ᴸᵃᵗcod 100 Arab Bo Syh: תעשה בן בקר 𝔐

15₂₈ fin B F V 72' f⁻²⁴⁶ n⁻⁷⁶⁷ x 59 ᴸᵃᵗcod 100 Aeth Arab Arm Sa] + (※ Gᶜ Syh^L; ÷ G*) και αφεθησεται (c var) αυτω (> 82) rell: + ונסלח לו 𝔐

15₃₂ τῇ ἡμέρᾳ] pr εν A 376 n⁻¹²⁷ x⁻⁵⁰⁹ 318 319 ᴸᵃᵗcod 100 Syh: ביום 𝔐

15₃₄ αὐτόν 2°] αυτω A F 29-58-72-376 414 b 75 121 68-120'-122ᶜ-628 55 59 319 ᴸᵃᵗcod 100 Arm^te Bo Syh: לו 𝔐

16₃ καὶ εἶπαν B V 72 d n t x 319 ᴸᵃᵗcod 100 Arm Bo^A] + προς (> 376*) αυτους (-τον 15-64*vid) rell: ויאמרו אלהם 𝔐

16₂₄ Κόρε] + (※ G 344 Syh; c var) και δαθαν και αβιρων A M' O'-29-82-707ᵐᵍ C''⁻⁵⁵²ᵗˣᵗ⁷⁶¹ b d⁻¹²⁵ 246 n⁻⁴⁵⁸ s t y z 55 319 624 799 ᴸᵃᵗcod 100 Aeth Arab Arm Bo Syh: קרח דתן ואבירם 𝔐

16₂₇ Κόρε] + (※ G Syh; c var) και δαθαν και αβιρων A O'-29-82-707ᵐᵍ C'' b d s t y⁻³⁹² 18'-126-628-630' 55 624 Arab Syh: קרח דתן ואבירם 𝔐

16₃₂ (καὶ) ὅσα B G-426 b 129 n⁻⁷⁶⁷ 509 319 ᴸᵃᵗcod 100 Arm Co] pr παντα rell: וכל אשר 𝔐

16₄₄ (Μωυσῆν) καὶ Ἀαρών] > A* 551 Sa¹²: משה 𝔐

17₁₀ σημεῖον B V 82 129 54-75' x Cyr I 673] pr και εις 246; pr et Bo; signi ᴸᵃᵗcod 100; > 319; pr εις rell: לאות 𝔐

18₁ (πατριᾶς) σου B V 58 529 129 x⁻⁵²⁷ 126 Cyr I 837 Arab Co] + (※ Syh) μετα σου (> 628) rell: אביך אתך 𝔐

18₅ (καὶ) οὐκ ἔσται B 82 129 730 x Bo] ουκετι εσται 381' b d n t 392 799 ᴸᵃᵗcod 100 MissMoz 85 Arm; + ετι (c var) rell: ולא יהיה עוד 𝔐

18₈ ἀπαρχῶν B V 82 129 x⁻⁶¹⁹ Cyr I 837 ᴸᵃᵗcod 100 Sa] + μου rell: תרומתי 𝔐

18₁₉ σοὶ δέδωκα] tr A F O''⁻⁸² C'' 56' s 619 y z 55 59 624 646 799 Cyr I 840 Aeth Arab Syh: נתתי לך 𝔐

19₅ τὸ δέρμα B 82 125 53'-129 x⁻⁶¹⁹ ᴸᵃᵗPsAug Serm Cai II 38.2] τα κρεα 319; + (※ G Syh^L) αυτης rell: את ערה 𝔐

19₈ τὸ σῶμα αὐτοῦ B F 29-82 129 392 Aeth⁻ᴳ] pr υδατι 628; αυτου sub ※ Syh^L; + (※ G Syh) εν υδατι O⁽⁻³⁷⁶⁾ Syh; + υδατι rell: בשרו במים 𝔐

19₁₆ ἀνθρωπίνου] ᾱνου A oI C'' s y⁻³⁹² 55 646: = α' 344ᵗˣᵗ

19₁₉ τῇ ἡμέρᾳ 3°] pr εν A 82 414-550' 54'-75 318 55: ביום 𝔐

20₁₉ (καὶ) τὰ κτήνη B V 82 d n⁻⁷⁶⁷ t x⁻⁶¹⁹ Phil II 87ᵗᵉ Sa¹²] pecora nostra ᴸᵃᵗcod 100 Aeth; + μου rell: ומקני 𝔐

20₂₈ Ἀαρών 2° B F oII 414-529 125 f 71-509 392 z 59 799 ᴸᵃᵗcod 100 Aeth⁻ᶜ Arab Arm Co] pr εκει 551 b⁻¹⁹; + (※ Syh) εκει rell: אהרן שם 𝔐

21₁ Χαανίς] χαναναιος A 72-426 56*(vid)-129-664 n⁻⁵⁴ 527 Procop 856 ᴸᵃᵗcod 100 Arab Arm^ap Bo Sa¹⁰¹²: = οι λ' 108 Syh

22₁₇ (καὶ) ὅσα] παντα α M' 426-oI'⁻²⁹ cI-52'-313-417ᶜ-422 56 28-30'-85-130ᵗˣᵗ-321'ᵗˣᵗ-343-344ᵗˣᵗ y⁻³⁹²* 799; pr παντα A Fᵃ O⁻⁴²⁶ 16-46-414' 246 619 z 55 59 Aeth Arab Bo Syh: וכל אשר 𝔐

22₂₅ Βαλαάμ] + (※ Syh^L) προς (εις 344ᵐᵍ) τον τοιχον A O'⁽⁻¹⁵⁾-82 C''⁽⁻⁴⁶ ⁷³' ⁵²⁹⁾ 246 s⁽⁻³⁴³⁾ 619 y⁻³⁹² z⁽⁻⁶²⁸⁾ ᴸᵃᵗAug Num 50 Arab Syh: + אל הקיר 𝔐

22₂₈ (καὶ) λέγει] ειπε(ν) A M' 82-376-oI C'' s⁻¹³⁰ᵐᵍ ³²¹'ᵐᵍ y⁻³⁹² 55 319 ᴸᵃᵗcod 100 Bo: ותאמר 𝔐

22₃₀ (τῆς) σήμερον ἡμέρας] ημερας ταυτης A: היום הזה 𝔐

22₃₃ τρίτον τοῦτο] tr A V 29 118'-537 106 129 767 30 t 319 Or IV 409 Aeth Arm Syh: זה שלש 𝔐

22₃₃ ἐξέκλινεν 2° B d 129 n t x⁻⁶¹⁹ 319 Aethᶠ Co] + απ εμου rell: נטתה מפני 𝔐

22₃₄ ἐν — συνάντησιν] (c var) εις συν. μοι εν τη οδω A F M' O''⁻⁷² C'' 56' s 619 y z 55 59 624 799 Aeth Arab Sa Syh: לקראתי בדרך 𝔐

24₂ πνεῦμα θεοῦ / ἐπ' αὐτῷ] tr A F O''⁻⁸² C'' 56' n⁻¹²⁷ s 527-619 y z 55 59 799 Latcod 100 Ruf Num XVII 2 Aeth Arab Syh: עליו רוח אלהים 𝔐

24₅ σου / οἱ οἶκοι] tr A F M' O''⁻⁸²³⁸¹' C''⁻⁵⁵²⁷⁶¹ s 619 y⁻³¹⁸ z⁻¹²⁶ 55 319 799: אהליך 𝔐

24₁₀ τρίτον τοῦτο] tr A F M' O'⁻³⁷⁶-29-707 C''⁻⁵²'³¹³⁷⁶¹ 19 d 53'-56 s 527 y z⁻⁶⁸'¹²⁰ 59 799 Arm Bo Syh: זה שלש פעמים 𝔐

25₄ τῷ Μωυσῇ] προς μωυσην (-ση M'; μωσει 72) A M' 58-72-oI d s t 619 y 55 319: אל משה 𝔐

25₄ κυρίῳ B V 82 d 53' n⁻⁷⁵* t 71-509 319 Cyr I 908 IV 300] > 75*; pr (※ G) τω rell: ליהוה 𝔐

26₅₈ δῆμος ὁ Κόρε B V 963 82 129 n 730 t⁽⁻³⁷⁰⁾ x⁻⁶¹⁹ 319 Latcod 100 Arm Bo Sa⁵] > Sa¹²; post Μουσί tr rell: משפחת המושי משפחת הקרחי 𝔐

27₂ συναγωγῆς] pr της A V 58-72-426 551 b d⁻¹⁰⁶ 129-246 458 121 126-128-628-630' 59: העדה 𝔐

27₂₀ οἱ (υἱοί) 963] > A* 707 b⁻¹⁹ 75 30-343 126 319: בני 𝔐

28₉ ἀναπεποιημένης ἐν ἐλαίῳ B V 963 15-82 d f n t x⁻⁶¹⁹ 121 319 Cyr I 1113 Latcod 100 Arm Bo Sa¹] post θυσίαν tr rell: מנחה בלולה בשמן 𝔐

29₂₀ τῇ ἡμέρᾳ] pr και A 129 54 509 392 18 646 Aeth Arab Arm BoᴮꞘ ביום 𝔐

30₆ καὶ τοὺς ὁρισμούς] + (※ Syh) αυτης A O-82-381' b 106⁽ᵐᵍ⁾ n 134 y⁻³¹⁸ Cyr I 1060 Latcod 100 Aug Num 57 Co Syh: ואסריה 𝔐

30₁₂ (οἱ ὁρισμοί) αὐτῆς 963] sub ÷ G; > A F 15'-58-618*(c pr m)-707 C'' 125 53'-56 s⁽⁻⁸⁵ᵗˣᵗ⁾ y⁻³⁹² z⁻⁴⁰⁷ 55 59 416 624 646 LatAug Num 59.2ᵗᵉ: אסר 𝔐

30₁₅ ὁρισμούς] + αυτης (αυτους 107*) A 426 d 127-458 730 t Armᵃᵖ Sa: אסריה 𝔐

31₁₈ πᾶσαν B O⁻³⁷⁶-82 129 x⁻⁵²⁷ 407 319 Syh] pr και rell: וכל 𝔐

31₂₇ συναγωγῆς 963] pr της (τη 75) A O⁻⁴²⁶-381' 414 106⁽ᵐᵍ⁾ 129 n t⁽⁻³⁷⁰⁾ 527 Cyr I 333 bis: העדה 𝔐

31₃₂ (καὶ) ἑβδομήκοντα] + (※ G) χιλιαδες (c var) A Fᶜ ᵖʳ ᵐ M' G-29-426-707-oI C'' b⁻¹⁹ 246 s y⁻³⁹² z⁻¹²⁶⁴⁰⁷⁶⁶⁹* 55 624 Syh: ושבעים אלף 𝔐

31₃₆ τριακόσιαι 963] + (※ G) χιλιαδες (c var) A F M' O''⁻⁷²⁸² C'' 56' 28-85'-321'-344* 509 y z⁻¹²⁶⁴⁰⁷ 55 59 624 799 Aeth Arab Bo Syh: שלש מאות אלף 𝔐

32₉ κύριος αὐτοῖς B V 82-381' 414 19' d 129 n t x 318 407] αυτους κ̅ς̅ 120; om αὐτοῖς 18; tr rell: להם יהוה 𝔐

32₂₉ οἱ (υἱοὶ Γάδ) 963] > A 15 44'-125 56 75' 318 126-628 319: בני גד 𝔐

32₃₃ Ἀμορραίων] pr των A 58-376 73' b d f⁻¹²⁹ n⁻⁴⁵⁸ t 55 799: האמרי 𝔐

33₃ ἀπῆραν] pr και A O' y⁻³¹⁸ 18'-126-628-630' 55 799 Aeth Sa Syh: = o' οἱ λ' 344

33₁₄ ἦν] + εκει A F O' C'' b 53'-56 s⁻³⁰ y⁻³¹⁸ 18-68'-120 59 Latcod 100 Aeth Arab Sa Syh: היה שם 𝔐

33₁₄ πιεῖν ἐκεῖ B*] ωστε πιειν 343-344ᵐᵍ; ποιε(ι)ν 767; tr Bᶜ M' V 15' d 129-246 t x⁻⁵²⁷ 126-128-407-628-630'; om ἐκεῖ rell: לשתות 𝔐

33₅₃ πάντας (τοὺς κατοικοῦντας τὴν γῆν) B Fᵃ M' V 58-72-426 d n t x 407 Latcodd 100 104 Bo Sa¹] > rell: cf את הארץ 𝔐

33₅₄ (τὴν γῆν) αὐτῶν B⁽ᵐᵍ⁾ M' V 963 (vid) 58-376'-oI 56ᵐᵍ-129-664 n t⁽⁻⁸⁴⁾ 509-527 z 319 Latcod 100 Bo Sa¹] ταυτην 799; sub ÷ G Syh; > rell: את הארץ 𝔐

34₇ τὰ ὅρια / ὑμῖν B 963 44'-107-610ᶜ t⁽⁻⁸⁴⁾ 509 407 319 Sa¹] τα ορια υμων 125-610*; υμιν ορια 82 799; om ὑμῖν 53' 126; tr rell: לכם גבול 𝔐

35₃ αὐτοῖς / αἱ πόλεις B Fᵃ V 529 b d 129 n⁻⁷⁵* t x 120' 319 Cyr I 864 Latcodd 100 104 Arm] αυτοις πολει 75*; αι πολ. αυταις 29; αι πολ. αυτων 72 53' 121 68'-128-669; tr rell: הערים להם 𝔐

35₂₈ καταφυγῆς B V 82 106 129 n⁻⁷⁵ t x 407-630 319 Sa] φυγης αυτου M'; -φυλης αυτου 618; + αυτου rell: מקלטו 𝔐

It is obviously not suggested that all the variants in list 7 are recensional in origin, since some of the correspondences are only formal. On the other hand, it is quite apparent that the A text has been substantially influenced by hex.

Many popular hex readings are present in A, whereas B has only a few. In the case of widespread hex readings B usually supports the non-recensional text, whereas A supports the variant text. The contrast between this list and list 4 is indeed noteworthy in this respect.

C. It remains to be determined whether B and A represent different text types within the text tradition. List 8 details instances in which A witnesses to Num, and B along with no more than four text groups (random support being disregarded) supports a variant tradition. Support of a reading by a group means support by at least half the members of the group. The group support is in each case summarized in parentheses.

List 8

1_2 (x) om υἱῶν B x Bas II 145 Lat cod 100

1_2 (d n t x) om αὐτῶν 1° B 414′ d n⁻⁷⁶⁷ t x 18 Bas II 145 Cyr VI 453 X 624 Lat cod 100 PsBas *Is* I 5 Arm

1_2 (d n t x) om αὐτῶν 2° B V d n⁻⁷⁶⁷ t x 18 319 Bas II 145 Cyr VI 453 X 624 Lat cod 100 Hi *Eph* II 3 PsBas *Is* I 5 Arm

1_2 (d t x) om αὐτῶν 3° B 19 d 127 t x 18 319 Cyr VI 453 X 624 Lat cod 100 Arm

1_{16} (n x) om αὐτῶν B V n⁻⁷⁶⁷ x⁻⁶¹⁹ 18-628 319 Lat cod 100 Arm Bo^B = Ra

1_{33} (d t) διακόσιοι] τριακοσιοι B d⁻¹⁰⁶ᶜ 54′ t 392 799 Lat cod 100 Arm

1_{44} (d t) ἐπεσκέψατο] -ψαντο (επισκ. 107′) B Fᶜ ᵖʳ ᵐ M′ d 127ᶜ 74ᶜ-76′ Aeth Arm Bo^ABᶜ Sa¹ Syh = Ra

1_{53} (d n t) ἐναντίοι] εναντιον κυριου B* M′ ᵐᵍ V d 54-75′ t = Ra

2_3 (x) πρῶτοι] κατα νοτον (νωτον 619) B x Lat cod 100

3_{32} (d t) υἱός] pr o B V 19 d⁻¹²⁵ t 126 646 Bo = Ra

3_{40} (n x) om αὐτῶν B 54-75′ x⁻⁶¹⁹ Lat codd 100 104 = Ra

4_{14} (x) αὐτά] αυτο B x⁻⁶¹⁹ 392 18′-126-669 Cyr I 852

4_{19} (y) εἰσπορευέσθωσαν] προσπορ. B V 82 551* 509 y⁻¹²¹ 55 Lat cod 100 = Ra

4_{25} (b) κατακάλυμμα] καλυμμα B M V 707 b 84ᵗˣᵗ(c pr m) 121 126 319 = Ra

4_{26} (b x) om καί 4° B b x⁻⁶¹⁹ 392 319 Lat cod 100 Aeth^M Arm Bo Sa⁴ = Ra

4_{35} (f x) om τὰ ἔργα B f x⁻⁶¹⁹ 319 Lat cod 100 Sa = Ra

4_{36} (x) ἑπτακόσιοι] διακοσιοι B 82 x⁻⁶¹⁹ Sa = Ra

4_{46} (x) om αὐτῶν 1° B x⁻⁶¹⁹ Lat cod 104(vid) = Ra

5_{10} (s) ἑκάστου] -στω B* 29 52′-313-414-417 28-30′-85-130ᵗˣᵗ-321*-343′-346⁽ᵐᵍ*⁾ 18-628 319 646

7_{15} (f n x) ἕνα 3° 963] > B F*(c pr m) V 29-82-707ᵗˣᵗ f n⁻⁷⁶⁷ 730 x⁻⁶¹⁹ 126-628 319 Lat cod 100 Aeth⁻ᶜ

7_{77} (oI x) Φαγαιήλ 963] φαγεηλ B V oI⁻¹⁵ 77 127 30 76 x⁻⁵⁰⁹ 392 Co

7_{86} (oII b f) πλήρεις] -ρης B F 381′-oII⁽⁻⁷²⁾ b⁻⁵³⁷ 44 f⁻⁵⁶ 767 30-85*-343 84 71 628

8_{16} (f) πάντων] + των B* f⁻¹²⁹

8_{17} (C) ἀνθρώπου 963ᶜ ᵖʳ ᵐ] α‾ν‾ω‾ν‾ (α‾ν‾ω‾ 509) B cΓ′⁻⁴⁶ 509 646

8_{21} (d t) ἔπλυναν] -ναντο B M′ 15-376 d 56 127 t = Ra

9_8 (n) πρὸς αὐτούς] post Μωυσῆς tr B* 16-46 n 730 527 318

9_{13} (n z) ἄν] εαν B 29 129 n 527-619 z Cyr I 1081 = Ra

9_{13} (O) μακράν] -ρα B V O⁻³⁷⁶-72 16ᶜ-46-422 75-127 76 509 392 Lat cod 100 Arm Syh (vid) = Ra

9_{14} (n) om οὕτως B 129 n⁻⁷⁶⁷ 71-509 Aeth Arab Arm Co = Ra

10_3 (z) σαλπιεῖς] σαλπισεις B* 619 z = Ra

10_5 (b d) παρεμβάλλουσαι] -βαλουσαι B* V 72-618 52′-73′-551-616*-739 b d 56 54-767 370 71 18-126 55 59 646

10_{32} (C s) ἄν] εαν B* F 58-82-707 C′′⁻⁵²⁸ s 392 59 = Ra

11_4 (C) κρέα] κρεας B* 618* C′′ 458* 71′ Chr I 476

11_{12} (O f n x) τὸν πάντα] tr B V O⁻⁵⁸ 422 f n x⁻⁶¹⁹ Phil III 6 Chr I 476 Tht *Nm* 204ᵃᵖ = Ra

11₂₆ (x) om τό B x⁻⁶¹⁹

11₂₉ (x) μοι] εμε B x⁻⁵²⁷ 392

11₃₄ (x) om ὅτι B x

11₃₅ (O n x) om τῆς B F V O'⁻²⁹ ⁵⁸ 129 54-75' x 392 59 319 799 = Ra

12₁₀ (d n t x) πρός] επι B V d 129 n⁻⁷⁵ 321'ᵐᵍ t x 319 Arab Arm Co = Ra

13₃ (x) ἀποστελεῖς] -στειλας B x⁻⁵⁰⁹

13₈ (x) Ἰγαάλ] ιλααλ B x

13₁₃ (x) Γαμαλί] γαμαι B x 319 Arm

13₁₆ (d) Γουδιήλ] τουδιηλ B 107'-125 319

13₂₀ (f n) εἰ 1°] η B F 29 528⁽ᵐᵍ⁾-529* f⁻¹²⁹ 54*-458-767 30 84ᶜ ᵛⁱᵈ 509* 392* 68'-120 55*

13₂₀ (d f n) εἰ 2°] η B 15-29-707 d⁻⁴⁴ f n⁻¹²⁷ 509 55 319 799 ᴸᵃᵗcod 100

13₂₁ (f x) εἰ 2°] η B F 29-82-381' 313* f 458-767 x⁻⁵²⁷ 68'-120' 319 799

13₂₃ (x) Ἐνάκ Fᵇ] εναχ B F 129 x Sa = Ra

13₂₈ (C) ἤλθομεν] ηλθαμεν B G C'⁻⁵²⁸ ⁶¹⁶ᶜ ⁷⁶¹ᶜ-52*-313-417-551-615 343* 509 = Ra

13₂₉ (d n t x) om αἱ B F*(c pr m) V 29 d n⁻⁷⁶⁷ t x Cyr I 373

13₂₉ (x) Ἐνάκ] εναχ B 129 x Sa = Ra

13₃₃ (x) ὑπερμήκεις] + εκει B x⁻⁵⁰⁹ ᴸᵃᵗcod 100

14₁₀ (x) om ἐν 3° B x Aeth

14₁₃ (t x) ἐν] τη B 44' 129 127-767 t x⁻⁵⁰⁹ = Ra

14₂₃ (C) οὐκ 3°] ουχ B* C⁻⁷⁷-52-73'-313-615*-761* 392 126 319 799

14₂₄ (x) om καί 2° B V 72 106 x 55 Cyr II 609 ᴸᵃᵗcod 100 Aeth Arm Co = Ra

14₂₇ (d t) om ἄ B* V d⁻⁴⁴ 75 t 318 319 ᴸᵃᵗcod 100 Sa

14₂₇ (b) μου] εμου B V 108-118-314* 30'-321'ᶜ 121 319 = Ra

14₄₅ (C) Ἑρμά] ερμαν B V 376 C'' 130* 509 = Ra

15₁ (d t x) ἐλάλησεν] ειπε(ν) B V d 129 t x Cyr I 1029 = Ra

15₃ (d t x) κάρπωμα] ολοκαυτωματα B d t x Cyr I 1029 = Ra

15₃ (d n t x) ὁλοκαύτωμα] ολοκαρπωμα (-μαν 509) B d 129 n t x 319* Cyr I 1029 = Ra

15₆ (O) εἰς 1°] pr η B O⁻⁵⁸ 509-527 Syh = Ra

15₁₂ (d t) οὕτως] ουτω B M d⁽⁻⁶¹⁰⁾ 54 t 509 128-628-630' = Ra

15₂₀ (x) ἅλωνος] αλω B x⁻⁵⁰⁹ Cyr VI 568 = Ra

15₂₄ (oII f) ποιήσει] -ση B* F K M' 15'-oII⁻⁸² 46-422-500*-528-616ᶜ f⁻¹²⁹ 127 527 669*

15₃₃ (f n t) ξύλα] + (+ εν 54-458) τη ημερα των σαββατων B f n⁻⁷⁵ t 527 799 = Ra

15₃₉ (d n t x) om ὀπίσω 2° B V d 129 n⁻⁷⁶⁷ t x 319 Tht Nm 211 ᴸᵃᵗcod 100 Arm Co

16₃ (C) Μωυσῆν] -ση B* 707 C''⁻⁴⁶ ⁴²² 19 28-30'-85 55

16₉ (x z) συναγωγῆς 2°] σκηνης B Fᵃ 56' x z 799 Cyr I 860 Sa

16₁₈ (s) ἐπ' αὐτά 2°] επ αυτο B* V s⁻³⁰' ³⁴³ Aeth = Ra

16₂₆ (d t x) ὅσα] ων B Mᵗˣᵗ V 376 d 129 t x = Ra

16₄₁ (n) ἐπαύριον] αυριον B n⁻⁷⁶⁷ 509-527

18₉ (d n t x) om τῆς B 82 d n⁻⁷⁶⁷ t x⁻⁶¹⁹ Cyr I 837 = Ra

18₁₀ (cII) φάγεται] φαγετε B 58 46-52'-417-616ᶜ 130* 71 630 Bo

18₁₂ (x) om καί 2° B 426 x⁻⁶¹⁹

18₂₇ (x) ἅλωνος] αλω B 426 x⁻⁶¹⁹ Cyr I 844 = Ra

18₂₇ (x) om ὡς 2° B 129 x⁻⁶¹⁹ 319 Cyr I 844 Bo Sa¹ = Ra

18₂₈ (oII b s z) ἄν] εαν B F 58-oII⁻⁸² b 56' s 619 392 z 59ᶜ 319 Cyr I 844 = Ra

18₂₉ (x) ἀπό 2°] pr η B V 129 x⁻⁶¹⁹ 392 Cyr I 844 Sa¹ = Ra

19₂₀ (d n t) ἄν] εαν B 376' 413 d n t 71 799 Eus VI 12 Tht Nm 215ᵗᵉ = Ra

20₄ (t) ἀνηγάγετε] -γαγες B* 129 74-76-84 71-509

20₈ (d) ἐναντίον] εναντι B M' 82 d⁻¹⁰⁶ 71-509 646 = Ra

20₂₇ (O f n) αὐτούς] αυτον B V O⁻⁵⁸ 414 f⁻⁶⁶⁴ n 71-509 Arm Bo Sa⁴ Syh = Ra

20₂₈ (b d) om τόν 1° B 16-46-414-552-761 b 107'-125 129 84 71-509 392 55ᵗˣᵗ(c pr m) 319 = Ra

21₉ (oI n) ἔδακεν] εδακνεν B oI⁻¹⁵-29 537 n⁻⁷⁶⁷ 71' 392 Cyr II 637 Arm Syh = Ra

21₁₁ (oI f) κατ' (ἀνατολάς)] κατα B M' 72-376-oI 16-46-422 537 610 f⁻⁵⁶ 458-767 84 527' 126-669 799 = Ra

21₁₂ (d t) Ζαρέδ] ζαρετ B 52* d t 318*(vid) = Ra

21₁₃ (f) πέραν] περα B* 53'-129

21₁₉ (z) Νααλιήλ 1°] μαναηλ B* V 376 129* 509 z Arm Sa

78

21₁₉ (z) *Νααλιήλ* 2°] *μαναηλ* B* V 509 z Arm
21₂₂ (f) om *ἄν* B 53'-129 71-509 55 = Ra
21₂₃ (b) *ὁρίων*] *ορειων* B* b⁻⁵³⁷
22₂₂ (O d f t) *ἐπορεύετο*] -*ρευθη* B V O d 53'-129 458 t 71-509 = Ra
22₂₂ (z) *ἐνδιαβάλλειν*] -*βαλειν* B Fᵇ V 82-426 125 30-343-344ᶜ 509 18'-126-628-630'
22₂₄ (f) *ἀμπελώνων*] -*λων* B V 53'-129 71(vid)-509 Or IV 409 = Ra
22₂₅ (b) *ἑαυτήν*] *αυτον* B V b 127 71-509 319 ᴸᵃᵗcod 100
22₃₃ (b x) *νῦν*] + *ουν* B b x⁻⁶¹⁹ ᴸᵃᵗcod 100 = Ra
23₁₂ (b t) *ἄν*] *εαν* B V 58 73' b 106 127 t 71 59 = Ra
23₁₇ (C) om *καί* 2° B* 15-58-72-82-618 C-46 53' 767 527 ᴸᵃᵗcod 100 Bo
24₂ (b) *ἐπ'*] *εν* B b⁻¹⁹ Tht *Nm* 221 = Ra
24₇ (t z) om *αὐτοῦ* 2° B 107' 129 76-84-134 71-509 18'-126-628-630-669* Eus VI 409
    Or IV 250 Arab Boᴬ Sa
24₁₆ (f n t) *ὑψίστου*] pr *παρα* (*παρ* 664; + *του* 84*) B V 82-376 106 f⁻⁵⁶* n t 71-509 392 319
    Phil III 191 ᴸᵃᵗcodd 91 92 94—96 100 Bo = Ra
24₂₁ (b y) *Καιναῖον*] *κεναιον* B 72 b 85 527-619 y⁻³¹⁸ 68'
24₂₂ (n) *νοσσία*] *νεοσσια* B* 82-426* 54'-75 = Ra
25₂ (O) *τὰς θυσίας*] *ταις* (> Bas) *θυσιαις* B V O⁻⁵⁸-82 127 Bas II 629 Cyr III 397 Or I 7
    = Ra
25₆ (n) *ἐναντίον* 2°] *εναντι* B* n⁻¹²⁷ 121 55 319 = Ra
26₄ (O n x) *καί* 2°] pr *συ* (*σοι* 767) B V O n x⁻⁶¹⁹ 407 ᴸᵃᵗcod 100 Arm Syh
26₂₇ (n t) *τεσσαράκοντα*] pr *τεσσαρες και* B F M' V 29-58-82 129 n⁻⁴⁵⁸ 130ᵐᵍ-321'ᵐᵍ-344ᵐᵍ
    t 509 318 407 59 Arm
26₂₈ (b) *Ἰεσουί* 1°] *ιεσου* B* V b Arm = Ra
26₅₁ (d) om *καί* 3° B* 417 d 767 84 128-669 319
26₅₉ (x) *Ἀμράμ* 1°] *αυτον* B V 82-376' 129 x⁻⁶¹⁹ Arm Sa Syhᵗˣᵗ = Ra
27₁₂ (C b s) *ὄρος* 2°] pr *το* B* C''⁻¹⁶⁴⁶ b 127-458 s⁻³⁰' 509 392 59*(vid) 646
27₂₂ (f) *ἐναντίον* 2°] *εναντι* B* 72-376 f = Ra
28₁₁ (b f n) *νουμηνίαις* 963] *νεομ.* (-*νιαι* 19) B 58-426 b f n Cyr I 1116 = Ra
28₁₉ (d f n t) *κάρπωμα*] -*ματα* B* K 58-82-426 d⁻⁴⁴ f n⁻⁴⁵⁸ 74'-370 624 = Ra
28₂₀ (oII f) om *ποιήσετε* B F V oII⁻²⁹ f 71 120-128-630' 319 Cyr I 1088 Aeth Arm
    Co= Ra
29₁₂ (f n) *ἑορτάσετε* 963] -*σατε* B 82-376-618* 537 f⁻⁵⁶ n⁻¹²⁷ 30-343 134 392* 59 319 624
29₁₃ (n) *κάρπωμα* 963] -*ματα* B* 58-82 n⁻⁴⁵⁸ Arm Sa = Ra
29₁₅ (f x) *τέσσαρας καὶ δέκα*] *δεκα τεσσαρας* (c var) B M' 82-376 77 f x 126-407 319
29₁₇ (f t x) idem B M' V 963 82-376' 77-417 106 f t x 18-407-669
29₂₀ (d f t x) idem B M' V 82-376 77 d⁽⁻¹⁰⁶ᵗˣᵗ⁾ f t x 18-126-407
29₂₆ (d f t x) idem B V 58-72-82-376 77 d f t x 407 416
30₃ (b) *ἄν* 2°] *εαν* B G b 129 54 121 = Ra
30₁₃ (z) *ἄν* 2° 963] *εαν* B G 509 18'-68'-120-630' 646 = Ra
31₁₀ (O) *κατοικίαις*] *οικιαις* B O⁻⁵⁸ 129 509 319 = Ra
31₂₈ (x) *ὄνων*] *αιγων* B Fᵃ V 82 129 x⁻⁵²⁷ 407 319 Arm Sa = Ra
31₃₆ (x) *πεντακόσια*] -*σιαι* B 127(vid) x⁻⁵²⁷ 407
31₄₈ (x) *καθεσταμένοι*] *κατεστ.* (-*μμενοι* 767; -*σπαμ.* 527) B V 129 767 x⁻⁵⁰⁹ 407 319
31₅₀ (f) *χλιδῶνα*] pr *και* B* 58 f⁻¹²⁹ 319 Cyr I 340 Aethᶜ Bo
32₆ (t) *πορεύσονται* 963] *πορευονται* B V 82 129 74'-76 509 18-407 55 ᴸᵃᵗcod 104 = Ra
32₂₅ (x) *ἐντέλλεται*] *εντελειται* B* x⁻⁵⁰⁹
32₃₀ (f) *διαβιβάσετε*] -*σατε* B 422-529 f 130-344* 527 392 120 55
32₃₁ (b n x) om *αὐτοῦ* B F 29-72 b n⁻¹²⁷ 30'-344 x 392 120' 59 319 ᴸᵃᵗcodd 100 104
32₃₃ (oI z) om *τῆς* 1° B* oI-29 413 18'-126-628-630' 799
32₃₉ (x) om *εἰς* B x
33₃ (x) *Ῥαμεσσή*] -*σσων* (-*σων* 527; -*μαισων* 619; -*σσω* 509) B x
33₅ (f t) *Σοκχώθ*] *σοχωθ* B* M' 82-376ᶜ 53'-129 54 730 74'-76-84*(c pr m) Sa¹²
33₁₇ (O f x) om *τῆς* B M' V O'⁻⁵⁸⁷² f x⁻⁵⁰⁹ = Ra
33₂₀ (x) *Λεβωνά*] *λεμωνα* (-*ννα* 509) B 767 x 407 = Ra
33₂₁ (x) *Λεβωνά*] *λεμωνα* (*λαιμ.* 619; -*ννα* 509) B 767 x 407 = Ra
33₂₂ (d t) *Μακελάθ*] -*λλαθ* B M' V G 44-107' 129 t 509 407 319 Arm = Ra

79

33_{23} (t) idem B M' V^c G 107' 129 t 509 407 Arm = Ra
33_{29} (d n t x) Ἀσελμωνά] σελμ. B d^{-125} 129 n$^{-54•\,767}$ t x 18 799 Arm Sa = Ra
33_{30} (d n t) idem B F^a V 44-107' 129 n t 799 Arm Sa = Ra
33_{31} (n x) Βαναιακάν] βαναια B V 376 54'-75 x 319 Sa^1 = Ra
33_{32} (n) idem B V 54'-75 71' Sa^1 = Ra
33_{35} (b d n t) ἐξ Ἐβρωνά] εκ σεβρ. (ξεβρ. 118) B M' 376 19'-118 d n t 71 392 59
33_{35} (n) Γεσιών] γεσσ. B* F^a 54-75' 84 392 Lat^{cod} 104
33_{43} (n) Ὠβώθ] σωβωθ B V 54'-767 71-509 319
33_{44} (n x) ἐξ Ὠβώθ] εκ σωβωθ (c var) B M' 58-72 n x 59 Sa^1
33_{54} (n) ἄν] εαν B* n^{-75} = Ra
33_{55} (n t) ἄν] εαν B* V 376 106 n t 619 68'-120 319 = Ra
34_{13} (d n t) κύριος] + τω μωυση (μωση n) B* d$^{(-44)}$ 246 n t Syh = Ra
34_{23} (b n) Οὐφίδ] σουφι B M' 376 b 129 n^{-127} 71-509* Lat^{cod} 104 Arm^{ap} Sa
35_{7} (x) om ἅς B V 82 129 344^{txt} x 407 319 Lat^{cod} 100 Arm = Ra
36_{7} (x) προσκολληθήσονται 963] pr και B x

Many of the variants in the above list are noted as "= Ra." For a discussion of their secondary nature cf chapter 6.

A more precise statement on the relations of the B text to the text tradition can now be made by noting the number of instances in which the B variant is supported by the individual text groups. To make the statement more complete those instances from list 4 in which no more than four text groups support a B reading are added to the statistics from list 8.

In the table below the vertical column designated A shows the number of instances a single text group supports a B reading; column B shows the number of instances in which a B reading is also supported by two text groups; column C, by three text groups, and column D, by four such. The last column gives the total number of these instances. Throughout this table random support is disregarded. No distinction has been made among the catena groups, i.e. among sub groups and/or C. Among the hex witnesses support by one or both sub groups but not by O is given separately.

	A	B	C	D	Total
O	4	2	8	5	19
oI or oII	2	6	1	1	10
C	7	1	1	—	9
b	8	7	4	3	22
d	3	12	11	16	42
f	8	10	10	6	34
n	11	13	14	13	51
s	2	1	1	1	5
t	3	17	13	16	49
x	37	15	12	14	78
y	1	1	—	—	2
z	5	5	—	1	11

From this table it is obvious that oI/oII C'' s y and z are only tangentially influenced by a B type text. As has already been mentioned in chapter 1 above,

x is closely related to B; it is clear from the above table that the relationship is closer than that of any other group. Thus out of 91 instances in which the B reading is supported by only one group it is x 37 times, whereas the next in order is n with only 11. From the total number in the final column it appears that the Byzantine groups are also significantly related to B in the text tradition, n being represented 51 times, t, 49, and d 42 times. Group f comes next with 34, followed by b with 22, and O with 19. The remainder, as indicated above, is insignificant.

In the final list the same conditions imposed on the B variants in list 8 are here imposed on variants found in codex A. As for list 8 the support by groups is summarized in parentheses. For the s group a majority of $85'^{mg}$-$321'^{mg}$-344^{mg} is included as an s reading as well.

List 9

1_5 $(C\ f\ s)$ Σεδιούρ] εδιουρ A G $C''^{-46\,52'\,413\,528}$ 53'-56c-246 s 121

1_{30} (x) υἱοῖς 2°] υιος A* x^{-509} 121 55

1_{47} $(oI\ C\ s)$ om φυλῆς A oI-29 $C''^{-131c\,(414')}$ s 121 55 424 624

2_2 $(oI\ y)$ κατά 2°] και (> 318 416) κατα τας A M' oI y^{-392} 55

2_2 $(C\ d\ s\ z)$ ἐναντίοι] εναντιον $\overline{κυ}$ A 82-707c C'-46 107'-125 127 85'-321-343'-346c 76 121 $z^{-122*\,126}$ 646

2_9 $(b\ s)$ ἐξαροῦσιν] αναζευξουσι(ν) A M'^{mg} b^{-537} $85'^{mg}$-$321'^{mg}$ 121 319

2_{11} (b) ἐπεσκεμμένοι] ηριθμημενοι A b 121 319 ^{Lat}cod 100

2_{13} (b) idem A b 121 319 ^{Lat}cod 100

2_{16} $(oI\ C\ b\ s)$ idem A oI-29 C'' b 30'-$85'^{txt}$-321-343'-346^{txt} 121 55 319 646 ^{Lat}cod 100

2_{16} $(oI\ b\ z)$ ἑκατὸν πεντήκοντα μία] μια και (> 68'-120') πεντ. και εκατον A M' oI-29 b 121 $z^{-18\,126}$ 55

2_{16} $(b\ s)$ ἐξαροῦσιν] αναζευξουσιν A M'^{mg} b $85'^{mg}$-$321'^{mg}$ 121 319

2_{18} $(O\ C)$ παρά] κατα A F^a M'^{mg} V O C''^{-131c} 767 121 126-128-628-669 55 319 646

2_{21} $(d\ n\ t)$ διακόσιοι] τριακοσιοι A*(vid) V 413*(c pr m) d n^{-767} t 55 799 ^{Lat}cod 100 Arm

2_{24} $(oI\ C\ b\ s)$ ἐπεσκεμμένοι] ηριθμημενοι A oI-29 C''^{-551} $b^{(-19)}$ 30'-$85'^{txt}$-321'-343' 121 55 319 646 ^{Lat}cod 100

2_{24} $(b\ s)$ ἐξαροῦσιν] αναζευξουσιν A M'^{mg} b 130^{mg}-$321'^{mg}$-344^{mg} 121

2_{26} $(d\ t\ x)$ δύναμις] -μεις A 376-707* d 56c 458-767 321 t x 68'-120' 55

2_{26} (b) ἐπεσκεμμένοι] ηριθμημενοι A b 319 ^{Lat}cod 100

2_{28} $(d\ t\ x)$ δύναμις] -μεις A* 376 d^{-44} 56c 458-767 t x 68'-120' 55

2_{31} $(C\ b\ s)$ ἐπεσκεμμένοι] αριθμηθεντες A 15-29 C'' 118'-537 s 121 55 319 624 646

2_{31} $(oI\ C\ s)$ ἑκατόν — χιλιάδες] επτα και πεντηκοντα και εκατον χιλιαδες A M' 29-58-oI C'' s^{-343mg} 121 55 319 624 646

3_1 $(d\ n\ t)$ ὄρει] pr τω A 72 d 246 n t 121

3_3 $(oI\ z)$ ἱερατεύειν] pr του A M' oI-29 121 z 55 646

3_{15} (b) ἐπισκέψῃ] αριθμησονται A b

3_{16} $(oI\ C\ b\ s)$ ἐπεσκέψατο] ηριθμησεν A oI-29-$707^{(mg)}$(vid) C'' b 28-30'-85-130^{txt}-$321'^{txt}$-343' 121 55 319 624 Sa^4

3_{16} $(oI\ b)$ ὃν τρόπον] καθα A oI-29 b 54 121 55 624

3_{25} (f) om τῆς θύρας A* 16-46 56'-129 509 18-126-628 55^{txt} 799 Arm

3_{27} $(d\ t\ y)$ Ἰσααρίς] σααρεις A G-426 d t y^{-318} 55 59 Arm

3_{36} $(d\ t)$ αὐτῆς 3°] αυτων A*(vid) d t Aeth

3_{37} $(b\ y)$ κάλους] κλαδους A b y^{-392}

4_5 (C) κιβωτόν 803] σκηνην A V 833 C''^{-528} 125-610 730 76 18 319 424

4_{11} $(b\ n)$ δερματίνῳ 803] -ματι A 707 b $n^{(-767)}$ Aeth

4_{12} $(b\ n)$ δερματίνῳ 803] -ματι (bis scr 118') A b n Aeth

4₁₄ (C) ὅσοις] οσοι A C''⁻¹⁶⁴⁶⁷⁷⁵²⁸⁵²⁹ᶜ 19′ 121 126 59

4₂₃ (z) ἐν τῇ σκηνῇ] τῆς σκηνῆς A 121 z Arm

4₂₄ (b f n) om τοῦ 2° A G-376 52-417-552 b 125 f⁽⁻¹²⁹ᵗˣᵗ⁾ n⁻⁷⁶⁷ 121 55

4₂₅ (C f n s) κάλυμμα 1°] κατακαλ. A Bᶜ F M′ 58-64-381 C''⁻⁵²⁷⁷*³²⁰⁴¹⁴⁵²⁸ 56-129-246ᶜ n⁻⁷⁵ s⁻³²¹*⁽³⁴³⁾ 318 59

4₂₅ (oI f y) αὐτῆς 2°] αυτην A M′ 29-58-72-oI f 71 y⁻³⁹² 55 59 646

4₃₃ (oI f y z) υἱοῦ] pr του A 426-oI f 619 y⁻³⁹² z 646

4₃₅ (oI) ἐν τῇ σκηνῇ] τῆς σκηνῆς A M′ 29-58-oI 619 121 68′-120 55 59 Aeth

4₃₆ (z) ἑπτακόσιοι] τριακοσιοι (-σια 18) A 15 121 18′-126-628-669 55

4₄₄ (oI' C n s) ἐγενήθη] εγενετο A F 58-oI' C'' n s 619 392 68′-120′ 55 59 319 646 799

4₄₄ (oI) om αὐτῶν 1° A 58-oI⁻⁶⁴ᵗˣᵗ 414 125 767 619 318 55 59

5₇ (oI C s) ἐποίησεν] ημαρτε(ν) A M′ᵐᵍ oI C'' 28-30′-85′ᵗˣᵗ-321′ᵗˣᵗ-343′ 55 646

6₁₂ (C s y) ἡγιάσθη] ηγιασε(ν) A 707 C'' 127-767 28-30′-85-130ᵗˣᵗ-343-344ᵗˣᵗ y⁻¹²¹ᶜ 55 319 624 Cyr I 1041

7₅₁ (n) ἕνα 3° 963] > A V 82-707 54-75′ 28-130-343′ 509 68*-120-122 ᴸᵃᵗcodd 100 104 Aeth⁻ᶜᴴ

7₅₇ (f n) ἕνα 3° 963] > A 707 f⁻²⁴⁶ 54-75′ 343-730 509 120′-122 ᴸᵃᵗcodd 100 104 Aethᴹ

7₆₃ (n y) om ἕνα 3° A V 82-707 413 54-75′ 343 509 y⁻³¹⁸ ᴸᵃᵗcodd 100 104

7₇₅ (x) ἕνα 3° 963] > A V 82 16-46-528 767 x⁻⁶¹⁹ 18-126

7₈₁ (n x) ἕνα 3° 963] > A* V 29ᵗˣᵗ(c pr m)-82 529 107′ 56 n⁻⁷⁶⁷ x⁻⁶¹⁹ 392 120 319 ᴸᵃᵗcod 100

8₁₃ (oI C s y) ἔναντι κυρίου 2°] κ͞ω A oI C'' s⁻⁸⁵′ᵐᵍ ³⁴⁶ᵐᵍ y⁻³⁹² 55 319 624 ᴸᵃᵗcod 100 Aeth

8₂₄ (C s) τοῦτο] τουτ (του 28*) A F 15*-707 C''⁻⁴⁶ 28-85-343′-730 121 68′-120′ 59 424

9₁₇ (oI d n t) παρενέβαλον] -λλον A F M′ 15-29-58-64ᶜ-381-707 57-313-422 125′-610ᶜ 56 54′-458 321′-344-730 t 121 Aeth Arm Sa

9₂₀ (oI C s y) ἀπαροῦσιν] εξαρουσι(ν) A M′ oI C''⁻⁴¹⁴ 127ᶜ 28-30′-85′ᵗˣᵗ-321′ᵗˣᵗ-343′ 619 y⁻³⁹² 55 319 646

9₂₂ (C) om τῆς νεφέλης σκιαζούσης A F 376 cI⁻⁵⁷-551 121

10₉ (oI C s y) σημανεῖτε] σαλπιειτε A Mᵐᵍ V oI C'' 44 s⁻¹³⁰ᵐᵍ ³²¹′ᵐᵍ y⁻³⁹² 126 55 319 416 ᴸᵃᵗOr Matth 52

10₁₄ (oI C s y) υἱῶν] pr των A 58-oI C''⁻⁽⁵⁷⁾⁵²⁹ s 619 y⁻³⁹²

10₂₅ (oI C s) Ἀμισαδαΐ] μισαδαι A oI⁻⁶⁴ C''⁻⁷³* s⁻³⁰ 121 55

10₃₀ (O C s y) ἀλλά] αλλ A V O⁻³⁷⁶-15-72′ C''⁻⁴²² ⁵²⁹ 75 s⁻³²¹* 509 y⁻³⁹² 18 55 59 319

10₃₁ (O f n y) ἐγκαταλίπῃς] -λειπης A F M′ O-29-64-381-618*-707 52′-313-417 f 54-75′ 30-343′ 134* 509 y⁻³⁹² 55 319

11₁₀ (C f n) ἕκαστον] -στος A C''⁻⁵²⁸ f 54-75′ 509 669* 55 Or II 388

11₁₂ (oI y) om τήν A oI y⁻³⁹² 55 624

11₁₃ (oI y) om μοι A M′ oI y⁻³⁹² 55 624

11₁₅ (z) οὕτως] ουτω A 619 z⁻¹²⁰′ 646 Cyr II 461

11₂₅ (oI C s y) ἐλάλησεν] + κυριος A M′ oI C''⁻⁴¹⁴* 610 75 s⁻⁷³⁰ y 55 624 Arm

11₃₁ (C n) om τῆς 1° A C'' 54-75′ 121 799

11₃₂ (b f) τήν 4°] τη A Fᶜ 58-72-381′ 529 b⁻¹⁹ f⁻¹²⁹ 54-75 121 59

12₁₄ (n) ἀφορισθήτω] -θησεται A 54-75′ 799 Cyr II 592 Tht Nm 209ᵗᵉ

12₁₄ (b f z) om ἑπτὰ ἡμέρας 2° A F V 29-58-72-376 b 44 f⁻¹²⁹ 458-767 130 619 121 z 55 59 799 Cyr II 592 Tht Nm 209

13₁₉ (f n) εἰ 1°] η A F M′ 29 f 54-75*-458 71′ 319 799

13₂₄ (C b f s) ᾖραν] ηρον A F M′ 15-58-707 C''⁻⁴⁶⁷⁷⁴¹⁴⁵²⁸⁷⁶¹ᶜ b f⁻²⁴⁶ s⁻³²¹′ᵐᵍ 509 121 59

13₂₉ (oI) Ἐνάκ] αιναχ A 58-oI⁻¹⁵ᶜ 127-458 121 18 319

13₃₀ (b y) τῇ 2° Fᵃ] > A F 58-72-82 417 b 56 30 509-527 y⁻³¹⁸ 59 799 ᴸᵃᵗBeda Sam 273 Arm

13₃₂ (oI' C s y) αὐτοῦ] αυτων A F M′ oI'⁻⁷² C'' 127 s⁻³⁴³ ³⁴⁴ᶜ y 55 59 624 Aeth

14₁₄ (oI) ὀφθαλμοῖς] -μους A M′ G-oI 57-77 610* 127 130* 370 527 121 55 799 Syh

14₁₇ (d n t) ἰσχύς] χειρ A M′ 29-72-376 16-46 d 129 n t 392 59 799 Eus VI 240 ᴸᵃᵗQuodv Prom II 17 Arab Arm

14₄₅ (b) ἐτρέψαντο] -ψατο A b⁻¹⁹ 54 318 55 59

15₂₁ (d t) ἀπαρχήν] -χης A 58-72 414 44-107′ 458 t⁻¹³⁴

15₂₂ (y) διαμάρτητε] -ρτυρητε A y⁻³¹⁸

15₃₈ (f n) ἐπιθήσετε] -σεται A V G-82-376 313-615 19 107* f⁻¹²⁹ 75′-767 28*-30 509 55 319 799

16₁₁ (b s y) τίς] τι A M′ 46ˢ b 28-85′-321′-730* 509 y⁻³⁹² 68′ Aeth Syhᵐᵍ

16₄₆ (s) ἀπένεγκε] -γκαι A F 15-58-376 16-46*-77-414-422-616 129 s⁻³⁰′ 84 619 121 128-669 55 59 319*

17₈ (C) Ἀαρών 2° Fᶜ] pr η A F M′ V G-82-426-707 C′′⁻⁵⁷ ⁷³′ ⁴¹⁷ ⁴²² ⁵²⁸ ⁵⁵¹ 106 56 54 85-321′ 74-370 527 55

18₅ (oI s y) φυλάξεσθε] -ξετε A oI 16-46-414-616-761 30′-130-343′-346 y⁻³⁹²

18₁₄ (b) υἱοῖς] pr τοις A b 121 128-669

18₁₅ (C s y) μήτραν] pr πασαν A M′ 15′-58 C′′⁻¹⁶⁴⁶⁵⁵²ᵗˣᵗ s 619 y⁻¹²¹ 55 Procop 845

18₁₈ (d n t) om κατά A 618*(c pr m) d 54-75′ t ᴸᵃᵗcod 100 Arm

18₁₈ (oI C s y) σοὶ ἔσται] tr A M′ oI C′′⁻¹⁶⁴⁶ s y⁻³⁹² 55 319 624 Aeth Arab Bo

18₂₄ (C s) υἱῶν 2°] pr των A C′′ 246 s 318 319 624

18₂₈ (f n) δώσετε] -σεται A V 72*-82-376 19 106 56′-664 75′-767 509 55 319

18₃₀ (C s) ἐρεῖς] ερειτε (c var) A 707 C′′⁽⁻⁵⁵⁰′⁾ s 121 55

19₂ (oI d n t) αὐτῇ] εαυτη A 376-oI 528-761ᶜ d⁻⁶¹⁰* 54′-767 t⁻⁸⁴ 318

20₃ (oI C s y) ἀπεθάνομεν] απωλομεθα A F M′ᵐᵍ oI⁻⁶¹⁸-29-707 C′′⁻¹³¹⁵⁰⁰⁵⁵⁰′⁵⁵¹ s⁻³⁴³⁷³⁰ 619 318 z⁻¹²⁶⁶²⁸ 319 646 Cyr II 488

20₂₄ (O b f n) δέδωκα] εδωκα A V O′⁻¹⁵³⁷⁶-72 52′-313-414′-422 b 53′-129 n⁻⁴⁵⁸ 74-76 527 121 55 59 646

20₂₄ (oI C s y) Ἰσραήλ] + εν κατασχεσει A F M′ V 58-72-oI C′′ 246 s 619 y⁻³⁹² 18-126-628 55 59 319 646 ᴸᵃᵗAug Num 39

21₃ (s t y z) Χανανίν] χανανι A M*(vid) 30′-130-321′-344 t 71-509 y⁻³⁹² 18′-126-628-630′ 416 646

21₃ (s) ἐπεκάλεσαν] -σε(ν) A 85′ᵐᵍ-321′ᵐᵍ-343-344ᵐᵍ 68′-120′ 799

21₁₂ (oI) Ζαρέδ] ζαρε A oI 121

21₁₉ (s) Μανθαναίν] -νειν A 707ᶜ 77-313-422-615 s⁻³⁴³³⁴⁴ᵐᵍ 624

21₂₅ (oI C s y) αὐτῇ] αυταις A M′ 58-oI C′′ s 619 y 55 624

21₂₇ (n) ἔλθετε] ελθατε A V 29-58 129 n 121(2°)-392 55*(c pr m) 624 799

22₅ (b d t y) Βεώρ] βαιωρ A 426 b d 127 t 71 y⁻³⁹² 55 319

22₂₃ (oI) τῇ ῥάβδῳ] εν τη ραβδω αυτου A oI

22₃₀ (b f) ἀπό] εκ A 29 b 53′-246 458 55

22₃₁ (C s z) Βαλαάμ] pr του A C′′⁻⁵² s 619 121 z 319

22₃₂ (oI C s y) εἶπεν] λεγει A M′ oI-82 C′′ s⁻⁸⁵′ᵐᵍ³²¹′ᵐᵍ y⁻³⁹² 55 319 624

22₃₈ (b f s) λαλήσω] φυλαξω λαλησαι A 82-707 b f⁻¹²⁹ 85′ᵐᵍ-321′ᵐᵍ-344ᵐᵍ 121 319 624ᵐᵍ 799 Aeth

23₈ (y) κύριος] pr ο A M′ 15 30′-343′ y⁻³⁹²

23₁₉ (oI′ n y z) οὐδέ] ουδ A F 58-oI′⁻⁸² 56′ 54-75′ 619 y⁽⁻³⁹²⁾ z 55 624 799

24₁ (d t y) ἔναντι] εναντιον A F 64-72-381 d t 619 y⁻³¹⁸ 630 55

24₃ (d t y) Βεώρ] βαιωρ A 106-107′ t 71 y⁻³⁹² Sa⁴

24₉ (C s y) εὐλόγηνται] ηυλ. A M′ 29 C′′⁻¹⁶⁴⁶⁵²⁹* 30′-85-130ᵗˣᵗ-321′ᵗˣᵗ-343-344ᵗˣᵗ y⁻³¹⁸ 669 55 59

24₁₅ (t y) Βεώρ] βαιωρ A 106 t 71 y⁻³⁹² 55 Sa⁴

24₂₂ (t y) idem A 15 125 t y⁻³⁹² 55

25₃ (oI y) ἐτελέσθη Ἰσραήλ] ετελεσθησαν A M′ oI⁽⁻¹⁵⁾ y⁻³⁹² Eus VI 404 Or I 7ᵗᵉ

25₆ (n y) ἐναντίον 1°] εναντι A 15-58-376 n y⁻³⁹² 126 55 319

25₁₅ (oI′ n s y) Ὀμμώθ] σομμωθ A F(vid) M′ 58-oI′⁻⁸²⁶¹⁸ 56′ 54′-458 s⁻¹³⁰³⁴³ y⁻³⁹² 55 799 ᴸᵃᵗcod 100

26₂ (d t z) συναγωγῆς] pr της A d 458-767 t⁻⁸⁴* 18′-120-628-630′

26₃ (oI d y) om ὁ ἱερεύς A oI⁻¹⁵ d⁻¹⁰⁶ y⁻³⁹² 55 319 Aeth

26₁₈ (x) τῷ] του A 85 x⁻⁷¹ 121 68′-120 Bo Syh

26₂₅ (oI z) Ἀζενί 1°] αζαινι A F M′ oI⁻⁶¹⁸ 56 121 18′-126-628-669

26₂₅ (oI z) Ἀζενί 2°] αζαινι A F M′ oI⁻⁶¹⁸ 121 18′-126-628-630′

26₄₄ (y) Νοεμάν 1°] νοεμα A 15-82 y 55

26₄₈ (oI b y) Γαννί 1°] γωννι A M oI-29-707 52 b 664 321-346* 619 y 55

26₄₈ (oI y) Γαννί 2°] γωννι A F M′ oI-707 52 130ᶜ-321′ 619 y 55

26₄₉ (oI y) Ἰέσερ] ιεσρι A oI y⁻³⁹²

26₄₉ (oI) Ἰεσερί] ιεσρι A oI 121

26₅₇ (oI) Γεδσών] γεδσωνι A oI 318

26₅₈ (oI b y) δῆμος 2°] pr και A M′ oI 551 b 246 619 y 68′ 55 624 ᴸᵃᵗcod 100 Aeth Arab Co

26₅₈ (n t) Χεβρωνί] χεβρων A n⁻⁷⁶⁷ t⁽⁻³⁷⁰⁾ 121 624 Co

26₅₈ (oI b t z) Μουσί] ομουσι A M′ oI⁻⁶⁴*⁻⁷⁰⁷ 52 118′-537 56′ 54-458 321′ 74′-76 121 18′-126-628-630′ 55 624 Boᴮ

27₁₄ (b d t) Σίν 1°] σινα A K M 376-707 550′ b d 767 t 121 59 319 ᴸᵃᵗcod 100 Aeth⁻ᶜ Co

27₁₇ (oI) ὡσεί 963] ως A M′ oI 121 126 55 Phil II 104ᶠ

27₂₁ (C) ἐπερωτήσουσιν 963] -σωσιν A 58 C″⁻⁵²⁷⁷⁴¹⁴⁴²²⁷⁶¹ 53′ 127 28-85 392 68 319 416

27₂₂ (C n s) ἐναντίον 1°] εναντι A 15-72 C″⁻⁵²′³¹³ 125 129 n 28-30′-85⁽ᵐᵍ⁾-343-344ᵗˣᵗ 84* 121 55 646

28₂ (d n) διατηρήσετε] -σατε A M′ d⁻¹⁰⁶ n 121 Phil I 247ᵃᵖ II 57ᵃᵖ 296ᵗᵉ Aeth

28₁₆ (y) ἡμέρᾳ 963] ⌒(17) A 72-618 y⁻¹²¹ᵐᵍ 59 624

28₁₇ (y) om ἑπτά — fin A 15 121ᵗˣᵗ-318 624

28₁₈ (f) ποιήσετε] -σεται A K V 82-376 56′-664 75′ 30-130* 509 120 55 624

28₃₁ (oI y z) τοῦ 2°] (c var) τῆς νουμηνιας και η θυσια αυτων και το ολοκαυτωμα το A M′ 58-oI 127 619 y z⁻⁴⁰⁷ 55 624 646

29₈ (O C s y) om κυρίῳ A F M′ O′ C″⁻⁵²′¹³¹ᶜ⁴¹⁴ s y 55 624 Syh

29₂₃ (oI C s y) τέσσαρας] -ρες (-ρεις 64) A F 29-58-426-707-oI C″⁻⁽⁷³′⁾⁷⁷ 54′ s⁽⁻¹³⁰⁾ y⁻¹²¹ 18′-630′ 59 646

29₂₆ (oI C s z) idem A F 29-426-707-oI C″⁻⁷⁷ s 392 18-68′-120-630 59 646

30₁₁ (oI C s y) κατά] pr o A oI-72-707ᶜ C″⁻⁵²′³¹³⁵⁵¹ s⁻³⁰ y 68′ 55 416 624 646 ᴸᵃᵗAug Num 59.2

30₁₅ (oI x y) (ἐπ’) αὐτῆς] αυτη A 72-426-oI⁻¹⁵ 53′ 134 x⁻⁵⁰⁹ y 407 55 416

31₈ (y) Βεώρ] βαιωρ A 15 767 71′ y⁻³⁹² 624

31₈ (oII b n y) τοῖς 2°] ταις A oII⁻⁷⁰⁷ 131-417-761 b 53 75′-767 84* y⁻³⁹² 68′-120 55 416

31₁₈ (d n s y) οἶδεν] εγνω A F 15-29-72 107′-125 129 n 130ᵐᵍ-321′ ᵐᵍ y⁻¹²¹

31₄₁ (C s) καθά 963(vid)] καθαπερ A 15′ C″⁻⁴¹⁴ 28-85′-321′ 318 55 624

31₄₃ (oI s y z) τῆς] pr το A M′ oI⁻⁶¹⁸ 52′-313 28-85ᵗˣᵗ-130-321′ᵗˣᵗ-343′ y⁻³⁹²* 18′-628-630′ 624 = Ra

32₃ (C s y) Ἀταρώθ] -ρων A 58-72 C″ s y⁻³¹⁸

32₄ (oI y z) om τῶν A M′ oI-82 y⁻³⁹² 18′-126-628-630′

32₇ (oI C s y) διανοίας 963] καρδιας A M′ 376-oI C″ s y 55

32₁₆ (f) ἡμῶν 1°] υμων A 417-422-528-551* 53′-246 527

32₁₉ (f) ἐν αὐτοῖς] εαυτοις A 413-414 f⁻¹²⁹ 121

32₂₁ (y) ὁπλίτης Fᶜ] οπλιστης (c var) A F G-72 129 509 y⁻¹²¹ 55

32₂₅ (d x) ἡμῶν] ημιν A d⁻¹⁰⁶ x⁻⁵⁰⁹ Sa¹²

32₂₇ (oI s y) καί 963] > A M′ oI-707 85′ᵗˣᵗ-321′ᵗˣᵗ-343-344ᵗˣᵗ y 18-628 55 624 Aeth

32₃₂ (C s) ἐνωπλισμένοι] post κυρίου tr A C″ s

32₃₆ (b y) Ναμβρά] αμβραν A 381′ 52′-414′-528-529 b 54 y⁻³⁹² 55

32₄₁ (C t) Ἰαὶρ 2°] ιαηρ A 58-72-82-376 C″⁽⁻⁵²⁸⁾ 106 53′ 127*-458* 28-85-343-730 74*-76-84 59 319 799

33₆ (x) ἀπῆραν] απαραντες A V G-82-426 129-246 x⁻⁵⁰⁹ 68′-120′ Arm Syh

33₁₅ (C s y) Σινά] pr τη A F 58 C″⁻⁴²²⁵²⁹⁷⁶¹* 118′ 129 s y⁻³¹⁸ 68′-120 59

33₃₁ (y) Βαναιακάν] βανικαν A y⁻³⁹² 407

33₃₂ (y) idem A y⁻³⁹² 407

33₄₁ (O f) εἰς] εν A Bᶜ M′ O-29-707 56′-129 509 121 68′-120′ 59

33₄₇ (C s y) Δεβλαθάιμ] δαιβλ. A G C″⁻⁴⁶⁵⁷⁴¹⁴⁵²⁹⁽⁵⁵¹⁾⁵⁵² 127 28-30-85-321′-344 84* y⁻³¹⁸ 407

33₄₉ (C s) Αἰσιμώθ] ασιμωθ A G*-29-58-72 C″⁻⁴¹³⁴¹⁴′⁴¹⁷⁴²²⁷⁶¹ s⁻³²¹³⁴³ 59

33₅₀ (C) παρὰ τὸν Ἰορδάνην] επι του ιορδανου A C⁻⁵²⁹-46

33₅₅ (oI C s z) οὕς] οσους A oI C″ 246 28-85′-321′ 121 18′-126-628-630′ 55

34₄ (oI C f t) Σέννα] σεενναк A oI⁻⁶¹⁸ C″⁻⁵²³²⁰⁴¹³⁴¹⁴⁴¹⁷⁵²⁸ f⁻¹²⁹ 28-85-343 121 126-128-628-669

34₅ (n) Ἀσεμώνα] σελμωνα A 72 131⁽ᵐᵍ⁾ 129-246 n⁻¹²⁷ 30 84 71′ 318 669 55* 59 Bo

84

34_6 (b) ἡ 1° 963] > A 82 b 121

34_{28} (O b z) Βεναμιούδ] αμιουδ A F O′$^{-376}$-72 73′-529-552-615*-616* 19′-314 30′-321* z$^{-18\,68′}$ 55 59

34_{29} (oII f s) καταμερίσαι 963] -μετρησαι (c var) A F oII^{-82} f^{-129} 130^{mg}-321′^{mg} 121 68′ 59 ^{Lat}codd 100 104 Aeth

35_{11} (oI x) φυγεῖν] φευγειν A oI 129 30′ x^{-509}

35_{15} (x) idem A 29 129* x^{-509}

35_{31} (oI z) περί] επι A V oI 414 246 121 18′-126-628-669 55

35_{34} (d t) ἐν ὑμῖν] επ αυτης A d t 55

35_{34} (oI b f) κατασκηνῶν] pr o A oI-82 b 53′-246 18′-628-669 Arm Bo

In the following table variants from list 7 in which no more than four text groups support an A variant are also included. Vertical column A gives the number of instances in which one text group supports an A variant; column B, two text groups; column C, three, and column D, four text groups. The final column gives the total number of instances of a text group supporting a variant also supported by codex A. The sub-groups oI/oII have been differentiated only when O is not involved. The C groups have not been kept apart. The s readings supported by the majority of 85′^{mg}-321′^{mg}-344^{mg} have been included.

	A	B	C	D	Total
O	—	3	5	7	15
oI/oII	9	14	18	33	74
C	6	9	18	29	62
b	8	14	15	12	49
d	1	6	16	5	28
f	4	8	8	6	26
n	5	15	11	12	43
s	3	9	21	34	67
t	—	9	15	7	31
x	5	5	4	—	14
y	10	14	20	28	72
z	3	6	11	9	29

The affiliations of A are quite different from those of B. The clearest picture of A's affinities is found in the totals of the last column. At the head of the list stands oI (and oII) with 74 instances of agreement, followed by y with 72, s with 67 and C'' with 62. These are then followed by b with 49, n with 43, t with 31, z with 29, d with 28 and f with 26. At the end of the list are O (as distinct from its sub groups with 15 and x with 14.

Over against this agreements with B found y as farthest removed from B with only 2 agreements. This was followed by s with 5, C'' with 9 and oI/oII with 10; i.e. the four which head the list in agreeing with A are at the bottom of the list of agreements with B. On the other hand, x stood closest to B, but is farthest removed from the A type text.

It would then appear that it is not entirely false to speak of an A type text over against a B type text as far as the text history of Numbers is concerned.

Chapter 5 Papyrus 963 As Textual Witness

963 is our oldest substantial Greek witness for Numbers; its outstanding importance is illustrated by the fact that it was copied before the time of Origen, i.e. it must represent a so-called prehexaplaric text. Because of its age its text has on occasions been taken as determinative for the text of Num, e.g.

26₆₅ υἱός 2° 963] ο του B M′ V 29-82-376′ b d⁻¹²⁵ 129 n t x⁻⁶¹⁹ Cyr I 348 352 Syh = Ra

In designating the immediate ancestry of Caleb and Joshua Num fluctuates apparently without reason between υἱός and ὁ τοῦ; for all others υἱός is standard. Since no pattern of translation is discernible it seemed best to follow the oldest witness, particularly since codex A also supports the reading.

Not that one should exhibit undue reverence for 963 just because of its age. The copyist was not overly careful as the following list of unique readings shows.

List 1

5₁₃ μετ᾽ αὐτῆς 1°] μετα ταυτης 963
5₁₃ μετ᾽ αὐτῆς 2°] μετα ταυτης 963
5₁₉ ἀπὸ τοῦ] [. . .] 963
    Probably 963 omitted τοῦ in view of the next variant.
5₁₉ om τοῦ 2° 963
5₂₁ om ἐν 1° — γυναικί 963ᵗˣᵗ
    This was simply the result of carelessness. The word before ἐν is γυναῖκα.
5₂₇ πρησθήσεται] πρηθησεται 963
6₄ ἀμπέλου] απελου 963
6₅ ξυρόν] λυτρον 963
6₅ κόμην] κοιμην 963*(c pr m)
6₁₁ ἁγιάσει] α[γι]ηση 963*(c pr m)
6₁₂ τὰς ἡμέρας] τη ημερα 963
6₁₄ ὁλοκαύτωσιν] -τησιν 963*(c pr m)
6₁₇ om θυσίαν 1° 963
6₁₈ ἠγμένος] ηυγμε 963*(|)
6₂₀ ἐπίθεμα] επι το θεμα 963
6₂₁ αὐτοῦ 3°] αυτης 963
7₃ ἕξ] pr και 963
7₅ πρὸς τὰ ἔργα] bis scr 963*(c pr m)
7₉ λειτουργήματα] + τα 963ᶜ
7₁₂ Ἀμιναδάβ] αμειναδεβ 963
7₁₃ τὸ δῶρον αὐτοῦ] om τό 963
7₁₃ φιάλην] φιελην 963
    963 consistently spells φιάλην with

an ε in this chapter. The reading is also extant in vv. 19, 25, 37, 43, 49, 55, 61, 67, 73 and 79; in each instance the spelling is unique.
7₁₈ Ναθαναήλ] ναν, αθαηλ 963ᶜ(vid)
7₁₈ Σωγάρ] σωγαδ 963
7₂₉ Ἐλιάβ] ελειαβ 963
7₃₀ Σεδιούρ] σεδειουρ 963
7₃₁ τριάκοντα] pr και 963*(c pr m)
7₃₅ Σεδιούρ] σεδειουρ 963
7₄₁ Σουρισαδαί] σουρεισαιδαι 963
7₄₅ om ἐνιαύσιον 963
7₄₈ om τῶν 963
7₄₈ Ἐφράιμ] εφρεμ 963*(c pr m)
7₄₈ Ἐμιούδ] εμειουδ 963
7₄₉ ἀργυροῦν] -ρον 963
7₅₃ Ἐμιούδ] εμει[ο]υδ 963
7₅₄₋₅₉ bis scr 963*
7₅₄ Φαδασούρ] φαδεσσουρ 963
7₅₈ om περί 963(1°)
7₅₉ om ἐνιαυσίας 963
7₅₉ Γαμαλιήλ 963(2°)] ελεισαμα 963(1°)
7₅₉ Φαδασούρ] φαδεσσουρ 963(2°); εμειουδ 963(1°)
7₆₀ Ἀβιδάν] αβειναδαν 963
7₆₂ θυΐσκην] pr εις 963*
7₆₃ om ἐκ — (64) καί 963
7₇₀ ἕνα] εν 963*(c pr m)

7₇₃ ἀργυρᾶν] -ρην 963
963 consistently has αργυρην for
ἀργυρᾶν in ch. 7; cf comment at 7₁₃
φιάλην above.

7₇₇ Ἐχράν] [ε]χθραν 963
7₈₆ εἴκοσι] pr και 963*(c pr m)
7₈₇ μόσχοι] μοσχους 963*(c pr m)
8₃ om ἑνός 963
8₈ om ἐκ βοῶν 1° 963
8₁₁ ἀφοριεῖ] -ρει 963*(c pr m)
8₁₂ τῶν] αυτων 963*(c pr m)
8₁₃ ἔναντι 4°] -ντιου 963*(c pr m)
8₁₇ ἀνθρώπου] -πους 963*(c pr m)
8₁₇ γῇ] τη 963
26₁₂ Ἰαμινί] . . .]εινει 963
26₃₃ Μαχίρ 1°] ⌒2° 963
26₆₄ τῶν] τω 963*
26₆₅ ἐξ αὐτῶν] om ἐξ 963
27₁₇ om πρό (προσώπου) 1° 963*
27₁₇ πρό 2°] απο 963*
27₂₂ ἐναντίον 1°] ⌒2° 963*(vid)
29₁₂ ἡμέρᾳ] τημερα 963

29₁₄ om καί 1° 963*(vid)
29₂₃ om τῇ ἡμέρᾳ 963*
29₃₅ om οὐ 963*
29₃₆ ἐνιαυσίους] pr ε̄ 963
29₃₈ πλὴν τῆς] bis scr 963*(c pr m)
30₇ γενομένη] γονομε[. . . 963
30₈ στήσονται 2°] συστη[. . . 963
30₁₄ εὐχή] ευχην 963*(c pr m)
30₁₆ μετὰ τήν] μετ αυ[τη]ν 963
30₁₆ om ἦν 963*
31₁₂ Μωάβ] μοα[β] 963
31₂₆ ἀνθρώπου] pr του 963*(c pr m)
31₄₀ δύο] pr και 963
31₄₈ χιλίαρχοι] pr και 963
32₁₂ συνεπηκολούθησεν] συνηκ. 963*
32₁₃ ἐπί] pr και 963*(c pr m)
32₁₅ ἀποστραφήσεσθε] [απ]οστραφησθε 963
32₂₉ εἰς] εν 963*
33₅₃ κατοικήσετε] [κατο]ικησεσθε 963
33₅₄ κατακληρονομήσετε] -μησε 963*(c pr m)
34₅ Ἀσεμώνα] σεμωνα 963
35₂₅ κατέφυγεν] κατεφευ[. . . 963

None of these unique readings needs to be taken seriously. Most of them represent careless errors on the part of the copyist, often resulting in an impossible text. Nonetheless in view of the age of the ms they have all been recorded in the apparatus.

It may be noted that 963 like B has a preference for the itacistic ει for ι. This is particularly obvious for proper names; cf 7₂₉ ₃₀ ₃₅ ₄₁ ₄₈ ₅₃ ₅₉ ₆₀. Since the variant is valueless for text criticism it will be disregarded in subsequent lists.

List 2 gives all the remaining secondary readings in 963 (except for the itacistic ει spelling for ι) with the exception of those which could have been the result of mediate or immediate Hebrew influence.

List 2

5₁₃ λάθῃ] λαβη 963 77 68′
5₁₃ ᾖ 1°] ην 963 82 b 68′-120′
5₁₄ ἤ] και 963 319
5₁₇ λαβών] αναλαβων 963(vid) b
5₂₄ καί 1°] ⌒2° 963 52′-413-414-528 d 767 370 126-669 Aeth
5₂₅ πρός B V b d 54′-75 t 71 319 Cyr I 909 Latcod 100] εις 458; επι 963(vid) rell
5₂₉ ᾧ] ο 963 707
5₃₀ ἄν S] εαν A B F 963 G-58-72′-82-oI⁻¹⁵ 77-417-529 19 54-458 134 71′ 392 z 59 319 = Ra
6₄ οἶνον] οινον 963*(c pr m) 319
6₅ om τῆς εὐχῆς B 963 664 54-75′ 28-85 x⁻⁶¹⁹ 628 799 Cyr I 1041 Arm Sa⁴
6₇ ἐπί 2° A B* V G-29-72-376-oI⁻¹⁵ b d⁻¹²⁵ n 130ᵐᵍ-321′ᵐᵍ t 619 318 55 319 Aeth⁻ᶜᴳ Arm] > 963 rell
6₇ om αὐτοῦ 1° 963 72 52′ 53′ 75 71 628 Latcod 100 Arm
6₈ κυρίῳ A B V G-29-426 761 n⁻⁷⁶⁷ 509 55 Cyr I 1041] pr τω 963 rell
6₁₃ ἡμέρας] -ρα 963 707ᵐᵍ(vid) 767 730 71 68′-120′ 59
6₁₄ σωτήριον] -ριαν B* Vᶜ 963 552ᵗˣᵗ-616*(vid) b 44 767 628 624

87

6₁₅ θυσίαν] θυσια (-σι 963*) B 963 n⁻⁴⁵⁸ x⁻⁶¹⁹ = Ra

6₁₅ σπονδήν] σπονδη (c var) B 963 n x⁻⁶¹⁹ = Ra

6₁₆ om τό 1° 963 ᴸᵃᵗcod 100

6₁₉ ἕν] ενα B* 963 16-46 246

6₁₉ ἡὔγμένου] ευγμ. (εγμ. 458) 963 G*-15'-29-426ᶜ ᵖʳ ᵐ-707 56-129ᵗˣᵗ(c pr m) n⁻⁷⁵ᶜ 28-30-85'-321'*-343' x⁻⁶¹⁹ 319

6₁₉ τὴν εὐχήν B 85'ᵐᵍ-321'ᵐᵍ-344ᵐᵍ x⁻⁶¹⁹ 319 ᴸᵃᵗcod 100 Arab] pr την κεφαλην 75'; τη κεφαλη 126; την κεφαλην 963 rell

6₂₀ ἅγιον] αγια 963 Sa⁴

6₂₀ ἡὔγμένος] ευγμ. A*(vid) F V 963 G*-15'-29-426-707 54'-458-767ᶜ s⁻¹³⁰ᶜ ³²¹ᶜ x⁻⁶¹⁹ 319

6₂₅ om σε 2° B 963 x⁻⁶¹⁹

6₂₆ ἐπὶ σέ] ∩(27) 963 16-46-414-422 75-127 392 68'-126 59 Cyr I 772 Sa¹²

7₃ παρά 2°] παρ V 963 376-oI C'' 54-75' s 392 126

7₁₀ τὸ δῶρον Aeth] τα (> 19) δωρα 963 rell = Ra
   Cf the discussion in ch 6 Sect 8b.

7₁₁ ἡμέραν 1°] ∩2° Fᵇ 963 58-72-82*(c pr m) cI-52'-313ᶜ-414'-422 108-118-537 44'-107 75-127-767 730 t 509 y⁻¹²¹ 669 59 Bo

7₁₂ Ναασσών] νασσων 963 Bo

7₁₃ ἀργυρᾶν] -ρην 963 130ᵐᵍ

7₁₉ ἀργυρᾶν] -ρην (-ριν 458-767) 963 G 44 458-767 130ᵐᵍ 71 319

7₂₄ Χαιλών] χελων F V 963 15-72-82-376 77-414 b 125-610 f⁻⁵⁶ 54-75' 130* 76-84 x 318 669 319

7₂₅ ἀργυρᾶν] -ρην (-ριν 458) 963 458 509 319

7₃₁ idem 963 130ᵐᵍ 319

7₃₃ om ἕνα 3° A V 963 82-376-oI⁻⁶⁴ C''⁻⁵²' ⁵²⁸ s⁻³²¹ᶜ ⁽³⁴³⁾ 71 18 ᴸᵃᵗcod 100 Aeth⁻ᶜᴴ

7₃₅ ἐνιαυσίας] -σιους F*(c pr m) 963 376* t⁻⁸⁴ 71 18-126-628

7₃₅ υἱοῦ] υιος V 963 458-767

7₃₇ ἀργυρᾶν] -ρην 963 130ᵐᵍ

7₄₁ ἐνιαυσίας] -σιους 963 52 56 619 18-126-628

7₄₁ υἱοῦ] υιος 963 29-707* 30-343' 74' 392

7₄₃ ἀργυρᾶν] -ρην K(vid) 963 130ᵐᵍ

7₄₇ om τό 963 413

7₅₅ ἀργυρᾶν] -ρην 963 130ᵐᵍ

7₆₁ idem 963 130ᵐᵍ

7₆₅ Γαδεωνί] γεδεωνει 963 129 127

7₆₇ ἀργυρᾶν] -ρην (-ρον 963*) 963 130ᵐᵍ

7₇₉ ἀργυρᾶν] -ρην 963 130ᵐᵍ 509 319

7₈₆ πλήρεις] -ρη V 963 15-376 106 458 130 509 392 68'-120' 55

7₈₈ κριοί] pr και B* 963 Aeth Arab Bo

7₈₈ ἀμνάδες] -δας 963* 72 509 121

7₈₈ ἐγκαίνισις] -νησις (ενκ. 30; -σεις 319) 963 O⁻⁴²⁶-29-707 16'-616* b d⁻¹⁰⁷ f⁻¹²⁹ 54-458 30-130 84-134 71 y 68'-120*-128-628 319

7₈₉ κυρίου] pr τον 963 458 84

7₈₉ χερουβίμ] -βειν F 963 15*-64-707 30-85'-343'

8₁ Μωυσῆν] μωσην 963 426 n Cyr I 608

8₁₄ ἐμοί] μοι 963 619 68'-120'

8₁₇ om ὅτι ἐμοί 963 72 509

25₁₈ Μαδιάν B 82-426 Syh] maziam ᴸᵃᵗcod 100; -νει G; μαδιαμ 963 rell

26₄₇ τετρακόσιοι] φ 963 129

26₄₉ Ἰεσερί] ιεσσερει V 963 129

26₄₉ Σελλήμ] σελημ 963 58-376-381*-618 77 b⁻¹⁹ 129 30 71 318 59

26₄₉ Σελλημί] σελημει 963 77 129 71

26₅₀ om πέντε καί B Fᵃ V 963 129 n t x⁻⁶¹⁹ 319 Arm Bo

26₅₀ τετρακόσιοι O 30' 619 68'-120'-128-630 59 319 Arab Bo Syh] sup ras 669; εξακ. 343; τριακ. 963 rell

27₃ διά] δι F K M' V 963 O'' C''⁻⁵²⁸ d⁻⁶¹⁰* f n s⁻⁷³⁰ x⁻⁶¹⁹ y z 59 319 646 Phil II 309

27₁₈ ἄνθρωπον] -πος 963 15*(c pr m)-376 616 19 75' 28 121*(c pr m)

27₁₈ αὐτόν] ⌒(₁₉) 963* 130-321'

27₂₁ οἱ (υἱοί)] > 963 246 619 68'-126 319

28₁₁ κυρίῳ] pr τω B 963 72-82-426 550*-551-552 d 346* t 509 319 424 Cyr I 1116 = Ra

28₁₄ ὁλοκαύτωμα (-τω 509) B F V O'⁻³⁷⁶-29-72 458 x⁻⁶¹⁹ 18'-126-628-630' 59 624] pr το 963 rell

28₁₆ κυρίῳ] κυ̅ Bᵗˣᵗ 963 82-426 127 55 319 Latcod 100 Aeth

29₂₃ τέσσαρας καὶ δέκα] δεκα τεσσ. (c var) B V 963 72-82-376 77 44' ƒ x 407 416

29₂₉ idem (-ρες B* 82; -σσερεις 664) B V 963 58-72-82-376 77 d⁻⁴⁴ ƒ⁽⁻⁵³⁾ t x 407 416 = Ra

29₃₀ κατά 1°] κατ 963 G-426 417 664 54-75 126

29₃₂ τέσσαρας καὶ δέκα] δεκα τεσσ. (c var) B V 963 58-72-82-376 77 d ƒ t x 407 416

29₃₆ om ἀμώμους 963 72

29₃₇ κατά 1°] κατ 963 G-426 54-75 126

29₃₉ καί 1° — ὑμῶν 3°] post ὑμῶν 4° tr V 963 d 56ᵐᵍ-129-246 t 319 Arm Sa

30₃ ἤ ὁρίσηται / ὁρισμῷ] tr B Fᵃ 963 82 d 129 n t x 407 319 Or II 306 Latcod 100 Arm

30₁₃ κύριος] pr o 963 458

30₁₃ καθαριεῖ F Fᵇ] -ρισει B Fᵃ(vid) 963 426 509 = Ra

30₁₆ λήμψεται A B* F V G-82 56* 509 624] ληψη 46ˢ; ληψ. Fᵇ 963 rell

31₆ σημασιῶν] σημειων 963 72-426

31₇ Μαδιάν B 509 Syh] madianitas Arm; μαδιαμ 963 rell

31₁₇ ἀποκτείνατε 1° Fᵃ] απεκτ. F 963 707 53 54-458 y⁻¹²¹ 407 799 Sa

31₂₁ ὅ 963*(vid)] ον V 963ᶜ 129 z⁻⁴⁰⁷

31₃₆ ἑπτακισχίλια] -λιοι (-χειλιοι 963 G) V 963 G-82-618 528 19' 59

31₃₈ om δύο 963* 108*(c pr m)

31₄₀ ἓξ καὶ δέκα] εκκαιδεκα B 963 15-82 = Ra

31₄₃ τῆς 72-618 C'ʼ⁻⁵²'³¹³ 509 392* 68-126 55 319 799 Latcodd 100 104 Arab] pr το απο 730; pr το A M' oI⁻⁶¹⁸ 52'-313 28-85ᵗˣᵗ-130-321'ᵗˣᵗ-343' y⁻³⁹²* 18'-628-630' 624; pr απο 963 rell

31₄₃ ἑπτακισχίλια] ζ χ(ε)ιλιαδες 963ᶜ 376 246

31₄₉ (πολεμιστῶν) τῶν] > 963(vid) 15 417 319

32₁₁ ὤμοσα] -σε(ν) B 963 G-82-426 414 129-246* x 407 Aeth

32₁₂ υἱός] pr o 963*(c pr m) 72 52'-313 x⁻⁵⁰⁹

32₁₅ καταλιπεῖν] -λειπειν (-πην 30; -πιν 767) F M' 963 G-29-376 129 75'-767 30 509-527 392 407-628 55 319

32₁₆ οἰκοδομήσωμεν] -σομεν Bᶜ F 963 G-426-707ᶜ C'ʼ⁻⁴¹³ ⁴¹⁷ ⁶¹⁵ 108 28-85-343' 509 318 18'-68'-120ᶜ-126-630' 624 Cyr I 404 Latcod 100 Co

32₂₁ ὁπλίτης] ο πολιτης 963 624

32₂₉ ἐνωπλισμένος] ενοπλισαμενος (c var) 963 C'ʼ⁻⁷³' ⁴¹⁷

33₅₅ ἔσται] εσονται 963 58-376 d n 344ᵐᵍ t 799 Latcod 104 Aeth Arm Sa Syh

34₁₂ ἡ ἁλυκή] om ἡ Bᶜ V 963 52* 129 x 59 319

34₂₃ Οὐφίδ] σουφει V 963 G-82 127 509ᶜ 407

35₅ ἔσται] εσονται 963 Latcod 100 Bo

35₆ om ἅς 1° B V 963 82 b ƒ x 407 319 Cyr I 865 = Ra

Many of these are obviously secondary, and can be dismissed out of hand. In a number of cases 963 does support a popular variant. Thus 963 proves the antiquity of the μαδιαμ spelling for Μαδιάν; cf 25₁₈ 31₇.

More problematic are a few readings which seem to show recensional influence even though the papyrus is pre-Origen in date. In the following list all instances of variant readings witnessed by 963 which either equal 𝔐 or equal a known hexaplaric reading are given.

List 3

27₉ θυγάτηρ αὐτῷ] tr V 963(vid) O⁻⁵⁸-82 414 b d 129 n t x⁻⁶¹⁹ 55 624 LatRuf *Num* XXII 1 Syh: לו בת 𝔐

27₉ κληρονομίαν] + αυτου V 963 O⁻⁵⁸-82 C'' b d 129 n s⁻³⁰ t 392 z 319 624 646 Arm Co Syh: נחלתו 𝔐

28₁₁ ὁλοκαυτώματα] -τωμα 963 72-426-oI⁻¹⁵ 551-615 54-458 28-346*-730 619 z Cyr I 1116 Aeth Sa Syh: עלה 𝔐

29₃₃ αἱ θυσίαι αὐτῶν] pr και 963 426 Arab Arm Sa: ומנחתם 𝔐

30₁₃ περιελών] περιαιρων F 963 29-72-426-707*(vid)-oI⁻¹⁵ᶜ 56' 127 130ᵐᵍ-321' ᵐᵍ 509 121 z⁻¹²⁶⁴⁰⁷ 59 416 646: = o' περιαιρῶν 344

30₁₆ idem A F 963 29-426-oI⁻¹⁵ᶜ b⁻¹⁹ 56' 127 130ᵐᵍ-321' ᵐᵍ 121 z⁻¹²⁶⁴⁰⁷ 416 624 646: = o' περιαιρῶν 344

32₁₃ ἐξανηλώθη] εξαναλ. A Fᵇ 963 G 422(vid) 129 767 s⁻³⁰' x⁻⁵⁰⁹ y⁻³⁹² 68'-120' 799: = σ' ἐξαναλωθῇ 344ᵗˣᵗ

35₁₅ τῷ ἐν ὑμῖν] om τῷ 963 129 Arm: בתוכם 𝔐
This is probably mere coincidence since the τῷ follows παροίκῳ and might easily be omitted because of homoioteleuton.

Only the first two instances in the list need in my opinion be taken seriously. The change in word order in 27₉ could be coincidence since it makes no difference as far as the Greek context is considered. The clause reads ἐὰν δὲ μὴ ᾖ θυγάτηρ αὐτῷ. Nor is the addition of a genitive pronoun after κληρονομίαν in the apodasis of the verse all that compelling, since τῷ ἀδελφῷ αὐτοῦ follows κληρονομίαν in the Num text. That an αυτου was added by the 963 copyist may be due to the fact that αὐτοῦ occurs frequently in the context; cf especially κληρονομίαν αὐτοῦ τῇ θυγατρὶ αὐτοῦ of the preceding verse. The text of 963 need not be due to Hebrew influence at all.

It is, however, in its positive witness to Num that the real value of 963 lies. In list 4 are presented all instances in which 963 has the Num text, but A and B do not.

List 4

6₂ ἄν 963] εαν A B n 318 Or II 316 Tht Nm 197ᵃᵖ = Ra

6₄ στεμφύλων 963] -λλων A B 707 56'-129 54-75' s⁻¹³⁰ᵐᵍ ³⁴³ y 126 646

8₁₄ τῶν 963] > A B O⁻⁵⁸ d 127-767 t x⁻⁶¹⁹ 121 = Ra

29₁₇ init 963 b 509] pr και rell = Ra 𝔐

29₃₅ init V 963 46 129-246 121 630 59 ᴸᵃᵗcodd 100 104] pr και rell = Ra

29₃₆ κάρπωμα 963*] -ματα A B 963ᶜ 58-82 129 509 y⁻³⁹² z 646 Sa = Ra

31₂₇ ἐκπεπορευμένων Fᵃ 963] εκπορευομ. A B* F V O''⁻⁸² 52-73'-77-422-528-529 b 44 f⁻¹²⁹ 54-75' x⁻⁵²⁷ y 68'-126-669 55 59 319 624 799 = Ra

31₄₅ καί 1° 963 O'⁻⁵⁸-72 C-46 118ᶜ n⁽⁻⁷⁵⁾ t ᴸᵃᵗcodd 100 104 Aethᶜ Arab Arm Bo Syh] > rell = Ra

32₂₅ ἐντέλλεται Bᶜ F M' V 963 O⁻³⁷⁶-29-72' 616 b f 343'-730 509 318 407 55 59 624 ᴸᵃᵗcodd 100 104(vid)] εντελειται B* x⁻⁵⁰⁹; εντεταλται (c var) rell

34₇ καταμετρήσετε 963] -σεται (c var) A B M' V 376 57-73'-313-615-761ᶜ 53*-56' 75' 509 55 319 799 Aeth

36₇ πατρικῆς 963] πατριας A B Fᵃ Fᵇ M' oI'⁻⁸²⁷⁰⁷ C'' 246 s⁻⁸⁵ᵐᵍ ³⁴⁴ᵐᵍ x y z⁻¹²⁰ 55 59 319 Cyr IX 900 = Ra

Most of the instances in this list represent improvements to the Ra text and are discussed in chapter 6 below. The other instances are fairly obviously early errors already found in the old uncial witnesses.

List 5 represents instances where 963 confirms the reading of A+ over against the secondary reading of B+.

List 5

5₁₃ ἦ 2° 963] ην Β Cyr I 909 = Ra

5₂₇ ἐν 963] > Β S* 68′ 799 Cyr I 909 Arm^ap

5₂₉ ἄν 963] εαν Β G 19 458 319 = Ra

6₂₁ τόν 963] > Β M′ V 16-46 19 130-321′ x^{-619} 319 Cyr I 1053 = Ra

6₂₆ ἐπιφάναι 963] pr καὶ Β* 121 ^Latcod 100 FirmMat *Consult* II 5 Aeth Arab Arm

7₁₅ ἕνα 3° 963] > Β F*(c pr m) V 29-82-707^{txt} f n^{-767} 730 x^{-619} 126-628 319 ^Latcod 100 Aeth^{-C}

7₂₀ πλήρη 963] -ρης Β S 84 59

7₂₉ τράγους πέντε 963] > Β^{txt} F*(c pr m) 30-343

7₄₁ τράγους πέντε 963] > Β^{txt} F*(c pr m) 29 318 18 ^Latcod 104

7₆₇ πλήρη 963] -ρης Β 707 767 84

7₇₂ Φαγαιήλ 963] φαγειηλ Β V G-72-707*-ol^{-15} 77 118′-537 125 54-458 30 76 x 392^c 319 Co

7₇₇ Φαγαιήλ 963] φαγειηλ Β V ol^{-15} 77 127 30 76 x^{-509} 392 Co

7₈₇ αἱ θυσίαι 963] pr καὶ Β* 707 d f^{-129} n t 319 Arm Sa = Ra

8₆ τῶν 963] > Β O^{-58} d^{-610} 127-767 t^{-84} 509 55 319 = Ra

8₈ σεμίδαλιν 963] -λεως Β 71 68′-120′ 59 = Ra

26₂₂ ὁ 3° 963] > Β 413-414* 246* 767

28₁₁ νουμηνίαις 963] νεομ. Β 58-426 b f n Cyr I 1116 = Ra

28₁₃ δέκατον δέκατον 963] semel scr Β* F 58-ol′ C″ b d f n s t x^{-509} z 55 59 319 624 Aeth^{-C} Bo = Ra

28₁₅ κυρίῳ 963] κ̅υ̅ Β*

29₁₂ ἑορτάσετε 963] -σατε Β 82-376-618* 537 f^{-56} n^{-127} 30-343 134 392* 59 319 624

29₁₂ κυρίῳ 963] κ̅υ̅ Β*

29₁₃ κάρπωμα 963] -ματα Β* 58-82 n^{-458} Arm Sa = Ra

30₁₃ καὶ παρασιωπήσῃ 963] > Β*

31₄₂ τοῦ 963] > Β*

33₅₄ ὑμῶν 1° 963] αυτων Β 381*(vid) 16-46 458 84* 392 319

35₁₅ καὶ τῷ 2° 963] om καί Β* 509 319

35₂₅ κατοικήσει 963] -ση Β 29 19′ 630-669* ^Latcod 100

35₃₂ τῶν 963] > Β* V 53′-129

36₇ προσκολληθήσονται 963] pr καὶ Β x

In this list 963 and codex A both support Num, whereas B represents a variant text. For those variant readings in the list which Rahlfs adopted as his text cf the discussions in ch. 6.

In the final list 963 confirms the B text as Num, whereas A constitutes a secondary text.

List 6

5₁₈ τοῦ ἐπικαταρωμένου τούτου (τουτο 458) Β 963 n x^{-619} 319 Cyr I 909 Tht *Nm* 196 Arm Bo] *quae abicietur* ^Latcod 100; το επικαταρωμενον (καταρ. 126; + ÷ Syh) τουτο (sub ÷ G; > 58 b Aeth = 𝔐) rell

5₂₁ κύριός σε Β F 963 O′^{-376} d f t x^{-619} y z^{-68′ 126} 59 799 Chr II 917 ^Latcod 100] σε ο κ̅ς̅ 552; σοι κ̅ς̅ 616^c 54 Tht *Nm* 197^{ap}; om σε 376 68′; tr rell

5₂₇ ἐάν Β S 963 O^{-58} 417^{txt} f^{-246} x^{-619} 319 Chr II 917 Cyr I 909 Sa Syh] ει (εν 707) μεν 72-707*; + μη 528; + μεν rell

6₅ τοῦ ἁγνισμοῦ Β 963 58 C″ 127 30′ 84 x^{-619} Cyr I 1041 Arm Bo] pr *et* ^Latcod 100; αφαγν. 44; αγνισμου αυτου b; > 72 319; + (※ G; ÷ Syh mend) αυτου rell = 𝔐

6₅ ὅσας 963] ας A

6₉ ἀποθάνῃ (-νει 75^c-458) Β 963 376 d f^{-246} n^{-767} t x^{-619} 68′-120-126 Phil II 131 III 134 Clem I 92 Cyr I 1048 Arm Co] + θανατω 319 = 𝔐; pr θανατω rell

6₁₀ καὶ τῇ Β V 963 O^{-58} d f n t x^{(-619)} Cyr I 1041 1048 Bo Sa⁴] om καί 392; τη δε rell

6₁₀ νοσσούς (νοσσους G-707*) Β F V 963 G-15′-426-707 127 30-130-321′-343′ 134 55] νεοσσους (c var) rell

6₁₂ αἱ πρότεραι Β M′ 963 O^{-58} 246 n 321′^c x^{-619} 318 624 Phil I 65 II 131] οι προτεροι 19; αι προτεροι F b^{-19}; αι προ^{τε} 126; om αἱ V f^{-246}; αι (> 64) προτερον rell

91

6₁₄ ἕνα 2° 963] > A 72 529 44 121 55 319 624

6₁₈ ὑπό B 963 44′ 74-76′-134ᶜ 509 392ᶜ Cyr I 1053 ᴸᵃᵗcod 100 Sa] επι rell

6₁₉ ἕνα ἄζυμον 963] tr A V 376′-707-oI C′′ ⁻⁴⁶ˢ b s y⁻³¹⁸ 55 319 624 799 ᴸᵃᵗcod 100 Aeth
= 𝔐

7₁ ᾗ ἡμέρᾳ B V 963 O⁻⁵⁸-707⁽ᵐᵍ⁾ b n 84 x⁻⁶¹⁹ 55 Cyr I 705] ημ. ογδοη 44; τη ημ. τη ογδοη
125; tr 68 59; + η 72 74′-76; + η ογδοη 106-107′ 370; τη ημ. η rell

7₃ προσήγαγον B 963 O⁻⁵⁸ b d n t x⁻⁶¹⁹ Cyr I 705 856] προσηνεγκαν rell

7₈ υἱοῦ B 963 376 509 126 Cyr I 856] pr του rell

7₅₁ ἕνα 3° 963] > A V 82-707 54-75′ 28-130-343′ 509 68*-120-122 ᴸᵃᵗcodd 100 104
Aeth⁻ᶜᴴ

7₅₇ ἕνα 3° 963] > A 707 f⁻²⁴⁶ 54-75′ 343-730 509 120′-122 ᴸᵃᵗcodd 100 104 Aethᴹ

7₇₅ ἕνα 3° 963] > A V 82 16-46-528 767 x⁻⁶¹⁹ 18-126

7₈₅ τῶν ἁγίων B 963 458 x⁻⁶¹⁹] τω αγιω rell = Ra

8₇ ἁγνισμόν 963] αγνιασμον A

8₇ πᾶν 963] > A

8₁₂ χεῖρας 963] + (※ Syh) αυτων A O⁻⁵⁸ b 18′-126-628-669 ᴸᵃᵗcod 100 Arm Co
Syh = 𝔐

26₄₀ Σουτάλα 963(vid)] θουσαλα A 53′ 68

26₅₈ δῆμος ὁ Κόρε B V 963 82 129 n 730 t⁽⁻³⁷⁰⁾ x⁻⁶¹⁹ 319 ᴸᵃᵗcod 100 Arm Bo Sa⁵] > Sa¹²;
post Μουσί tr rell = 𝔐

26₅₈ δῆμος 3° B V 963(vid) 82 129 n t⁽⁻³⁷⁰⁾ x⁻⁶¹⁹ 319 ᴸᵃᵗcod 100 Bo] pr και rell = Sam

26₅₉ καὶ τό B V 963(vid) 82 x⁻⁶¹⁹] om τό 343; το δε (δ 126) rell

26₆₅ κύριος 963] > A 319

27₁ Μανασσή 963] μανν. A 458 121

27₁₇ ὡσεί 963] ως A M′ oI 121 126 55 Phil II 104ᶠ

27₁₉ ἐντελῇ 2° 963] εντειλαι (c var) A M′ oI C′′ 28-30′-85′ᵗˣᵗ-321′ᵗˣᵗ-343-344ᵗˣᵗ 619 y 68′
55 ᴸᵃᵗRuf Num XXII 4 Aethᶜ

27₂₀ οἱ 963] > A* 707 b⁻¹⁹ 75 30-343 126 319

27₂₁ ἐπερωτήσουσιν 963] -σωσιν A 58 C′′ ⁻⁵²⁷⁷⁴¹⁴⁴²²⁷⁶¹ 53′ 127 28-85 392 68 319 416

28₄ ποιήσεις 1° 963] -σετε (c var) A F K M′ 58-oI′ ⁻⁸² C′′ ⁻⁶¹⁶* s 619 y z 55 59 646 Aeth

28₄ ποιήσεις 2° 963] -σετε (-ται A K M*) A F K M′ 58-oI′ ⁻⁸² C′′ s⁻¹³⁰ 619 y z 55 59 646
Aeth

28₉ ἀναπεποιημένης ἐν ἐλαίῳ B V 963 15-82 d f n t x⁻⁶¹⁹ 121 319 Cyr I 1113 ᴸᵃᵗcod 100
Arm Bo Sa¹] post θυσίαν tr rell = 𝔐

28₁₀ ὁλοκαύτωμα 963] -ματος A F M′ V O′-29-707ᶜ C′′ b s⁻³⁴⁶* 527-619 y z 55 59 319
624 646

28₁₀ σαββάτων 963] -του (σεβαστου 15) A F K M′ V O-15′-29-72-707ᵐᵍ C′′ b 28-85ᵗˣᵗ-
130-321′-343-344ᵗˣᵗ 619 y z 55 59 319 624 646

28₁₁ καί 2° B F V 963 O′⁻⁵⁸⁷² 118′-537 129 509-619 z 319 Cyr I 1116 ᴸᵃᵗcod 100 Aeth
Arm Co Syh] > rell

28₁₆ ἡμέρᾳ 963] ⌒(17) A 72-618 y⁻¹²¹ᵐᵍ 59 624

28₁₇ τούτου 963] + ποιηθησεται A

28₂₄ ποιήσετε 963(vid)] -σεται (-σηται 458 319) A K V 82-376 56′-664 75′ 509* 120 55
319

28₂₇ ἑπτά 963] post ἐνιαυσίους tr A F M′ 15′-58-oII⁻⁸² C′′ b n s 619 y⁻³¹⁸ z⁻¹²⁶⁴⁰⁷ 624 646
ᴸᵃᵗcod 100 Aeth Arab Co

28₃₁ τοῦ 2° 963] + (c var) της νουμηνιας και η θυσια αυτων και το ολοκαυτωμα το A M′
58-oI 127 619 y z⁻⁴⁰⁷ 55 624 646

29₆ καί 4° B V 963 426 131⁽ᵐᵍ⁾ 129 n⁽⁻⁴⁵⁸⁾ t 407 Aethᶜᴹ Bo Syh] > rell

29₁₅ init B M′ V 963 O′⁻⁵⁸-82 f⁻²⁴⁶ x 407 319 Cyr I 1120 Aeth Syh] pr και rell = 𝔐

29₃₉ κυρίῳ 963] pr τω A F 58-oI′⁻⁸² C′′⁻⁵² f⁻¹²⁹ s y z⁻¹⁸⁴⁰⁷ 59 416 646

30₂ Ἰσραήλ B V 963(vid) 15-oII⁻²⁹ 53′ x y⁻³⁹² 126-407 ᴸᵃᵗcodd 100 104] > 392; pr των
υιων (> 610) G C′′ d⁻¹²⁵ n s t 424 646 Cyr I 1060; pr υιων rell = 𝔐

30₆ πάσας 963] > A V 129-246

30₁₂ αὐτῆς 3° 963] sub ÷ G; > A F 15′-58-618*(c pr m)-707 C′′ 125 53′-56 s⁽⁻⁸⁵ᵗˣᵗ⁾ y⁻³⁹²
z⁻⁴⁰⁷ 55 59 416 624 646 ᴸᵃᵗAug Num 59.2ᵗᵉ = 𝔐

30₁₄ ψυχήν 963] αυτην A

30₁₇ γυναικός B V 963 O⁻⁵⁸-82 d 53 n t x 319 ᴸᵃᵗcod 100 Sa Syh] pr ανα μεσον rell

31₁₂ υἱούς B V 963 G-29-426 19′ 129 54′ 121 407 55 319] pr τους rell

31₂₇ συναγωγῆς 963] pr της (τη 75) A O⁻⁴²⁶-381′ 414 106⁽ᵐᵍ⁾ 129 n t⁽⁻³⁷⁰⁾ 527 Cyr I 333bis = 𝔐

31₃₆ τριακόσιαι 963] + (※ G) χιλιαδες (c var) A F M′ O′′⁻⁷² ⁸² C′′ 56′ s⁻³⁴³³⁴⁴ᶜ 509 y z⁻¹²⁶⁴⁰⁷ 55 59 624 Aeth Arab Bo Syh = 𝔐

31₄₁ καθά 963(vid)] καθαπερ A 15′ C′′⁻⁴¹⁴ 28-85′-321′ 318 55 624

32₁₁ κακόν 963] et ἀγαθόν tr A F M′ O′′⁻⁸² C′′ b f⁻¹²⁹ n s 509 y z⁻¹²⁶⁴⁰⁷ 55 59 624 799 Aeth Arab Bo Syh

32₁₃ ἕως 963] + αν A oI C′′ b s x⁻⁵⁰⁹ y⁻¹²¹ 18-407-628

32₂₀ ἐξοπλίσησθε 963] -πλισθησεσθε (c var) A 59 319

32₂₇ καί 963] > A M′ oI-707 85′ᵗˣᵗ-321′ᵗˣᵗ-343-344ᵗˣᵗ y 18-628 55 624 Aeth

32₂₉ οἱ υἱοί 2° 963] om οἱ A 15 44′-125 56 75′ 318 126-628 319

32₂₉ Γάδ 963] γαλααδ A

33₅₄ αὐτῶν 1° B⁽ᵐᵍ⁾ M′ V 963(vid) 58-376′-oI 56ᵐᵍ-129-664 n t⁽⁻⁸⁴⁾ 509-527 z 319 ᴸᵃᵗcod 100 Bo Sa¹] ταυτην 799; sub ÷ G Syh; > rell = 𝔐

33₅₄ ἐν κλήρῳ 963] κληρωτι (-τη 618; -τει 392) A F oI⁻¹⁵-29-707 C′′ b 56ᵗˣᵗ s⁻³⁴³³⁴⁴ᶜ y 18-628

33₅₅ ἐπί 2° B 963 129 x 407 319 Sa] pr υμων 707* 458 18; pr adversos vos ᴸᵃᵗcod 100; pr υμιν rell = 𝔐

33₅₆ ὑμᾶς B M′ V 963 15-82 246 30′-344ᵐᵍ x z⁻⁶⁸′¹²⁰ 319] υμων 799; υμιν rell = Ra

34₂ τήν 2° B* 963 O⁻⁵⁸ 129 n⁻⁷⁵ 799] > rell = Ra

34₃ λίβα 1° 963] βορρα A; βορραν 55

34₄ Ἀσεμώνα 963(vid)] ασελμωνα A F M′ 29-58-72-376-oI 500-cI′⁻⁴⁶⁵² b d 129-246 127 s t y⁻³¹⁸ 18′-126-628-630′ 55

34₆ ἡ 1° 963] > A 82 b 121

34₆ τὰ ὅρια 2° 963] το οριον A = 𝔐

34₇ τὰ ὅρια /ὑμῖν B 963 44′-107-610ᶜ t⁽⁻⁸⁴⁾ 509 407 319 Sa¹] τα ορια υμων 125-610*; υμιν ορια 82 799; om ὑμῖν 53′ 126; tr rell = 𝔐

34₇ τὸ ὄρος 2° B 963 G*-426 d⁻⁴⁴ 246 n t x Arm Syh] οθρος 82; > rell

34₂₉ καταμερίσαι 963] -μετρησαι (c var) A F oII⁻⁸² f⁻¹²⁹ 130ᵐᵍ-321′ᵐᵍ 121 68′ 59 ᴸᵃᵗcodd 100 104 Aeth

34₂₉ τοῖς υἱοῖς 963] τους υιους A 15′ C′′ f⁻¹²⁹ 28-85-130ᵗˣᵗ-321′-343′ y⁻³⁹² z⁻¹²⁰′ 55

35₂₅ ἀποκαταστήσουσιν 963] αποκαταστησει (c var) A M′ 58-oI C′′ s y 18′-126-628-669 ᴸᵃᵗcod 100 Arm

35₂₅ αὐτοῦ 963] > A 707 84 Cyr I 581 VII 625 Aeth Arm

35₃₀ φονεύσεις 963(vid)] -σει A M′ V O′′⁻²⁹⁷⁰⁷ C′′⁻⁶¹⁶* b 53-56′ s⁻³⁰³⁴⁴ᵐᵍ³⁴⁶* 318 18′-120-628-669ᶜ 55

36₇ καί 963] > A

36₁₂ τοῦ 2° B V 963(vid) 129 x 319] υιων G-426 Aeth Syh; των υιων 407-630; > rell

36₁₂ ἐγένετο B V 963 O b 129 x⁻⁵⁰⁹ 407 319] -νοντο 509 630; εγεννηθη 82 46′-417*-528 767; εγενηθη rell

The length of this list compared to that of the preceding confirms the conclusion of chapter 4 that the B type text is a much better witness to Num than is the A type text.

The value of 963 for the Numbers text lies more in its confirmation of a Num text than in its establishment. It is unfortunate that no more of its text is extant since it is almost two centuries older than B. Furthermore its text is much more closely related to B than to A, which fact would also accent its value as an ancient and superior text, and of the highest importance for recovering the earliest from of the Numbers text.

Chapter 6   The Critical Text (Num)

As in earlier volumes of the Gottingen Septuagint certain general rules of thumb have been followed. Since the old uncial texts normally add the *νῦ ἐφελκυστικόν* wherever possible, this has been done throughout Num as well regardless of the practice of later scribes (and occasionally those of papyri).

A further general practice followed concerns the transcription of the gentilic ending. This has always been transcribed by *-ι* in spite of the fact that the oldest uncials commonly have *-ει*. It has been argued elsewhere (cf Gen 489ff) that the correct transcription of the Hebrew /i/ and /ī/ is "iota" in Hellenistic Greek and this system has been followed throughout. Accordingly the masculine plural gentilic is regularly transcribed by *-ιμ* and a masculine plural noun form by *-ιμ*.

The classical future stem for *λαμβάνειν* is *ληψ-*, i.e. without a nasal. As is well-known from papyri from the third century B.C. onwards the Hellenistic stem *λημψ-* became popular; cf Mayser I. 1, 166f. Since the oldest uncials, A B and S, all attest to the future form with nasal infix, it has been the common practice to accept such forms throughout for the critical text. With the appearance of Deut in the Gottingen series this practice, though continued, is no longer as certain. Papyri earlier than Codex B are not uniform in attesting to the Hellenistic form. For Gen mss 911 961 and 962 all attest to the Hellenistic form, although 963 occasionally witnesses to the classical form (Num 30₁₆ Deut 2₆ 5₁₁ 28₃₀ 30₄), but to the stem with "mu" at Num 5₁₇ ₂₅ ₃₁ 6₁₉ 8₈ Deut 5₁₁). Apparently 803, a Qumran fragment, witnesses to the Hellenistic stem at Num 4₁₂, but 848, which is certainly of Egyptian origin, has the classical stem throughout (Deut 21₃ 22₆ ₇ 26₂). In spite of one's uncertainty on the matter the Hellenistic stem has been retained throughout Num.

1. That Num and Deut are the products of different translators is apparent from their respective attitudes towards their parent text. The demands of the target language play a greater role in Num than in Deut which is often literalistic in its renderings. Thus prepositions are much less literally rendered in Num than in Deut. The Numbers translator also reflects a much freer attitude towards the Hebrew in rendering repetitive phrases; in census reports or in repeated offerings Num tends to stylize his renderings according to a pattern, regardless of minor differences in the Hebrew.

The linguistic demands of Greek are respected to a greater extent in Num than in Deut. To cite but one such, the case and number of relative pronouns are observed much more carefully. Whereas in Deut the inflection of the relative pronoun was often the result of attraction to its antecedent, such inflections are comparatively infrequent in Num, the inflection being determined by the syntactic demands of the relative clause.

Another marked characteristic of Num in contrast to that of Deut is the comparative infrequency of δέ constructions as compared to those with καί. Num does not avoid δέ for paratactic constructions; it simply prefers καί.

It is thus clear that problems concerning the critical text must first of all be established through the patterns of usage and of translation within the book itself rather than from the Pentateuch as a whole, and only secondarily from the wider context of the Greek Pentateuch and the LXX as a whole.

2. The usage of the particle ἄν in Num is the same as that which was established for Deut; cf THGD, ch. 7, Sect. B. Within relative clauses ἄν, but never εαν, is accepted as critical text since such usage predominated in the time of the translator. The long form became popular in the early centuries of our era at times almost completely supplanting ἄν; in fact at 23₂₆ all mss have εαν rather than the original ἄν. Usually ἄν is read in the majority of our witnesses. Since Codex B, being a fourth century ms, commonly reads the longer form, Ra often adopted εαν in his text. He must be corrected at 5₆ ₁₀ ₂₉ ₃₀ 6₂ 9₁₀ ₁₃ 10₃₂ 15₁₂ 17₅ 18₂₈ 19₁₆ ₁₈ ₂₀ ₂₂ 22₆bis ₈ ₁₇ ₃₅ ₃₈ 23₃ ₁₂ ₂₆ 24₁₃ 30₃ ₁₃ 31₂₃ 33₅₄ ₅₅.

As in Deut ἕως occurs with ἄν when introducing the subjunctive mood. ἕως ἄν is normal in the papyri, ἕως without ἄν occuring only in late Ptolemic times (Mayser II, 3, p. 79). In a few instances the ἄν has been lost in much of the tradition; thus at 10₂₁ only V b d n 85′ᵐᵍ-321′ᵐᵍ(vid) t 319 support ἄν; at 14₃₃, A B* F* 707 77 b 44 f⁻¹²⁹ 458-767 x⁻⁵⁰⁹ y 126 55 319 624 om ἄν, and at 23₂₄, only V 58-72-82 d 127-767 t 55 59 have it. ἕως also occurs with the indicative two times (12₁₅ 32₁₃), but of course without ἄν.

3. ἔναντι, ἐναντίον and ἐνώπιον.

As in Deut so in Num the translator used all three of these as prepositions governing the genitive with no discernible semantic distinctions. Certain observations on usage can, however, be made. Whenever the genitive is κυρίου (or τοῦ θεοῦ) the preposition is always (50 times) ἔναντι regardless of the Hebrew text. The usual Hebrew preposition is לפני, but בעיני (24₁ 32₁₃), ל (8₁₃ 32₂₃), את (20₁₃) also occur, as well as מן (32₂₂) and even באזני (11₁ ₁₈). In a number of instances there is no corresponding text in 𝔐 (8₁₃ ₁₅ 32₃₀), and at 31₃ 𝔐 represents a different text.

If the governed nominal is a pronoun ἔναντι is normally avoided in favor of ἐναντίον or ἐνώπιον; in fact, only one case (27₁₄) of ἔναντι with a pronoun has been accepted as Num. The textual evidence is as follows: ἔναντι (αὐτῶν) B F K M′ V 963(vid) oI-72′ d 129 s⁻²⁸ ⁸⁵ t x⁻⁷¹ y z⁻⁶³⁰ 59 624 799] εν μεσω C″ 28-85 55 646; εναντιον rell: לעיני 𝔐. All the uncials except A, including 963(vid), support ἔναντι and this would appear to be Num, though a case for εναντιον could well be made, particularly in view of the following two cases.

20₈ ἐναντίον (αὐτῶν)] εναντι B M′ 82 d⁻¹⁰⁶ 71-509 646 = Ra
25₆ ἐναντίον (πάσης συναγωγῆς)] εναντι B* n⁻¹²⁷ 121 55 319 = Ra

In all three instances the Hebrew equivalent is לעיני. In the last two instances the B variant has only minority support and the less common word is likely original. It should be added that these are the only instances in Num involving לעיני.

That the translator preferred not to use ἔναντι with pronouns is particularly clear from 27₁₉ in which לפני occurs three times. In the first two instances (governing Ἐλεαζάρ and συναγωγῆς resp.) ἔναντι occurs, but the third instance, governing αὐτῶν, is ἐναντίον. The text of Num is substantially supported in the tradition:

ἔναντι 1° 963] -τιον K 29-64 y 59 Tht Nm 224
ἔναντι 2° 963] -τιον A 29-58-oI d n t 619 y⁻³⁹² 68′ 55 319 Tht Nm 224
ἐναντίον 963] εναντι 72 509

It would otherwise seem unlikely that the translator would have varied the preposition in coordinate phrases; thus in 8₁₃ and 27₂ ἔναντι occurs four times; in 32₂₂ and 36₁ it occurs three times, and in 3₄ 27₂₁ twice, whereas the rare ἐνώπιον occurs twice in 13₃₄ (otherwise occurring only at 17₁₀ 19₃ 32₄ ₅).

The translator apparently tended to use the same preposition within an immediate context. Thus at 27₂₂ it seems unlikely that Ra represents the original text. Ra has ἐναντίον Ελεαζαρ τοῦ ἱερέως καὶ ἔναντι πάσης συναγωγῆς. The relevant facts are as follows:

ἐναντίον 1°] εναντι A 15-72 C″⁻⁵²′³¹³ 125 129 n 28-30′-85⁽ᵐᵍ⁾-343-344ᵗˣᵗ 84* 121 55 646 = Compl
ἐναντίον 2°] εναντι B* 72-376 f = Compl Ra; > 106-125 126 319

It would seem likely that ἐναντίον is the original preposition in both places in this verse.

ἔναντι was certainly the favored of these prepositions; it occurs 73 times in Num, whereas ἐναντίον occurs 19 times, and ἐνώπιον only 6 times.

1₅₃ ἐναντίοι] υπεν. C″ 646; -ντιον (ενατ. 59*; -τιων 108) 19′ 321ᶜ 527 318 126 59 799; εναντι 53′ 509; εναντιον (-τιων 458) κυριον B* M′ ᵐᵍ V d 54-75′ t = Ra; εναντι κυριον 55 127; sub ÷ G Syhᵀ; > 58-376 Arm Bo = 𝔐; + κυ Bᶜ

V. 53 contrasts the position of the Levites with that of the other tribes who are to pitch their tents ἀνὴρ ἐν τῇ ἑαυτοῦ τάξει καὶ ἀνὴρ κατὰ τὴν ἑαυτοῦ ἡγεμονίαν; the Levites are to encamp ἐναντίοι κύκλῳ the tent of testimony. 𝔐 simply has סביב, but the translator has added ἐναντίοι in order to emphasize the contrast. That Ra's text is not original is clear from the fact noted above, viz. that ἐναντίον was never used to govern κυρίου. Furthermore ἐναντίον (as well as ἔναντι) is used in Num only as a preposition, so that here ἐναντίοι must be original.

Elision of the final vowel of prepositions is common in Hellenistic prose with pronouns and common phrases such as κατ' ἀνατολάς or ἀπ' ἀνατολῶν, but is otherwise regularly avoided in Num. Thus in 4₄₉ κατὰ ἄνδρα is probably original as is διὰ ἁμαρτίαν in 27₃, the variant short forms in the tradition being the result of haplography. On the other hand, κατ' ἀνατολάς in 21₁₁ and ἀπ' ἀνατολῶν in 23₇ (the latter in poetry) are instances of elided prepositions probably original to the translator.

24₂ ἐπ' (αὐτῷ)] εν B b⁻¹⁹ Tht Nm 221 = Ra

That the phrase ἐπ' αὐτῷ is original to Num is clear from the Hebrew which has עליו. The variant was palaeographically determined. What is not immediately evident is its position in the verse. In Num it appears at the end of the verse. In 𝔐 עליו precedes rather than follows רוח אלהים. The following witnesses place the phrase in front of πνεῦμα θεοῦ: A F O'ᵉ⁻⁸² C'ᵉ 56' n⁻¹²⁷ s 527-619 y z 55 59 799 ᴸᵃᵗcod 100 Ruf Num XVII 2 Aeth Arab Syh. This change in word order is probably the result of Origen's work; note the witness of the O mss, Arab and Syh.

14₁₃ ἐν] τη B 44' 129 127-767 t x⁻⁵⁰⁹ = Ra; τα 509; > 500

The preposition occurs in the context ὅτι ἀνήγαγες ἐν ἰσχύι σου τὸν λαὸν τοῦτον and the clause reproduces 𝔐 literally. Codex B* uniquely also substitutes ηγαγες for ἀνήγαγες. This can hardly be original in view of the transitivity of the verb העלית in 𝔐; ἄγειν is never used as a rendering for העלה in the Pentateuch. The text of B is questionable in this clause, and the preposition is undoubtedly original and the article is not.

4. *Pronouns.* The presence or absence of a third person pronoun in Num is often formulaically determined.

1₂ om αὐτῶν 1° B 414' d n⁻⁷⁶⁷ t x 18 Bas II 145 Cyr VI 453 X 624 ᴸᵃᵗcod 100 PsBas Is I 5 Arm
— om αὐτῶν 2° B V d n⁻⁷⁶⁷ t x 18 319 Bas II 145 Cyr VI 453 X 624 ᴸᵃᵗcod 100 Hi Eph II 3 PsBas Is I 5 Arm
— αὐτῶν 3°] sub ÷ G; > B 19 d 127 t x 18 319 Cyr VI 453 X 624 ᴸᵃᵗcod 100 Arm

Phrases such as κατὰ συγγενείας, κατ' οἴκους πατριῶν and κατὰ ἀριθμὸν ἐξ ὀνόματος are set phrases in Num which are almost always modified by αὐτῶν even when 𝔐 has no pronominal suffix. The text of B omits αὐτῶν 1° 2° 3° in this verse but this is secondary as Ra also recognized. This is rendered doubly certain by the fact that αὐτῶν 3° is sub obelo in G, there being no suffix present in the Hebrew. In vv. 16 and 44 αὐτῶν is similarly omitted by codex B against the normal pattern; the omission would appear secondary.

4₄₆ δήμους αὐτῶν] om αὐτῶν B x⁻⁶¹⁹ ᴸᵃᵗcod 104(vid) = Ra

The word δῆμοι is inevitably followed by a genitive modifier in Num, except for the specific listing of various δῆμοι by name throughout chapter 26. The B text adopted by Ra must be understood as secondary.

3₄₀ αὐτῶν 803(vid)] > B 54-75′ x⁻⁶¹⁹ ᴸᵃᵗcodd 100 104 = Ra; post ὀνόματος tr O⁻⁵⁸
Bo Syh

The context for the pronoun is τὸν ἀριθμὸν αὐτῶν ἐξ ὀνόματος for the Hebrew
מספר שמתם. The transposition of αὐτῶν after ὀνόματος was effected by Origen
and corresponds exactly to the Hebrew. Ms 803 must have had an αὐτῶν in
its text, since the length of the line demands it but its position is not clear.
Since the transposed order is clearly hex, 803 probably supports Num. It
seems likely therefore that it is original.

2₂₂ ἐχόμενοι αὐτοῦ 376′ f(+ ras 1 litt 56) z Syh] sub ÷ Syhᴸ; εχομ. αυτων G-58 Arm
Bo; > ᴸᵃᵗcod 100; om αὐτοῦ rell = Ra

In the ch. 2 account of the tribal encampments over against the tent of
testimony the tribes are divided into four groups of three each. The second
tribe is introduced in 𝔐 by והח(ו)נ(י)ם עליו מטה in each case (vv. 5, 12, 27)
except for the third group (v. 22) where 𝔐 omits החנים. The third tribe is
introduced simply by ומטה (vv. 14, 22, 29) or מטה (v. 7). The Greek in each
case has the longer formula καὶ οἱ παρεμβάλλοντες ἐχόμενοι to introduce both
the second and third tribes but varies the rest of it depending on whether αὐτοῦ
occurs after ἐχόμενοι or not, i.e. either occuring as ἐχόμενοι αὐτοῦ (φυλή) or as
ἐχόμενοι (φυλή). The evidence for αὐτοῦ (with some variation in number) is
clear in vv. 12 14 27 where all witnesses, except for mss 618* 19 which omit
αὐτοῦ in v. 14, attest to the pronoun. In v. 22 αὐτοῦ is weakly attested but it
is included under the obelus in Syh, i.e. the αὐτοῦ is at least preOrigen and is
probably to be regarded as original. Where no αὐτοῦ obtained the tradition
has added either αυτου or αυτων.

Since ἐχόμενοι in the sense of "adjacent to" often governs the genitive,
φυλή easily became φυλης in the tradition, though what this was intended to
mean is not clear. Even when αὐτοῦ was present in the text a large part of the
text tradition attests to the genitive which could hardly be original. Accordingly φυλή as predicate nominative is to be read throughout. Oddly Ra accepted
φυλης throughout; cf vv 5 7 12 14 20 22 27 29.

18₃ σκηνῆς σου] σκ. του μαρτυριον Fᵇ d f⁻¹²⁹ n t 527 126-628 799 Arm; + του μαρτυριου
376; σου sub ÷ Syhᵀ; om σου B V 58-82 x⁻⁵²⁷ z⁻¹²⁶⁶²⁸ 319 646 Aethᶜᴳ Sa = Ra 𝔐

The σου is apparently original in view of the evidence of Syh; it was probably added by the translator due to the influence of the coordinate φυλακάς
σου in the same verse.

On the other hand, Ra was probably correct in not adopting the genitive
pronoun after γυναῖκες at 21₃₀ with B V 82 54-75′ 71-509 319 Phil passim
ᴸᵃᵗcod 100. 𝔐 has נשים; thus there is no textual justification for the majority
reading γυναικες αυτων. The pronoun came into the tradition through the influence of the parallel construction of v. 30a: τὸ σπέρμα αὐτῶν.

14₂₇ μου] εμου B V 108-118-314* 30′-321′ᶜ 121 319 = Ra

In contrast to normal usage with the so-called true prepositions (cf Mayser I. 2. 62f), the short form of the first singular pronoun is to be preferred after ἐναντίον, possibly through analogy with the second singular pronoun; cf ἐναντίον σου at 11₁₁ or ἐνώπιόν σου at 32₅. The phrase ἐναντίον μου also occurs at 22₃₂, where, however, a substantial number of witnesses do attest to the long form εμου.

16₆ (ὑμῖν) ἑαυτοῖς] αυτοις B 29 122* 55 Cyr I 860 = Ra

The use of a reflexive pronoun rather than the simple third person pronoun to intensify a first or second person plural pronoun occurs only here in Num. The simple pronominal intensifier does not occur in Num at all but is common in Deut, particularly in the phrase ἐξ ὑμῶν αὐτῶν; cf also Exod 12₂₁ Lev 26₁ and elsewhere. It would be difficult to explain ἑαυτοῖς as secondary, it being the lectio difficilior. The reading of B on the other hand is easily understood as an adaptation to better Greek usage.

1₅₄ ὅσα A O⁻ᴳ-72 b f 85′ ᵐᵍ-321-346ᵐᵍ 121 18′-126-628-669 59 319 624] α rell = Ra
16₂₆ ὅσα] α n⁻⁷⁶⁷; ων B Mᵗˣᵗ V 376 d 129 t x = Ra

In both cases ὅσα must be original, since the antecedent is an inflected form of πᾶς. The translator always uses ὅσα when its antecedent is πᾶς except of course in the collocation πᾶς ὅς of 19₁₆ (as well as παντὸς οὖ in 19₂₂, a somewhat different construction).

4₉ ὅσοις] οσοι A 72 551 30′ 121 18 59; οις B M′ᵗˣᵗ V 509 318 Cyr I 852 = Ra; εν οις d n t 71; οσα 529 b ᴸᵃᵗcod 100(vid); > 53′-56-129⁽ᵐᵍ⁾

The context is τὰ ἀγγεῖα . . . ὅσοις λειτουργοῦσιν ἐν αὐτοῖς; in v. 14 the same relative clause occurs but the antecedent is τὰ σκεύη. In the latter the variant οις is found only in one ms, 318; ὅσοις is clearly original in v. 14 and the grammatically correct dative is also original in v. 9. A similar case of grammatical correctness occurs in the following case.

6₂₁ ἦν B x⁻⁶¹⁹ Cyr I 1053] η[. . . 963; ος 537; ης rell

The context reads τῆς εὐχῆς αὐτοῦ ἦν ἂν εὔξηται. The accusative is grammatically correct as modifying ευξηται, but case attraction, as in the majority reading, is well-attested already in Classical times. The translator, however, only seldom allowed case attraction to predominate over grammatical correctness. In fact only the following cases in Num are clear cases of such attraction.

14₁₁ σημείοις οἷς ἐποίησα
30₁₅ ἡμέρᾳ ᾗ ἤκουσεν

The reverse trend is characteristic of Num, and Ra was correct in following B in 6₂₁.

5. Since Num is a translation document the paratactic character of the Hebrew original is reflected in it. The presence or absence of the conjunction καί for the original text is not always easily determined since Num does not always agree with 𝔐. Thus at 4₂₃ such a disagreement occurs.

4₂₃ λειτουργεῖν καὶ ποιεῖν] om καί B x⁻⁶¹⁹ Arm Sa = 𝔐

The collocation "to serve (a service) to do" occurs in 𝔐 of Numbers at 4₃ ₂₃ ₃₅ ₃₉. At v. 3 it is literally rendered by λειτουργεῖν ποιῆσαι; when the translator used the present infinitive ποιεῖν in the other three instances he inserted the conjunction in spite of the fact that none obtains in the Hebrew. It should be added that the reading καὶ ποιεῖν is attested by all witnesses in vv. 35 and 39; the omission of καί in v. 23 seems to be secondary.

7₈₇ αἱ θυσίαι 963] pr και B* 707 d f⁻¹²⁹ n t 319 Arm Sa = Ra 𝔐

The pattern αἱ θυσίαι αὐτῶν καὶ αἱ σπονδαὶ αὐτῶν (or its equivalent in the singular) also occurs at 6₁₅ 29₆ (twice) 11 16 18 19 21 22 24 27 28 30 31 33 34 37 38. In all but 29₁₆ ₂₄ ₃₁ ₃₄ ₃₇ 𝔐 has the conjunction introducing the pattern. Except for 6₁₅ and 29₆ the translator did not render the conjunction. In view of this general pattern it would seem that the και of the variant text is not original. It should also be noted that the και intrudes between δώδεκα and αἱ and may independently have been formed by partial dittography.

4₃ ἕως] pr και B F M′ V 833 O-29-707 19 d⁻¹²⁵ t x⁻⁶¹⁹ 392 z 59 799 Syh = Ra 𝔐

The translator made no distinction between עד and ועד in his work. He renders them throughout by ἕως except at 9₁₂ where εἰς occurs, at 8₄ (twice), at 32₉ where עד has no equivalent in Num and at 14₁₁ where ועד is rendered by καὶ ἕως. At 14₁₁ the conjunction is necessary since it joins two clauses introduced by ἕως τίνος. All other instances of ועד are simply rendered by ἕως. Its introduction at 4₃ may well be hex.

4₂₆ καὶ ὅσα] om καί B b x⁻⁶¹⁹ 392 319 Latcod 100 AethM Arm Bo Sa⁴ = Ra

The immediate context is τὰ σκεύη τὰ λειτουργικὰ καὶ ὅσα λειτουργοῦσιν for כלי עבדתם ואת כל אשר יעשה in 𝔐. The relative clause containing λειτουργοῦσιν also occurs at 3₃₁ 4₉ ₁₂ 18₂₁; in these cases no καί precedes since the Hebrew has no ואת כל; that is, the relative pronoun has an antecedent. The omission of καί in the B tradition may have been influenced by such cases; this may also have been facilitated palaeographically since λειτουργικά occurs immediately before καί, the latter being omitted by haplography.

The tradition has also amplified the text through hex activity. All but B M′ V 82 16-46 b d n t x⁻⁶¹⁹ 319 Latcod 100 Arm Co have added αυτων after λειτουργικά. Furthermore hex activity is also apparently to be seen in the insertion of παντα between καί and ὅσα in V O⁻⁵⁸-29 619 Aeth Syh.

5₁₀ καὶ ἀνήϱ — fin Fᵃ] om καί B* = Ra 𝔐; om καὶ ἀνήϱ 707ᵗˣᵗ 392; sub ※ G Syh;
> F 29 131⁽ᵐᵍ⁾ 53′ z 59

The clause was apparently absent in Origen's parent text, it having been
omitted by parablepsis (i.e. ἔσται 1° ⌒2°), and then restored by hex. The text
of 𝔐 has איש for καὶ ἀνήϱ, the conjunction having fallen out through haplography after יהי. It is present in Sam and a number of Hebrew mss, and the
equivalence of B* and 𝔐 is coincidence, the καί being accidentally omitted
after ἔσται through homoioteleuton.

14₂₄ καὶ εἰσάξω] om καί B V 72 106 x 55 Cyr II 609 ᴸᵃᵗcod 100 Aeth Arm Co = Ra

The καί can only be interpreted on the basis of a Hebrew parent text since
it is barely intelligible in the Greek. The Greek begins with the nominative
ὁ δὲ παῖς μου Χαλέβ, then continues with the causal ὅτι clause "because there
was another spirit in him and he followed after me," after which καὶ εἰσάξω
αὐτόν is placed. This corresponds exactly to the Hebrew, but good Greek style
would not render the conjunction of 𝔐's והביאתיו by καί. The καί must be
original text.

29₁₇ init 963 b 509] pr καɩ rell = Ra 𝔐
29₃₅ init V 963 46 129-246 121 630 59 ᴸᵃᵗcodd 100 104 = Compl] pr καɩ rell = Ra

The successive days of the feast described in vv. 12 ff are introduced by the
conjunction in 𝔐 with the exception of the final (eighth) day, i.e. v. 35. Num
consistently begins each day's account with τῇ ἡμέϱᾳ τῇ . . ., i.e. without a
καɩ. The new evidence of 963 shows that the translator was indeed fully consistent in this practice, and it is now evident that an introductory καɩ is secondary in vv. 17 and 35 as well as for the intervening days.

31₄₅ καί 1° 963 O′⁻⁵⁸-72 C-46 118ᶜ n⁽⁻⁷⁵⁾ t ᴸᵃᵗcodd 100 104 Aethᶜ Arab Arm Bo Syh]
> rell = Ra

Ra could reasonably omit the καί for his text as being hex since most of the
usual hex witnesses attest to it and the older uncials did not, but the new evidence of 963 makes this impossible. The καί occurs in a list καὶ βόες . . . καὶ
ὄνοι . . . καὶ ψυχαὶ ἀνθϱώπων. In a list with three members the second is often
introduced without a conjunction in Greek as in English, i.e. as "cattle, oxen
and human beings." The omission of καί is probably stylistically inspired,
whereas the original text contained it because of the presence of a conjunction
in the parent Hebrew text.

15₆ εἰς 1°] pr η B O⁻⁵⁸ 509-527 Syh = Ra

The variant text which Ra adopted introduces the first of the alternatives,
i.e. εἰς ὁλοκαύτωμα ἤ εἰς θυσίαν. Greek often uses an ἤ . . . ἤ . . . construction,
though the first of these is not always present. In Num such alternatives are
never introduced by η, the conjunction only occurring between the two parts.

Our Greek text has no equivalent in 𝔐 here, but for an instructive example of usage in Num where an equivalent does obtain in 𝔐 cf v. 8.

6. A comparison of the Greek text with the Hebrew shows that the word order of the Greek translation is strongly determined by that of the Hebrew original. When problems of word order occur the text tradition may often be misleading because of Origen's work. Though Origen says nothing about word order the nature of the hexapla was such that the Greek word order was largely forced to coincide with that of the Hebrew; cf the discussion in THGG 59 and for some insight into the probable nature of the actual hexapla cf G. Mercati, Psalterii *Hexapli Reliquiae*. I. *Codex rescriptus Bybliothecae Ambrosianae 0.39 Supp. phototypice expressus et transcriptus.* Roma, 1958. When the tradition is divided between witnesses to the Hebrew word order and those to a different order, serious consideration must be given to the possible priority of the latter order. A good example of such is 16₉.

16₉ ὑμᾶς / ὁ θεὸς Ἰσραήλ] tr B O⁻⁵⁸ d 129 127 t 509 Cyr I 860 Syh = Ra 𝔐

𝔐 has אתכם ישראל אלהי (הבדיל). The translator preferred to bring the pronominal object next to the verb. Though he tended to follow the Hebrew order, he was by no means slavish in this regard as the study on hex corrections in word order (p. 56–58) indicates. The variant text is probably such a hex correction.

A similar case obtains at 19₁₀. The verb כבס is separated from its modifier בגדיו את by its subject הפרה אפר את האסף. The translator brings the object next to the verb rendering the clause by (καὶ) πλυνεῖ τὰ ἱμάτια ὁ συνάγων τὴν σποδιὰν τῆς δαμάλεως.

At times, however, close attention to the Hebrew text may solve problems of word order in quite a different way.

11₁₂ τὸν / πάντα (λαὸν τοῦτον)] tr B V O⁻⁵⁸ 422 f n x⁻⁶¹⁹ Phil III 6 Chr I 476 Tht Nm 204ᵃᵖ = Ra

Here the variant παντα τον λαον (τουτον) accepted by Ra is almost certainly secondary; it is probably due to the common expression "all the people" found elsewhere (e.g. in v. 13). The more unusual order of Num is due to the Hebrew העם כל את. The translator regularly rendered את by articulation and τόν placed before πάντα represents his attempt at rendering the Hebrew exactly.

A particularly complicated textual problem concerning word order obtains in 14₂₅.

14₂₅ ὑμεῖς / καὶ ἀπάρατε B V 129 x Co] om ὑμεῖς F* Aeth Arm; και εξαρ. υμεις (>75) αυτους (> 127) n 319; + αυτους d t; + vos ᴸᵃᵗcod 100; tr rell; + (⁂ G Syh) αυτοι O 18′-628-630′ Syh

In the context ὑμεῖς refers to the subject of the preceding ἐπιστράφητε, whereas the variant text supported by the majority makes ὑμεῖς refer to ἀπάρατε and is closer to 𝔐 which reads לכם וסעו פנו. It should be noted that d t add αυτους after the verb. Origen probably had the original word order in his parent text since he added αυτοι (sub ※ G) at the end (Syh has ※ *ipsi vos* ∠ for ὑμεῖς). Only the order accepted as original for Num can explain the various attempts to correct the text.

7. The problem of articulation of nouns is undoubtedly one of the most difficult textual problems facing the text critic of Numbers, since patterns of usage are often not present.

a) In the collocation "the desert of" plus proper name, the proper name is commonly not articulated (3₄ ₁₄ 9₁ 13₄ ₂₂ ₂₇ 20₁ 26₆₁ ₆₄ 27₁₄ (twice) 33₁₁ ₁₂ ₁₅ ₁₆ ₃₆ (twice) 34₃). A few instances are, however, problematic. At 11₁₉ occurs the phrase ἐν τῇ ἐρήμῳ τῇ Σινά; the article in question is attested in v. 1 at least as early as Origen since it is sub ob in G. In both instances the relevant article is omitted by some mss (in v. 1 by F* V 72 417-528 537 44-125 127-458 509 59* 319 799, and in v. 19 by oI⁻⁶⁴*-72 125 53′ 127-458-767 84*(c pr m) 18), but in view of its early attestation it has been adopted as Num.

At 9₅ Ra adopted του Σινα as his critical text on the basis of B although at v. 1 Σινά occurred without the article. Both instances occur in the phrase ἐν τῇ ἐρήμῳ Σινά and it is unlikely that the translator would have changed his normal pattern within the same context. Furthermore the unarticulated proper noun is attested by A 72-376 552 44′ 75′ 71-509 126 and is probably original. At 13₁ the original hand of B (and 376 761 44′-125) does not articulate Φαράν (Ra in opposition to his usual practice adopts the reading of Bᶜ here), and it seems wise to follow the common pattern here as well.

On the other hand at 10₁₂ the articulated proper noun is strongly supported. The collocation occurs twice within the verse, Ra articulating only the second. The evidence is as follows:

τοῦ Σινά] om τοῦ B V O⁻⁵⁸ 44′-125 x⁻⁶¹⁹ = Ra
τοῦ Φαράν] om τοῦ 44′-125 767; σινα 376*

In view of the strong support for the article, the article has been accepted in both cases.

b) *Articulation or non-articulation of the tetragrammaton.*

κύριος as rendering for the tetragrammaton occurs in the nominative case 176 times and is never articulated except once (14₉), where, however, the particle δέ intervenes. It occurs 14 times in the accusative and only once (16₃₀) is it articulated; in this case יהוה is preceded by את and τόν was undoubtedly intended by the translator to represent it. The text tradition throughout substantiates this lack of articulation for κύριον with the sole instance of 11₂ where ms 318 and Cyr I 381 read (πρὸς) τον κυριον.

The genitive κυρίου as substitute for the divine name occurs 125 times in Num, and it is here argued that the translator never articulated it. In all but 19 cases no extant witness obtains for του κυριου. For most of the 19 exceptions the evidence for later articulation is slight. In the list below only the evidence for articulation is given.

7₈₉ (φωνὴν) κυρίου] pr του 963 458 84
8₁₁ (ἔργα) κυρίου 963] pr του 422
9₁₃ (δῶρον) κυρίῳ] τον κυριου 381'
9₂₀ (προστάγματος) κυρίου] pr του 82
11₂₃ (χεὶρ) κυρίου] pr του Fᵇ V O⁻⁵⁸-82-707 C'' b⁻¹⁹ s z 646 799
16₉ (σκηνῆς) κυρίου] pr του 52'-313
16₁₉ (δόξα) κυρίου] pr του 319 799
16₄₁ (λαὸν) κυρίου] pr του 376 414
17₁₃ (σκηνῆς) κυρίου] pr του 528 318
19₁₃ (σκηνὴν) κυρίου A B M' V oI b d n t x⁻⁶¹⁹ 630 319] > 376; pr του rell
19₂₀ (ἅγια) κυρίου] pr του 458
20₉ (ἀπέναντι) κυρίου] pr του 392
21₇ (κατὰ) κυρίου M' 15-707 C''⁻⁷³' s⁻³⁰³⁴³ 318 z⁻¹⁸⁶³⁰' 59 Phil I 105] του θεου 426 75
    Bo Sa¹; pr του 1ell = Ra
21₁₄ (πόλεμος) κυρίου A 72* 121 630 55] pr του rell = Ra
22₁₈ (ῥῆμα) κυρίου] pr του 619
22₃₄ (ἀγγέλῳ) κυρίου] pr του 52'-313-422
31₃ (παρὰ) κυρίου F 58-72 C'' b⁽⁻¹⁹⁾ 129 85'-321' z⁽⁻¹²⁶⁾ 55 59 319 Hipp Balaam 491]
    θεου 125; του θεου V d⁻¹²⁵ t; pr του rell = Ra
31₂₉ (ἀπαρχὰς) κυρίου] pr του 426 b
31₄₇ (σκηνῆς) κυρίου] pr του 761*(vid) b 246ᶜ

In all but five instances (11₂₃ 19₁₃ 21₇ ₁₄ 31₃) the variant article is attested by only a few mss and may be regarded as insignificant, although in one case (7₈₉) the early 963 does support the articulation. Since 120 (or 119) out of the 125 occurrences of κυρίου were certainly unarticulated in Num it is plausible to suggest that κυρίου was never articulated by the translator.

The dative κυρίῳ occurs 72 times in Num, in all but a few cases representing ליהוה. In six cases (15₁₄ 18₂₈ ₂₉ 28₁₃ 29₁₁ 31₄₁) the unarticulated form is attested by all witnesses; in eighteen cases three or less mss support the article. The oldest ms witnesses usually support the unarticulated word. 963 is extant in 19 instances and supports the unarticulated word in all but one case (6₈) where A B V and G, however, all support the unarticulated κυρίῳ. Codex B supports the unarticulated word in all but three instances (5₉ 15₅ 18₁₂). Occasionally Origen was responsible for the addition of the article as the following instances prove.

6₆   κυρίῳ 963] pr (※ S G Syh) τω (το 376) Mᵗˣᵗ Sᶜ O-82 52'-313-414 d n 28-85' ᵐᵍ-
      321'ᵐᵍ-344ᵐᵍ t Tht Nm 198 Bo Syh
6₁₂   κυρίῳ 963] pr (※ G) τω F S O'⁻⁽⁵⁸⁾⁷⁰⁷ 619 z 59
25₄   κυρίῳ B V 82 d 53' n⁻⁷⁵* t 71-509 319 Cyr I 908 IV 300] > 75*; pr (※ G) τω rell
28₂₆ κυρίῳ 963] pr (※ Syh) τω O⁻⁵⁸ 422 f 407 55 Syh
29₁₃ κυρίῳ] pr (※ G) τω O⁻⁴²⁶ f⁻¹²⁹ Cyr I 1120
31₃₈ κυρίῳ 963] pr (※ G Syh) τω O-15 53'-56-246ᵐᵍ Syh

The addition of the article was probably intended to represent the preposition ל; puzzling is the fact that hex only shows this equation occasionally since the chief witnesses usually witness to the absence of the article. In any event, it would seem that the translator did not follow this practice but rendered ליהוה without the dative article to represent the preposition.

c) *Articulation of υἱοί as clan designation.*

Whenever υἱοὶ Ἰσραήλ occurs Num has the article before it. When it occurs in the genitive however, no discernible pattern obtains; even within one verse the pattern may vary. Thus in 8₁₉ υἱῶν Ἰσραήλ occurs but τῶν υἱῶν Ἰσραήλ occurs twice; cf also 18₂₄. In the accusative the article is lacking when πάντας precedes; otherwise it is present. In the dative the article is usually present, though not always (cf 15₃ 5₉ 8₁₇ ₁₈ 15₂₉ 18₁₄).

With clan names other than Israel the pattern is slightly different. The dative is always articulated but the accusative is not. The latter occurs only five times; twice the tradition is unanimous in attesting the article (3₁₅ 4₃₄) and twice in attesting its absence (16₁₀ ₁₂). At 24₁₇ the evidence is divided and the oldest witness has been followed. For both the nominative and the genitive the translator was quite arbitrary and no pattern seems to have been followed. Ra usually adopted the reading of his oldest witness; this same principle has been adopted for Num as well.

d) *Articulation of υἱός in patronymics.*

Ra does not normally accept an article before υἱός when υἱός intends clan designation. At 3₃₂, however, he accepts the article on the basis of Codex B. He also accepted articulation at 4₂₈.

3₃₂ υἱός] pr o B V 19 d⁻¹²⁵ t 126 646 Bo = Ra
4₂₈ υἱοῦ Ἀαρών 29-381′ 125 799] τον ααρων υιον 107′; > 319; pr τον rell = Ra

The pattern of usage in Num elsewhere is presented in the following list.

2₂₉ 7₂₄ ₃₀ ₄₂ ₄₈ ₅₄ ₆₀ ₆₆ ₇₂ ₇₈ 10₁₄ ₁₅ ₁₈ ₁₉ ₂₂ ₂₇ 13₅ ₆ ₇ ₈ ₉ ₁₀ ₁₁ ₁₂ ₁₃ ₁₄ ₁₅ ₁₆ ₁₇ 16₃₉ 22₂ ₁₀ 24₁₅
    25₇ ₁₄ 34₂₂ ₂₃ ₂₄ ₂₅ ₂₆ ₂₇ ₂₈ υἱός omn
3₃₀ υἱός] pr o 58 73′ 107′ 126
3₃₅ υἱός] > 799 ᴸᵃᵗcod 104
4₁₆ υἱός] pr o 392; > 628
4₃₃ υἱοῦ] pr τον A 426-oI f 619 y⁻³⁹² z 646
7₈ υἱοῦ B 963 376 509 126 Cyr I 856] pr τον rell
7₁₂ υἱός] o τον 319
7₁₇ υἱοῦ] τον 552; τω τον 319
7₁₈ υἱός] > 314
7₂₃ ₂₉ ₃₅ ₄₁ ₄₇ ₅₃ ₅₉ ₆₅ ₇₁ ₇₇ ₈₃ 25₇ ₁₁ 27₁bis 31₆ υἱοῦ omn
7₃₆ υἱός] pr οι 30; > 528
10₁₆ υἱός] o τον 319
10₂₆ υἱός] o τον b
10₂₉ 26₃₇ 32₄₀ υἱῷ omn
14₃₀ υἱός (Ἰεφοννή)] pr o C′-46-414-422; o τον 29
14₃₈ υἱός (Ναυή)] pr o 417; o τον V 29 55; τον 509; > 529 44 458 68′-120
14₃₈ υἱός (Ἰεφοννή)] o τον 29
16₁ υἱός 1° 2° omn
16₁ υἱοῦ 1° 2° omn
22₄ υἱός] pr o 53′
22₅ 31₆ ₈ υἱόν omn
24₃ υἱός] pr o 44
26₆₅ υἱός 1° 963] pr o 44-107′ 646 Cyr I 352
26₆₅ υἱός 2° 963] pr o 550
27₁ υἱοῦ 1°] τον o 458; τον 54-75-767

27₁₈ *υἱόν*] pr *τον* 739 126; > 53
32₁₂ *υἱός*] pr *ο* 963*(c pr m) 72 52′-313 *x*⁻⁵⁰⁹
32₂₈ *υἱόν* 963] pr *τον* 72 *C″* 53′ 28-85-130^txt.-321′txt; *τον τον* 799; *του* 126
32₃₉ *υἱός*] pr *ο* 422; > 707
32₃₉ *υἱοῦ*] pr *τον* 422^c; *ο υιος* 422*; *ο τον* 72
34₁₉ *υἱός*] *ο τον* F 130^mg.-321′ mg
34₂₀ *υἱός*] *ο τον* 130^mg.-321′ mg.-344^mg
34₂₁ *υἱός*] *ο τον* 130^mg
36₁ *υἱοῦ* 1°] *τον* 551
36₁ *υἱοῦ* 2°] pr *τον* V 16 *d t*

It is abundantly evident from the above list that in the collocation "N son of N" the translator never articulated "son," and that Ra's acceptance of *ο υιος* in 3₃₂ was incorrect. The instance at 4₂₈ might seem more problematic in view of the strong support in the tradition. It is reasonable to assume that Num did not make an exception here. The context reads *υἱοῦ Ἀαρὼν τοῦ ἱερέως* and the articulation of *ἱερέως* probably created the confusion in the tradition.

e) *Individual instances.*

3₁₀ *τὰ (ἔσω)*] > B 72-376 *x* Cyr I 845 Bo = Ra

This is part of a tradition explaining Aaron's *ἱερατείαν* which has no equivalent in 𝕸, viz. *καὶ πάντα τὰ κατὰ τὸν βωμόν* (for which a variant tradition obtains: *και παντα τα του θυσιαστηριου*) *καὶ τὰ ἔσω τοῦ καταπετάσματος*, "both all the things pertaining to the altar and the things within the veil." The tradition is based on 18₇ where Aaron is divinely ordered to guard his priesthood *κατὰ πάντα τρόπον τοῦ θυσιαστηρίου καὶ τὸ ἔνδοθεν τοῦ καταπετάσματος*. That the passages are related is clear. *πάντα τὰ κατὰ τὸν βωμόν* is an interpretation of *πάντα τρόπον τοῦ θυσιαστηρίου*, whereas *τὰ ἔσω* interprets *τὸ ἔνδοθεν*. If *τά* were not original the *ἔσω τ. καταπ.* phrase would be coordinate with *κατὰ τὸν βωμόν* rather than with *πάντα τὰ κ. τ. β.* Since in the 18₇ passage the second phrase must be coordinate with *πάντα –θυσ.* rather than with *τρόπον τ. θυσ.* the article in *τὰ ἔσω* must be original.

3₃₂ om *ὁ* 2° B *O*⁻⁵⁸-15-707* 44′-125 *f*⁻²⁴⁶ *n* 321* *x* *y*⁻¹²¹ 669* Syh = Ra

The article occurs in the phrase *ὁ ἄρχων ὁ ἐπὶ τῶν ἀρχόντων* for the Hebrew נשיא נשיא. *ο αρχων των αρχοντων* would be a literal rendering, but the translator avoided this as too much like "lord of lords," i.e. a divine title. The insertion of *ὁ ἐπί* rendered the term innocuous. The article was probably omitted through dittography due to the similarity of *ο* and *ε* in the uncial script.

11₃₅ *τῆς ἐπιθυμίας*] om *τῆς* B F V *O*′⁻²⁹ ⁵⁸ 129 54-75′ *x* 392 59 319 799 = Ra
33₁₇ *τῆς ἐπιθυμίας*] om *τῆς* B M′ V *O*′⁻⁵⁸ ⁷² *f* *x*⁻⁵⁰⁹ = Ra

The genitive phrase is part of the name of an encampment called *Μνήματα τῆς ἐπιθυμίας* (11₃₄), the rendering of the bound phrase קבר(ו)ת התאוה. The name also occurs in the preceding verses (11₃₄ 33₁₆) where Ra left it articulated. Obviously the translator would have rendered it consistently throughout.

Since in all four cases 𝔐 articulates תאוה the articulated form of the genitive is to be preferred throughout.

15₁₅ τὰς (γενεάς)] > B 129 509 = Compl Ra

The phrase εἰς τὰς γενεὰς ὑμῶν occurs seven times in Num (10₈ 15₁₅ ₂₁ ₂₃ ₃₈ 18₂₃ 35₂₉) and in all instances except 15₁₅ no witness omits the article. The omission is clearly secondary.

18₉ om τῆς B 82 d n⁻⁷⁶⁷ t x⁻⁶¹⁹ Cyr I 837 = Ra

The phrase καὶ ἀπὸ πάσης τῆς πλημμελείας αὐτῶν is one of a list of prepositional phrases of the pattern "from all their . . . ." In all these the nouns are articulated and it would be unlikely that this one should be left without an article. The omission of the article may well have been due to the fact that πλημμελείας is singular (as always in the Pentateuch) in contrast to the others in the list. It is, however, a collective, and does not actually contrast with the other items in the list; the articulated noun is to be preferred.

20₂₈ τὸν Ἀαρών] om τόν B 16-46-414-552-761 b 107'-125 129 84 71-509 392 55ᵗˣᵗ (c pr m)
    319 = Ra; > 376 Sa¹²

Though proper names are usually not articulated in Num except where the case relationship is in doubt, this one must be as 𝔐 shows in its את אהרן. The translator usually renders את by an article, and since he did not name the subject of the verb (i. e. Moses) as 𝔐 had done, the article is particularly necessary to avoid the possible misinterpretation that Aaron removed his own clothing, which is what the shorter text apparently means. Since ἐξέδυσεν can be modified either by one or two accusatives, the τόν is here necessary. That this was the interpretation intended by the translator is certain from the coordinate clause καὶ ἐνέδυσεν αὐτὰ Ἐλεαζὰρ τὸν υἱὸν αὐτοῦ where ἐνέδυσεν is expressly modified by a double accusative.

21₄ τὴν γῆν Ἐδώμ] om τήν B 82 54-75 = Ra

Here again τήν is the rendering for the Hebrew את; 𝔐 has את ארץ אדום. Its omission in the variant tradition is the result of haplography due to its similarity to γῆν.

23₂₂ ὁ θεός] om ὁ B (|) 509 = Ra
24₈ ὁ θεός] om ὁ B V 82-426 d⁻⁴⁴ t 71-509 319 Eus VI 409 Or IV 250 = Ra

θεός is always articulated in Num when it is nominative regardless of whether or not the corresponding word in 𝔐 is articulated. In other cases it is usually but not always articulated. That B twice omits ὁ before θεός may well be palaeographically inspired since all four letters of θεος in the uncial Bible hand are similar. Note that in 23₂₂ the word also occurs at change of line.

25₁₄ τῶν B 82 509 407] υιων 71; + υιων V d n t 319 Arm; οικου 344ᵐᵍ; > rell

The article modifies Συμεών and follows πατριᾶς. In spite of the small support the article is original. The context in 𝔐 is אב לשמעני. The article is an attempt to render the gentilic, for which cf ch. 26 passim in particular. The word πατριᾶς is modified by a proper name only here and in v. 15, where, however, the Hebrew context is somewhat different. There אב במדין הוא is rendered by πατριᾶς ἐστιν τῶν Μαδιάν; here the translator also used the article but in order to render a preposition governing a gentilic noun.

31₄₃ τῆς συναγωγῆς 72-618 C''⁻⁵²'³¹³ 509 392* 68-126 55 319 799 Latcodd 100 104 Arab] pr το απο 730; pr το A M' oI⁻⁶¹⁸ 52'-313 28-85ᵗˣᵗ-130-321'ᵗˣᵗ-343' y⁻³⁹²* 18'-628-630' 624 = Ra; pr απο 963 rell

There is no good reason for accepting the majority reading attested among others by B and 963. It has no basis in the Hebrew text, and is probably due to the number of ἀπό phrases in the immediate context, i.e. both immediately following συναγωγῆς as well as in the preceding verse.

The addition of the article το serving as a relative pronoun was accepted by Ra and is more noteworthy, but it too is not original. The notion of "half of the Israelites' possession" also occurs in v. 42 and v. 47. In both cases ἡμισεύματος is modified directly by a genitive construction, i.e. neither by a relative construction nor by an ἀπό phrase. In all three cases the construction in 𝔐 is a bound phrase. In v. 43 το has probably been introduced into the tradition under the influence of the immediately preceding τὸ ἡμίσευμα.

34₂ τήν 2° B* 963 O⁻⁵⁸ 129 n⁻⁷⁵ 799] > rell = Ra
36₃ om τήν B V G-82-426 d 129 n t x 319 = Ra

In both the above instances the article modifies κληρονομίαν. The Num translator always articulated this noun except for those instances where it is exegetically indefinite in meaning. This statement applies in all instances regardless of whether it is modified by another noun modifier or not; cf 32₁₈ 35₈ 36₂ ₄ ₇ (twice).

36₁₀ τῷ Μωυσῇ 58-82-376 b d 53' t⁻³⁷⁰ x⁻⁵²⁷ 392 407-630 799 Syh] τω μωυσ 126; τω μωση G n; τω μωσει 72-426; om τῷ B 527 = Ra; προς μωυσην rell

That the reading of B is secondary is clear from parallel passages. Whenever the formula "as/which the Lord commanded Moses" occurs (1₁₉ ₅₄ 2₃₃ ₃₄ 3₅₁ 4₄₉ 8₃ ₂₀ ₂₂ 9₅ 15₃₆ 17₁₁ 26₄ 27₁₁ ₂₃ 30₁ ₁₇ 31₇ ₂₁ ₃₁ ₄₁ ₄₇), Moses occurs in the dative with the article. This is the case both with ἐντέλλεσθαι and συντάσσειν. The reading of B must therefore be secondary. Nor is the popular variant to be considered as original text, since πρός phrases modifying συντάσσειν occur only twice (in 15₂₃) and never as προς μωυσην.

8. Nominal inflections.

a) A number of instances involving case inflection deserve special attention.

3₁₃ (ἐν γῇ) Αἰγύπτου] -πτω 29-72-376-oI 413-414'-417-528-552 b d⁽⁻¹⁰⁶⁾ 664 130*(c pr m)-343 t y⁻³⁹² 126 55 Phil I 250 255; αιγυπτ 82; > 761*(2°)
8₁₇ (ἐν γῇ) Αἰγύπτῳ] -πτου F*(c pr m) 376-707*(vid) 414-739 54'-75 509* 619 68'-120'; αιγυπτ 52 458-767
14₂ (ἐν γῇ) Αἰγύπτῳ] -πτου 56 54'-458 68'-120' Cyr I 373; αιγυπτ 82 314
33₄ (ἐν γῇ) Αἰγύπτῳ] -πτου F 82 414 53' n⁻⁷⁶⁷ 68'-120 Latcod 104

As in Gen the dative $Aἰγύπτῳ$ is preferred in the construction $ἐν\ γῇ\ ...,$ although the translator did apparently use the genitive in 3₁₃. There the dative is a minority reading, and all the oldest witnesses except Phil witness to the genitive. It would seem that the reading of B is in each case to be preferred as indicating the original text.

6₁₅ $θυσίαν$] $θυσια$ ($θυσι$ 963*) B 963 n^{-458} x^{-619} = Ra
— $σπονδήν$] $σπονδη$ (c var) B 963 n x^{-619} = Ra

The nominatives $θυσια$ and $σπονδη$ are old variants but can hardly have been intended by a translator. Along with $ἀμνόν, ἀμνάδα, κριόν, κανοῦν, ἄρτους$ and $λάγανα$, they explicate $τὸ\ δῶρον$ as object of $προσάξει$ in v. 14. The variants probably arose from a misreading of $θυσιᾱ$ and $σπονδῇ$ in parent texts.

8₈ $σεμίδαλιν$ 963] $σεμηδαλιαν$ 319; $σεμιδαλεως$ B 71 68'-120' 59 = Ra; $σεμιδλ$ 126; > 29 551

The reading of B is secondary, and probably due to the common occurrence of the genitive in the cultic laws; cf the recurring $πλήρη\ σεμιδάλεως$ in ch. 7, and $θυσίαν\ σεμιδάλεως$ in 15₄ ₆ ₉. The majority reading, also attested in 963, is the accusative demanded by the context; the word is here in opposition to $θυσίαν$ as the case of $ἀναπεποιημένην$ makes certain. It is after all the flour mixed with oil which constitutes the sacrifice.

9₁₃ $μακράν$] $μακρα$ B V O^{-376}-72 16ᶜ-46-422 75-127 76 509 392 ^{Lat}cod 100 Arm Syh(vid) = Ra

The word is under the obelus in Syh and is lacking in $\mathfrak{M}$. It occurs in the context $ἐν\ ὁδῷ\ μακράν$, i.e. as an adverbial accusative. It occurs in this same context in v. 10, where similarly the tradition attests change to adjectival from adverbial use; $μακρα$ there occurs in O^{-376}-72 414 56 75 Chr II 877 ^{Lat}cod 100 Syh(vid). The variant text simplifies the construction, though it may have been palaeographically conditioned, since a final nu is often indicated simply by a horizontal stroke over the vowel and is easily overlooked.

11₂₉ $μοι$] $εμε$ B x^{-527} 392

The B text is secondary as Ra also recognized. It represents the classical usage after $ζηλοῖς$, but Num is translation Greek and here represents literally the לי of the Hebrew parent text. Instructive is the translation pattern for modifiers of $ζηλόω$. In 5₁₄ (twice) ₃₀ $ζηλώσῃ\ τὴν\ γυναῖκα\ αὐτοῦ$ recurs for קנא את אשתו. In 25₁₁ $ἐν\ τῷ\ ζηλῶσαί\ μου\ τὸν\ ζῆλον$ is the rendering of בקנאו את קנאתי. On the other hand, in 25₁₃ $ἐζήλωσεν\ τῷ\ θεῷ\ αὐτοῦ$ renders קנא לאלהיו. When the preposition ל relates the modifier to the verb the dative is used, but when את is used the translator rendered it by the accusative.

16₃₃ $αὐτοῖς$] $αυτων$ B ^{Lat}cod 100 = Ra

The phrase כל אשר להם also occurs in v. 26 and v. 30. In each case להם is rendered literally by the dative $αὐτοῖς$ with no variants in the tradition. The phrase means "everything they possessed," and the change to the genitive does not change the sense of the phrase. It is probably merely a stylistic change, but in view of the literalism elsewhere as well as the small base of support for the genitive here, the genitive has been taken as secondary.

25₂ τὰς θυσίας] ταις (> Bas) θυσιαις B V O⁻⁵⁸-82 127 Bas II 629 Cyr III 397 Or I 7 = Ra

The accusative is the object of ἐπί and the phrase modifies ἐκάλεσαν. The majority tradition has εἰς τὰς θυσίας which is closer to 𝔐's לזבחי, but the lectio difficilior is probably to be preferred. I suggest that ἐπὶ τὰς θυσίας is here original since it could most easily explain both the change to the dative (possibly palaeographically inspired) as well as the change of ἐπί to εις.

28₃₁ αἱ σπονδαί] τα σπονδ(ε)ια (-δι 53) f; ταις σπονδαις (σποδ.*) 58; τας (τα 54-75 509 407) σπονδας B V 82-376′ d n⁻¹²⁷ t x⁻⁶¹⁹ 407 319 Cyr I 1092 = Ra

The phrase καὶ αἱ σπονδαὶ αὐτῶν was understood by the translator as coordinate to ἡ θυσία αὐτῶν of v. 28. This type of collocation is fully clear from chapter 29 where the same type of grammatical understanding recurs. Thus in 29₆ καὶ αἱ θυσίαι αὐτῶν καὶ αἱ σπονδαὶ αὐτῶν(1°) obtains as a nominative construction in exactly the same manner, i.e. as a continuation of the nominative construction ἡ θυσία αὐτῶν of v. 3; compare also 29₁₁ ₁₆ ₁₉ ₂₂ ₂₅ ₂₈ ₃₁ ₃₄ ₃₈ for the same construction.

The variant text which Ra accepted as text was conditioned by the immediate context; the occurrence of καὶ τὴν θυσίαν αὐτῶν ποιήσετέ μοι easily led to the change of αἱ σπονδαί to the accusative of the variant text. The lectio difficilior, however, is here to be preferred as original.

11₃₃ ἐν (> 52′-313-551) τῷ λαῷ A M′ V oI C″ 28-30′-85′ᵗˣᵗ-321-343-344ᵗˣᵗ-346ᵗˣᵗ y⁻³⁹² z 55 319 624 646] αυτους 125 75; > 509; τον λαον rell = Ra

𝔐 in context reads וַיִּךְ יהוה בעם. It is thus clear that ἐν τῷ λαῷ derives from a Hebrew source since good Greek would demand τον λαον. πατάσσειν is usually modified by the accusative in Num, but this is irrelevant since only here is the ב construction found in 𝔐 of Numbers. It might be argued that ἐν τῷ λαῷ is a hex correction. This is unlikely to be the case since no O ms, nor any d n t witnesses, attest to it. Thus it must be original text and the accusative a secondary improvement of Greek style; the variant text may also have been influenced by the occurrence of τὸν λαόν earlier in the verse.

b) Change in number in the nominal system within the text tradition is involved in a number of instances which invite discussion. Of particular interest are those involving the noun ὁλοκαύτωμα.

The words ὁλοκαύτωμα and ὁλοκαύτωσις are the usual renderings of עלה in Num. In the two instances where 𝔐 has the plural (10₁₀ 29₃₉) Num also has the plural. In all other instances 𝔐 has the singular, but the Greek tradition varies between singular and plural. If, however, עלה occurs in the phrase לעלה Num always uses the singular, and the entire tradition supports the singular with the exception of b^{-537} in 6₁₆ and d^{-106} 392 in 28₂₃.

Other instances of the singular in Num are as follows (only the plural variants are given).

8₁₂ (εἰς) ὁλοκαύτωμα 963] -ματα 44(2°)
15₃ ὁλοκαύτωμα] -ματα A B V 72 b d t x y 55 Cyr I 1029 = Ra

In 15₃ the singular must be original since its immediately following coordinate noun is also singular, i.e. ἡ θυσίαν (for או זבח). Ra also transposes the word with (ὁλο)κάρπωμα, but this is not to be taken seriously, as the Hebrew text makes clear.

Other instances of the singular in Num are:

15₆ (εἰς) ὁλοκαύτωμα with no equivalent in 𝔐
15₈ ₂₄ (εἰς) ὁλοκαύτωμα
28₆ ὁλοκαύτωμα] -ματα 106 509 318
28₁₀ ὁλοκαύτωμα] -ματα 707*(vid) 53-664⁽ᶜ⁾ 509 Cyr I 1116; -τωμαᵗ 72
28₁₄ (τοῦτο) ὁλοκαύτωμα
28₂₄ ₃₁ τοῦ ὁλοκαυτώματος
29₆ τὸ ὁλοκαύτωμα

In the remaining instances Num has the plural although 𝔐 is singular. These are

23₆ τῶν ὁλοκαυτωμάτων] της ολοκαυτωσεως F*(c pr m) Bo
28₁₁ ὁλοκαυτώματα] -τωμα 963 72-426-oI⁻¹⁵ 551-615 54-458 28-346*-730 619 z Cyr I 1116 Aeth Sa Syh
28₁₉ ὁλοκαυτώματα] (+ το 84) ολοκαυτωμα A 82 53′ 344*(c pr m) 84 71 121 59 Aeth
28₂₇ ὁλοκαυτώματα] -τωμα M′ 963 oI-29 C-46′-52′-57′-422-528′-550-551 125′ 246 127-458 x⁻⁵⁰⁹ 319
29₂ ὁλοκαυτώματα] -τωμα F 426-618 528 314 127 121 59 ᴸᵃᵗcod 100 Aethᴹ Armᵗᵉ
29₆ τῶν ὁλοκαυτωμάτων
29₈ ὁλοκαυτώματα B V 82 C′′⁻¹⁶⁴⁶⁵²⁸′ b d 56*(vid)-129 75 t x⁻⁶¹⁹ 18-126-407 59 319 ᴸᵃᵗcodd 100 104 Arm Co] pr εις 72; καρπωμα 761 130ᵐᵍ; ολοκαρπωμα 85ᵐᵍ-321′ᵐᵍ-344ᵐᵍ; (+ το F) ολοκαυτωμα rell
29₁₃ ὁλοκαυτώματα 963] -τωμα F 29-376-381′ n⁻¹²⁷ 28-85 84 ᴸᵃᵗcodd 100 104 Aeth Bo
29₃₆ ὁλοκαυτώματα] (+ το 84) ολοκαυτωμα F G-29-381′-707 d⁻¹²⁵ 56′ n t 319 Cyr I 1124 Aeth; -καρπωμα 53′; -τωμα k̄ω̄ 376

Except for 29₆ all of these are defined in the context as consisting of more than one sacrifice and the translator rightly understood עלה in a collective sense. In 29₆ τῶν ὁλοκαυτωμάτων is modified by τῆς νουμηνίας; the sacrifices of the new moon were detailed in 28₁₁—15 as plural, and the translator understood these as such here as well.

When the plural ὁλοκαυτώματα is described as κάρπωμα the number is not fully clear. In all instances κάρπωμα is the translator's rendering for אשה, i.e. the holocaust(s) are described as being a fire offering in 𝔐, this being regularly rendered in Num by κάρπωμα.

28₁₉ κάρπωμα] -ματα B* K 58-82-426 d⁻⁴⁴ f n⁻⁴⁵⁸ 74′-370 624 = Ra
29₁₃ κάρπωμα 963] -ματα B* 58-82 n⁻⁴⁵⁸ Arm Sa = Ra; > Bᶜ M′ V x⁻⁶¹⁹ 318 407
29₃₆ κάρπωμα 963*] -ματα A B 963ᶜ 58-82 129 509 y⁻³⁹² z 646 Sa = Ra; > F oI-72 53′ 458 59 416 ᴸᵃᵗcod 104

In each instance B supports the plural which Ra adopts. On the other hand, it is difficult to explain how an original plural would in each case have been changed into the linguistically more difficult singular in the majority tradition, whereas the impulse to an agreement in number with ὁλοκαυτώματα is easily explicable. The translator interpreted the holocausts as belonging to the class of κάρπωμα; this had the added advantage of exact equivalence in number to 𝔐. It should be noted that at 28₁₉ the present text of Num differed from 𝔐. 𝔐 has אשה עלה for which Num has ὁλοκαυτώματα κάρπωμα. Since κάρπωμα never renders עלה, but is normal for אשה it is clear that the parent text had עלה אשה. At 15₃ B along with *d n t x* Cyr I 1029 has transposed κάρπωμα and ὁλοκαύτωμα. In the former 𝔐 has אשה and in the latter עלה, and Ra cannot be correct in following B's text: ολοκαυτωματα κυριω ολοκαρπωμα.

עלה is not always rendered by ὁλοκαύτωμα, however, since ὁλοκαύτωσις also occurs. Thus the phrase עלת התמיד is normally rendered by a Greek expression with ὁλοκαύτωσις (28₃ ₁₀ ₁₅ 29₁₁ ₁₆ ₁₉ ₂₂ ₂₅ ₂₈ ₃₁ ₃₄ ₃₈ and compare also 28₂₃ where the parent text must have been עלת התמיד as well).

Four instances obtain in which ὁλοκαύτωσις is not modified by a genitive noun modifier.

6₁₄ (εἰς) ὁλοκαύτωσιν B V 963ᶜ ᵖʳ ᵐ *x*⁻⁶¹⁹ 319 Cyr I 1052] -τησιν 963*; -τωμα rell: עלה 𝔐
7₈₇ (εἰς) ὁλοκαύτωσιν] -τωμα 313-615 318; -τωματα 52: לעלה 𝔐
15₅ (τῆς) ὁλοκαυτώσεως] ολοκαρπωσεως *z*⁻¹²²*: העלה 𝔐
23₁₇ (τῆς) ὁλοκαυτώσεως (αὐτοῦ) = עלתו 𝔐
    Cf. also 15₈ ὁλοκαύτωμα A B V O⁻⁵⁸ *d* 129 *n t x* 121] -καρπωσιν 528; -τωσις rell: עלה 𝔐

There seems little doubt concerning the original reading of 7₈₇ 15₅ and 23₁₇. In the case of 6₁₄ and 15₈ the textual evidence is divided, but since semantically there is little to distinguish ὁλοκαύτωσις and ὁλοκαύτωμα the oldest witnesses must decide.

4₂₀ (ἰδεῖν . . .) τὰ ἅγια B V 29 *x*⁻⁶¹⁹ 318 Bo Syh] *sanctitatem sanctitatum* Arm; τα των αγιων αγια 610; + των αγιων *d*⁻⁶¹⁰ *n t*; το (τον 52) αγιον rell

The translator is quite inconsistent in the rendering of the singular substantive קדש, at times rendering it by the singular τὸ ἅγιον, but elsewhere by the plural τὰ ἅγια. In two instances, both in 18₉, the parent text may have been other than 𝔐. With little or no variants in the text tradition the singular is clearly original in 3₃₁ ₃₈ 4₁₆ 7₉ 18₁₀ 28₇. On the other hand, the plural is equally assured in 3₂₈ ₃₂ 4₁₂ ₁₅ (twice) ₁₉ 8₁₉ 16₅ 18₅ ₁₉. At 4₄ the phrase קדש הקדשים is rendered ἅγιον τῶν ἁγίων but with αγια for ἅγιον in *d n*⁻¹²⁷* *t* 646 Armᵃᵖ. That the translator was arbitrary in the matter of number is clear from his use of τὰς φυλακὰς τῶν ἁγίων at 3₂₈ and 3₃₂ but of τὰς φυλακὰς τοῦ ἁγίου at 3₃₈; cf also ἐν τῷ ἁγίῳ at 4₁₆ 28₇ but ἐν τοῖς ἁγίοις at 4₁₂. Since there is no apparent translation pattern in Num the plural which is attested by the oldest witness has been adopted for 4₂₀.

7₃ τὸ δῶρον B 963 x⁻⁶¹⁹ Cyr I 705 Aeth Sa] τα (> 72) δωρα rell = Ra
7₁₀ τὸ δῶρον Aeth] τα (> 19) δωρα 963 rell = Ra
7₁₁ τὸ δῶρον Aeth Bo] τα δωρα rell = Ra

Chapter 7 presents the presentation of the offerings (קרבן) for the dedication of the altar tribe by tribe on successive days. Each of the twelve tribes presents its קרבן as a series of offerings in identical terms. The collective term is rendered throughout the chapter (cf also 5₁₅ 6₁₄ ₂₁ 9₇ ₁₃ 15₄ ₂₅) by τὸ δῶρον rather than the plural regardless of the number of the subject and/or verb. In the above three instances the majority tradition is the result of the pressure of the immediate plural environment, i.e. in v. 3 by ἤνεγκαν τὸ δῶρον αὐτῶν, in v. 10 by προσήνεγκαν οἱ ἄρχοντες τὸ δῶρον αὐτῶν, and in v. 11 by προσοίσουσιν τὸ δῶρον αὐτῶν. The singular occurs eighteen times throughout this chapter but the plural is not used at all.

9₇ αὐτόν B 71-509 Cyr I 1081 Sa Syh] αυτων 426; αυτους rell

In v. 6 men approach Moses and Aaron, and a plural reference might therefore be expected in v. 7. 𝔐, however, has the singular; i.e. "those men said to him," viz. Moses, which Num reproduced correctly. That the singular is indeed correct appears from v. 8 where only Moses replies to the men. The plural of the majority tradition represents an attempt to harmonize v. 7 with the preceding verse.

11₁₂ αὐτούς 2°] αυτον B O⁻⁵⁸ d 56* n⁻⁷⁶⁷ t x⁻⁶¹⁹ Phil III 6ᵗᵉ Chr I 476 Tht *Nm* 204 Arm BoᴮSyh = Ra 𝔐

Since the antecedent is העם the pronoun is singular in 𝔐; Num uses a plural pronoun to refer to τὸν λαόν, since "the people" consists of individuals. This is clear from the reference in (ἔτεκον) αὐτούς where the pronoun in the Hebrew text is also singular, but only 628 799 Phil III 6ᵗᵉ Chr I 476 Tht *Nm* 204 have the singular variant αυτον. The referent is identical in the two cases, and the translator would hardly have changed the number of the pronoun in the very next clause. The variant is not necessarily due to Hebrew influence however; it may have been grammatically induced by λαόν, though it is not clear why αὐτούς 1° should not have been changed to the singular in the tradition to the same extent as αὐτούς 2°. It should also be observed that the plural reference in αὐτῶν at the end of the verse is unanimously supported in the text tradition.

20₂₇ αὐτούς] αυτον B V O⁻⁵⁸ 414 f⁻⁶⁶⁴ n 71-509 Arm Bo Sa⁴ Syh = Ra

The word occurs in the clause καὶ ἀνεβίβασεν αὐτούς and refers to Moses' execution of the Lord's command in v. 25 "take Aaron and Eleazar his son καὶ ἀναβίβασον αὐτούς to Mount Hor." In 𝔐 (ויעלו) the clause is intransitive with plural referent, i.e. "and they went up." The reading of B is certainly secondary in view of v. 25; it may be due to the exegetical consideration that in v. 26 the death of Aaron is predicted, and the ex post facto record would leave only Eleazar to be effectively "brought up" to the mountain by Moses.

9. Nouns are repeated in Hebrew in order to mark distribution. This is not the case in Greek normally but translation Greek may show this Hebrew characteristic.

28₁₃ δέκατον δέκατον A Bᶜ M′ V 963 O⁻⁵⁸ 509 y⁽⁻³¹⁸⁾ Cyr I 1116 Aethᶜ Arab Syh] δυο δεκατα 646; semel scr rell = Ra

The distributive עשרון עשרון occurs five times in Numbers (28₁₃ 21 29 29₁₀ 15) and it is always faithfully rendered by δέκατον δέκατον in the Greek. The majority text accepted by Ra is therefore the result of haplography. This could hardly have been original, since no Greek scribe would have repeated δέκατον and created such barbaric Greek. In fact at 29₄ the phrase δέκατον δέκατον also occurs with only a few supporting a single δέκατον:

29₄ δέκατον δέκατον 963] semel scr 414 44-125 56-129 Arab = Compl

Though 𝔐 has a single עשרון, the parent text of Num must have had the distributive.

No such regularity of translation appears for איש איש. The phrase occurs only five times in Num but there is no set pattern in the Greek.

1₄ ἕκαστος Fᵃ] + εκαστος A F G-29-426 56 y⁻³¹⁸ z⁻¹⁸ 59 624 Syh
4₁₉ ἕκαστον] pr ενα O Arab Syh; εκαστος f 75 28 59 319

In both cases the longer reading probably was the result of Origen's work. The other three instances are

4₄₉ ἄνδρα κατὰ ἄνδρα] om ἄνδρα 1° f⁻²⁴⁶
5₁₂ ἄνδρος ἄνδρος] semel scr V 72 529ᶜ d 53′ 75′-767 71 68′-126 799 Cyr I 909 Bo Sa¹²
9₁₀ ἄνθρωπος ἄνθρωπος] semel scr Fᵇ 72 d 75′ 126 319 Chr II 877 Cyr I 1081 ᴸᵃᵗcod 100 Bo Sa¹²

In these three instances the repetition of the Hebrew word is also shown in the Greek.

10. Numbers.

A great deal of variation obtains in the census report of ch. 26 in the text tradition and only a small minority, mainly from the O and z mss. witness to the original text. This is assured by the total given as 601,730 which is = 𝔐. In part the divergent tradition is influenced by the census reports of chapters 1 and 2. This seems to be the case in vv. 21, 31 and 45. In v. 21 the number for Issachar is given as 64,300, whereas in 1₂₇ 2₆ it is given as 54,400. A well supported variant reads 400 for 300. In v. 31 Asher is given as 53,400, but in 1₄₁ 2₂₈ as 41,500. Only O 128-630′ Aethᶜ Arab Syh witness to πεντήκοντα (χιλιάδες), all others reading τεσσαράκοντα. Similarly for Benjamin in v. 45 the majority reading of τριακοντα (χιλιάδες) instead of the correct τεσσαράκοντα supported only by O 767 619 z ⁻¹²⁶ ⁶²⁸ Arab Syh, may be due to the 35,400 of 1₃₅ 2₂₃ (instead of 45,600).

On the other hand, no such influence can be identified in such well-supported variants as πεντήκοντα for τριάκοντα in v. 7, in the addition of 4000 to the number in v. 27, of 62,000 instead of 52,000 in v. 38, in 500 for the correct 600 in v. 45, in 600 substituted for 400 in v. 47, or in 300 instead of 400 in v. 50. No particular rationale seems to lie behind these majority variants since the total number is supported by almost the entire tradition.

The only text tradition which adds up correctly is that adopted as original text here (as well as by Ra). It is also in all cases the same number which obtains in 𝔐.

29₁₃ τέσσαρας (-ρες 426 44′ n⁻⁴⁵⁸ t 646) καὶ δέκα G-426 d n t⁻⁸⁴ 646] om καὶ δέκα V 120*; δεκα και τεσσαρας 120ᶜ; δεκα τεσσαρας (c var) 963 rell = Ra

29₂₉ τέσσαρας καὶ δέκα] δεκα τεσσαρας (-ρες B* 82; -σσερεις 664) B V 963 58-72-82-376 77 d⁻⁴⁴ f⁽⁻⁵³⁾ t x 407 416 = Ra

Ra accepts τέσσαρας καὶ δέκα for vv. 15 17 20 23 26 but δεκα τεσσαρας for vv. 13 29, thereby following the text of B. B, however, usually uses the symbols ῑ for ten and δ̄ for four as does 963 and is therefore not a reliable guide. In v. 29 B has δεκα τεσσαρας spelled out but in v. 13 has ῑδ̄. It is most unlikely that the translator would have arbitrarily changed from δεκα τεσσαρας in v. 13 to τέσσαρας καὶ δέκα in vv. 15—26, and then back to δεκα τεσσαρας in v. 29. That τέσσαρας καὶ δέκα is original throughout is made virtually certain by the fact that in the context of v. 13 the μόσχους to be offered is given as τρεῖς καὶ δέκα and not as δεκα τρεις.

29₁₄ τρισὶ(ν) καὶ δέκα O⁻⁴²⁶-618 n⁻⁷⁵ z⁻⁴⁰⁷ 319 646] ȳ και (> 963*) ῑ V 963; τρισι και δυο 59; om καὶ δέκα 75; τρεις και δεκα A F M′ 29-82-707* 313 246 30-344 509 y⁻³⁹² ; τρισκαιδεκα rell = Ra

As for the instances detailed in the preceding note and as throughout Num, the ascending paratactic order for numbers from 13 through 19 has been accepted as Num text. It might be noted that usage in Num was quite different from Gen where a descending asyndeton order for the "-teen" numbers occurs throughout. This latter is also the expected order in Ptolemaic times (cf Mayser I. 2.75f.), but is hardly justified as Num in view of complete lack of support in the Greek tradition. The only possible alternative to the above text would have been the compound τρεισκαίδεκα (not the itacistic ordinal spelling τρισκαιδεκα chosen by Ra). Since uncial texts do not show space at word juncture in the earlier centuries, the early ms tradition is not germane; accordingly a consistent pattern of separate lexemes is employed in Num, and the inflected τρισίν is here considered to be original text.

11. Spelling of Proper Nouns.

3₁₉ Ἰσαάρ F V 44-610 458-767* 30′-343-346* 76 126 55 59 ᴸᵃᵗcod 100 Bo] ισσαρ cI⁻⁵⁷* ⁷³* ³²⁰-414′-417-422; ισαρ 73*-320 319; ιεσααρ 376; ιεσσαρ 246; ιεσσαχαρ 129ᶜ-664; ιεσαχαρ 56; ισσαχαρ 15 C⁻⁵²⁹-57* 129* 392; ισαχαρ 46-529 18; sahar Arm(vid); > x⁻⁵⁰⁹; ισσααρ rell = Ra

16₁ Ἰσαάρ Fᶜ ᵖʳ ᵐ 58-72 46-414-417 t 527 68′ 59 Cyr I 857] ιασσ. F*; ασσ. 44-125′; ασ. 610; σααρ V 54-75 55 319 Arm Bo; σισ. 82; ισσαχαρ 29; ααρων 458; ισσααρ rell = Ra

The translator would hardly have transcribed יצהר by a double sigma spelling; this is clear from the fact that he recognized the root as having ה as the second radical which he attempted to show by doubling the vowel. The popular ισσααρ variant is the result of dittography.

The gentilic form at 3₂₇ must then be Ἰσααρίς as attested but with itacistic ending -ρεις in only four mss 72 730 18-126 and Compl. The popular variant σααρεις led Ra to adopt Σααρις which would presuppose a parent text of הצהרי instead of 𝔐's correct היצהרי.

13₅ Σαμού 129 x Sa¹²] . . .]ον 963; σαμμου F 29-426 f⁻¹²⁹ 392; σαμουηλ B Syh; σαμουτος 799; σαμιηλ 68'; σαλαμουηλ 82; σαμαλιηλ A 72-618 19; salamēl Sa⁴; σαλαμηηλ 30; σαλαμιηλ Fᵃ rell = Ra

That 𝔐's שמוע was also the parent text for Num is now made most likely by the reading of 963; the first part of the name is not extant but that ου was the end of the name is certain. The only uncertainty that remains is whether σαμου or σαμμου is original. The translator usually rendered the *qatūl* type name correctly; cf Ῥαφού, Ῥαγουήλ; Σαούλ, Ἰεσού. The popular variant adopted by Ra, σαλαμιηλ, was the name of the chief of the tribe of Simeon (2₁₂ 7₃₆ ₄₁ 10₁₉); here Shamoua is the spy sent from the tribe of Reuben.

13₆ Οὐρί 426 C'' f⁻¹²⁹ 28-85'-321' 319 Syhᵗˣᵗ

All other witnesses prefix a *sigma*, a reading which Ra adopts. 𝔐 has חורי, however, and the *sigma* is a dittograph from the immediately preceding τῆς.

13₂₂ Ἐμάθ occurs for חמת in the common phrase לבא חמת (cf also 34₈). Inexplicably the tradition confused it with the Euphrates as is shown in the εφρααθ of d n⁻⁷⁵ t x⁻⁵⁰⁹ and *ephrath* of Arm. This apparently led to the early error εφααθ attested in B 376 509 ᴸᵃᵗcod100 Sa¹ = Ra

13₂₃ Σεσί for ששי occurs in the tradition with two *sigmas* in medial position in B Fᵃ V 127 343 71'; A has σεμει, and Sa¹² *semeei*, all other witnesses having a single sigma. Since Masoretic pointing also witnesses to a single sibilant for the second consonant, there is no good reason to follow the minority reading σεσσι with Ra

21₁ Ἀθαρίμ for האתרים. Ra adopted αθαριν; variants with final *nu* obtain in B 82 71-509 Arm Co and in αβαριν (-ρην 527) of d⁻¹⁰⁶ t 527. Transcriptions of names with masculine plural endings ought to end in -ιμ; thus Βελσαττίμ in 33₄₉; Ἀβαρίμ in 33₄₇ ₄₈ and of the dual endings of Καριαθάιμ in 32₃₇ and Χεβλαθάιμ in 33₄₆ ₄₇.

In view of Βελσαττίμ above it would seem best to read Σαττίμ in 25₁ instead of the more popular σαττιν adopted by Ra; a final *mu* is attested only by F Fᵇ 29-72'-426 d 56' n 344ᶜ t 527-619 18-68'-120'-126 799 Cyr III 397 IV 300 Arab Arm Syh. On the other hand, עקרבים of 34₄ was almost certainly transcribed as Ἀκραβίν; the variant with final *mu* in 29*-381-426 16-46-528 54 Syh is probably a hex correction. Similarly an apparently original Ῥαφιδίν in 33₁₄ ₁₅ for the name רפידם (not a plural ending however) was revised to end with *mu* in 426 761 d t Syh (plus Armᵗᵉ in v. 15) probably by Origen. It appears that final nasalization may well not have been phonetically distinctive between labial and nasal positions; in any event /-m/ and /-n/ are not always clearly

116

kept apart. In 26₄₃ Σωφάν and its gentilic Σωφανί occur. 𝔐 has שפופם and
השופמי resp.; presumably the former read שופם in the translator's text. In
the text tradition only 58-426 Syh have changed the nu into mu, i.e. a hex
correction.

In v. 42 Ἀχιράν and its gentilic Ἀχιρανί occur for אחירם and אחירמי resp.
A correction of the nu into mu is witnessed for the former in 58-426-707 f⁻¹²⁹
54-75′ 318 Syh and for the latter in 58-426-707 f⁻¹²⁹ 54-75′ Syh, obviously hex
corrections. An early variant prefixed an iota, i.e. ιαχιραν and ιαχιρανι which was
adopted by Ra. Names with אחי as first element are always transcribed as αχι-.
The initial iota is the result of dittography from an uncial parent text since the
word preceding Ἀχιράν was ΤΩΙ.

In 33₆ ₇ the name "Etham" occurs, but in the first instance with the preposition ב, באתם, and in the second with מן, מאתם. The word is transcribed in
both places as βουθάν, though preceded by the preposition εἰς in v. 6. Origen
corrected the nu to mu, as the text tradition shows:

v. 6 Βουθάν] βουθαμ 58; ουθαμ 426 54-75; οθαμ 799; οθομ 82; b'tm Syh; σουθαμ
127-458

v. 7 Βουθάν] βουθαμ 58; οθαμ 799; σουθαμ 75′-127; ουθαμ 426 54; οθομ 82; b'wtm Syh

The last problem dealing with final nasals concerns the place name "Mi-
dian." 𝔐 has מדין throughout. The Greek evidence is as follows:

22₄ Μαδιάν 426 ᴸᵃᵗAug Num 46 Ruf Num XIII 5 Syh] mazyam ᴸᵃᵗcod 104; μαδιαμ
rell = Ra

22₇ Μαδιάν 426 Arab Syh] mazziam ᴸᵃᵗcod 100; μωαβ 53′; μαδιαμ rell = Ra

25₁₅ Μαδιάν B O⁻⁵⁸-82 ᴸᵃᵗAug Loc in hept IV 80(mazianᵃᵖ) Syh] maziam ᴸᵃᵗcod 100;
μαδιανιτων 59; μαδηναιων 799; μαδιαμ rell

25₁₈ Μαδιάν B 82-426 Syh] maziam ᴸᵃᵗcod 100; μαδιανει G; μαδιαμ 963 rell

31₃ Μαδιάν 1° B G ᴸᵃᵗRuf Num XXV 2 Syh] μαδιαμ rell; ⌒2° 19 54-75′ 126 | Μαδιάν
2° B ᴸᵃᵗRuf Num XXV 2 Syh] madie ᴸᵃᵗcod 100; μαδιαμ rell

31₇ Μαδιάν B 509 Syh] madianitas Arm; μαδιαμ 963 rell

31₈ Μαδιάν 1° B 82 Syh] -δειαμ V; -διααμ 422; madianitarum Arm; μαδιαμ rell | Μαδιάν
2° Syh] μωαβ G; μαδιαμ rell

31₉ Μαδιάν B 82 ᴸᵃᵗAug Num 62 Syh] αντων των μαδιανητων 416; μαδιαμ rell

It should be noted that the gentilic form also occurs frequently throughout
Num but always with a μαδιαν-stem, and there seems little doubt that the
translator transcribed Μαδιάν throughout in spite of the overwhelming witness
to μαδιαμ. Possibly copyists were influenced by the popular name Μαριάμ when
Μαδιάν occurred as an isolate, whereas such influence was void for the gentilic
form.

21₁₂ Ζαρέδ] ζαρετ B 52* d t 318*(vid) = Ra; ζαρεθ Fᵇ b⁽⁻⁵³⁷⁾ 127-767 343 509 318ᶜ(vid)
18-669 55 799 Bo; zireth ᴸᵃᵗcod 100; sared Sa; ζαρελ V; ζαρε A oI 121

Since 𝔐 has זרד the B text must be secondary. The Hebrew daleth is always
transcribed by delta in all names in Num regardless of position. For final position cf Ἐμιούδ, Ἐλδάδ, Μωδάδ, Ἀράδ, Σαλπαάδ, Ἰωχαβέδ and Βεναμιούδ.

21₂₄ Ἀμμάν 1°] αμμα 72; αμβαν 53; αμμων M′ V 426-707 417-528 b 767 30′ y⁻³¹⁸
68′-120′ 319 624 ᴸᵃᵗcod 100 Arab Arm Bo Syh | Ἀμμάν 2°] αμμων B V 426 b 246
767 30′ 18 319 ᴸᵃᵗcod 100 Arab Syh = Ra; amon Arm

Only an undue reverence for the text of B could have induced Ra to adopt two different spellings for this name within a single verse. That Ἀμμάν was the old pronunciation of עמון was argued in THGD 62. This is also clear from the LXX transcription of the gentilic form with *alpha*, not with *omega*.

14₄₅ Ἑρμά] ερμαν B V 376 C'' 130* 509 = Ra; αρμα 54*; ερμωνα 30(vid); ρημα 129*(c pr m)

The final nasalization of the variant text may have resulted from reading final *alpha* as -*ā* in a parent text. In any event it is not original as 𝔐's החרמה makes clear.

26₁₇ (τῷ) Ἰαμουήλ] -λει 319; ιαμοηλ 72; ιεμ. d t; iamu ᴸᵃᵗcod 110 Sa; αμουλ 426; ιαμουν B 82-376 129-664 71 407 = Ra; ιαμμουν 53; ιαμων 509; iamuni ᴸᵃᵗcod 100; amuni Bo; yḥmwl Syhᴸ; yḥmwʼyl Syhᵀ

𝔐 has לחמול but the parent text of LXX must have had לחמואל as Sam. The B reading is due to inner Greek error in the uncial scripts, with *H* copied as *N*. The following word is *ΔΗΜΟΣ* and the *Λ* was dropped by haplography to create ιαμουν. The gentilic then inevitably followed as ιαμουνι for Ἰαμουηλί. Whether the initial *iota* is original remains uncertain since except for the hex correction in 426 (cf also Bo) the tradition is unanimous in supporting such an *iota*.

26₂₀ Σαμράμ Bᶜ F 29-707*(vid) 56' 509 407 Syh] σαμαραν Ra. | Σαμραμί 56] σαμαρανι Ra.

𝔐 has שמרן and השמרני respectively. Presumably Rahlfs' conjecture is based on B* which has σαμαραμ for the first and σαμαρανει for the second. It stands alone, however, in reading a vowel before ρ, and this is unlikely to be original. More problematic is the question of the last consonant. *Nu* and *mu* are often confused palaeographically not only, but the translator also often transcribes final *m* by *nu* and final *n* by *mu*. Furthermore the forms with *mu* are also attested for α' and ϑ'. It is possible that the *nu* tradition derives ultimately from hex (note σαμραν in 82-426 767 and σαμρανει in 82-426ᶜ), and the dominant *mu* tradition is probably original.

26₃₄ Χέλεκ] χαλεκ 72 528 246 767 318 Bo; αχελεκ 54-75'; χελεδ 68'-120; chedek Sa; αχελει V; χελεβ 509; χελεχ F; χελεγ B 376 129 71 407 Arm = Ra; χελεεγ 82

𝔐 has חלק. The reading adopted by Ra is clearly wrong. The letter *qoph* is never rendered by *gamma* in Num but always by *kappa* (except at 34₂₂ Βαχχίρ for בקי where the parent text is uncertain). The gentilic Χελεκί must also be read (for החלקי) rather than χελεγι with Ra. This same generalization applies to Ἐνάκ for הענק at 13₂₃ ₂₉ where Ra adopted εναχ which B read; cf also Deut 9₂.

Μααλά occurs three times in Num; Ra adopted μαλα for two of them and *Μααλά* for one.

26₃₇ Μααλά] μαλα A B 72*-82 413 b 767 321 x⁻⁶¹⁹ 319 = Ra; μααλλα d 54-75 t; mḥlʼ Syh; machala ᴸᵃᵗcod 100; μαλαα 392; μααυλα 129; μαλααδ 127; βαλα 130; ααλλα 458; μααυα 550' 730; μαδαα 68'-120'; maada Sa; μαυαα 15

118

27₁ Μααλά] μαλα A B 82 129 509 = Ra; μααλλα d⁻⁴⁴ n⁻¹²⁷ 30 t; maali BoᴮB; μαλλα 53′; μαλαα 414 71*; μαλδαα 68′-120′; magala Latcod 100; μαλακ 319; βααλα 628

36₁₁ Μααλά 963(vid)] μαλα 72* 129 130* 509; μααλλα d⁽⁻¹⁰⁶⁾ n t; μαλαα A oI⁻⁶⁴ 392 120 624 Boᴬ; μααλ b 407-630; machala Latcod 100; mathala Latcod 104; mella Boᴮ; νααλα 799; μαλαδ 82; μααρα 246

Medial ḥeth with vowel when it represents a laryngeal rather than a velar (cf JW Wevers, Ḥeth in Classical Hebrew, Essays on the Ancient Semitic World Edited by J W Wevers and D B Redford [Toronto, 1970], 101—112) is variously rendered in Num but most commonly by a single or double vowel, as the following instances show: Ἀλλήλ (יחלאל), Σηών (סיחן), Ναβί (נחבי), Μοολί (מחלי), Ναασσών (נחשון), Ἀσιήλ (יחצאל), Νααλιήλ (נחליאל) and Ῥαάβ (רחב). Presumably the parent text for Ἀλλήλ and Ἀσιήλ had no initial yodh. Double vowel transcriptions apparently represent ḥeth in intervocalic position whereas single vowel transcriptions represent ḥeth with a single vowel either before or after the ḥeth. Since both maḥᵃlā and maḥlā are possible realizations for מחלה one can only depend on the text tradition. It would seem likely that the transcription should be the same in all three instances. Μααλά is probably to be preferred since ḥeth closing a syllable medially is attested elsewhere in Num only for Ναβί; furthermore for 36₁₁ both B and 963(vid) attest to the double vowel form.

32₃₆ Ναμβρά 707 74′-76] αμβρα d 370; ναβραν 84; ναβρα 799; ναβραι 82; nambram Latcodd 100 104; ναμραμ B; ναμβραν Ra.; ναμραν F 129 Aeth Arm; αμβραμ V 15 C⁻⁵²⁹-46-417-528 75′-127 130-346*(vid) 392 126-128-630 624; αμβρ[... 422; αμραν Μ′ 72 28 x 18; αβραν 246 767 68′ Bo Sa¹; ναμμαραν 319; αμραμ G-29-64 57′-73′-550-761 85-321-343′-346ᶜ-730 120′-628 59 Sa¹²; αβραμ 313-552 669; αμβαμ 376; αραμ 30; βηθ ναμρα 426 Arab Syh; βηθη αμραμ 58; βιθι αμραμ 56; βιθι αμαρμ 53′; αμβραν rell

A final nasal, though widespread, can hardly have been original. 𝔐 has בית נמרה, but Num's parent text apparently lacked בית which was then added by hex. The name נמרה also occurs in v. 3 where it was also transcribed as Ναμβρά. It should be noted that in the transmission of Ναμβρά of v. 3 some final nasalization is also witnessed in the tradition. The spelling without initial nu is due to haplography since the preceding word is τήν. Final nasalization may have been facilitated by the name of Moses' father Ἀμράμ.

32₄₂ Κανάθ] κανααθ F Μ′ 29-58-72-oI C′′⁻¹⁶⁴⁶⁴¹³⁵⁵¹ b 125-610 246 s y⁻¹²¹ 18′-126-628-630′ 59 624 Latcod 100 = Ra; κααναθ A 121; κανανθ 413; κααθ B 16-46 56; καμαθα 426; καδως 53′; ganath Sa¹²; gathanaath Bo; canathatha Latcod 104

There is no good reason to question the קנת of 𝔐 which is correctly transcribed by Num. κανααθ would presuppose either קנחת or קנעת and is secondary, the result of dittography.

33₂₀ ₂₁ Λεβωνά for לבנה. Ra adopted λεμωνα on the basis of B, a minority reading supported by only a few witnesses

33₂₂ ₂₃ Μαχελάθ for קהלתה. The parent text must have had a mim prefix since it is universally attested in the text tradition. Ra adopted μακελλαθ read by B M′ G 107′ 129 t 509 407 Arm in both instances as well as by V 44 319 in v. 22 and by V^c in v. 23. It can not be original, however, if *he* was the second consonant in the name, which would result in the syllable -κελ- or -κεελ- but never -κελλ-; cf also Μακηλώθ in vv. 25 26.

33₂₉ ₃₀ Ἀσελμωνά for חשמנה. The *lambda* is baffling but is apparently original since forms without it constitute a hex correction witnessed to by O and scattered *f* and *z* mss. Ra adopted σελμωνα on the basis of B. An initial *ḥeth* syllable is never elided by Num, however, as the names Ἀγγί, Ἐνώκ, Ἀσρών, Ἐσεβών, Οὐρί, Ὠβάβ, Ἐμάθ and Ἀνιήλ demonstrate.

33₃₀ ₃₁ Μασουρούθ] μασσουρουθ Ra. The Ra reading is based on the minority reading of B (though in v. 30 B has μασσουρωθ uniquely). The ms evidence for the dittograph is as follows: v. ₃₀ μασσουρουθ M′ 343 509 392; μασσουρωθ B | v. ₃₁ μασσουρουθ B M′ 509 392 Sa¹². Since the translator seldom transcribed intervocalic /s/ by a double sigma (as e.g. Δεσσά), the majority form is to be preferred.

33₃₁ ₃₂ Βαναιακάν for בני יעקן. In both occurrences the name is followed by the conjunction καί. The B text which Ra followed has βαναια and was the result of parablepsis BANAIAKANKAI becoming BANAIAKAI.

34₉ Ζεφρώνα for זפרנה. The translator always transliterated *zayin* by *zeta* and never by *delta*. Ra's adoption of δεφρωνα was based on B*'s unique reading, but does not merit serious consideration.

34₁₁ Χενέρεθ for כנרת. The name occurs only once elsewhere in the Pentateuch. At Deut 3₁₇ מכנרת is transliterated by Μαχανάραθ (codex B has μαχαναρεθ, which Ra adopted). The name is also found four times in Joshua. In Codex B these occur as κενερωθ in 11₂, χενερεθ in 12₃ and 13₂₇ and as κενερεθ in 19₃₅. The only other occurrence obtains at 1 Kg 11₂₀ where B uniquely has χεζραθ although the majority has either χενερεθ or χεννερεθ. In our passage B has χεναρα which Ra followed. It would seem that a transliteration with final *theta* must be correct here. Furthermore all witnesses which have final *theta* support the spelling with ε vowels throughout. Χενέρεθ is undoubtedly the original transliteration for כנרת here.

34₂₃ Οὐφίδ A F 58-707 *f*⁻¹²⁹ 121] ουφει F^a; εφιδ 72-426; σουφιλ 30′ 392; σουφηλ 381′; σουφιηλ 15′ 18′-126-628-630′; σουφιρ 106-125 *t*; σουφηρ 44-107′; *suphin* Bo; σουβηθ 343; σουφι B M′ 376 *b* 129 *n*⁻¹²⁷ 71-509* Lat^{cod} 104 Arm^{ap} Sa; ουφι Ra.; *sofi* Lat^{cod} 100; σουφει V 963 G-82 127 509^c 407; σουφη 527 319; σεφι 619; ’*pwr* Syh; σουφιδ rell

𝔐 has אפד, and the transcription with final *delta* is correct. The apocopated form is attested as early as 963 and B which led Ra to propose ουφι; it probably resulted from auditory assimilation of *delta* to the next syllable τῆς, i.e. ου-φιδτης → ουφι της. The prefixed *sigma* in most of the witnesses is of course a dittograph from the preceding υἱός.

Φαδασούρ for פדהצור occurs at 2₂₀ 7₅₄ ₅₉ 10₂₃. In each case the popular reading φαδασσουρ is attested among others by B and is accordingly adopted by Ra, whereas Φαδασούρ is retained by a minority of mss.

That the *he* is part of the first element of the name rather than representing the article of the theophoric element צור is clear from such names as פדהאל and עשהאל where the "he" clearly stands for the third grapheme of a ל'ה′ verb. Thus the transcription φαδασσουρ is certain to be secondary. The dittograph was probably facilitated by acquaintance with the well known Ἀσσούρ.

Ὠβάβ for חבב at 10₂₉ is clearly correct. In uncial mss it was preceded by ΤΩΙ and the *iota* was copied twice to produce the popular ιωβαβ variant which Ra adopted.

A number of names in Num remain which do not equal 𝔐; either the translator misread (such as *daleth* for *resh* or vice versa) or the parent text did not = 𝔐. Some of these were corrected by hex. They are listed here in the order of their first occurrence together with the reading of 𝔐: *Ραγουήλ* דעואל; *Ἀβιούδ* אביהוא; *Ἰαβί* ופסי; *Γουδιήλ* גאואל; *Ἀχελγαί* עיי; *Ζωόβ* והב; *Μανθανάιν* מתנה; *Ἰαζήρ* עז; *Ἀροήλ* ידו; *Γώγ* אגג; *Χασβί* כזבי; *Ἰαμουήλ* חמול; *Ἀδδί* ערי; *Ἀροαδί* ארוד; *Ἀριήλ* אראלי; *Ἰαμίν* ימנה; *Ἀχιέζερ* איעזר; *Συμαέρ* שמידע; *Τάναχ* תחן; *Ἐδέν* ערן; *Ασυβήρ* שבם; *Σωφάν* שפופם; *Ἀδάρ* ארד; *Σαμί* שוחם; *Ἀσιήλ* יחצאל; *Εὐίν* אוי; *Σεβαμά* שבם; *Σωφάρ* שופי; *Ραφακά* דפקה; *Δεσσά* רסה; *Μακελάθ* קהלתה; *χαραδάθ* חרדה; *Καταάθ* תחת; *Ταράθ* תרח; *Φινώ* פונן; *Γαί* עיים; *Βελσαττίμ* אבל השטים; *Ἀράδ* אדר; *Σαραδά* צדדה; *Ασερνάιν* חצר עינן; *Βηλά* ומחה; *Βακχίρ* בקי; *Σαβαθά* שפטן; *Ὀζά* עזן and *Ἀχιώρ* אחיחוד.

12. Verbal inflections.

a) *Number*

1₄₄ ἐπεσκέψατο] -ψαντο B F^c pr m M′ d 127^c 74^c-76′ Aeth Arm Bo^ABc Sa¹ Syh = Ra

3₁₆ ἐπεσκέψατο F V 72-82 44-610 56-129-664 75-127 130^mg y⁻¹²¹ z⁻¹²⁶ 59 646 799] επισκ. 246 54-458 321′ mg 126; ηριθμησεν A oI-29-707^(mg) (vid) C″ b 28-30′-85′-130^txt-321′ txt-343′ 121 55 319 624 Sa⁴; -ψαντο rell = Ra

The subject of the verb in 1₄₄ is Μωυσῆς καὶ Ἀαρὼν καὶ οἱ ἄρχοντες Ἰσραήλ, in 3₁₆ Μωυσῆς καὶ Ἀαρών. With compound subjects following the verb of which the first member is singular the verb is normally singular in 𝔐 as in these cases and the translator followed this same practice. When the verb (or participle as predicate) follows the compound subject it is commonly plural in Hebrew, and again the translator usually follows the Hebrew practice.

In the case of 3₁₆ the strongly attested plural in the text tradition should be seen in view of the related confusion in the preceding verse.

ἐπισκέψῃ F 82 392 z 646 Sa⁴] -ψαι (-ψε 318) 72 130^mg-321′ mg 318 59 Cyr I 848; -ψας 84*(c pr m); -ψει 799; αριθμησεις 29 Lat^cod 100; αριθμησον (-μισ. 739) oI-707^(mg) (vid) C″ 28-30′-85-130^txt-321′ txt-343′ 55 319 624 Aeth; αριθμησονται (καταρ. 121) A b 121; recensebitis Bo; -ψασθε (c var) rell = Ra

The popular plural variant accepted by Ra is grammatically incorrect since it is part of God's command to Moses alone, i.e. ἐπίσκεψαι ... επισκεψασθε αὐτούς (for Hebrew פקד ... תפקדם). The plural tradition both here and in v. 16 arose through the confusion as to who was responsible for the census. The actual numbering of the people was the work of both Moses and Aaron, not of Moses alone. The plural verb is, however, not original.

The following cases are exceptions:

1. With verbs preceding the subject

4₁₅ καὶ συντελέσουσιν (Ἀαρὼν καὶ οἱ υἱοὶ αὐτοῦ) for 𝔐: וכלה

31₁₃ καὶ ἐξῆλθεν (Μωυσῆς καὶ Ἐλεαζάρ) for 𝔐: ויצאו

The plural was probably used in 4₁₅ since the preceding verses had been discussing the duties of Aaron and his sons in plural terms and a singular in

v. 15 would be obtrusive. In the case of 31₁₃ it seems likely that the parent text of the translator had the singular as has Sam.

A Greek singular verb for a plural in 𝔐 also obtains in the following instances.

20₁₀ ἐξεκκλησίασεν (Μωυσῆς καὶ Ἀαρών)] εκκλησιασαν 527 ᴸᵃᵗcod 100 Aeth Arm Bo Sa¹² = 𝔐

22₇ ἐπορεύθη (ἡ γερουσία Μωὰβ καὶ ἡ γερουσία Μαδιάν)] -θησαν 85′ ᵐᵍ-344ᵐᵍ-346ᵐᵍ 319 Arm = 𝔐

34₁₄ ἔλαβεν (φυλὴ υἱῶν Ῥουβὴν καὶ φυλὴ υἱῶν Γάδ . . . καὶ τὸ ἥμισυ . . .)] -βον d t 799 Aeth Bo = 𝔐

In all these cases it would appear that the translator followed his normal practice of using the singular for a verb preceding a compound subject rather than strictly following the Hebrew text.

2. For verbs following a compound subject

In only one case does the translator use a singular verb after a compound subject, viz. at 13₃₀ ὁ Χετταῖος καὶ ὁ Εὑαῖος καὶ ὁ Ἰεβουσαῖος καὶ ὁ Ἀμορραῖος κατοικεῖ, undoubtedly due to Hebrew influence, since 𝔐 reads יושב. In one other instance 𝔐 reads a singular predicate with a coordinate subject preceding,' 14₂₅ והעמלקי והכנעני יושב, but here the translator followed his common practice of using the plural when the predicate follows the compound subject.

31₅₄ εἰσήνεγκαν] -γκεν A B F 376′ C′′⁻⁵²⁹⁷⁶¹ᶜ 127 s⁻³⁰′ 84 x 59 Cyr I 340 = Ra

When a compound subject immediately follows a verb the verb is singular if the first element is singular, but in the following narration the verb is in the plural. Thus 1₁₇ 12₁ 14₄₅ 17₁₁ 20₆ 22₇. In 20₁₀ an apparent exception occurs: καὶ ἐξεκκλησίασεν Μωυσῆς καὶ Ἀαρών . . . καὶ εἶπεν. But here the context makes clear that it is only Moses who is the subject of εἶπεν since the pronoun in the message is singular: ἀκούσατέ μου. In 31₅₄, however, the verb must be plural as in 𝔐 since both Moses and Eleazar are involved in the action.

4₂₃ ἐπίσκεψαι B M′ V 127 x⁻⁶¹⁹ Co] pr και d⁻⁶¹⁰ n⁻¹²⁷ t Arm; και επισκεψον 610; -ψεσθε 19; -ψασθε (aut -σθαι) rell

Num correctly renders the singular of 𝔐, but in vv. 29 30 uses the plural in spite of the singular in 𝔐. In v. 32 both Num and 𝔐 use the plural, probably in anticipation of v. 34 where it is said that Moses and Aaron and the leaders of Israel were responsible for the census. The majority text with the plural verb in v. 23 is an attempt at consistency. It cannot be original, however, in view of v. 21 and v. 22. Only Moses is addressed by the Lord, and he is ordered λάβε . . . ἐπίσκεψαι. The variant text interprets those addressed in v. 23 as Moses and the leader of the sons of Gedson.

8₂₄ εἰσελεύσεται Phil I 273] pr και 458; και εισελευσονται V; -λευστ 126; -σονται (-σωνται 376; ειλενσ. 529*) rell = Ra

𝔐 has singular verbs throughout vv. 24 25 with which Num agrees. Ra had adopted the plural for v. 24 but the singular throughout v. 25 creating an inconsistent text. The passage is introduced by τοῦτο τὸ περὶ τῶν Λευιτῶν; as a result the plural easily predominated the tradition through attraction to τῶν Λευιτῶν, but the more unusual singular supported only by 458 and Philo seems to be original as the text of 𝔐 shows. In any event it would have been odd for Num to have begun with the plural and then continued with the singular.

21₂₆ ἔλαβεν] -βον B F 72-82-426 422 53'-129 71 z ᴸᵃᵗcod 100 = Ra

The plural variant can hardly be considered seriously as 𝔐 shows. The coordinate clause reads καὶ οὗτος (i. e. Sihon) ἐπολέμησεν βασιλέα Μωὰβ τὸ πρότερον, and καὶ ἔλαβεν follows immediately—obviously with the same subject. The variant text is based on confusion of ο/ε in a parent uncial text.

b) *Hellenistic inflections*

The Hellenistic tendency to inflect second aorist stems with first aorist endings is particularly apparent with εἶπον which is throughout Num consistently inflected as εἶπαν (cf also εἶπα 24₁₁). In the text tradition the classical form is always a minority tradition except for the following:

14₃₇ κατείπαντες (καθ. G*) A B M' V G-29-64* b⁻¹⁹ 56 55*] -ποντες rell
22₇ εἶπαν] -πον Fᵇ 72'-376-381' C''⁻⁵²'³¹³ d 53'-129 n⁻⁴⁵⁸ 28-85-130ᵐᵍ-321' ᵐᵍ-344ᵐᵍ
   t x⁻⁶¹⁹ y⁻¹²¹ 126-128-628 59 319; ειπεν 52'-313 Syhᴸ; λεγουσιν b 458
22₁₄ εἶπαν B 426 53'-129 71-509 319] ειπεν 528 75; ειπ 458; ειπον rell
32₂ εἶπαν] ειπον 72-376-oI⁻¹⁵ C''⁻⁴¹³⁷⁶¹ 19 d 53' n⁻⁷⁵ s x⁻⁵⁰⁹ 392 18'-126-628-630' 319
   799 Cyr I 404; ειπε 75

In each of these cases the oldest witness attests to the hellenistic form, and since in all other cases the hellenistic form is not only the majority reading but also supported by the oldest witnesses it must be original.

For ἔρχεσθαι and its compounds the opposite is the case though in a few cases the text-tradition is not as clear as in the case of εἶπαν.

8₂₂ εἰσῆλθον (-θων 376) B V O⁻⁵⁸ 550* b d n⁻⁴⁵⁸ t x⁻⁶¹⁹ 319 799] -θεν 458; -θοσαν (c var)
   rell
12₅ ἐξῆλθον] ηλθον 552; εισηλθον 392; -θοσαν (-θωσαν 319) A B* 130ᵐᵍ-321' ᵐᵍ 319
   = Ra
13₂₄ ἦλθον (ειλ. 767; ηλθεν 509*) B G-426 n x 55 Cyr I 373] -θοσαν rell = Ra
13₂₈ ἤλθομεν] ηλθον 59*(c pr m); ηλθαμεν B G C'⁻⁵²⁸ ⁶¹⁶ᶜ ⁷⁶¹ᶜ-52*-313-417-551-615
   343* 509 = Ra

At 12₅ and 13₂₈ the hellenistic form is a minority reading and was chosen by Ra because it was attested by B. The dominance of the classical form throughout Num must outweigh these rare occurrences of support for the hellenistic forms in B. The other two instances (8₂₂ 13₂₄) find the hellenistic -θοσαν ending in the majority of witnesses. In both instances B supports Num, with Ra singularly not following the B form at 13₂₄.

In the case of πίπτειν the evidence is divided but the classical form is probably to be preferred. Only the following cases are relevant.

16₂₂ ἔπεσον Fᵇ] -σαν A B F M' O'⁻⁷² 77 f⁻¹²⁹ 28-85'-321-344-346* x y 122 55 59 624 799 = Ra
16₄₅ ἔπεσον] -σαν Bᶜ G-29-426 x⁻⁵²⁷; -σεν M'
20₆ ἔπεσον Bᶜ Fᵇ M' V G-426-oI⁻⁶⁴ 73'-414-528-761ᶜ(vid) b d 53'-129 n 85*-321-343-346ᶜ t x⁻⁵⁰⁹ y⁻¹²¹ z 319 646 799] -σεν 59*; -σαν rell = Ra

The translator consistently used the hellenistic form only for εἶπαν, and probably followed the classical forms for all other stems. At 16₄₅ the classical form seems assured; the other two instances are more problematic. B has the hellenistic form at 16₂₂, but Bᶜ changes the original hellenistic form to the classical at 20₆. The classical form as the more conservative has been adopted in all three cases for Num.

c) *Tense*

10₃ σαλπιεῖς] σαλπισεις B* 619 z = Ra
30₁₃ καθαριεῖ F Fᵇ] -ρισει B Fᵃ(vid) 963 426 509 = Ra

The translator avoided the uncontracted -ισω future which became more and more popular in later stages of the language in favour of the Attic (and Ionic) contracted forms for verbs in -ιζω. In Num the following future forms of -ιζω verbs occur: ἀναθεματιῶ 21₂, ἀφαγνιεῖς 8₆, ἀφαγνιεῖτε 31₂₀, ἀφοριεῖ 8₁₁, ἀφοριεῖτε 15₂₀, καθαριεῖ 14₁₈ 30₆ ₉ ₁₃, καθαριεῖς 8₁₅, ποτιεῖ 52₄ ₂₆, ποτιεῖτε 20₈, σαλπιεῖτε 10₅ ₆(three times) ₇ ₁₀ , σαλπιοῦσιν 10₆ ₈ , but cf σαλπίσωσιν 10₄. For the Attic future of -ιζω verbs cf Schwyzer I 785, and for Hellenistic usage cf Mayser I 2. 128.

21₇ ἡμαρτήκαμεν] -τοκαμεν 58; -τησαμεν C''⁻⁴¹⁴; -τομεν (aut -τωμεν) B V O⁻⁵⁸-381' d 53'-129 n 30 t x⁻⁶¹⁹ 392 55 = Ra

The perfect tense as the people's confession is the more exact equivalent of 𝔐's intent than is the aorist, and it probably stems from the translator. Since the object clauses of the verse contain an aorist verb (ὅτι κατελαλήσαμεν), the tradition easily adopted an aorist for the main verb as well. The reading of B is likely to be the result of such adaptation.

21₉ ἔδακεν] εδακνεν B oI⁻¹⁵-29 537 d n⁻⁷⁶⁷ t 71' 392 Cyr II 637 Arm Sa Syh = Ra

The majority tradition with the aorist is to be preferred to the imperfect since the action of snake bite is punctiliar. It is also clear from the coordinate ἐπέβλεψεν.

Precisely at this point the text tradition shows a number of uncertainties as well. Thus d 53'-129 t Sa place ὄφις before the verb, and Fᶜ ᵖʳ ᵐ M' 72-376-618 b 53' 127-767 71 y⁻¹²¹ z⁻⁶⁸' ¹²⁶ 59 319 Cyr II 637 articulate the noun. Neither variant is original. The imperfect is, however, probably palaeographically rather than exegetically rooted.

22₂₂ ἐπορεύετο] επορευθη B V O d 53'-129 458 t 71-509 = Ra

That the imperfect tense is original seems clear from the Hebrew הוא ההולך which it represents adequately. More surprising is the imperfect in v. 23 where καὶ ἐπορεύετο renders ותלך, since the preterite is commonly rendered by the aorist. The translator may have been unconsciously influenced by his

124

use of the tense in v. 22. In v. 22 the accent is precisely on the fact that Balaam was journeying, that is, that he continued on the way, and the aorist would be inappropriate. The variant is easily explicable since the aorist tense is far more common in Num than the imperfect.

22₂₈ πεποίηκά] εποιησα B O⁻⁵⁸ 106 n t 527 = Ra

The phrase in context reads τί πεποίηκά σοι for the Hebrew מה עשיתי לך. The perfect is clearly intended in view of the recurrence of the tense in the ὅτι clause which follows: ὅτι πέπαικάς με τοῦτο τρίτον. The variant text of B is easily explicable in view of the frequency of the aorist in Num; cf also 23₁₁.

23₈ ἀράσομαι] αρασωμαι B 75-767 = Ra
    καταράσομαι] -σωμαι B 767* 30 = Ra; επικαταρασωμαι 75

The quasi-subjunctive forms are clearly secondary. The form is future indicative, and though aras- as an aorist stem is theoretically possible it is highly implausible; cf LS sub voce.

23₈ ἀρᾶται] αρασεται 767; καταραται B 58 52′ 55 = Ra

Why Ra should here have followed the B text is difficult to understand since the simplex form is clearly original. 𝔐 pairs אקב with קבה, and אזעם with זעם. The first of these pairs is rendered in Num by ἀράσομαι and ἀρᾶται resp., and the second pair, by the compound forms καταράσομαι and καταρᾶται. That the translator should have used the compound verb for three of the four is of course highly improbable.

31₂₇ ἐκπεπορευμένων Fᵃ 963] εκπορευομ. A B* F V O″⁻⁸² 52-73′-77-422-528-529 b 44 f⁻¹²⁹ 54-75′ x⁻⁵²⁷ y 68′-126-669 55 59 319 624 799 Cyr I 333(2°) = Ra

This participial form also occurs in v. 28 in exactly the same context (τῶν πολεμιστῶν τῶν ἐκπεπορευμένων εἰς τὴν παράταξιν), and in a similar context in v. 36. In both cases Ra adopted the perfect rather than the present form. The witness of 963 for the perfect participle in v. 27 makes clear that the translator rendered היצאים consistently.

32₆ πορεύσονται 963] πορευονται B V 82 129 74′-76 509 18-407 55 Latcod 104 = Ra; προπορευονται 527

𝔐 has the imperfect יבאו and the future renders its intent. That this is original seems clear from the coordinate verb καθήσεσθε rendering תשבו. It should also be noted that our oldest witness, 963, supports the future for both verbs as well. The variant text which Ra adopted is palaeographically inspired, i.e. uncial ΣΟ → Ο.

d) Two instances which need discussion involve voice.

28₂₀ ποιήσετε] -ται A K M* 376 75′ 30 55; ποιηθησεται b⁽⁻¹⁹⁾; > B F V oII⁻²⁹ f 71 120-128-630′ 319 Cyr I 1088 Aeth Arm Co = Ra

Syntactically ποιήσετε is peculiar, since the sentence seems to contain a hanging nominative ἡ θυσία αὐτῶν. This is to be taken as a nominal clause with σεμίδαλις as predicate. Then τρία δέκατα becomes the object of ποιήσετε. That this was not always understood is clear from passive variants in the tradition on the one hand, and the omission of the verb on the other. The verb is, however, a literal rendering of תעשו, and is original to Num.

8₂₁ ἔπλυναν] επλυναντο (επλην. 376) B M′ 15-376 d 56 127 t = Ra

The aorist active must be original here as is obvious from the context: καὶ ἔπλυναν τὰ ἱμάτια for 𝔐: ויכבסו בגדיהם. The intent of the clause is simple transitive action. The variant text could indeed be understood as involving some advantage to the subject, but it is secondary, probably due to the influence of the following τά. The variant tradition is especially misleading since it would most naturally be understood as passive in sense, i.e. quite at variance with the parent text.

13. Lexemes. Some of these textual problems concern variant elements in compound words.

1₄₇ οὐ συνεπεσκέπησαν] ου συνεσκ. C″⁻⁵²′ ⁽⁴¹⁴′⁾ ⁴¹⁷ 628* 424 646; ουκ (ου G) επεσκ. (επισκ. 53) B O⁻⁵⁸ f 75 x⁻⁵²⁷ 319 = Ra

The usual rendering for √ פקד throughout the book is ἐπισκέπτειν (cf especially chh. 1—4), but for the Levites Moses is ordered not to count them along with the other Israelites and the compound is particularly well chosen to emphasize that fact. So too in v. 49 this verb obtains without exception in the tradition (cf also 2₃₃). The variant easily entered the tradition ex par, but it can hardly be considered original.

4₁₉ εἰσπορευέσθωσαν] πορ. 610; προσπορ. 72 71; προσπορ. B V 82 551* 509 y⁻¹²¹ 55 Latcod 100 = Ra

𝔐 has יבאו which was correctly rendered by Num. The variant is the result of textual simplification. Earlier in the verse the Levites are referred to with respect to their activity when they approach the most holy things; προσπορευομένων αὐτῶν is an appropriate rendering of בגשתם. Here, however, it is Aaron and his sons who are to come in—εἰσπορευέσθωσαν—and appoint the Levites to their tasks. The variant is due to a misunderstanding of this contrast, which was fully clear in the Hebrew and to the translator.

7₈₅ τῶν ἁγίων B 963 458 x⁻⁶¹⁹] τω (το 376* 615) αγιω rell = Ra

The phrase בשקל הקדש occurs regularly throughout the chapter modifying שבעים שקל (12 times) and is in each case rendered by κατὰ τὸν σίκλον τὸν ἅγιον. V. 85 is part of the summary statement and the relevant phrase is not rendered by a κατά construction but by the literalistic ἐν construction. Since the translator apparently intended this literalism, the genitive would fit better in view

126

of the bound construction of the parent text. The majority variant text is then the result of the recurring τὸν σίκλον τὸν ἅγιον construction. Also relevant is the fact that in v. 86 the phrase obtains in 𝔐 but was omitted in Num; it was, however, added by hex as εν τω σικλω τω αγιω and this text may have been influential in creating the popular variant in v. 85.

7₈₈ ἐγκαίνισις] -νωσις (ενκ. 509) B 426 509 = Ra

The root is ἐγκαινίζειν and the noun formation ἐγκαίνισις is expected. 963 has the itacistic variant εγκαινησις, i.e. it witnesses to the majority reading. In vv. 10, 11 and 84 Num has ἐγκαινισμός. Since neither ἐγκαίνισις nor the B variant is attested elsewhere in LXX it would be unwise to adopt the sparsely supported B variant, particularly in view of the fact that our oldest extant witness supports the majority text.

31₁₀ κατοικίαις] οικιαις (οικειαις 319) B O⁻⁵⁸ 129 509 319 = Ra

The phrase ἐν ταῖς κατοικίαις αὐτῶν renders 𝔐's במושבתם. κατοικία is the standard rendering for מושב in the Pentateuch (cf Exod 35₃ Lev 3₁₇ 7₁₆ 23₃ ₁₄ ₁₇ ₂₁ ₃₁ Num 24₂₁ 35₂₉), whereas the simplex οἰκία never renders מושב throughout the entire LXX. The B reading is clearly secondary.

4₂₅ κάλυμμα 1°] κατακ. A Bᶜ F M′ 58-64-381 C′′⁻⁵²⁷⁷* ³²⁰ ⁴¹⁴ ⁵²⁸ 56-129-246ᶜ n⁻⁷⁵ s⁻³²¹*⁽³⁴³⁾ 318 59; καταλυμμα (-λημμα 509*) 72-618 52-77*-528 75 509; καταλυμα 71
κάλυμμα 2° B M′ V 426-707 b 121 68′-120′-126-669 55 319] καταλ. 72-82-618 52 106-107 75′ 509 392*; καταλυμα 71; κατακαλ. rell
κατακάλυμμα] καλυμμα B M V 707 b 84ᵗˣᵗ(c pr m) 121 126 319 = Ra; καταλυμμα 72-82 52 75 509; καταλυμα 71

That κάλυμμα and κατακάλυμμα have approximately the same lexical content is clear. The translator, however, used them carefully to distinguish the Hebrew מכסה and מסך. In 4₂₅ מכסה occurs twice and is rendered by κάλυμμα, whereas מסך, occurring once, is rendered by the compound. In 3₂₅ ₃₁ κατακάλυμμα renders מסך, whereas in 3₂₅ 4₈ ₁₀ ₁₁ ₁₂ κάλυμμα is the rendering for מכסה. In no case are the equations reversed. Once (4₁₄) κάλυμμα occurs for כסוי, and in 4₆ it is κατακάλυμμα which renders כסוי. All other occurrences of either word (4₁₄ and three times in secondary expansions in v. 31) have no equivalents in 𝔐.

8₂₂ καθά] καθως B* 58-72 59 = Ra

The clause "as the Lord commanded Moses" (and variations of it) occurs 19 times in Num but is never introduced by καθως. It is introduced by καθάπερ at 27₂₃, and otherwise by ὃν τρόπον (1₁₉ 3₁₆ ₅₁ 4₄₉ 26₄ 31₄₇ 34₁₃ 36₁₀) or by καθά (8₃ 9₅ 15₂₃ ₃₆ 17₁₁ 20₉ ₂₇ 27₁₁ 31₄₁). In each instance 𝔐 has כאשר or אשר, as it does at 8₂₂; καθά must therefore be original here as well.

11₅ σικύους] σικυας (c var) A B* F 58ᶜ-72 528 ƒ 54-75′ y⁻³¹⁸ 55 59 646 799 Phil III 19ᵗᵉ DialTA 80 = Ra

Though קִשֻּׁאִים occurs only here in the OT the word is generally accepted as meaning "cucumber"; cf for example the learned discussion with references in Dillmann's commentary. This was correctly rendered by Num as σικύους. The feminine variant is the word for the common gourd; cf LS sub voce.

11₈ ἥ V *b* 319 ᴸᵃᵗcod 100 Bo] καί rell = Ra

The coordinate clauses καὶ ἤληθον αὐτὸ ἐν τῷ μύλῳ and ἢ ἔτριβον ἐν τῇ θυείᾳ refer to alternative, not successive, actions, as 𝔐 clearly indicates; the manna was either ground in the mill or crushed in the mortar, not both. The variant is a thoughtlessly created error, which crept into the tradition because of the numerous καί clauses in the verse.

15₁ ἐλάλησεν] ειπε(ν) B V *d* 129 *t* *x* Cyr I 1029 = Compl Ra

λαλέω is the standard rendering for √דבר, whereas εἶπον is used for √אמר. In fact out of the large number of instances in which εἶπον occurs in Num only eight obtain where 𝔐 has √דבר (14₂₆ 16₃₆ 22₇ ₃₅ 23₂ 24₁₃(twice) 27₁₅). The reverse pattern, i.e. λαλέω for √אמר in 𝔐 only obtains at 15₃₅ 18₂₀ 26₁ 27₆ ₁₈ 30₁ and 31₂₅. The equation is so carefully maintained that in each of these cases another parent text is probably to be presupposed. At 15₁ 𝔐 reads וידבר and there is no reason to question it as parent text for Num.

15₂₀ ἅλωνος] αλω B *x*⁻⁵⁰⁹ Cyr VI 568 = Ra
18₂₇ ἅλωνος] αλω B 426 *x*⁻⁶¹⁹ Cyr I 844 = Ra
18₃₀ ἅλωνος] αλω B G 71 Cyr I 844 = Ra

The terms ἅλως and ἅλων are synonymous and can be used interchangeably. They occur elsewhere in the Pentateuch only as ἅλων (Gen 50₁₀ ₁₁ Exod 22₆ ₂₉ Deut 16₁₃), and there is no good reason for adopting the sparsely supported reading of B as original text.

16₂₇ τῶν σκηνῶν B V *d* *f*⁻¹²⁹ *t*⁻⁸⁴ *x* *z* 799] τῆς σκηνῆς 84 Aeth⁻ᶜᴳ Bo Sa¹; > Sa¹²; των σκηνωματων (c var) rell

That τῶν σκηνῶν is original is clear from the preceding verse where secular אהלים is also rendered by σκηνῶν, only *b* 392 witnessing to σκηνωματων. σκηνή is used throughout Num for אהל both for the sacred tent (usually σκηνὴ τοῦ μαρτυρίου) and the secular; cf also 24₅. In fact, σκήνωμα does not occur at all in Num.

16₄₀ μηθείς B *d* 129 127-767 *t*⁻⁷⁶ *x* 319] μηδε εις O⁻⁵⁸; ουδεις 126; μηδεις rell

The classical μηδεις was largely replaced by the dialect form μηθεις during the third to the first centuries B.C., then again to be replaced wholly by the *delta* spelling; cf Mayser I, 1, 448f and especially J. Wackernagel's explanation of the *theta* form in *Kleine Schriften* II 1054. The dominance in the tradition of the *delta* form is secondary and due to the fact that the Hellenistic μηθεις was completely replaced by μηδεις in the first centuries of our era.

18₃₂ ὅταν M^mg V G 52 *d n* 30'-344^mg *t* 392 55 319 416 ^Latcod 100 Arm Bo] οτι 58-*o*II⁻⁷⁰⁷ 53'-129 71 121 Syh; οτι εαν 246; οτι αν (+ οτι αν 56) rell = Ra

Whether ὅταν or οτι αν is original is immediately apparent from 𝔐 בהרימכם, which was rendered in Num by ὅταν ἀφαιρῆτε, i.e. a temporal, not a causal, construction. οτι αν is simply due to palaeographic confusion of τ and τι in an uncial parent text.

21₁₅ κατοικῆσαι F^b] -κεισαι (-σε V) F V 29 129 767 30; οικησαι 624; κατοικιαν *o*I⁻¹⁵ *d t* 619 55^c; *habitationes* Bo; -κισαι A B M' 56' 54' 344 121 Syh = Ra

The transitive κατοικισαι is clearly secondary here since 𝔐 has לשבת. As Schleusner says under the entry κατοικίζω concerning this passage: ubi lectio κατοικίσαι est fortasse vitiosa, et reponendum κατοικῆσαι. Since the variant is homophonous to κατοικῆσαι in Hellenistic and later Greek, it easily entered the text tradition, but it remains secondary.

21₃₂ ὄντα] κατοικουντα B V *O*-82 *d* 53'-129 *n t x*⁻⁶¹⁹ Arm Syh = Ra

ὄντα cannot be taken as a hex correction since *O*-82 Arm Syh all attest the variant text which was thus earlier than Origen. The phrase τὸν ὄντα ἐκεῖ exactly reproduces the Hebrew אשר שם, whereas the variant text seems to be an exegetical smoothing out of the text, possibly influenced by the common collocation of "the Amorite who was dwelling there."

22₈ ῥήματα M' 458-767 130^mg-321'^mg ^Latcod 100] pr τα *f*⁻¹²⁹ = Compl; ρημα 75 Aeth = 𝔐; πραγμα A 426*(c pr m) Cyr I 440; προσταγματα 730; πραγματα rell = Ra

ῥῆμα and πρᾶγμα are often confused in the LXX tradition. Since the semantic field of the Hebrew דבר includes both "matter, thing" as well as "word, message," both occur as renderings in LXX. In 22₈, however, only the latter meaning is possible. It modifies ἀποκριθήσομαι, and the phrase is intended to reproduce והשבתי דבר. Whenever ἀποκρίνειν is used to represent השיב and has an object modifier either ῥῆμα or λόγος is used in the LXX for דבר but never πρᾶγμα. Unusual here is the use of the plural since it is the singular which commonly occurs. The plural, though unusual, here refers to the awaited words of God; it can also be defended on text traditional grounds, since it would more easily lead to the variant singular text of the majority tradition than would the reverse process.

22₂₄ ἀμπελώνων] αμπελων B V 53'-129 71(vid)-509 Or IV 409 = Ra

That ἀμπελώνων is original and the variant text the result of haplography seems assured from the Hebrew. ἄμπελος is the standard rendering of גפן, i.e. the grape vine, whereas ἀμπελών is the standard rendering for כרם "vineyard." Contrast 6₄ 20₅ with 16₁₄ 20₁₇ 21₂₂.

22₃₁ τοῦ θεοῦ] $\overline{κυ}$ B *O*'⁻⁸² *b f* 85'^mg-321'^mg-344^mg 71' 392 *z* 59 Aeth Arm Syh = Ra; > 509 Phil II 93^F

References in 𝔐 to the angel of Yahweh are always rendered by ὁ ἄγγελος τοῦ θεοῦ. In fact although 𝔐 usually refers to Balaam's God as Yahweh throughout ch. 22 the Greek consistently renders it by "God" except for v. 34. The reason may well have been theological, since Balaam was a bad seer who eventually came to a violent end and the translator may have intentionally downplayed the fact that it was Yahweh who ordered Balaam about. It should be noted, however, that the Targums do not do this. It seems, however, quite clear that τοῦ θεοῦ is original here. At v. 34 κυρίου has been accepted as Num because of the textual evidence, only ms 54 and Bo attesting to του θεου for κυρίου in the phrase τῷ ἀγγέλῳ κυρίου.

31₂₈ ὄνων] αιγων B Fᵃ V 82 129 x⁻⁵²⁷ 407 319 Arm Sa = Ra

The context in 𝔐 reads ומן הבקר ומן החמרים ומן הצאן for which Num has four items καὶ ἀπὸ τῶν κτηνῶν καὶ ἀπὸ τῶν βοῶν καὶ ἀπὸ τῶν προβάτων καὶ ἀπὸ τῶν ὄνων, the second item apparently a doublet to the first, with the last two in reverse order to 𝔐. A number of witnesses add και απο των αιγων after προβατων, viz 58-72 131ᶜ b f⁻¹²⁹ 59 and Bo. חמרים is represented by ὄνων and not by αιγων which would presuppose שעירים. It should be added that Sam has the text of 𝔐 plus ומכל הבהמה at the end.

32₁₃ κατερρέμβευσεν] κατερομβ. B Gᶜ; κατερρομβ. = Ra

Why Ra should have been misled by the reading of B is not clear. The root ρομβευω means "to spin," whereas the root ρεμβευω means "to roam or rove." Since 𝔐 has the Hiphil of the root נוע the majority form is obviously correct here, and the reading in B G simply a spelling error based on a confusion of *omicron* and *epsilon* in an uncial parent text.

34₁₂ καὶ τά] κατα G Latcodd 100 104(vid)

The variant text seems at first blush to find support in 𝔐 which reads לגבלתיה (הארץ), which the translator rendered by καὶ τὰ ὅρια αὐτῆς. The word also occurs in a similar context in v. 2 as ארץ כנען לגבלתיה rendered by γῆ Χανάαν σὺν τοῖς ὁρίοις αὐτῆς in Num. In other words, the translator understood the prepositional phrase in the sense of "together with its borders" rather than as "with reference to" or "according to its borders."

35₁₅ φυγαδεῖον 82-426-707-oI b⁻³¹⁴ n⁻⁴⁵⁸ 121ᶜ z⁻⁴⁰⁷ = Sixt] -δευτηριον 29 458 Syh; -δευτηρια 246; -διον (-διων 376) rell = Ra

φυγαδεῖον, not φυγάδιον, is the correct spelling here, since it is derived from φυγαδεύω. The itacistic variant adopted by Ra would presuppose a derivation of *φυγαδεω which does not obtain. Cf LS as well as Walters 43.

36₇ τῆς πατρικῆς V 963 O⁻³⁷⁶·707 d f⁻²⁴⁶ t 120 799 Arm Syh] του πατρος 82-376 b n 85ᵐᵍ·344ᵐᵍ Latcodd 100 104 Co; *patrum* Aeth; om πατρ. F; της (> 509) πατριας (+ ας Fᵃ) Fᵃ Fᵇ rell = Ra

אבת as "family clan(s)" is normally rendered by πατριας (-ων), but here and in v. 8 πατρική is apparently original text. This is assured in v. 8 where the entire tradition (except for V which has του πρς) supports τὴν πατρικήν. In v. 7 πατρικῆς, though the more unusual rendering, is to be preferred particularly in view of the support of 963 as the oldest witness. The variant reading is to be explained as ex par.

14. Instances where the longer text is to be preferred

2₃₁ σὺν δυνάμει αὐτῶν] post ἐξαροῦσιν tr 246; sub ÷ SyhᵀT; > B V O⁻⁵⁸-707 b f⁻²⁴⁶ x 392 Cyr I 724 ᴸᵃᵗcod 100 Aeth Arab Co Syhᴸ = Ra 𝔐

The first two chapters contain a great deal of repetitive materials and the translator renders them in almost formulaic fashion adding set phrases even when they are occasionally absent in 𝔐. In the parallel passages 2₉ ₁₆ ₂₄ this phrase occurs both in 𝔐 and in Num. In v. 31 it is absent in 𝔐 but present in Num. That it is original to Num is now made even more certain by the witness of Syhᵀ where the passage is under the obelus. The phrase could of course have crept into the text ex par, but it is too much to expect the obelus to have been added as well and that coincidentally corresponding exactly to the situation in 𝔐.

3₂₃ οὗτοι Bᶜ V O⁻ᴳ d f n t x 799 Arm Bo] sub ÷ G Syh; > rell = Ra 𝔐

The word seems to have been original; it was in any event present in the preOrigenian text as the obelus in G and Syh demonstrates. It should also be noted that it is preceded by καί which also has no equivalent in 𝔐 and is also under the obelus in G and Syh. Since οὗτοι is followed by υἱοί which in the text tradition has been articulated the originality of οὗτοι is not fully certain. Palaeographic confusion could have introduced the word into the text prior to Origen.

9₁₄ οὕτως] > B 129 n⁻⁷⁶⁷ 71-509 Aeth Arab Arm Co = Ra

That the shorter text might conceivably be seriously considered as original text could only arise out of an undue reverence for the witness of B. Num always represents the כן of 𝔐 correctly by οὕτως and there is no good reason why he should have failed to do so here.

9₂₁ om καὶ ἀναβῇ ἡ νεφέλη ἀπαροῦσιν (22) ἡμέρας ἤ B 129 71-509 Sa = Ra

The shorter text can hardly be original as the abrupt transition from ἡμέρας ἤ νυκτός to μηνός without an expected ἤ particle makes clear. Furthermore the text represents 𝔐 adequately and there is nothing palaeographically obvious in the Hebrew which might have promoted the omission by the translator. The omission is explicable within the Greek tradition as a lapsus oculi, skipping from νυκτός to μηνός in the collocation ἡμέρας ἤ μηνός.

18₂₇ ὡς 2°] εις 246; > B 129 x⁻⁶¹⁹ 319 Cyr I 844 Bo Sa¹ = Ra

The translator often tends to repeat the preposition in paratactic constructions in accordance with 𝔐. Thus ἔναντι is repeated four times in 27₂. For chapter 18 repetition of the preposition is attested in v. 3 πρὸς τὰ σκεύη τὰ ἅγια καὶ πρὸς τὸ θυσιαστήριον, v. 9 ἀπό . . . καὶ ἀπό . . . καὶ ἀπό . . ., as well as in v. 30 ὡς γένημα . . . καὶ ὡς γένημα. The omission of ὡς 2° is a stylistic improvement within the text tradition but is not original.

21₅ τούτῳ] > B 29-426-707* 16-46 71-509 68'-120' Arab Arm Sa = Ra

The word in question is part of the phrase ἐν τῷ ἄρτῳ τῷ διακένῳ τούτῳ. The pronoun has no counterpart in 𝔐, but it is apparently under the obelus in Syh^L and is thus at least as early as Origen. Furthermore its omission is only sparsely supported in the text tradition.

26₃ μετ’ αὐτῶν] μετ αυτου 72 318 Aeth^-C; *ad illos* Lat^cod 110; αυτοις 𝔐^txt o*I* C'' d n 30'-85'^txt-321'^txt-343' t 392 z^-68' 120 55 319 646 Lat^cod 100 Bo; > B 58-82 71-509 Aeth^C Arm Sa = Ra

The context of the phrase is καὶ ἐλάλησεν Μωυσῆς καὶ Ἐλεαζὰρ ὁ ἱερεὺς μετ’ αὐτῶν. The phrase in question represents אתם in 𝔐. The rendering is not fully unambiguous as the text tradition shows. Thus the modifier ὁ ἱερεύς is omitted by A o*I*^-15 d^-106 y^-392 55 319 Aeth. The ambiguity lies in the fact that μετ’ αὐτῶν could modify either the verb or ἱερεύς. One strand in the tradition voided the ambiguity by changing the phrase to αὐτοῖς; the other, by omitting it. The ambiguous phrase must have been original.

35₆ om ἅς 1° B V 963 82 b f x 407 319 Cyr I 865 = Ra
35₇ om ἅς B V 82 129 344^txt x 407 319 Lat^cod 100 Arm = Ra

The relative pronoun follows τὰς πόλεις and was easily lost through homoioteleuton. Decisive is the Hebrew text which has הערים אשר. In v. 6 the original ἅς was lost as early as 963, i.e. before the time of Origen whose parent text also lacked the pronoun; he restored it under the asterisk which ms G attests. That the translator did not intentionally omit ἅς in this type of context is clear from v. 4 where ἅς follows πόλεων; there its omission obtains only in 82 b 54-75' 509 318 628(2°), and it is undoubtedly original; cf also v. 8 where the pronoun is present in all witnesses except 407 319 and its originality is unquestioned.

15. Finally a number of passages obtain in which Ra adopted a longer text than that of Num.

4₁₄ ἐν αὐτοῖς] pr επ αυτο (αυτω Cyr) B V O^-58 x^-619 Cyr I 852 Arm Syh = Ra 𝔐; + επ αυτο 44'-125(2°) 127 t Sa; + επ αυτων n^-127

Both vv. 9 and 14 contain the same clause ὅσοις λειτουργοῦσιν ἐν αὐτοῖς. In v. 9 the tradition contains the following variant: ἐν αὐτοῖς] pr αυτη O Syh = 𝔐, clearly a hex addition. The translator obviously felt that επ αυτο / αυτη as literal renderings of עליו and לה resp. would be otiose in Greek. In both cases Origen amplified the text in order to give a one for one equation for the Hebrew phrases.

4₂₃ τὰ ἔργα] + αυτου B V 29 b d f n 130^{mg}-321′^{mg} t x^{-619} 318 319 ^{Lat}cod 100 Bo = Ra

4₃₅ τὰ ἔργα] > B f x^{-619} 319 ^{Lat}cod 100 Sa = Ra

Both of these occur in the context "(his) works in the tent of meeting," a phrase occurring seven times in ch. 4. Twice (vv. 31 33) 𝔐 has עבדתם, and Num faithfully renders the suffix by αὐτῶν. In all the other occurrences (vv. 3 23 35 39 47) the Hebrew word is without suffix, and the Greek is throughout faithful to the Hebrew. It is most unlikely that v. 23 should be an exception. Nor does the translator ever fail to render the word for "work" by τὰ ἔργα. For v. 35 the τὰ ἔργα must be original as the exact parallel in v. 39 shows.

4₂₉—₃₃ constitutes a statement on the duties of the Merarites in the service of the tent of testimony. The text adopted as original agrees in details and is a restatement of the ἡ ἐπίσκεψις ἡ φυλακὴ υἱῶν Μεραρί given in 3₃₆ ₃₇ and represents 𝔐 adequately.

Ra adopted a considerably longer text in accordance with the manuscript tradition. The list of duties which detail the αὐτούς of ἐπισκέψασθε αὐτούς (v. 30) in Ra are as follows (I leave unaccented the secondary materials): τὰς κεφαλίδας τῆς σκηνῆς καὶ τοὺς μοχλοὺς αὐτῆς καὶ τοὺς στύλους αὐτῆς καὶ τὰς βάσεις αὐτῆς καὶ το κατακαλυμμα και αι βασεις αυτων και οι στυλοι αυτων και το κατακαλυμμα της θυρας της σκηνης (32) καὶ τοὺς στύλους τῆς αὐλῆς κύκλῳ και αι βασεις αυτων και τους στυλους του καταπετασματος της πυλης της αυλης καὶ τὰς βάσεις αὐτῶν καὶ τοὺς πασσάλους αὐτῶν καὶ τοὺς κάλους αὐτῶν καὶ πάντα τὰ σκεύη αὐτῶν . . . .

One comment should be made on the primary materials in Ra. Ra on the basis of the minority reading of B omitted αὐτῆς after μοχλούς in v. 31 (supported by B V d 54-75′ t x^{-619} 319 ^{Lat}cod 104 Arm Sa^{12}). This is unlikely to be correct since the accent lies on the contrast in genitive pronouns; that is, the μοχλούς, στύλους and βάσεις of v. 31 belong to the σκηνῆς, whereas the pronouns of v. 32 (αὐτῶν throughout) refer to the τοὺς στύλους τῆς αὐλῆς κύκλῳ. This is consistent with the Hebrew text as well.

It is immediately evident that there are secondary materials present in the text of Ra. In v. 31 και αι βασεις αυτων και οι στυλοι αυτων are both nominative phrases and are modified by plural pronouns. This doublet probably was due to the influence of the tabernacle account of Exod 27₉-₁₉.

Also secondary in v. 31 is και το κατακαλυμμα και το κατακαλυμμα της θυρας της σκηνης which entered the text tradition from 3₂₅; that is, these were part of the φυλακή of the Gedsonites (Gershonites 𝔐), and not of the Merarites. Why this should have entered the text tradition at this point is not obvious.

That the Ra text of v. 32 also contains secondary materials is clear from και αι βασεις αυτων with the noun in the nominative case which does not fit into the context. This grammatical difficulty bothered the tradition and 72

b d^{-44} 127-767 t^{-84} Arm changed $\alpha\iota$ to $\tau\alpha\varsigma$. The phrase occurs correctly in $\varkappa\alpha\grave{\iota}$ $\tau\grave{\alpha}\varsigma$ $\beta\acute{\alpha}\sigma\epsilon\iota\varsigma$ $\alpha\mathring{\upsilon}\tau\tilde{\omega}\nu$ to which it is a doublet.

Not as obviously secondary is $\varkappa\alpha\iota$ $\tau o v\varsigma$ $\sigma\tau v\lambda o v\varsigma$ $\tau o v$ $\varkappa\alpha\tau\alpha\pi\epsilon\tau\alpha\sigma\mu\alpha\tau o\varsigma$ $\tau\eta\varsigma$ $\pi v\lambda\eta\varsigma$ $\tau\eta\varsigma$ $\alpha v\lambda\eta\varsigma$, though it too has no equivalent in $\mathfrak{M}$. It constitutes in all likelihood an exceptional amplification (or doublet) to $\varkappa\alpha\grave{\iota}$ $\tau o\grave{v}\varsigma$ $\sigma\tau\acute{v}\lambda o v\varsigma$ $\tau\tilde{\eta}\varsigma$ $\alpha\mathring{v}\lambda\tilde{\eta}\varsigma$ $\varkappa\acute{v}\varkappa\lambda\omega$. The $\varkappa\alpha\tau\alpha\pi\acute{\epsilon}\tau\alpha\sigma\mu\alpha$ $\tau\tilde{\eta}\varsigma$ $\pi\acute{v}\lambda\eta\varsigma$ $\tau\tilde{\eta}\varsigma$ $\alpha\mathring{v}\lambda\tilde{\eta}\varsigma$ are referred to in 3$_{26}$ as part of the charge of the Gedsonites. That there were $\tau o\grave{v}\varsigma$ $\sigma\tau\acute{v}\lambda o v\varsigma$ $\tau o\tilde{v}$ $\varkappa\alpha\tau\alpha\pi\epsilon\tau\acute{\alpha}\sigma\mu\alpha\tau o\varsigma$ was well-known from the tabernacle account; cf Exod 38$_{18}$. It is, however, most unlikely that the translator was responsible for this amplification. He did not tend to amplify the parent text, nor is it likely that his parent text, or any Hebrew text for that matter, contained this gloss. The Hebrew text is fully consistent with the parallel tradition of 3$_{36}$, and so was Num.

9$_7$ $\pi\varrho o\sigma\epsilon\nu\acute{\epsilon}\gamma\varkappa\alpha\iota$ ($-\gamma\varkappa\epsilon\iota\nu$ 127 527 Chr) B V 127 x^{-619} 126 319 Chr II 877 Cyr I 1081 Bo] pr $\tau o v$ b; pr $\omega\sigma\tau\epsilon$ $\tau o v$ 619 68$'$-120$'$; pr $\omega\sigma\tau\epsilon$ ($-\tau\alpha\iota$ 75$'$) rell

Ra was undoubtedly correct in rejecting $\omega\sigma\tau\epsilon$ for marking the complementary infinitive. Num used $\H\omega\sigma\tau\epsilon$ only three times in a similar grammatical context (5$_8$ 7$_1$ 8$_{11}$) and commonly left the infinitive unmarked. For an excellent parallel the collocation $\H v\sigma\tau\epsilon\varrho\acute{\eta}\sigma\eta$ $\pi o\iota\tilde\eta\sigma\alpha\iota$ in 9$_{13}$ is convincing (cf also 9$_4$ $\pi o\iota\tilde\eta\sigma\alpha\iota$).

11$_{21}$ $\delta\acute{\omega}\sigma\omega$ $\alpha\mathring{v}\tau o\tilde{\iota}\varsigma$] + $\varphi\alpha\gamma\epsilon\iota\nu$ B = Ra
15$_{33}$ $\xi\acute{v}\lambda\alpha$] + (c var) $\tau\eta$ $\eta\mu\epsilon\varrho\alpha$ $\tau\omega\nu$ $\sigma\alpha\beta\beta\alpha\tau\omega\nu$ B M$'$ 528 f n^{-75} t 527 121 799 Arm = Ra

In neither of these two instances is the text of B to be taken seriously since the intrusive gloss comes from a parallel passage. The $\varphi\alpha\gamma\epsilon\iota\nu$ variant in 11$_{21}$ has no basis in the Hebrew and is an intrusion from 11$_{18}$ $\varkappa\alpha\grave{\iota}$ $\delta\acute{\omega}\sigma\epsilon\iota$ $\varkappa\acute{v}\varrho\iota o\varsigma$ $\H v\mu\tilde{\iota}\nu$ $\varkappa\varrho\acute{\epsilon}\alpha$ $\varphi\alpha\gamma\epsilon\tilde{\iota}\nu$. The variant in 15$_{33}$ also has no support in $\mathfrak{M}$. It constitutes a gloss taken from the preceding verse where it is the original text.

22$_{33}$ $\nu\tilde{v}\nu$] + $o\nu\nu$ B b x^{-619} ^{Lat}cod 100 = Ra

$\mathfrak{M}$ has עתה גם, and $\nu\tilde{v}\nu$ is the standard equivalent for עתה, but גם is usually not rendered at all, and when it is, $\varkappa\alpha\acute{\iota}$ is used. The $o\nu\nu$ of the variant text is simply a partial dittograph and not to be taken seriously.

24$_{16}$ $\H v\psi\acute{\iota}\sigma\tau o v$] pr $\pi\alpha\varrho\alpha$ ($\pi\alpha\varrho$ 664; + $\tau o v$ 84*) B V 82-376 106 f^{-56*} n t 71-509 392 319 Phil III 191 ^{Lat}codd 91 92 94—96 100 Bo = Ra

The originality of the preposition is questionable in view of the context. The verse contains three parallel constructions, $\lambda\acute{o}\gamma\iota\alpha$ $\vartheta\epsilon o\tilde{v}$, $\mathring{\epsilon}\pi\iota\sigma\tau\acute{\eta}\mu\eta\nu$ $\H v\psi\acute{\iota}\sigma\tau o v$ and $\H o\varrho\alpha\sigma\iota\nu$ $\vartheta\epsilon o\tilde{v}$. These are present in $\mathfrak{M}$ as אמרי אל, דעת עליון and מחזה שדי, all bound constructions adequately rendered in Greek by noun plus genitive modifier. That the translator who usually rendered the second element in a bound phrase by a genitive should in the second instance use a prepositional phrase is unlikely. One suspects that the divergence was exegetically inspired, one making explicit that the $\mathring{\epsilon}\pi\iota\sigma\tau\acute{\eta}\mu\eta\nu$ as well as the $\lambda\acute{o}\gamma\iota\alpha$ were to be understood as finding their source in the deity and not their object.

25₄ τοὺς ἀρχηγούς] pr παντας B Fᵃ O⁻⁵⁸-82 d 53′ n 130ᵐᵍ t 71-509 799 Phil III 223
Cyr I 908 IV 300 ᴸᵃᵗcodd 91 92 94—96 100 Co Syh = Ra 𝔐

A number of text critical considerations indicates that the variant text is
not LXX but rather hex. Ms 344 indicates on the margin that παντας is an
o′ reading; such an indication is usually a reference to the hex form of the
Septuagint text. Furthermore ms 58 has added παντας before rather than after
λάβε, i.e. at the wrong place. This ms often shows evidence of post Origenian
activity. In any event all O mss witness to the variant. So too, the marginal
notes on the Vulgate mss 91 92 94—96 are often hex type Latin notes. The B
text must here be considered secondary.

26₄₄ Νοεμάν 1⁰] + (+ ※ Syh; c var) τω αδαρ δημος ο αδαρι M′ O′⁻³⁷⁶ ⁶¹⁸ᵗˣᵗ 56′ 619 18′-
126-628-630′ Boᴮ Sa Syh = Ra

That the shorter text is original is clear from the asterisk in Syh. The plus
added by Origen does not exactly represent 𝔐 which has משפחת הארדי (M′
omit τω αδαρ and more closely equal the text of 𝔐); Sam, however, has לארד
משפחת הארדי and it would appear that the Hebrew text of Origen contained
an equivalent for τω αδαρ. That such a text was the likely parent text for
Origen is apparent from the coordinate לנעמן משפחת הנעמי in 𝔐 (as well as
Sam).

The confusion of *daleth/resh*, palaeographically similar in the Hebrew script,
led to Ἀδάρ for ארד but cf אדר in 1 Par 8₃. Which spelling is to be preferred
is uncertain.

34₁₃ κύριος] + τω μωυση (μωση n) B* d⁽⁻⁴⁴⁾ 246 n t Syh = Ra

The variant gloss is part of the formulaic clause "which the Lord commanded
Moses." Here, however, 𝔐 simply has אשר צוה יהוה. The fuller clause occurs
many times in Num and Deut (cf THGD 95), and entered the tradition ex
par. The omission of an original τω μωυση in the text tradition would be highly
unlikely.

Index

23	108, 111, 127	13	10, 11, 95, 124	12	61, 103
28₃	112	14	50	13	61
10	112	16	94	14	116
13	56, 104, 114	17	108	15	103, 116
15	112	31₃	95, 104	16	103, 106
17	50	5	11	17	106
19	112	7	89, 108	20	119
20	125f	8	26	21	119
21	26, 114	9	11	22	119
23	112	10	127	23	119f
28	108	13	121f	29	120
29	114	19	10	30	120bis
31	110	20	124	31	120bis
29	110	21	108	32	120
29₁	128	23	95	36	103
3	110	25	128	38	20
4	114	27	125	46	116
6	100, 110, 111, 124	28	11, 125, 130	47	116bis
9	124	31	108	48	116
10	26, 114	32	26	49	116
11	100, 104, 110, 112	36	10, 125	54	9, 11, 95
12ff	101	37	26	55	95
13	10, 115, 124	41	104, 108, 127	34₂	108, 130
14	115	42	108	3	26, 103
15—26	115	43	10, 108	4	26, 116
15	56, 99, 114, 115	45	101	7	26
16	100, 110, 112	47	108bis, 127	9	29, 120
17	101, 115	48	11	10	11, 29
18	25, 100	52	10	11	120
19	100, 110, 112	54	31, 122	12	10bis, 11, 130
20	115	32₂	123	13	127, 135
21	10, 25, 100	3	11bis, 119	14	25, 122
22	10, 100, 110, 112	4	11, 96	16	10
23	115	5	96, 99	20	61
24	100	6	125	22	10, 11, 118
25	10, 110, 112	9	29, 100	23	11, 120
26	115	12	10	26	11, 61
27	100	13	95bis, 130	28	11bis
28	10, 100, 110, 112	14	11	29	107, 127
29	115	15	10bis	35₄	132
30	10, 100	17	11	6	26, 50, 132
31	10, 100, 110, 112	18	26, 108	7	10, 26, 132
33	10, 100	20	26	8	108, 132
34	10, 100, 110, 112	21	10	15	10, 130
35	101	22	95, 96	30	10
37	100	23	95	34	11, 22
38	100, 110, 112	25	10	36₁	96
39	10, 50, 110	27	10	2	25
30₁	108	30	9, 11, 95	3	22, 50, 70, 108
2	10	36	119	4	108
3	11, 95	37	116	5	10
5	19	39	10, 50	6	9
7	10	42	119	7	10bis, 108, 130f
9	11	33₃	11, 26	8	31, 131
11	10, 26	6	117	10	108, 127
		7	25, 29, 117	11	9, 119
		11	103	12	10, 22